THE CANADIAN WAY

The Canadian Way

———————— ✄ ————————

Shaping Canada's Foreign Policy 1968-1984

IVAN L. HEAD

PIERRE ELLIOTT TRUDEAU

Canadian Cataloguing in Publication Data
Head, Ivan, 1930–
    The Canadian way: shaping Canada's foreign policy 1968-84

Includes bibliographical references and index.
ISBN 0-7710-4099-7

1. Canada – Foreign relations – 1945-
I. Trudeau, Pierre Elliott, 1919-   . II. Title.

FC625.H4 1995   327.71'009'045   C95-931710-4   FI034.2.H4 1995

The publishers acknowledge the support of the Canada Council and the Ontario Arts Council for their publishing program.

Typesetting by M&S, Toronto
Printed and bound in Canada on acid-free paper

McClelland & Stewart Inc.
The Canadian Publishers
481 University Avenue
Toronto, Ontario
M5G 2E9

1 2 3 4 5   99 98 97 96 95

"... when a certain Spartan king had said, Happy that republic which has for its boundaries the spear and the sword, Pompey corrected him, and said, Happy rather that which has justice for its boundary."

Hugo Grotius
1583–1645

CONTENTS

—————————— →← ——————————

PREFACE

This is a personal journal, but one that we hope will be of some public interest nevertheless. Its intention is to be reflective as well as reminiscent, necessarily selective rather than chronologically exhaustive. As the title reveals, the contents relate to Canada's international roles and experiences during the often tumultuous years from 1968 to 1984. Persons desirous of insights into Canada's domestic history in that period will not find them here – except for those events directly related to activities offshore.

The structural frailties of such an enterprise are obvious: the narrowness of view and partiality of observation that actors necessarily bring to the description of events in which they have participated; the possibility that hindsight and subsequently gained knowledge will combine to colour those descriptions. We readily acknowledge the inevitability of the former, yet express the immodest hope that historians will find these accounts useful as they engage in their important task of assessment and balance. The second circumstance, though obviously real, is one that we have steadfastly endeavoured to avoid; we concede nevertheless that our joint and individual powers of recall are as subject to unconscious colouration as are those of any human. In each instance, we earnestly solicit readers to bring to bear their individual judgement of our success.

Within the international community, Canada has never claimed the status of a major power. Notwithstanding, in the course of many years it has been extraordinarily influential. One of the reasons, stated Adlai Stevenson, Jr., in 1955, has been the ability of Canadians to retain some vestige of perspective and common sense,

. . . a patient and level-headed poise in a world in convulsion. If
we are to ride out the tests and trials, the storms, of our time on
earth, we need the kind of built-in gyroscope which you
Canadians seem to have. It is a great national virtue to be able
calmly to endure what cannot be immediately remedied.

Mr. Stevenson's model, and the authors' mentor in matters of this
kind, was that most decent of Canadians, and Nobel Peace Prize
winner, former prime minister Lester B. Pearson. It is Mr. Pearson who
coined the phrase "middle power" to describe Canada's international
stature. With the greatest of respect to him, our preference in the world
of the late sixties and thereafter was that Canada should function as an
"effective power." Whether the term is an accurate description of the
period under review will be for others to decide. It is offered here,
however, as a standard for reference by all readers.

The formulation of foreign policy in a country as diverse as Canada
is not a simple task. Nor is the implementation of that policy eased
when the country is wedged between two superpowers locked in an
ideological struggle of epic proportions. Yet those challenges only
made the trying more necessary, and the successes, when achieved,
more satisfying. Both efforts and accomplishments were shared with an
extraordinary group of professionals – those men and women engaged
in one of the many public-sector elements of the foreign and defence
services. Agreement was not always easily reached with these dedicated
persons, and sometimes never was, yet their devotion to Canada should
be a matter of pride to all Canadians. For us, the most respectful of
relationships with many of those persons has been one of the enduring benefits of the experiences related here.

The challenge to us as authors of this volume extended not only to
the selection of the material but to the style of its presentation. After
considerable experimentation, we chose to employ the third person as
the most efficient way to distinguish our separate involvements. The
disadvantage of this written style is the degree of formality that it intro-
duces, and the possible impression that we are distancing ourselves from
the events chronicled. This latter is quite unintended, as is another: the
assumption by some readers that the events described here are exhaustive of all Canadian international activities in the years 1968 to 1984.

That is far from the case. Those selected nevertheless represent, we believe, the most important of events, those that best reflect the flavour of the period.

This book is the most recent product of a collaboration between us that began in 1967, shortly following Trudeau's appointment as minister of justice. Head, then a professor of law at the University of Alberta, joined him in Ottawa as an associate counsel for what each of us thought would be a single year. In the course of three subsequent decades, the association has grown ever richer. The book was written in the same fashion as were so many of our joint enterprises over the years. Utilizing archival materials, and stimulated by frequent conversations with Trudeau, Head produced preliminary drafts of chapters that would become the subject of intense examination, review, and spirited debate between us. Trudeau's criticisms and additions would then be absorbed into the final text. Nordhoff and Hall, we know, laboured in different fashion, but they had the luxury of an isolated tropical island on which to work. We were separated by three thousand kilometres for much of the period, and each was engaged in other, full-time, activities.

We acknowledge gratefully the assistance of a number of persons in the course of this extensive enterprise: Peter Dauvergne, Debby Gupta, and Martha Nelems, research assistants; Judy Myer, librarian at the Canadian Embassy in Washington, D.C.; Ann Head, who skilfully typed every word of every draft; and Douglas Gibson and Pat Kennedy, whose editorial support in the final phases added much to the quality of the work. Finally, a genuine word of thanks to all those friends and associates who encouraged us throughout this lengthy exercise: one, Gérard Pelletier, deserves special mention.

Ivan L. Head
– Vancouver

Pierre Elliott Trudeau
– Montreal

May 1995

CHAPTER ONE

The Inheritance

I

One of the more colourful statements attributed to Winston Churchill is his observation that "History is just one damn thing after another." Practitioners of foreign relations understand well the passion behind those words. Events that are often unexpected, infrequently amenable to constructive influence, and seemingly always capable of simplistic interpretation by someone, cascade unceasingly onto foreign-office desks. They compete for attention, demand responses of one kind or another, and all too often threaten to disrupt the carefully considered agendas on which governments rely. Thus does reality differ from expectation. The desirable presence of insightful scenarios, prudent policy proposals, and soundly prepared alternative courses of action tend all too often, unfortunately, to be of greater application in academic treatises than in cabinet deliberations. The challenge to governments thus becomes twofold: one, not to be daunted by the seeming novelty of events as they arise and, two, not to be tempted to address them in a fashion so pragmatic as to forsake unconsciously the values and interests of one's own society.

In a world where distinctions between the domestic and the international become increasingly irrelevant, the maintenance of balance is not a simple or easily acquired skill. National "interest" often takes on a magnitude and definition quite novel, making coherence of activities the more challenging. And all the while the momentum of events is both unpredictable and disorderly. Day after day, originating elsewhere, transparently communicated, comes "one damn thing after another," without heed to previously fixed budgets or agendas or commitments.

Seldom can these "things" be safely ignored, even when they appear most benign. The obvious, immediate inclination in such circumstances, encouraged by the media, by the parliamentary opposition, and by public-interest groups, is to do *something*. Governments quite properly are assailed for indifference or indolence. Nevertheless, the often less obvious, yet much more important, challenge is to probe beyond symptoms, to address underlying causes, to build international legal regimes where appropriate, to develop the stamina to stay the course. To be effective.

The state of public awareness of international events is often as unpredictable as is the level of expressed concern. The year 1968 revealed that. Canadians in the mid-sixties were far from indifferent to offshore issues, but were not on the whole particularly seized by any of them. Without doubt, they expected their government to act prudently and honourably in the discharge of its international responsibilities, but generally left the impression that that expectation was satisfied. The election of 1968, not surprisingly, focused on domestic issues, and so international themes did not enter the campaign as a major element.

In large measure this could be explained by the fact that the decade had turned from a fractious period of Canadian self-doubt into an era of unexpected self-confidence. The buoyancy burgeoned from one region to another as Quebec's *"révolution tranquille"* was matched by generally high employment rates in most parts of the country, and was capped by the triumph of Expo 67 in Montreal. Expo attracted the favourable attention of the world and prompted an unusual burst of genuine pride – all the more so because it was modest – from coast to coast. The new Canadian flag flew prominently throughout the country and was seen in places far and wide all over the world, stitched onto the backpacks of young Canadians who were assisting newly independent countries in their fledgling steps towards development or roaming confidently in regions both familiar and remote. Throughout Canada there was an impression of a new era, yet, as with most impressions, the boundary between old and new was more apparent than real. Particularly was this the case in the sector of foreign policy.

International relations, perhaps more so than much other human activity, are part of a continuum. No matter how tempting or convenient is the tendency to compartmentalize into a fixed period this or that event — wars, droughts, plagues, even love affairs — a thorough examination of each reveals preliminary circumstances and consequential effects well outside the boundaries arbitrarily selected. The Trojan War, the Industrial Revolution, and the Ming Dynasty all appear in history books with neatly bracketed dates marking their beginnings and ends. Historians know, however, that no matter how authoritatively these dates are presented, they are simply devices to assist us in our ability to catalogue and relate. These are the labels on history's filing cabinets, not definitive milestones of absolute legitimacy. For the same reason, chronological descriptions of this or that civil administration or government are bound to be misleading if the impression is left of definitive starts and stops, elections notwithstanding. The edges of periods in office tend more often than not to be blurred and indistinct, not sharply defined and clear.

And so it must be understood in the descriptions that follow that events are seldom singular or isolated; they overlap, interact, and rebound. The Canadian federal election of June 25, 1968, did not instantly mark the opening of a new era in Canadian history, much as it was attractive for observers to report this, or convenient for some of us then to suggest it. More accurately, that election gave to Pierre Elliott Trudeau and his associates the opportunity to influence Canadian foreign policy by broaching preferences and exercising options of a kind and in a way not previously pursued. These policies were not entirely novel, however, nor were they introduced into an international vacuum.

The sixties had been turbulent and contradictory, witness to a wide range of extraordinary accomplishments — from the launching of humans into space to the ultimately successful campaign to eliminate smallpox — as well as to a tragic litany of human frailties and barbarism. Among the latter were the assassinations of President John Kennedy (and, later, his brother Robert) and Martin Luther King, Jr.; several bloody conflicts in Africa and Asia; the increasing incidence of major environmental catastrophes of human origin; and the spread of nuclear arsenals. One could not pretend that Canada and Canadians were unaffected by these events, no matter how distant from Canadian shores any of them may have seemed. Equally, no matter how diminutive one regarded Canada's influence in the world, the basic instinct of

Canadians was to participate responsibly in an endeavour to seek reasoned outcomes whenever it seemed appropriate.

That instinct was not, of course, universal. It varied from region to region and from one age group to another. It found root in a number of circumstances, not all of them well understood and seldom clearly enunciated, yet influential nevertheless. Among them: Canada's economic dependency on export markets; the presence within the country of so many Canadians of diverse origins; the searing experience of participation in the two world wars; the positive post-1945 contributions of Canada within the several organs and institutions of the international community; and a growing awareness of the immense disparities in living standards from one part of the globe to another.

One group of Canadians was quite clear in declaring its opinions. Those dedicated to the study and practice of international affairs were exceedingly articulate in their support of a vibrant foreign policy. These people understood that the international interests, indeed the international reputation, of a state depended for their safeguarding upon an active participation and an effective contribution in world affairs. Their views were influential and contributed to the general expectation among Canadians that their governments would not neglect either international responsibilities or international opportunities. In 1968, the new government was thus well aware that its international policies and practices would sooner or later be subject to careful public scrutiny and criticism. As luck would have it, events abroad brought the spotlight to bear more quickly than had been anticipated.

Prominent among those events, not unexpectedly, were the continued hostilities in Vietnam, including the political drama being played out in the U.S. election campaign, all reported in vibrant detail in the Canadian news media. The decision of President Lyndon Johnson not to seek re-election was evidence of the deep social turmoil that this most controversial of wars had unleashed in America. Though characteristically more subdued in Canada, public expression on university campuses and in newspaper columns was nevertheless untiring in its commentaries and demands upon the government. Johnson's retirement acted as a stimulus to those opposed to the war.

Entirely unexpected, by contrast, was the reaction of Canadians to a civil war in a part of Africa so remote that it had scarcely gained attention anywhere in the immediate aftermath of the first claims to secession by a discontented army colonel, but which suddenly rose to such prominence that it dominated Question Period in the House of Commons month after month before disappearing from view as quickly as it had arrived.

Some of the scrutiny, on the other hand, was prompted by internal Canadian circumstances. One such was the fact that the 1968 election was the first in a decade to return a majority government, one not constrained in its decision-making by the fear of a parliamentary blockage. Another was the withdrawal from active public life of Prime Minister Lester Pearson, a person whose lengthy career as a diplomat and foreign-affairs actor lent to him a well-deserved international credibility. Trudeau, in contrast, was a largely unknown persona in the international arena, and therefore the object of considerable curiosity and quite overblown expectations on the part of the Canadian public. Another kind of curiosity, one laced with apprehension, centred in the many members of the foreign-service community whose entire careers had been shaped in association with Pearson in one or another of his capacities. They now found to their dismay that the closest to "one of their own" in the Prime Minister's Office was Ivan Head, whose brief experience as a junior foreign-service officer in the Department of External Affairs had concluded some years earlier, when he resigned in favour of teaching international law at the University of Alberta.

The prime ministership gave to Trudeau the opportunity to practise what instinct and training had both long encouraged in him: the conscious sequencing of policy-making and policy-implementation; and the identification of desired goals and their pursuit in light of circumstance. This was his intention in the international, as well as the domestic, sphere. In each, he well recognized, a number of forces were at play quite beyond the ability of any Canadian government to shape decisively, sometimes even to predict accurately. That very circumstance made it all the more necessary in Trudeau's view that policy goals and preferences be well considered, accurately defined, and consciously pursued to avoid the ignominy of allowing events to dictate policies and priorities. The very fact that the number and weight of variable factors were greater in the international domain than in the domestic was reason to identify most certainly there Canadian values, interests, and goals, lest these be unduly manipulated by outside events. In the absence of a well-defined policy framework, the hurly-burly of international events so colourfully referred to by Churchill will inevitably dominate. When that occurs does one rely on the atavistic instinct to remain afloat, to muddle through, to make the best of it with colourful but empty comments and gestures?

In the superpower world of the sixties, the excesses of ideological polarity complicated the scene even more. In Washington and Moscow, circumstances were often made subject to the most simplistic (sometimes the most complicated) of Cold War interpretation and argument. Demands were made, expectations aroused, priorities reordered. "Principle" was always asserted, yet unconscionably abused all too frequently behind smoke screens of adversarial rhetoric.

No country in the world was invulnerable to these rushing tides of influence and manipulation. The range of susceptibility varied, however, as some states competed to be included as unquestioned partners in the grand design, while others, so powerless as to be impotent, were simply swept along. Great Britain fell into the first category. Cruelly treated by the Second World War, this still-proud country emerged into the postwar period denuded of its economic strength, soon to be stripped of its overseas possessions, yet determined to command recognition as an important actor and the occupant of a "special relationship" with the United States. Tanzania was an example of the second category. One of the many newly independent states endeavouring to overcome horrendous economic and social frailties, wholly incapable of influencing the tides of history that were so indifferent to its interests, it could only appeal to the consciences of others, which it did with eloquence. President Julius Nyerere recounted a Swahili proverb to express his country's vulnerability: "It matters not whether the elephants are fighting or making love, they still trample the grass."

Canada's position was neither of these, and, to the credit of all postwar prime ministers, had remained distinctive in the face of often intense pressures. Sometimes naïvely, but with unquestioned sincerity, Canadians on the whole retained their own vision of the world. It was a vision that featured decency, fair play, and a role for rational initiatives. An interpretation of that vision was shared in remarkable detail by Trudeau and Head even though we had been raised in quite distinctive parts of Canada, one in Quebec, the other in Alberta. In 1968, the year of the optimism of the Prague Spring and the bitter agony of its cruel repression, another year of a less-than-fully-representative United Nations and broadly unfulfilled expectations in the developing regions of the world, a year of mounting foreign adventurism by some Canadian provinces, Trudeau called for a fresh look at Canadian foreign policy. There was no anticipation on his part that there would be an avalanche of dramatic departures from past directions. There was, however, a belief in the value of a comprehensive reappraisal of the world as it then was, of a careful examination of Canada's interests and undertakings, and of a systematic consideration of a range of alternatives.

The intention was not to challenge Pearson's concept of Canada as a "middle power," but to explore opportunities that would ensure that Canada would function as an "effective power." Without doubt, there was a degree of intellectual curiosity evident in the call for such a review. There was as well, however, a healthy admiration of the extraordinary contributions that Canada had made in the "shaping of peace,"[1] John Holmes's term for the architectural design of the Bretton Woods and United Nations institutions and processes, and a desire to continue that tradition. In those instances, as in the drafting of the North Atlantic Charter creating NATO, the Canadian vision of a decent, fair, and stable international community was expressed by brilliant, competent public servants of an earlier generation. Persons such as Louis Rasminsky, Hume Wrong, Escott Reid, Jules Léger, Hugh Keenleyside, Norman Robertson, Georges Vanier, and Mike Pearson had combined concept and resolve with skill and language to reflect high purpose and practical techniques in an optimistic era of global constitution-making. Canada had found its calling in this newborn world of diplomatic negotiation, and, as a result, had engendered respect abroad and support at home.

A quarter-century later, encouraged by a new generation of public servants, Trudeau recognized that a fresh look was needed in light of world circumstances dramatically different from those of that earlier age. Canada, by choice, had withdrawn from its 1945 status as a significant military power and a major maritime flag state; the countries of Western Europe had emerged from their period of reconstruction;

Japan was now a formidable economic power; and the countries of the "Third World" were rapidly increasing in number and in influence.

The review Trudeau called for was in part a follow-on to a similar, but incomplete and rather unsatisfactory, exercise launched by Prime Minister Pearson in 1967 on the eve of the announcement of his intention to resign. A preliminary element of the new review was to be an examination of Canada's defence commitments. The expectation was that this initial exercise could be concluded within a few months, permitting the main foreign-policy review to proceed smoothly in light of all facets of Canadian interests and obligations. The government could then set its priorities early on in its mandate, confident that it was in possession of all relevant information, and seized of a holistic view of the contemporary world.

These expectations proved to be quite unrealistic. Completion dates were extended several times, tests of will between public servants and ministers emerged frequently, and cabinet solidarity was severely tried. A quite unexpected outcome of these skirmishes and struggles was the bonding of the two of us into a rare partnership. Over a period of several months, there evolved a relationship that ensured no major foreign- or defence-policy decision or initiative would be taken, conference attended, or speech delivered by the prime minister without Head's involvement.

The arrangement was not entirely one of happenstance, nor was it unprecedented, either in Canada or elsewhere. In a Westminster system of responsible government, however, certain conventions as well as personal sensibilities were obviously potentially at risk. Not surprisingly, varying levels of apprehension were voiced from time to time, some rational and to be heeded, others ill-informed or opportunistic, yet not to be ignored. Against these, the relationship would be measured constantly to ensure it demonstrated relative advantage.

An early test had arisen prior to the 1968 election. That spring, the president of the University of Alberta had extended invitations to the secretary general of the United Nations, U Thant, and Trudeau (then minister of justice) to accept honorary degrees in a special convocation marking the sixtieth anniversary of the university. In the interval between invitation and event, Trudeau had been chosen leader of the Liberal Party and, thus, prime minister of Canada. Each man had accepted the invitation; Trudeau would deliver the main convocation address, and U Thant would be the principal speaker at a gala banquet the same evening. As the event neared, Head was given the task of drafting a speech, in light of his continuing association with the university as professor of law on leave.

The occasion was clearly an opportunity for remarks relating to the international community, and took on added significance in view of Trudeau's decision to seek dissolution of Parliament. The event would be the first public address delivered by him in his new capacity as prime minister. An election campaign was technically under way, but no thought was given to a partisan theme. Instead, the subject chosen was the relationship of Canada with the developing countries. It was a theme that would remain constant in Canadian foreign policy throughout the several Trudeau administrations. The message delivered that sunny spring afternoon in Edmonton in the presence of the UN secretary general would emerge again and again in the years following:

> We must recognize that, in the long run, the overwhelming threat to Canada will not come from foreign investments, or foreign ideologies, or even – with good fortune – foreign nuclear weapons. It will come instead from the two-thirds of the peoples of the world who are steadily falling farther and farther behind in their search for a decent standard of living.

He emphasized that it was Canada's moral obligation, and in Canada's interest, to cooperate with those countries in their quest for self-improvement. This dedication to international equity would lead to the creation of novel development-assistance mechanisms, to quite unexpected Commonwealth initiatives, to co-chairmanship of the Cancun Summit, and to numerous international interventions.

There were no major events outside Canada in the summer of 1968 that demanded the immediate involvement of the prime minister, as distinct from appropriate ministers. An eye would have to be kept on the U.S. election campaign, of course, because of the critical importance of virtually any American decision to so many things Canadian. Because the polls suggested a Republican presidency, the first since that of Dwight Eisenhower, the likely attitude of a new American administration towards Canada–U.S. trade, and particularly the recently concluded Auto Pact, was important, as was any posture about Vietnam War objectors crossing into Canada. The continuing drama of Britain's possible entry into the European Community would affect Canadian exports in unknown ways should British policy become clear and an agreement be struck. The ongoing drama of Rhodesia's unilateral declaration of independence, on the other hand, was not an issue engaging Canada in major fashion. The potentially cataclysmic nuclear standoff in Europe was one that needed attention, but not instantly, notwithstanding the Soviet invasion of Czechoslovakia. The initial response was properly one for the NATO alliance.

The Canadian ministers keeping an eye on all of this were both competent and experienced. The trade minister was Jean-Luc Pepin; the secretary of state for external affairs was Mitchell Sharp. Both had served under Pearson, both were sensitive to the dominant issues, especially those with an economic content. In an earlier phase of his career, Sharp had been employed by Brazilian Traction, Light and Power Company, and had retained a keen sense of the potential benefits to Canada of closer relations with the countries of South America. He proposed to lead a series of business missions through that continent as an early initiative of the new government, and Trudeau agreed.

From a different source, some evidence of unwelcome activity, while not critical, demanded a watching brief nevertheless. The arrogance of President Charles de Gaulle's meddling remarks in Montreal a year earlier were by no means an isolated incident. For reasons best known to itself, the French government continued to engage in unfriendly provocations of a kind alien to relations between two mature states, and found – as it knew it would – individuals in Quebec who delighted in their newfound roles as international bit players. Trudeau understood the potential damage of this kind of sideshow and was determined not to be intimidated by Paris. He had recognized months earlier the hazards implicit in the international pretensions of Quebec and had accordingly encouraged Pearson to take an unequivocal stand on the Gabon incident at a time when the Department of External Affairs appeared indifferent to the stakes involved.[2] Normally, the foreign minister would bear the responsibility of watching this brief. Sharp, however, was not a Quebecker, nor did he speak French.

The assignment was given to Marc Lalonde, the prime minister's principal secretary, who had served in the same capacity for Pearson.

In addition to these "watching" activities, and the launching of the foreign- and defence-policy reviews, the order was given to pursue two areas deemed susceptible to major Canadian initiatives. It was well understood that each would require patience and stamina, and should proceed independent of the foreign-policy review. The first sought a means of formal diplomatic recognition of the People's Republic of China and a legal relationship with the Beijing government. The second anticipated a major increase in Canada's official development assistance and an enhancement of involvement in the developing countries, so many of them newly independent. Each of these sectors reflected a long-standing commitment by both Trudeau and Head, and had been the subject of several searching conversations between us in earlier months.

The China issue had long been a simmering irritant to many Canadians and a clear example of an international anomaly in the minds of each of us. The manipulation of the UN Credentials Committee by the United States was as blatant as it was unconscionable and self-defeating. Pearson had wanted to do something that might rectify the situation, but his minority position in Parliament (where John Diefenbaker was unalterably opposed to any weakening of support for the Nationalist government in Taiwan and its claim to be the legitimate government of all China), and the unambiguous signals of opposition to such a move from Washington, combined to discourage any initiative. Trudeau resolved to try. There was, of course, no guarantee that Beijing was even interested in talking to Canada or, if it were, that those discussions would have any impact on the credentials blockage in the United Nations. Nevertheless, if one believed in the universality of the United Nations, and in the primacy of international law fairly applied, this exercise was desirable and defensible. And so it began.

A less important recognition issue was pursued in tandem, this one to establish diplomatic relations with the Holy See. The intention here was simply to gain access, through formal diplomatic relations, to the rich global network of Vatican representatives. The effort was not without detractors, nevertheless. As there were Canadian critics reluctant to engage with communists, so were there those opposed to engagement with the Roman Catholic Church. Trudeau had anticipated the latter and was determined to appoint a prominent Protestant as Canadian ambassador should the discussions conclude successfully, as they did early in 1970. After both Frank Scott and Eugene Forsey had declined the nomination, another distinguished Canadian, John E. Robbins, president of Brandon University, became Canada's first representative to the Vatican.

Canadian policies towards the developing countries had assumed a new importance during the Pearson governments. The independence of so many former colonies of European powers prompted Canada to establish a number of new diplomatic missions. Trading policies, especially with the Caribbean, were re-examined, and new development-assistance programs were launched, even though aid flows remained minuscule.[3] These budgets and programs would be clustered by Trudeau into a specially created unit in 1968, the Canadian International Development Agency (CIDA), under the presidency of Maurice Strong, who had been recruited from the private sector. Strong proved to be extraordinarily adept in this role. He supervised Canada's entry into the emerging sector of multilateral assistance programs and encouraged the creation of a novel, independent organization to foster the scientific and technological competence of the developing countries. This pioneering concept would take form in 1970 as the International Development Research Centre (IDRC) and become the model for similar initiatives launched by a number of countries. Early on, Trudeau pledged that funds dedicated to Official Development Assistance (ODA) would be one of only two budget items not subject to freezes or reductions.[4]

The late sixties may have appeared to observers of the Canadian scene as the beginning of a new, more confident era, but there was little evidence that the world as a whole viewed events in the same light. The Cold War dominated the international landscape and gave no sign of easing. The earlier optimistic expectations of those countries emerging from colonial rule were already dampening under the harsh realities of the responsibilities of independence. The seemingly intractable tensions in the Middle East were seldom, if ever, out of sight and would shortly spawn quite unprecedented levels and forms of violence and terrorism. The admitted advantages of the Kennedy Round of tariff negotiations served to reveal the range of still-remaining trade irritants and barriers and the likelihood of more difficult negotiations if further tariff reductions in the Tokyo Round, then beginning, were to be achieved. And all the while the technology associated with ever more lethal forms of nuclear warfare continued to evolve.

Canada was not uninterested in any of these circumstances. Nor was it bereft of policy options related to them. The extent of its leverage varied considerably, however. In the course of the first few months following the 1968 election, certain principles nevertheless emerged which, while not always new or unorthodox, gave to the government fresh incentives to act with some certainty.

The era of intercontinental ballistic missiles and the promised emergence of defensive technology placed Canada in the distinctly uncomfortable geographic position of lying beneath the trajectories of the first, and the fallout of the second. Whatever could be done to ease superpower tensions in a constructive way was obviously of appeal.

The difficult circumstances in which so many developing countries found themselves, and the potential this offered for instability and human tragedy, was becoming increasingly apparent. These circumstances might respond positively to more imaginative and dedicated assistance programs.

The likelihood that Britain would renew its application for membership in the European Community, and so place in jeopardy much of Canada's favoured trading advantages with it, would have to be faced sympathetically, with the long-term interests of both countries in mind, not with the hyperbolic opposition voiced by Prime Minister Diefenbaker at an earlier date.

It seemed clear to us the applicable principles in these and other instances should preferably relate to the orderliness of international political and legal regimes, and to the concepts of fairness and equity, not to immediate nationalistic or political advantage. How to proceed was much more difficult than stating the obvious, however. The balance of principle with interest can seldom be sharply defined. A major consideration, the response of such important international actors as the United States, is not always ascertainable. Above all, commitments would be necessary. After all, if the mark of a responsible power is one that does not turn away from challenge, that of an effective power is one that does not posture hollowly. Constructive influence would be the criterion of measurement.

II

In an ideal world, the design of foreign policy and the conduct of foreign relations would form the two sides of a single coin. Foreign policy would be the long-term, enlightened agenda of a country's goals, reflecting its needs and its aspirations; the conduct of foreign relations would consist of the short- to mid-term actions and investments necessary for the implementation of that policy.

In the real world, however, no state, no matter how large or powerful, is able so to function. From within, an inevitable mix of shifting interests, both sectoral and regional, bring incompatible and inconsistent demands and pressures to bear on the formulation of policy. From without, a myriad of international actors – some human, some natural – combine and compete to create unexpected circumstances, calling for novel responses and adjustments. Governments function in the real world, yet endeavour not to lose sight of the ideal.

Ironically, those governments that are most dedicated to their own image of the ideal – whether for ideological or nationalistic reasons – are most likely to deny the possibility of its achievement. When those same states are powerful, either globally or regionally, they create circumstances that force all others to adjust both policy and response. In another irony, the governments of the strongest states and the members of the weakest domestic constituencies often share and project similar attitudes. Each tends to portray a righteousness that assumes all other actors – foreign states, national governments, fellow citizens – would be better served if only they adopted a point of view identical to their own. And, all too frequently, each of these quite different actors is driven by the assumption that forceful perseverance will reward them in the realization of their goals.

There is still a further element with which governments must contend. It takes the form of the oft-times large domestic constituency that contends that foreign policy and foreign relations are of little, if any, relevance or have no impact upon one's own circumstances. From this source comes advocacy for withdrawal, for isolation, for acquiescence, for indifference, or some combination of these factors. The strength of this constituency is generally in inverse proportion to the health of the domestic economy; as well, it seems all too often to be in direct relation to the military strength of the state.

Subject to these vicissitudes, governments of all persuasions seek to chart their own courses within the international environment and to navigate the often unpredictable and sometimes tumultuous circumstances en route. Successive Canadian governments have become familiar with all of the above and have endeavoured in varying fashion to adjust appropriately. Those endeavours have been complicated in several aspects by the peculiarities of Canada's history, geography, and climate. Long after the Peace of Westphalia in 1648,[5] which settled the boundaries of most European states, Canada's territorial extent was not so much subject to contention as it was in large measure simply unknown. At the time of Confederation in 1867, much doubt still remained about the outlines of the Arctic land masses and bodies of water, notwithstanding centuries of exploration by daring navigators. When, in 1880, Britain ceded to Canada at Canadian request the balance of its colonial territories in these regions, it did so not with precise geographic coordinates but with artfully drafted language:[6] ". . . all the British possessions on the North American continent not hitherto annexed to any colony."

An official Canadian government publication much later speculated on the purposeful vagueness of this wording:[7]

> . . . the reason advanced by those who have studied the attitude of
> the British authorities is that it was finally considered inadvisable
> to define that which according to available knowledge was
> indefinite.

It was not until well into the twentieth century that modern surveying and mapping techniques, many of them conducted by the fledgling Royal Canadian Air Force, permitted accurate presentations of shorelines in the inhospitable Arctic regions, and not until 1930 that an amicable settlement was concluded with Norway that ceded to Canada the Sverdrup Islands, located west of Ellesmere Island.[8]

Canada's territorial boundaries, both land and sea, have been contested and negotiated through the years – in most instances with the United States but more recently with France and Denmark as well. By 1968, all land boundaries had long since been settled with Canada's only adjacent neighbour; several water areas would remain in dispute for years to come, however, and be the subject of sometimes contentious confrontation.

The social composition of Canada, moulded over the centuries, and the geographic propinquity of the United States have always been immensely important influences on Canadian foreign policy. The initial social contract, dating back to the eighteenth century, endeavoured to join in harmonious fashion the two distinct communities, one French-speaking (the longest resident), the other English-speaking. It did so by recognizing French civil law, including property rights, the seigneurial system, and the legitimacy of the Roman Catholic religion. It failed signally, however, in generating a constructive dynamic between the two groups, prompting Lord Durham's oft-quoted comment in his 1839 report about "two nations warring in the bosom of a single state,"9 and leading to Hugh MacLennan's astute description of "Two Solitudes" in 1945.10

The sociological determinants of this behaviour were not difficult to identify: a clerical encouragement of insular nationalism in Quebec, and an unwillingness on the part of an increasingly non-French-speaking majority to accept the linguistic reality of a minority community. The genius of a federal system of government both preserved the Canadian union and laid the groundwork for the kind of jurisdictional competitiveness that was rapidly gaining strength in the late sixties. Contributing to the tension of the circumstance was the growing segment of the Canadian population whose roots were neither British nor French. This *mélange* of proud, often non-communicating elements, posed a test to common sense and decency in human terms, and structural flexibility and wisdom in juridical terms, that would provoke in the majority of instances the most gracious, yet oft-times the most dismal and self-serving, characteristics on the part of Canadians.

All too often overlooked in the process were the circumstances and interests of the indigenous peoples, whose presence preceded by millennia the now-dominant immigrants. This combination of backgrounds and attitudes lent to the Canadian social experiment a dynamism and potential that made it a model of human governance. It also produced a sharply divergent spectrum of foreign-policy interests on the part of the several communities, ranging from military alliances, as in the two world wars, to human-rights issues in the Soviet Union, all of which required recognition and consideration by government. How to bring these disparate views together without sacrificing principle would pose a recurring challenge.

The most dominant factor in Canadian foreign policy is the ponderous presence of the United States. With its overwhelming influence on the economy and culture of Canada, the United States had been for much more than a century the single most important consideration in the design of successive Canadian foreign policies. There was an enduring tenaciousness among Canadians and their governments that sometimes bemused, sometimes irritated, U.S. administrations: the commitment to a social and political distinctiveness. This instinctive belief in the worth of Canadian values and institutions prevailed alongside the immense respect and admiration that most Canadians, including we two, held for so many American traits and accomplishments. Each of us had travelled widely in the United States, each of us had pursued graduate studies at an American university (Harvard in each case), each of us recognized implicitly the extraordinary dynamism and resourcefulness of American society, yet each of us believed deeply in those attributes of Canadians – pluralism, decency, fairness, respect for law, among others – that gave to Canada its own personality and to Canadians their own sense of human dignity and worth.

Still another circumstance, this one with constitutional roots reaching back to Westminster in the age of empire, was increasingly perplexing to those engaged in the practice of foreign relations. To understand this factor, one must remember that the British North America Act of 1867, for more than a century Canada's constitution, was a statute of the British House of Commons.[11] Its original purpose was not at all intended to grant independence to Canada, but only to mark formally the articles of Confederation agreed to by the three colonies of Canada, Nova Scotia, and New Brunswick, and in the process to fortify certain elements of "self" government – all of them local. In the catalogue dividing legislative competence between the new Dominion of Canada and the four provincial constituent parts (to be Ontario, Quebec, Nova Scotia, and New Brunswick), no mention was made purposely of constitutional amendment, of the locus of power of representation abroad, of treaty negotiation, or of defence. The BNA Act was silent in these respects, because the new Dominion remained a colony. Britain exercised all these responsibilities in its own interest for decades to come. Not until the Statute of Westminster in 1931 – another act of the British parliament[12] – were these functions abandoned by the imperial power. In that sixty-four-year interval, Canada realized on many occasions how indifferent to Canadian interests the colonial power could be.

Perhaps the incident with the most far-reaching impact was one of the earliest – the 1903 Yukon–Alaska boundary arbitration – when British interests far removed from those of Canada proved to be the most influential. As in the much earlier negotiation to fix the British Columbia–Washington boundary, geographic aberrations became permanent. Unlike that outcome, however, the 1903 decision still remains as an irritant in Canada–U.S. relations, because of the maritime dimensions of the territory. A portion of the body of water lying between the Alaska "panhandle" and the Queen Charlotte Islands of British Columbia is claimed by both countries, who both cherish its fishery.

The principal enduring effect of the BNA Act in international-relations terms, however, has been internal. The price Canada paid to be the first British colony to gain a degree of independence is evident from the constitutional language of the second colony in the process. Australia is a product of the Australia Act, 1900,[13] a British statute which states:

(i) Trade and Commerce with other countries. . . .
(vi) The naval and military defence of the Commonwealth. . . .
(xxix) External Affairs. . . .
all fall within the exclusive competence of the Commonwealth
(i.e., the federal) government.

In the absence of similar provisions in Canada's constitutional document, this country had witnessed a continuing series of assertions by provinces (principally, but by no means only, Quebec) intent to demonstrate that they are possessed of an international quality and competence. Over the years, this provincial pretentiousness has puzzled and delighted foreign powers, who have used it to their own advantage, most often in the economic sector, where one province has been played off against another to the disadvantage of each. It would be an exaggeration to suggest that the international activities of Canadian provinces have on the whole diminished Canada's stature internationally – by far the greatest number of them have been proper and appropriate – but in all too many instances the internal wrangling has been exceedingly unpleasant and time-consuming. In the result, this structural weakness in the Canadian framework has been much more than a mere aggravation to successive Canadian governments, and has undoubtedly led to enhanced job descriptions on the part of numerous provincial politicians and a lesser number of provincial officials.

A distinct, and this time entirely appropriate, effect of the Canadian federal constitution is evident in the field of treaties. Subject areas that clearly fall within provincial jurisdiction, such as education (exclusively) or agriculture (shared), require the involvement of provincial governments should they be addressed internationally. In such instances, the negotiation and the ratification of treaties becomes a more complex, and likely more thoroughgoing, process in federal states such as Canada than in unitary states such as France. As well, the end result in terms of understanding and of support has been strengthened. For these reasons, Canada was deeply engaged in the negotiation of the "federal state" clause in the UN Convention on the Law of Treaties, concluded at Vienna in 1969.[14]

In the late sixties, a peculiar variation of this sharing of jurisdiction arose, this time involving language. It took the form of efforts on the part of some French-speaking nations and of Canada to replicate in some respects the most successful and quite venerable Commonwealth of Nations, the association of Britain and the English-speaking former British colonies.

The thought that some Canadian provinces should be engaged as full members of the Commonwealth had never arisen, largely because of the history of the association. When Senegal, Tunisia, and Canada proposed the creation of an association of francophone states, however, the argument was later made by Quebec that political units of varying kinds be included as full members. A contest immediately broke out as to which government, that of Canada or of Quebec, could legitimately represent the interests of French-speaking Canadians in international fora.

Consistent with the levels to which ambitious humans will descend, the manifestations of this contest became as absurd as they were serious. When representatives of French-speaking foreign powers landed at Montreal's international airports en route to Ottawa, federal welcoming parties would be shouldered aside by their zealous provincial counterparts in this contest for status. Provincial delegations travelling to foreign capitals would demand ministerial access, and then seek to exclude Canadian Embassy staff members from any meeting on the premise that the latter were eavesdropping on provincial business. With the exception of the Gaullist government in France, foreign states found these practices either amusing or embarrassing. Nevertheless, the energies and resources committed to these struggles elevated them from the comic-opera genre into something far more serious, and certainly unpleasant. These shenanigans were intended as symbolic steps in the struggle to create an international legal stature for Quebec, a necessary stage in the pursuit of independence. As such, they had to be countered. The time-to-time mimicking of some of these Quebec practices by certain other provincial governments may have contributed to the egos of the proponents, but was of considerably less seriousness.

The great value of federalism for a country of Canada's diversity is in no danger of being overcome by jurisdictional challenges and competitiveness on the part of its component parts. When there are mechanisms appropriate for the determination of these claims, as in the case of the Offshore Minerals Reference,[15] both the process and the outcomes are wholesome, whatever the result. In the absence of acceptable mechanisms (or in the failure to employ them), much more than Canada's international effectiveness is at stake, however: Canada's social well-being diminishes.

Geography and history should properly be beyond the reach of any government to redefine. The structure of its own institutions and the design of its own processes are quite different, however; in those respects do constitutional issues intersect with foreign relations.

It was this latter element of the inheritance that would demand constant attention throughout the several Trudeau administrations. Sadly, but not surprisingly in light of the social and historic dynamics involved, it would escape a final resolution satisfactory to all communities and all levels of government.

III

These, in broadest description, were the ingredients inherited by the new Trudeau administration as it began its mandate of governance in the summer of 1968. With the determination and confidence that is part of a majority electoral victory, and the innocence and inexperience that is inherent in any new government, Trudeau and his colleagues set to work to establish their priorities in a range of areas, and to address without delay the one issue that all regarded as the single most important challenge facing them and the country – that of Canadian unity. Individual ministers would supervise the departments of government reporting to them (in the foreign and defence sectors, the three senior ministers were Sharp, Pepin, and Léo Cadieux, minister of national defence), but major policies would be formulated and decisions be taken in the full collegiality of cabinet, where a number of other ministers soon exhibited a keen interest and a vigorous point of view in matters international. This would prove to be a mixed blessing: of considerable value, as fresh opinions were expressed from sometimes unconventional vantage points; of some concern, as delays in decision-making were occasionally engendered by unexpected debates.

Apart from our insistence that the recognition of China be explored with all due speed, that the special circumstances of the developing countries be accorded an understanding response, and that a deep intellectual investment be made towards the responsible reduction of tensions with the Soviet Union, neither of us were seized of a foreign-policy agenda. During our relationship in the Department of Justice in the Pearson government, we had often discussed informally and sometimes at length the ingredients that one or both regarded as essential in a functioning international community. As lawyers and teachers of law, it was not surprising that each of us was dedicated to the creation and extension of legal regimes, to the contribution of orderly and constructive processes for change, and to the fostering of cooperative techniques for dispute resolution. Each of us had observed from different perspectives the advantages to be gained from international cooperation, as well as the tragic evidence of inequitable circumstances among and within nations.

Trudeau had been a lifelong critic of nationalism, focusing most intensely on the expressions of those in Quebec who championed the cause of withdrawal or separation. Head had observed in the ferment of Southeast Asia the dangerous futility of naked assertions of sovereignty. Each of us accepted, as many observers had long argued, that many of the challenges, as well as the interests, of individual societies were simply not totally responsive to territorially explicit policies or solutions.

At the very moment that the international community was burgeoning with newly launched political units, each seeking to flourish within boundaries that were often the product of aberrant colonial decisions, forces and events oblivious of national borders were assuming increasing importance. Environmental pollution was one of these, the transmission of infectious disease and destabilizing political theories were others. Still another was the resurrection of sometimes long-quiescent ethnic or tribal rivalries that prompted large-scale migrations of persons and drove communities to seek relief. Most intrusive of all factors oblivious to national boundaries was the ease with which information flowed, most often in the sixties by means of radio transmission, but increasingly, in the age of satellites, through television. The most immediately threatening of these phenomena, of course, was the proliferation of weapons of mass destruction, often mounted as warheads on very long-range and increasingly accurate rocket-delivery systems.

The inadequacy of territorially explicit national governments to cope effectively with these issues and activities was coupled with a political culture incapable of responding to many of them adequately and in timely fashion. Neither education nor experience had prepared leaders or publics to accept the need for greater cooperation and

cession of sovereign pretensions. Moreover, the UN Charter emphasized that the sovereignty of member states was a founding principle of
the post-Second World War order.[16]

Though stout advocates of international law, each of us was sceptical of the viability of world federalism. We believed that, in the world
as it was organized in 1968, the nation-state provided both the legitimacy for action and the platform for advocating change. We accepted
without question the need to foster Canadian credibility if Canada's
influence were to be effective internationally. That credibility could
only be earned, we argued, by the responsible sharing of burdens in
multilateral fora, but, as well, we would insist, it could be earned by
principled demonstrations of goal-setting and goal-pursuit on a unilateral basis if that was the most likely path towards normative international standards. Because each of us came to government from
positions as university professors, we were deeply aware of the wealth
of effort and thought that had been directed to these issues by scholars
worldwide. From the outset, Trudeau encouraged debate of the most
far-reaching kind, insisting with Cartesian logic that argument begin
with first principles, and that the broadest range of policy alternatives
be examined and evaluated before decisions were taken. From the
outset, Head was encouraged to seek out the viewpoints of those
within Canada and without whose intellectual integrity and impressive
experience lent to them a respected voice.

One such person, Douglas Dillon, President Kennedy's secretary of
the treasury, spoke to Head in 1968 with the seriousness that only a
veteran statesman can bring to bear. The error of far too many heads
of government, he insisted, lay in their willingness to champion international reforms only following their retirement from political office,
at a time when their legitimacy and influence were in rapid decline.
Dwight Eisenhower could have been immensely influential in com-
bating the military-industrial complex had he laid siege to it during his
presidency, Dillon argued, rather than referring to the problem for the
first time in his farewell address. Pearson could have been much more
effective in meeting the needs of the developing countries had he
addressed them with the same vigour while prime minister as he did
shortly thereafter as chairman of a World Bank commission of which
Dillon was a member. Take it upon yourself as a personal mission,

Dillon advised Head, to encourage Trudeau to speak out and act upon these issues at the height of his power, while in office.[17]

This advice confirmed Trudeau's own instincts. In his career to this moment he had spoken out vigorously and acted upon any number of public issues about which he felt strongly. He would welcome Head's references to Dillon's views in years to come.

CHAPTER TWO

Manhattan Comes to the Arctic

I

Canada's land mass is vast, second only to that of Russia. It is roughly triangular in shape, as deep from south to north as its base is broad from east to west. Lester Pearson once pointed out to an American audience that the Port of Churchill, home to polar bears and located far north of the major settled areas of Canada, lies only a third of the distance between the U.S. border and the tip of Ellesmere Island, Canada's northernmost point.[1]

The far-northern regions of Canada long represented one of the world's geographic mysteries. For longer than most other parts of the world, the Arctic was regarded as being the territory of no state: *terra nullius*. So extensive is the Arctic, and so forbidding the terrain and the climate, that some of the Arctic islands, straits, and topographical features were unknown until the twenties, when the advent of aerial photographic surveys permitted the commencement of systematic examination and accurate charting. Maps that now portray with considerable precision the interfaces of land and water are virtually a post-Second World War phenomenon. Their predecessors were often as vague and uncertain as the surface explorations that produced them.

The combination of vast distances and frigid temperatures had challenged Arctic explorers and deterred mapmakers for centuries. Though an immense amount of detailed local knowledge rested with the Inuit, who had made the Arctic their home since crossing over from Asia almost a millennia ago, this information was inadequate for the purposes of navigational charts or geological surveys. Some broad features, of course, had long been known, albeit imprecisely. Among

them was the existence of ice-choked narrow bodies of water separating the continental land mass from the islands of the archipelago.
Through these channels, since the arrival of Sebastian Cabot in 1497,
had sailed a number of largely British navigators, seeking to find a
route to the Pacific, a "Northwest Passage" to the legendary riches of
Cathay. In the course of their courageous endeavours, these men penetrated ever farther westward, leaving their names on prominent geographic features. Between 1576, when Martin Frobisher sailed into
the bay that bears his name, and 1846, when Sir John Franklin and his
expedition perished off King William Island, these waters and this
quest attracted men such as Davis, Hudson, Baffin, Parry, and Ross.
None made it through successfully. It was not until 1942, three and a
half centuries following Frobisher's first attempts, and then from west
to east, that the passage was undertaken to conclusion. The successful
vessel was the Royal Canadian Mounted Police schooner *St. Roch*,
under the command of Sgt. Henry Larsen.[2]

In the years immediately following the *St. Roch*'s epic voyages, the
Northwest Passage continued to be more evident on maps than
through usage. Supply ships and icebreakers utilized the brief summers
to deliver foodstuffs and building materials to the tiny communities
that had sprung up around trading posts, mine sites, and military bases
on the various islands of the archipelago; the passage itself went
unchallenged. One reason was the increased reliance placed upon the
airplane, unhindered as it was by the massive ice floes and pack ice that
deterred maritime traffic.

Not surprisingly, perhaps, little of this activity seized the attention
of the Canadian public. Whereas in past decades the daring accomplishments of bush pilots such as "Wop" May or "Punch" Dickens,
and the almost mythical activities of the RCMP, were the stuff of
Canadian legends, the brooding presence of the Arctic had passed
from the daydreams of young adventurers and into the boardrooms of
mining and construction companies. Geologists now travelled with
relative ease – often flying in Canadian-designed and -built aircraft
such as the Beaver and Otter – where Inuit had used dogsleds. Not
one Canadian in ten thousand was likely able to locate and identify by
name more than two or three of the major archipelagic islands.
Occasional notice would be taken, of course, of unusual happenings.

One such was Prime Minister John Diefenbaker's popular initiative in the late fifties to ensure that the Canadian flag flew over each of the scattering of airfields, weather stations, and radar sites that had sprung up in cooperation with the United States to ensure surveillance of Soviet activities beyond the Pole.

Generally, however, in the cities of the South, there was little awareness of the extraordinary and sometimes heroic endeavours of northern Canadians. Most southerners would likely have been surprised at the successful efforts that had been expended to ease the isolated lifestyles of northern dwellers. Launched in the early seventies, for example, were the world's first satellites dedicated to the provision of domestic TV and communication services.[3] These were a far cry from the romantic image of isolated Hudson's Bay Company trading posts and solitary RCMP patrols. Mineral and hydrocarbon exploration was widespread; scheduled air service to a number of remote settlements began to supplement the infrequency of bush-plane flights; and the comprehensive Polar Continental Shelf scientific research project got under way in 1967. To those relatively few Canadians deeply interested in the Arctic, the universe probably seemed to be unfolding as it should: in relative obscurity.

This indifference, however, was about to change dramatically with the discovery in 1968 of immense quantities of oil beneath the waters of Prudhoe Bay on the north slope of Alaska. Suddenly there was reason to seek a low-cost means of transporting the crude oil to the refinery markets thousands of kilometres to the south. Because seaborne oil can be landed at a much lower cost than that from a pipeline, the principal owners of the Alaskan oil cast about for a water routing. With a greater knowledge of maps than of the terrain itself, they decided to test the feasibility of the Northwest Passage as a year-round supertanker route from Alaska to the Atlantic seaboard.

The ship selected for the first test run was the 145,000-ton Humble Oil Company tanker *Manhattan*. This vessel was approximately half the size of the tankers that would be used regularly should the scheme prove feasible, but was nevertheless far larger than any ship that had ever ventured into these waters. To prepare for this experimental voyage, the *Manhattan*'s hull was strengthened, and a special icebreaking bow was fitted to it. A straightforward maritime trial, similar to dozens of others conducted around the world, was what was intended. How misguided were those expectations, few could have predicted.

Certainly the owners did not anticipate the furies their activities were about to unleash. The Arctic became front-page news as long-dormant Canadian nationalism found cause and focus. Before the sequence of events concluded, the Northwest Passage was destined to arouse within Canada an unprecedented volume of popular outcry, and to place the Canadian and U.S. governments on a most uncomfortable adversarial footing. As a quite unexpected consequence, it provided the Trudeau administration with an early opportunity to implement its own views on the position and role of Canada within the international community. Without warning, there were created the circumstances for innovative government initiatives to test in practice some of the foreign-policy theories tentatively aired in the spring of 1968. The exercise would prove to be far from smooth, however. With greater vehemence than the government was able fully to apprehend in the early months of 1969, the public demonstrated convincingly that its mood was in direct conflict not only with the attitudes of previous Canadian governments but, as well and dangerously, with fundamental U.S. interests. An unsavoury, and altogether uncharacteristic, jingoism swept across Canada.

More by good luck than good management, Trudeau and Head had much earlier prepared themselves for the forthcoming trials – one between the forces of populism and those of reason, the other between the U.S. navy and the will of the Canadian government. Over the years, Trudeau had travelled extensively north of the Arctic Circle and had canoed on its many stretches of magnificent white-water rivers. He had long been deeply impressed with the pristine beauty of these lands and waters, and early in the life of the new administration he had actively encouraged Jean Chrétien to move quickly to establish Canada's first far-northern National Parks.[4] Head had chosen the legal status of the Canadian Arctic as the subject for his graduate research dissertation while studying at Harvard Law School.[5] Neither had anticipated an early challenge to Canadian Arctic jurisdiction, yet each was dedicated to the proposition that Canada must be a serious and credible actor in any designation of responsibilities in the Arctic, whatever claims or assertions might be made from elsewhere.

Each of us, too, was deeply aware of the potential military significance of these distant regions that separated the two Cold War superpowers, and of the very limited abilities of Canada to deter the United States or the Soviet Union from probing the Canadian sector, either in the sky or beneath the ocean. Each of us knew as well that neither superpower was in the habit of disclosing the intended transit routes of its nuclear-powered submarines, even in certain instances when these routes took them into waters claimed by others.[6] Such voyages on the part of American submarines were consistent with the long-held and aggressively practised policies of the U.S. navy to exercise its presence as broadly as international law and custom permitted, everywhere in the world. In the late sixties, therefore, encouraged by the U.S. navy, the U.S. government opposed the increasingly frequent extension of national territorial seas from the three-mile norm that had prevailed since the eighteenth century. Five years prior to the *Manhattan*'s voyage, for example, in bilateral discussions, the United States had objected strongly when Canada proposed drawing straight baselines seaward from its coasts, from which the territorial seas would then be measured. In the result, Canada did not act. There was no doubt in the mind of either Trudeau or Head, therefore, that in 1969 the U.S. government would oppose vigorously any endeavour by Canada to hinder or regulate the passage of the *Manhattan* on any basis whatever.

Though Humble Oil had much earlier signalled its intention to run the *Manhattan* trials in the summer of 1969, and had commenced structural alterations to the hull of the vessel for that purpose, the proposed voyage did not publicly enter parliamentary debate until February 28, 1969, when questions were posed in the House of Commons.[7] That same day the Canadian Press reported allegations by a former chairman of the Canadian Chiefs of Staff that some official U.S. maps designated the islands of the Canadian Arctic archipelago as "disputed territory."[8] Former prime minister John Diefenbaker was quick to ask if the Canadian government would respond by asserting Canadian sovereignty. Supplementary questions followed, asking about this new "*Manhattan* project."[9]

It was from these beginnings, fuelled by intense media interest and speculation, that the national outcry began. With a suddenness wholly uncharacteristic of Canadian public mood swings, a cacophony of anti-American sentiment threatened to replace any feeling of good neighbourliness on the eve of Trudeau's visit to Washington for his first meeting with President Richard Nixon. Quickly, therefore, were official inquiries made of the U.S. State Department. Not unexpectedly, these revealed that nothing was known in Washington of the alleged maps, and, if any such existed, they were without official American status.

Gordon Robertson, clerk of the Privy Council (and former deputy minister of northern affairs), and Head took the lead in counselling Trudeau on this issue preparatory to the Washington trip. Head prepared memoranda detailing the international law relative to territory in remote areas, as well as recounting the often perplexing, sometimes contradictory, and occasionally overinflated statements made over the years by successive Canadian governments when referring to the Arctic. He cautioned against further offhand ministerial statements about the extent of Canadian claims or about the juridical character of the water, ice, and superjacent airspace. Robertson wisely counselled against pressing any territorial proposals upon Nixon during the first meeting. The U.S. reaction, after all, was predictable, and there were other, more immediate, subjects to be addressed during this important initial meeting. In the result, the issue was mentioned only in passing during the White House discussions, raised by Trudeau in order to acquaint Nixon with the apparent volatility of Canadian public opinion, and the importance to Canada of a wholesome Arctic.

Thereafter began a period of intense activity. Led by the three Toronto daily newspapers (the *Star*, the *Globe and Mail*, the *Telegram*) and by members of Parliament from all parties, a jingoistic cry for assertive Canadian territorial claims began to build, which would reach crescendo pitch at the time of the voyage. Within the government, a number of departments wasted no time in declaring their particular interests. As could be expected, these were far from homogeneous. They reflected, among other things: a desire to ensure the continued access of Alberta oil to U.S. markets and the possible construction of a pipeline across Canadian territory as the preferred mode of transportation of Alaska oil; a concern that Canadian fishing grounds off the Atlantic and Pacific coasts not appear to be treated as any less important than Arctic fisheries; an expectation that active U.S. maritime participation would hasten the installation of necessary navigational aids and so open the Northwest Passage to an economic future as a major shipping channel; a worry that the close military collaboration between Canadian and U.S. armed forces might somehow be placed in jeopardy; an insistence that the interests of the Inuit and the wholesomeness of the environment not be sacrificed; and an assumption that Canada would not act other than in accordance with long-established multilateral processes. Quite clearly, not all of these interests could be accommodated, nor, in the interest of an enlightened policy, should they have been.

In examining the emotional content of what was being said, inside as well as outside of government, the mythical attraction of the "sector theory" was clearly a major factor. In a memorandum to Gordon Robertson in mid-March, Head endeavoured to remove the theory from active discussion. He asked how much longer the Government of Canada would continue its long-practised pretence of issuing official maps that depicted the boundaries of Canada in heavy magenta lines following the meridians of longitude north to the Pole from the Yukon–Alaska boundary on the west and from Ellesmere Island on the east. This vast pie-shaped sector enclosed tens of thousands of square kilometres of open sea, far distant from any Canadian shores. It represented no formal claim by any government of Canada, had no basis in international law, and was certainly not taken seriously by the international community. But, mystery of mysteries, it had long appeared on official Canadian maps, and it gave Canadian nationalists a heaven-sent premise for inflated assertions of sovereignty, which they actively pursued. Robertson agreed with Head's arguments, commenting that there was no more magic to an imagined wedge in the Arctic Ocean than to one in the Atlantic.[10]

As newspaper shrillness increased and public calls for Canadian assertiveness in the Arctic became more frequent, government ministers began speculatively to voice their own proposals for the assertion of this or that form of Arctic sovereignty. The minister of fisheries, for example, claiming to be alarmed about maritime priorities, moved publicly and without cabinet authorization to assert his intention to declare broad, exclusive fisheries-protection zones off the Atlantic and Pacific coasts through the device of fisheries closing

lines. The secretary of state for external affairs was advocating the
need to establish baselines surrounding the archipelago that would
serve as the Canadian seaward boundary.

In light of this nationalistic musing, the U.S. government, not surprisingly, decided that the time was ripe to issue a cautionary warning.
Early in April 1969, the U.S. Embassy in Ottawa delivered an *aide-
mémoire* to the Department of External Affairs, stating that the United
States would be concerned about the effects of any extension of maritime jurisdiction. A cautious Canadian response reflected the high
road. It affirmed that there was not, nor would there be, any conflict
between Canada's policies and Canada's international responsibilities.
By choosing so formal a means of communication, the Americans
made clear, if there had been any doubt, that Washington was keeping
a close eye on boundary issues, and that the failure of Nixon to emphasize that point during the earlier March discussions in the White House
should not be construed by Canada as indifference. Neither Trudeau
nor Head had the slightest doubt that such was the case.

As the weeks passed, and the sailing date approached, public interest gave no sign of diminishing. Journalists and politicians could not
remember any incident in the past that had so aroused the chauvinism
of the Canadian public. These emotional outpourings were healthy,
insofar as they aroused awareness of the geography and ecology of the
high Arctic, but were distressing to the extent there was a distinct
anti-American bias to them. Unfortunately, the fires of contention
were being fuelled on both sides of the border. Members of
Parliament and journalists would convey their interpretations of
Canadian concern to U.S. officials and members of Congress, only to
be told of the resolute attitude of the United States, and particularly
of the U.S. navy, towards any steps taken by any country that could
reduce the extent of ocean open to free navigation by American
vessels. All of this would in due course be repeated either in parliamentary committees or in the press, leading to wholesale Canadian
accusations of timidity, indecision, or weakness on the part of its own
government. Outrageous arguments were put forward in support of a
stalwart Canadian position, often claiming to be authoritative interpretations of history or international law or practice elsewhere.
Seldom did they prove to be so. On one occasion, for example, Head

was solemnly told during a meeting with the editorial board of a major Canadian newspaper that no self-respecting Canadian government should allow waters separating parts of its territory to be navigated freely by foreign ships. Head expressed the hope that other countries would not heed similar advice; there was a lot of ocean between the states of California and Hawaii, for example.

By this stage, albeit reluctantly, Trudeau accepted that this particular issue would demand his own intensive involvement. His commitment to participatory cabinet decisions remained, as did his insistence that ministerial responsibility be exercised. The various departments of government would therefore be called upon to express their own views and defend their own interests, but in the final analysis the policy would be the prime minister's if cabinet continued to be so uncertain about the most appropriate policy. Trudeau's brief statement in the House of Commons in May was designed to quell the most fearsome of allegations and to emphasize that the government was closely engaged in the *Manhattan* project as a means of protecting Canadian interests.

> . . . the legal status of the waters of Canada's Arctic archipelago is not at issue in the proposed transit of the Northwest Passage by the ships involved in the *Manhattan* project. . . .
>
> The oil companies concerned and the United States Coast Guard have consulted with appropriate Canadian authorities in the planning of the operation. The government will support the trials with the Canadian Coast Guard ice-breaker *John A. Macdonald* . . . and will also provide aerial ice reconnaissance and assume responsibility for the coordination of such reconnaissance. The government has also selected and appointed an official Canadian government representative on board the SS *Manhattan* who will act as technical adviser and as coordinator of Canadian support for the operation.[11]

Far from quieting public concern, the statement was attacked as inadequate and cowardly. From within and without government, advocacy continued to build for Canadian territorial aggrandizement, through non-lethal means admittedly, but little different nevertheless from the often automatic and emotional outbursts of nationalism in other parts of the world, which for centuries had limited progress towards a rational and cooperative international system.

Trudeau by instinct and by intellect was much opposed to this form of national behaviour. To him, sovereignty for sovereignty's sake was a hollow and self-defeating concept. In this respect he found vibrant support from Head and from Allan Gotlieb, a brilliant young public servant who had recently left the Department of External Affairs to become deputy minister of the new Department of Communications. Like Head, Gotlieb was a student of international law and an advocate of an international community that paid heed to assumptions of responsibility along functional lines. Each felt it important to assess realistically Canada's Arctic interests and then to ensure that, for the protection of those interests, policies be designed that would draw upon the strength and advantage of sound international legal practices. These were not visionary impulses; the aim was to protect Canadian interests by utilizing the support of the international community and not through trumpeted assertions of national might or hollow pretensions to an enhanced sovereignty.

During the summer of 1969, public agitation and pressure for firm action continued unabated. Several members of the Liberal caucus wrote to the prime minister, deploring what they perceived to be his "weak" public statements.

The *Manhattan* proposal had spurred opposition in the United States as well, but largely of quite a different character. Those promoting a U.S. pipeline for the transportation of Alaskan oil were working at an accelerated pace. Their preferred option was not a geographically direct route across Canada, linked to the international oil pipelines already in place in the heartland of the continent, but, instead, a line across the mountainous and geologically unstable terrain of central Alaska, exiting on the Pacific at the port of Valdez. At that point, the oil would be loaded onto large tankers and taken by sea down the Pacific seaboard to the continental United States. Not surprisingly, this enterprise was viewed with alarm by environmentalists, who pointed out the hazards of catastrophic spills from pipeline haemorrhages and tanker groundings or collisions, all the more dangerous if the southern terminal were to be located in the traffic-congested Puget Sound.

The supporters of the trans-Alaska project, envisaging the economic benefits to that state, were undeterred, however, and quickly shifted into high gear. Playing on the always present xenophobia rooted in the American public, they warned dolefully of the shortsightedness of making a strategic resource such as oil hostage to a foreign country. (This at a time when much of the oil, and most of the natural gas, entering U.S. western markets was of Alberta origin, regarded by no one as "undependable.") But the pipeline supporters did not rely on argument alone. Long before the necessary public hearings were complete and licences issued, pipe had been ordered and delivered from Japanese steel mills. The first load arrived in September. By the time construction was formally approved many months later, the weight of the immense lengths stacked in storage pressed the lower levels into unusable ovals. And so began the many unnecessary and costly charges to American consumers prompted by U.S. petroleum nationalism.

In September, too, the U.S. government chose to issue still another warning to Canada with respect to the Arctic waters. Canadian Ambassador Ed Ritchie was handed a note from the State Department, asserting that the United States "could not accept any extension or exercise of jurisdiction not clearly justified by international law" and demanding "adequate consultation" before any such were taken.

II

September marked the actual voyage of the *Manhattan*. Never had an Arctic expedition been so closely monitored by the media. Aerial photographs of the giant vessel, which was accompanied by two icebreakers – the U.S. Coast Guard vessel *Westwind* and the much larger Canadian Coast Guard vessel *Sir John A. Macdonald* – were front-page fare. A group of MPs flew north to greet the convoy at Resolute Bay on Cornwallis Island, near the site of a recent accident that had involved the loss of an oil barge caught in shifting ice. Editorial insistence that something be done continued throughout, most often assuming that the Canadian government was bereft of policy, interest, or conviction. "Just a bunch of patsies," sniffed one column.[12]

The test passage revealed clearly the formidable challenge faced by the proponents of this route. Even in September, the month when ice conditions were least difficult, the giant tanker was slowed and halted. Again and again it had to be broken free by the powerful *Sir John A. Macdonald*. As it neared the western terminus of the passage, a major route change was found necessary. The preferred course through the broad waters of M'Clure Strait had to be abandoned, because of the impenetrable ice. The much narrower Prince of Wales Strait was navigated in its stead, a channel less than six nautical miles wide at its eastern entrance, narrow enough to be embraced within the three-mile Canadian territorial seas. The convoy finally emerged at the western terminus of the passage, Sachs Harbour, on September 15. All this newly acquired knowledge of weather and ice conditions, hull and engine performance, time and cost factors, was carefully recorded, to be analysed with care in the months to come by those responsible for the immense financial commitments required should the tests be taken to a further stage. Temporarily, the issue of the legal status of the Northwest Passage passed from daily newspaper and television headlines into the relative obscurity of government and corporate offices.

Quite clearly, however, even in those offices, it was realized that the Canadian government faced an issue much more complex than popular indignation or even Canada–U.S. relations. There was now the very real possibility that these distant and dangerous waters could one day be home to frequent maritime passages, with all of the attendant, and still-unknown, hazards and challenges to the environment that these might bring.

Canada, of course, was far from alone in pondering these and related issues. Foremost among the American concerns at this time was the worry that other archipelagic states might be tempted to follow any Canadian precedent. Should Canada make extensive claims, and the Philippines or Indonesia take similar steps, for example (and each at the time was claiming as its own vast stretches of the Sulu Sea and adjacent waters), some of the world's strategic shipping routes could be affected. An extension seaward need not be very great in order to give some juridical colour of right to the closing of certain straits; many of these bodies of water – the Strait of Sunda between the islands of Sumatra and Java, for example, or the Strait of Hormuz at the entrance to the Persian Gulf – are quite narrow and so could, in theory, be affected by even modest increases in the breadth of the territorial sea.

The territorial sea, in 1969, was exhibiting remarkable elasticity off a number of countries. The traditional three-mile limit was still heeded by Britain, the United States, Canada, and some others, but twelve miles was becoming the norm. While not likely offending international law, twelve miles nevertheless could not demand formal recognition by the international community as a whole. In the autumn of 1969, a count revealed that fifty-four countries had extended their territorial sea to twelve miles, while only twenty-seven countries followed the traditional practice. Another twenty-three had territorial seas ranging from four to two hundred miles. Of major importance, however, was the fact that no major shipping state claimed more than three miles. Although the then-authoritative 1958 Geneva Convention proclaimed the right of innocent passage through territorial seas, that right was subject to challenge if any individual voyage could be claimed to be prejudicial to the "peace, good order and security" of the coastal state.[13] This condition worried the U.S. navy, particularly so if territorial seas were to be broadened, because naval vessels were everywhere the subject of coastal state concern, and submarines were legally required to transit territorial seas on the surface, not submerged.

Within the cabinet, the solution to the situation proved to be far more challenging than simply asserting some modest form of response, no matter how effective that might be in theory. The government had been in office scarcely more than a year. Among those ministers who had previously served in the Pearson cabinet, there had emerged from time to time an expression of ruefulness, because their accustomed independence was eroding in the face of new government-wide planning-and-decision mechanisms. Indeed, one veteran, Paul Hellyer, had already resigned, in despair that his own priorities were required to give way to those of the cabinet as a whole. Among the newer ministers, there was a feistiness and an impatience relating to several foreign-policy issues, among them the Arctic and NATO. While collegiality prevailed, there was no doubt that these several personalities and the constituencies they represented required heed and care. Equally, other countries were watching this perceived contest between unequals – Canada, with its reputation for good international citizenship, and the United States, which was accustomed to protecting its own interests – and considering their own options. Each of these various players and observers had to be considered in light of overall Canadian and global interests. The evolution of any Canadian policy required tact and skill, not simply demonstrations of decisiveness or bravado. The tasks being undertaken by the government throughout this period endeavoured to employ the former. Just as in the preparations for the *Manhattan* voyage itself, it was important that no step be taken and no statement be issued that would either precipitate an absolute clash with the United States or jeopardize the long-term interests of Canada in the high Arctic. Public pronouncements and diplomatic communications alike were accordingly drafted with considerable care, and cleared before issuance by senior ministers.

External Affairs had become champion of a proposal to extend Canadian territorial seas to twelve miles, claiming that this would effectively enclose several narrow stretches of the Northwest Passage (but not all[14]) under the blanket of Canadian sovereignty, and thus give Canada authority to regulate shipping there. Such a step would permit the further argument to be made – because the passage had not historically been used for international navigation – that traditional rules of innocent passage would not be applicable. External proposed this extension as the first step towards an eventual closure of the entire archipelago by extended baselines (which would have the effect of making the archipelagic waters "internal," of the same legal quality in most instances as Lake Winnipeg).

Head, Gordon Robertson, and Allan Gotlieb were all firmly opposed to these proposals, and not simply in anticipation of the United States' reaction. Robertson worried that External's presentation to cabinet contained no hard analysis of what Canada's real objectives were, and was perhaps motivated by chauvinism. Gotlieb observed that our three-mile zone already effectively blocked the passage at the western end (at the narrow Prince of Wales Strait), and that all a twelve-mile claim would accomplish would be to rile the United States and perhaps prompt the Canadian assertion to be challenged in the International Court of Justice. Head argued that baselines had two effects: they claimed what lay within them, but explicitly relinquished interest in what lay beyond. Because international law had evolved mightily in the past, encompassing the concept of the Continental Shelf, for example, he conjectured that this process might continue in the future and to Canada's benefit; assertions of boundaries now could possibly jeopardize claims to future benefits. The three men were troubled, as was Trudeau, by the simplicity of proposals that were seemingly devoid of content apart from the assertion of sovereignty.

At this point, Head was encouraged by Robertson to expand upon an idea he had earlier encouraged: the creation of Arctic pollution-control zones. These would permit Canada to promulgate regulations restricting shipping as needs arose, and compared in quality to those declared from time to time by the United States and the U.S.S.R., warning shipping away from vast tracts of open ocean in advance of test-missile firings. The Canadian zones, in contrast, would be entirely benevolent and permanent. Head argued that such a policy would provide to Canada an opportunity, on behalf of the community of nations, to perfect and advance a new international legal concept, one addressed to functional jurisdiction. The proposal was to extend international standards into the hitherto unfrequented area of environmental protection. Such a proposal faced a daunting challenge, however: to gain the support of the international community, a community heavily influenced by major maritime powers outspokenly resistant to environmental regulations.

At the heart of the proposal, therefore, was the concept of international trusteeship. In the forefront of the development of international law, Canada would assume responsibility for protecting the vast and threatened Arctic ecological resource off its northern coasts, working all the while for appropriate international mechanisms to be designed and set in place. We would do this by pursuing two simultaneous goals: (i) the passage of protective legislation designed to prevent oil spills and other deleterious activity; and (ii) the negotiation of accepted international standards to embrace and further the Canadian position. We would emphasize that we were not acting in *breach* of international law, rather, in the special Arctic circumstances, we were acting on behalf of the international community in the *absence* of applicable law.

This novel proposal was first revealed in language drafted by Head for the forthcoming Speech from the Throne, which would open a new session of Parliament in late October 1969. In a meeting in the prime minister's East Block office, the room that had been occupied by Canadian prime ministers for almost a century, Head read out to the small group of persons who were privy to the speech process his suggested wording. Following a remarkably brief discussion among these senior advisers, Trudeau declared his support of the concept and gave his approval for the policy to be included in the Throne Speech text and then refined to the state of precision necessary to permit legislation to be drafted. In the interim, of course, he would have to convince his cabinet and caucus of the wisdom of this approach. It would not prove to be an easy task.

On October 23, 1969, therefore, a little more than a month following the passage of the *Manhattan*, the Governor General addressed senators and commoners in the Senate chamber, gathered to hear the Speech from the Throne opening the second session of the twenty-eighth Parliament:

> . . . we must fulfill our responsibility to preserve these [Arctic] areas, as yet unspoiled and essentially in a state of nature. The Government will introduce legislation setting out the measures necessary to prevent pollution in the Arctic Seas. . . .
>
> Through the United Nations and its agencies Canada is seeking to establish a system to combat the pollution of international waters which threatens so many forms of life on this planet.[15]

The following afternoon, in the opening hours of the formal debate on the Speech from the Throne, Trudeau spoke:

> . . . Canada regards herself as responsible to all mankind for [the preservation of] the peculiar ecological balance that now exists so precariously in the water, ice and land areas of the Arctic archipelago.
>
> We do not doubt for a moment that the rest of the world would find us at fault, and hold us liable, should we fail to ensure adequate protection of that environment from pollution or artificial deterioration. Canada will not permit this to happen, Mr. Speaker. It will not permit this to happen either in the name of freedom of the seas, or in the interests of economic development. We have viewed with dismay the abuse elsewhere of both

these laudable principles and are determined not to bow in the Arctic to the pressures of any state. In saying this, we are aware of the difficulties faced in the past by other countries in controlling water pollution and marine destruction within their own jurisdictions.

Part of the heritage of this country, a part that is of increasing importance and value to us, is the purity of our water, the freshness of our air, and the extent of our living resources. For ourselves and for the world we must jealously guard these benefits. To do so is not chauvinism, it is an act of sanity in an increasingly irresponsible world. Canada will propose a policy of use of the Arctic waters which will be designed for environmental preservation. This will not be an intolerable interference with the activities of others; it will not be a restriction upon progress. This legislation we regard, and invite the world to regard, as a contribution to the long-term and sustained development of resources for economic and social progress.

We also invite the international community to join with us and support our initiative for a new concept, an international legal régime designed to ensure to human beings the right to live in a wholesome natural environment. In pursuit of this concept I shall be holding discussions shortly about this and other matters with the Secretary General of the United Nations.[16]

On November 11, Trudeau flew to New York to disclose to U Thant, the secretary general of the United Nations, his Arctic proposal. Notice of the purpose of the trip had been given well in advance, and U Thant was fully briefed on the international state of play concerning oceans. This was a third meeting between Trudeau and U Thant (the second had taken place in October of the previous year when the Nigerian civil war was the main topic of discussion), and they were comfortable and candid in their conversation. Canada had long been among the most ardent of UN supporters, and the work of Lester Pearson had contributed much to the reputation of Canada within the organization, as well as to the effectiveness of the UN itself. Nevertheless, two visits of a head of government to UN headquarters in a period of thirteen months, each dedicated to consultations with the secretary general on a specific topic of global concern, was a rarity. The Canadian decision to seek the advice of U Thant and his staff was intended as a clear signal to persons inside and outside Canada that Trudeau took seriously the views of the international community and was seeking to formulate Canadian policy well within the spirit of the UN Charter.

Posing for the obligatory photographs before the luncheon meeting on the thirty-third floor of the Secretariat Building, U Thant questioned Trudeau about the significance of the poppies worn in his lapel and in those of Head and Canadian Ambassador Yvon Beaulne. He was told of the Remembrance Day tradition in Canada and of the famous poem of Canadian soldier-physician-poet John McCrae that had launched the custom.[17]

Over lunch and following, the pollution-prevention proposal was examined in some detail. U Thant and his advisers confirmed that there was no imminent UN plan to launch a follow-on conference to update the three 1958 Geneva Conventions,[18] which were now rapidly being overtaken with the advent of new technologies and the needs and opinions of a host of newly independent states emerging from colonial status. The challenge for Canada, therefore, was to devise a legal regime that would serve Canadian interests, yet nevertheless be supported by a significant majority of the members of the international community. A conference of the traditional UN kind was not seen by Trudeau or Head as likely to give a timely endorsement to Canada's views. Neither, however, was there any wish to be seen to be functioning outside the UN ambit. Thant reassured Trudeau that he had no reason to caution him in these respects.

In the meantime, the U.S. government had not been idle. In the brief interval between the Speech from the Throne and the UN visit, Vice-President Spiro Agnew had publicly announced a major new program dedicated to arctic environmental research, and the State Department had delivered an *aide-mémoire* to Ambassador Ed Ritchie, prompted, the Americans said, by Trudeau's House of Commons speech. The *aide-mémoire* proposed consultations leading to the negotiation of an international agreement for the protection of the peculiar environment of the Arctic region. Thus revealed was the thrust of U.S. diplomacy for the months to come: bilateral consultations leading to the convening of an international conference. The Antarctic Treaty[19] was suggested as a model, one that placed a moratorium on national territorial claims and laid down principles within and beyond territorial limits regarding environmental protection, scientific cooperation, maritime navigation, and a range of related issues. The decision for Canada was whether to engage in such consultations, cognizant as the government was of the strong and largely contradictory opinions held on each side of the border.

The pressure from Washington would grow ever stronger in the months to come, and would be applied at frequent intervals. In late January 1970, Ritchie was called in by Undersecretary of State U. Alexis Johnson and handed a further *aide-mémoire*, encouraging an early start to the Arctic consultations. The proposal was set forth in altogether reasonable language, supportive of Trudeau's October 24 remarks in the Throne Speech debate, assuring Canada of the U.S. support for a wholesome Arctic environment, and proposing a range of undertakings to be considered in order to ensure that the needs of future navigation would be properly anticipated and effectively met. The United States quite clearly was apprehensive about any Canadian domestic legislation and wished to move immediately to the second element of the strategy – international negotiations. The challenge for the Canadian government was to retain control of the overall exercise. Not to do so would mean that the prevailing inadequate international agenda and standards of conduct – dominated as they were by the major maritime powers – would undoubtedly prevail.

A two-track Canadian exercise, formally launched with the public declaration of intent in the Throne Speech, was now under way in earnest. Within the government, a representative committee of very senior public servants was struck and given the responsibility of preparing the content of the promised legislation, a complicated and controversial task even following the Throne Speech pronouncement of policy. Internationally, Canadian diplomatic missions were instructed to inquire of several Arctic and maritime governments their attitudes towards pollution control. Of particular interest were the policies and views of the Soviet Union, which was far and away the most sizeable Arctic state, and those of the Scandinavian countries, whose affinity to Canada in the formulation of a number of UN policies was well known and deeply appreciated.[20]

As the months went by, the intensity of diplomatic activity increased. Both Canada and the United States engaged in a widespread campaign to convince other governments of the wisdom of their particular point of view. It was an exciting period; this was a serious issue, appreciated as such by a large number of countries, and so it attracted the attention of legal advisers and policy-makers in many capitals around the world. The skills and experience of Canadian diplomats were of immense value in this exercise. Twice in a period of months was the new Canadian government making a major departure from previous policies,[21] and twice were some of the most senior External Affairs officers instructed to carry out tasks that were contrary to the advice they had given the government. Not always in good grace, but always correctly, and always effectively, did they do so.

Within the government, there remained considerable differences of view about implementing the announced policy. A strong constituency argued that pollution-control zones should simultaneously be extended along the Atlantic and Pacific coasts, as well as to Arctic waters. Sympathetic as Trudeau was to the case for such legislation, he was forced to point out that the particular environmental circumstance of the Arctic was the basis for a distinctive regime there; the very real difficulty of obtaining international support in the Arctic would be well-nigh impossible should a more ambitious scheme be proposed in this early stage of environmental awareness. Another constituency seemed primarily motivated by a wish to stand up to the United States. Additionally, and not surprisingly, the many departments involved viewed with apprehension any omnibus bill that might be seen as diminishing their own authority. Transport wanted to retain responsibility for all aspects of shipping, such as regulations for hull design and construction; Energy, Mines and Resources was concerned about its supremacy in circumstances of mineral exploitation and conservation; Fisheries had an agenda entirely its own, which its minister was publicly advocating; Northern Development had long regarded the Arctic as virtually exclusively within its own jurisdiction, and was reluctant to concede entry to others. Finally, External Affairs continued to promote the wholly orthodox concept of broadening the territorial seas from three to twelve miles, a concept fatally flawed in the views of the Prime Minister's Office. Because most of these internecine struggles were

conducted at an official level, it fell on Robertson and Head (with considerable discreet assistance from Gotlieb) to keep the process on course
and on time. The domestic task was proving to be hardly less difficult
than the international one.

By late January 1970, the first outlines of a legislative bill were
ready for consideration by cabinet. They addressed themselves to three
major elements: (i) prohibition of certain types of conduct likely to
cause pollution; (ii) preventive measures establishing minimum standards of conduct; and (iii) provisions for financial responsibility and
liability in the event of injury. By coincidence, the House of
Commons chose this same period of time to debate a report of its
Standing Committee on Indian Affairs and Northern Development, a
report that reflected the views of all parties in Parliament. This report
included language similar to that employed in the press during the
Manhattan's voyage, illustrating that the political furore of the previous
summer had far from dissipated:

> Your Committee considers that the waters lying between the
> islands of the Arctic Archipelago have been, and are, subject to
> Canadian sovereignty historically, geographically and geologi-
> cally. . . .
> Your Committee recommends that the Government of Canada
> indicate to the world, without delay, that vessels, surface and sub-
> marine, passing through Canada's Arctic Archipelago are and
> shall be subject to the sovereign control and regulation of
> Canada.[22]

Not only regulation of tanker traffic, but the navigation of American and Soviet nuclear submarines as well, was the recommendation.
The task of making such regulation credible and enforceable was not
surprisingly left to the government.

In mid-February, John R. Stevenson, the legal adviser to the U.S.
Department of State, delivered a major address to the Philadelphia
World Affairs Council. He chose as his subject the law of the sea. In
his speech, Stevenson emphasized U.S. dedication to the multilateral
solution of the many issues that now separated the interests of coastal
states and those of maritime states. He reflected on the inability of the

1958 Geneva Conference to fix an accepted breadth of the territorial sea, and argued that this issue, plus those such as fishing zones and environmental concerns, were proper subjects for future international negotiation; he hinted at another international conference to settle them. "The United States is prepared to lead the way towards a true internationalism in the oceans," he said.[23] As if to emphasize that the United States was not about to recognize any unilateral moves in these respects, the *New York Times* reported a few days later a State Department press release stating, "The United States supports the twelve-mile limit as the most widely accepted one, but only if a treaty can be negotiated which will achieve widespread international acceptance and will provide for freedom of navigation through and over international straits."[24]

III

The time was now ripe to respond to the United States' invitation to consult. Diplomatic courtesy dictated that Canada propose the time and place for a meeting; Washington was suggested as the site, at an early date convenient to both parties, and the afternoon of March 11 was agreed upon. Head and Alan Beesley, newly appointed legal adviser in the Department of External Affairs (and later to become Canada's chief negotiator at the UN Law of the Sea Conference) flew down to Washington, where they briefed Marcel Cadieux, Canada's recently arrived ambassador and a former legal adviser, on the written instructions that had been sent down to him in advance. Cadieux and Ed Ritchie had exchanged jobs a few weeks earlier, each replacing the other in the important positions of undersecretary (deputy minister) of state for external affairs and Canadian ambassador to the United States. Cadieux was a spirited public servant, a tough negotiator, with a keen sense of humour and a reputation for speaking his mind. He had expressed considerable opposition while in Ottawa to each of the Arctic and the NATO policies, as much to the process that was being employed as to the substantive policies themselves. On this, his first major assignment since arriving in Washington, Cadieux was uneasy that he should be accompanied by Head and Beesley, both of whom had been his juniors at External Affairs. He emphasized to them in the privacy of his office that, in his role as ambassador, he would be the primary Canadian spokesman on this mission.

The American side consisted of U. Alexis Johnson, undersecretary of state, whose reputation for outspokenness and toughness as a negotiator was legend; John Stevenson, legal adviser, well known to Head and Beesley from meetings of the American Society of International Law; and several others. Cadieux ably presented the Canadian position: the deep sensitivity of the Canadian public to the issues at hand and the long-standing Canadian claim to sovereignty to the waters of the archipelago; the environmental fragility of the area and its vulnerability to ill-planned economic development; and the need for prompt, effective action to deter and prevent any large-scale pollution. He referred at some length to Trudeau's remarks in Parliament and then proceeded to outline in broad fashion the alternative courses of action open to the government in order to ensure that these interests would be protected. The views of the United States with respect to each were earnestly sought.

There then followed a broad-ranging but intensive discussion of baselines, territorial seas, and pollution zones (all of which were still being championed within the cabinet by different ministers) in the kind of legal detail that would have fascinated the finest law-school faculty, yet all pursued with the seriousness of purpose employed by diplomats who realized that their remarks were being recorded in detail on each side, to be transcribed, widely circulated among colleagues, and scrutinized with the greatest of care in preparation for the next round of talks. Nothing so contributes to mature discussion by negotiators as the awareness that historians in decades to come will be examining statements with a critical eye.

The Canadian delegation emphasized that the pollution-control-zone alternative was one that arose from the inadequacy of international law in the peculiar circumstance of rapid technological change in an environmentally fragile region, and was designed to bolster – not flout – sound legal principles. It was emphasized that the Canadian legislation was intended to lead the international community, and to protect the environment in the interim – an "interim injunction" against irresponsibility as Head described it. He introduced as well the analogy to Air Defence Identification Zones, which were employed by the United States and Canada as an exercise of their security interests, even though nothing of the specific sort had ever been sanctioned by international law, and of the Truman Declaration of 1945, which anticipated by thirteen years the later adoption by the international community of the concept of the Continental Shelf.

The discussion was friendly and very candid. The Americans revealed their keen awareness of the Canadian public mood, evidence of the professionalism of the U.S. Embassy in Ottawa. Head emphasized that the government's timetable expected the introduction of the legislation as early as Easter. The Americans for their part left no doubt of their aversion to domestic legislation and their preference for an international conference that included the maritime powers as well as the circumpolar states.

Discussed as well, much more briefly because it was a less controversial measure in the minds of the Americans, was the likelihood of legislation to create a series of fisheries closing lines to enclose coastal waters. The United States was less concerned about such an act, because these measures were contemplated in the Geneva Conventions, and international law guaranteed the continuance of fishing by those states enjoying historic access to the waters in question. American fishermen would thus be protected in all their traditional fishing areas, should Canada legislate such lines.

The two delegations undertook to brief their own political masters, and to continue discussions in the future.

Fully aware as ministers now were of the U.S. position, cabinet was ready to take its final decision on the path to be followed. By this time all ministers were alert to the hazards of oil pollution. The immense size of the current generation of supertankers and the extraordinary damage that sometimes resulted from breaches and spills was a matter of popular concern. The foundering of the *Torrey Canyon* in the English Channel in 1967 was the first major example of the modern perils of large-volume sea transport of oil. The *Torrey Canyon*'s cargo was 118,000 tonnes. It was not until February 4, 1970, however, when the Liberian registered tanker *Arrow* went aground in Chedabucto Bay, Nova Scotia, that Canadians were alerted to the fact that these spills could happen anywhere.

The *Arrow* was a relatively small vessel by industry standards, but large enough to discharge 15,500 metric tonnes of oil along an attractive shoreline. The photographs of this spill were carried in newspapers and on television from coast to coast to coast; the vivid images reinforced the long-standing concern of biologists that oil could cause enduring injury to wildlife and to maritime food chains. Though actual experience was limited in the cold waters of the polar regions, the bulk of scientific opinion cautioned that oil spills there could be even more damaging and their effects of much longer duration than in warmer climes. Warnings of this kind, combined with the romantic image of the Arctic still held by most Canadians, produced a strong public reaction to the very possibility of a severe oil spill. Trudeau had referred to these concerns in the House of Commons the previous October.

> In the Canadian Arctic are found the breeding grounds, sometimes the only breeding grounds, of many species of migratory birds. Bylot Island is the nesting ground of the total population of the Greater Snow Goose. It is the site as well of the nesting colonies of some six million sea birds. Along twelve miles of the coast of Somerset Island are the nesting grounds of four million birds. Large numbers of air-breathing mammals – whales, seals, walrus – inhabit the waters lying throughout the Canadian archipelago. The existence of these and other animals and birds is dependent upon an uncontaminated environment; an environment which only Canada can take the lead in protecting. The beneficiaries of this natural life are not only Canadians; they are all the peoples of the world.[25]

In the months that followed, Trudeau would refer again to these particular Arctic circumstances. In Toronto:

> [There is not] now known any technique or process which can control, dispel, or reduce vagrant oil loose in Arctic waters. Such oil would spread immediately beneath ice many feet thick; it would congeal and block the breathing holes of the peculiar species of mammals that frequent the region; it would destroy effectively the primary source of food for Eskimos and

carnivorous wildlife throughout an area of thousands of square miles. . . .

Because of the minute rate of hydrocarbon decomposition in frigid areas, the presence of any such oil must be regarded as permanent. The disastrous consequences which the presence would have upon the marine plankton, upon the process of oxygenation in Arctic North America, and upon other natural and vital processes of the biosphere, are incalculable in their extent.[26]

In Canberra, Australia:

The break-up and sinking of oil tankers . . . make ludicrous the word "spill." These are monumental disasters. . . .

If governments do not prevent . . . this sort of activity, we are all in peril. Oil, phosphate detergents, and effluents act to inhibit, overextend or destroy the photosynthetic production of oxygen in the oceans. The issue is not simply one of littering, or of offensive smells, as some industrialists would have us believe. The issue is one of life itself.[27]

By early March, therefore, there was little resistance in cabinet to legislation designed to deter Arctic pollution. The issue that faced, and divided, ministers was the content of that legislation. Encouraged by thousands of constituents demanding a firm territorial statement in response to the *Manhattan* initiative, a number of voices around the cabinet table championed a sovereignty "solution." None of those advocating such a policy believed that this would extend Canada's boundaries. They were of the opinion that the archipelagic waters already were Canadian, and that a declaration to this effect was simply a technical recognition of existing circumstance. It was not surprising that they held this view, given the lengthy existence of official Canadian maps purporting to encompass land and water all the way to the Pole. These maps were one of those mysteries of bureaucracy that lend to governance a sense of bemusement. They had been issued over the years without any formal cabinet authorization. Head's efforts to determine how they came to be published (as they had been for several decades) came to naught. All that was clear was that these were manifestations of the seductive "sector theory" first put forward by a Canadian Arctic explorer, Joseph Bernier, in a speech to the Arctic Club in New York shortly after the turn of the century.

The theory might well have been forgotten then and there had it not been referred to in 1909, in a debate in the Senate of Canada. Senator Pascal Poirier on that occasion resolved that Canada make a formal declaration of possession of "lands and islands" extending to the North Pole. He cited in considerable detail several arguments in support of his resolution – discovery, cession, occupation – all well-accepted and understood international principles. Then, almost as an afterthought, he referred to Bernier's sector theory. He proposed that "every country bordering on the Arctic regions [Norway, Russia, the United States, Canada, and Denmark] would simply extend its possessions up to the North Pole."[28] Alas, Poirier's resolution was not even seconded, let alone carried by a vote. That scarcely seemed to matter, however, for the impression was gained in many quarters that the Canadian government had made its Arctic claims on a sector basis. Far from it. Prime Minister Sir Wilfrid Laurier, when asked in the House of Commons to comment on the Bernier proposal, replied, ". . . if Captain Bernier spoke as he is reported to have spoken, all I can say is that I think he had better keep to his own deck."[29] The theory would not disappear, however. In 1938, the minister of mines and resources told the House of Commons, without any supporting evidence, that the theory was "now very generally recognized" and that "our sovereignty extends right to the pole within the limits of the sector."[30] In 1946, in a journal article, Lester Pearson, then an official with the Department of External Affairs, employed extraordinarily expansive language, again without authority:

A large part of the world's total Arctic area is Canadian. One should know exactly what this part comprises. It includes not only Canada's northern mainland, but the islands and the frozen sea north of the mainland between the meridians of its east and west boundaries, extended to the North Pole.[31]

Ambassadorial articles, even when written by one as distinguished as Lester Pearson, do not necessarily reflect government policy, and this one certainly did not. But they can contribute to mythology, and this one did.[32] By the time the *Manhattan* transited the Northwest Passage in 1969, the myth had become a reality in the minds of many. In some respects, however, the several confusions – about the state of the law and about the Canadian interests involved – eased ministerial opposition to Trudeau's pollution-control-zone proposal. He was assisted in this respect by the increasing opposition of the U.S. government to any unilateral Canadian initiative.

On the afternoon of March 17, U.S. President Richard Nixon telephoned Trudeau to encourage a cooperative solution. Nixon expressed his awareness of the political pressures bearing upon the Canadian government, but revealed that Canadian legislation could raise trouble in Washington. He announced that he was dispatching to Ottawa a delegation of senior officials to continue discussions of the earlier proposed international conference. The eleven-person delegation arrived a few days later, led by U. Alexis Johnson, and it included, significantly, the assistant secretary of the navy. As evidence of the seriousness with which these issues were regarded in Canada, the Canadian side was led by Mitchell Sharp and included two other ministers, Donald Macdonald and Jean Chrétien, as well as a number of senior officials, including Gordon Robertson, Ed Ritchie, Alan Beesley, and Head.

The American position was much the same as it had been. Concern was expressed: that any Canadian act would be seen as a precedent by others, no matter how special were the Canadian circumstances; that any restrictions on air or naval movements would diminish the security of both countries; that a proliferation of pollution, fisheries, or other functional zones would make unlikely the conclusion of a new law of the sea treaty. The Americans, courteous, as diplomatic practice and friendship demanded, were nevertheless uncompromising in their firm opposition to any Canadian assertion of either sovereignty or jurisdiction. They proposed an interim U.S.–Canada joint commission to regulate the planned second voyage of the *Manhattan*, pending the negotiation of an international convention dealing with Arctic maritime issues.

For the first time, a series of objections were raised about fisheries closing lines, most of them related to their allegedly precedential nature and the likely unprincipled adoption by others of similar measures. The

Canadians were left in no doubt that the United States regarded Canada's contemplated legislation – not yet drafted – as threatening vital U.S. interests. Acquiescence would not be possible; the United States would protect its position should Canada act on its own. Tough words from a tough country, which meant at the very least that Canadian legislation would likely be challenged in the International Court of Justice.

When acquainted with this most recent exchange, cabinet was even more reluctant than previously to abandon the proposed legislation and to submit the fate of either the government or the country to a conference organized by the United States and bound to reflect the interests of the major maritime powers. There was a clearer realization, moreover, of just how intense would be U.S. pressure should Canada undertake any action with respect to jurisdiction, no matter how altruistic Canada's stand might be made to appear. For that reason, ministers decided, albeit most reluctantly in face of the principled opposition of Paul Martin and Mitchell Sharp, to deposit a reservation to Canada's acceptance of the compulsory jurisdiction of the International Court of Justice. The reservation would exclude from the court's jurisdiction any litigation challenging the pollution and fisheries-zones legislation.

Paul Martin, in particular, regarded such a step as a weakening of Canada's traditional support for the international rule of law. He was clearly aggrieved, but had no other adequate response to the likely U.S. challenge. Nor did he seem fully to accept the arguments that had been made in recent weeks by Head, in particular that Canada's proposed legislation was not a breach of international law but a bold step to create international law. In any event, several respected Canadian professors of law had concluded that a reservation, sad as it may be in concept, was absolutely necessary if Canada were to prevail in the face of an undoubted attack by the major maritime powers.[33] Head and Allan Gotlieb were both persuaded by the weight of these arguments, as was Donald Macdonald, who had been advised by Professor Ronald St. John Macdonald, one of Canada's most eminent international legal scholars and dean of the faculty of law at the University of Toronto.

Cabinet agreed as well, in order to blunt the expected animosity of the United States, that any regulations provided for in the legislation should exempt "sovereign" (i.e., naval) vessels. This decision was a recognition of two realities: the influence of the U.S. navy on U.S. government policy-making, and the total inability of Canada to interdict (likely even to detect) submerged nuclear-powered submarines. The exemption was not open-ended, however. Subsection 12(2) demanded "standards substantially equivalent," and the exercise of "all reasonable precaution."

The bill proclaimed Canadian jurisdiction seaward one hundred nautical miles from Arctic coastlines. It described the maritime zone as seas liquid or frozen, and prescribed civil responsibility on an absolute basis for pollution damage, as well as criminal offences and penalties for a range of polluting activities. Provision was made for regulatory powers extending to: (i) the financial responsibility of those active in the Arctic seas or the seabed beneath; (ii) the creation of safety-control zones for shipping; (iii) minimum standards of vessel construction and operation (e.g., hull and fuel-tank construction, equipment requirements, navigational aids and escorts); and (iv) the removal or destruction of vessels in distress that are depositing polluting materials.

The stage was now set for legislation to be introduced in Parliament. Notice was duly given to the House of Commons, Canada's ambassador to the UN was instructed to deposit with the secretary general an instrument containing the International Court of Justice reservation, and Canada's ambassador to the United States was instructed to disclose to the State Department the contents of the legislation. Only one diplomatic step was still necessary; Trudeau felt obliged to communicate with Nixon. His reasons arose from an unfortunate set of circumstances. Immediately prior to the final cabinet decision on the legislation, Sharp had instructed Marcel Cadieux to assure Alexis Johnson that Canada would likely reflect in the legislation several points sought by the United States. Johnson could be expected to have so informed Nixon. When cabinet subsequently refused to endorse all Sharp's recommendations, it became necessary to persuade the president that he had not purposely been misled.

Trudeau telephoned Nixon for this purpose on April 7, the day before Bill C-202, "The Arctic Waters Pollution Prevention Bill," was introduced into the House of Commons, and the text publicly revealed for the first time. In preparation for that call, he reviewed the draft talking points prepared by Head a few days earlier in anticipation of a final meeting between Canadian and American officials in Washington. Such a meeting proved not to be necessary, but the arguments were held in readiness for future use and, on Head's urging, to reassure any hesitant Canadian ministers that the United States' legal position was far from unassailable.

The telephone call could not immediately be completed because of the president's schedule. Secretary of State William Rogers quickly called back instead. Rogers was a courteous and most affable person, who had met Trudeau earlier during the official visit to Washington. The conversation continued for some forty-five minutes. Trudeau assured Rogers that, with the introduction of the bill, formal and extensive consultations could now take place with the United States with respect to the content of the all-important regulations. He also volunteered Canada's intention to participate fully in any appropriate international conference, with the aim of setting acceptable international standards. The exercise of pollution jurisdiction should be seen as an endeavour to block environmental damage in the interim, as well as to withstand the immense Canadian public pressure for an assertion of sovereignty.

Rogers was not about to be persuaded that America's stated interests could be thwarted by Canada. He stated that the United States would be forced to defy the Canadian position with any available means, including a submarine, if that were necessary to prove the point. This uncharacteristic threat of force enraged Trudeau. He replied that Canada's pollution concerns stemmed from oil tankers, not submarines. "Mr. Rogers, if you send up a tin can with a paper-thin hull filled with oil, we'll not only stop you, we'll board you and turn you around. And if we do so, Mr. Rogers, we'll have the world on our side."

The tone of the call thereafter quickly reverted to one in keeping with diplomatic courtesy. Rogers expressed surprise that Canada had moved as it had. He said the United States was caught off-balance as a result of Cadieux's discussion with Johnson. Trudeau revealed his embarrassment at the incident, and acknowledged how the message might have been misconstrued. The call concluded on a friendly and courteous note, with Rogers accepting Trudeau's invitation to convey the contents of the conversation to Nixon.

The following day, after first reading – and damning criticism of inadequacy from the two opposition leaders, Robert Stanfield and David Lewis – Trudeau emphasized to the press that the proposed legislation, combined with a companion bill creating fishing zones and extending Canadian territorial waters from three to twelve miles (by now accepted as the norm by the overwhelming majority of the international community), was a carefully composed package, which would protect Canadian and international interests by addressing the two key issues of pollution and fisheries conservation.[34]

> We're not taking a chauvinistic or jingoistic view on sailing in the North. . . . We just want to make sure that the development is compatible with our interests as a sovereign nation, and our duty to humanity to preserve the Arctic against pollution. . . . I'm sure this action may accelerate the convening of international meetings by many nations to do multilaterally, by international law, what, as of now, we've had to do alone because nobody else can act in the Canadian Arctic if we don't.[35]

In the interim, the environment would be protected.

IV

The draft legislation reduced to almost zero Canadian public apprehension about the second voyage of the *Manhattan* in the spring of 1970. It was escorted once again by the *Sir John A. Macdonald*, and this transit established even more firmly than the first the formidable ice conditions that faced any endeavours to engage in year-round navigation. There was still need, however, to convince the international community. Now began an intense period of diplomatic activity in many capitals to acquaint governments of the beneficial intent of the legislation. It was important that others fully understood the Canadian plan to call for consultations prior to the fixing of regulations and of the intentions to respect reciprocal and historic fishing rights pending any negotiated changes. Instructions were sent to a large number of Canadian diplomatic missions to present this information, as well as copies of the bills, to the governments to which they were accredited. It was particularly important to reassure powers that were traditionally friendly to Canada yet were major maritime actors, countries such as Britain, Holland, and the Scandinavian states.

Another country of compelling importance on this issue was the Soviet Union. With the longest Arctic coast of any state, and with the world's largest fleet of heavy icebreakers, the attitude of this country towards the Canadian legislation would be crucial. If Canada were to be successful in encouraging the evolution of new international legal principles and practices, it was essential that the states most active in the development of international law not actively oppose the Canadian proposals before they were fully spelled out.

No time could be lost in this diplomatic exercise, because the United States was prompt in making public its opposition. On April 9, the State Department expressed formal regret at the Canadian action, adding that,

> The United States does not recognize any exercise of coastal state jurisdiction over our vessels on the high seas and thus does not recognize the right of any state unilaterally to establish a territorial sea of more than three (nautical) miles or exercise more limited jurisdiction in any area beyond twelve (nautical) miles.[36]

That public statement was followed a few days later by a note delivered to the Canadian Embassy in Washington, repeating the message but announcing as well the American intention of calling an international conference to discuss and negotiate Arctic issues and expressing the hope that Canada would participate. The note concluded, irony of ironies in light of the United States' long-standing refusal to accept the jurisdiction of the World Court except on a case-by-case basis when it so suited it, by expressing disappointment in Canada's apparent lack of confidence in the international judicial process. The note avoided, not unexpectedly, any reference to the many unilateral initiatives taken by the United States over the years, either to advance international law or to demonstrate its own interpretation of international law. In a somewhat sanitized form, the note was later published by the State Department in the form of a press release.

On April 15, the United States delivered invitations to its conference in a number of capitals. The reference in the note to the Arctic was not limited to maritime issues, and so raised questions in Ottawa about the real extent of the U.S. agenda. In the meantime, Canada had replied at length to the note, employing many of the arguments contained in Head's draft talking points. Shortly thereafter, a Canadian *aide-mémoire* was delivered, addressed to the proposal for an Arctic conference, seeking clarification of the agenda and the scope; what did the State Department mean by "assets both living and non-living"? And on April 19, Trudeau spoke to the nation on CBC television. After describing the susceptible nature of the Arctic environment and the responsibility of Canada to protect it, he described the legislation to be "as exciting and as imaginative a concept as this government has undertaken."[37]

Happily, the reaction of the Canadian media was almost unanimously laudatory, a distinct reversal of its mood leading up to the legislation. Equally as important, the influential Washington *Post* stated in an editorial:

There will be much sympathy with Canada's move to protect the Arctic from pollution without waiting for the niceties of international law to be spelled out. Prime Minister Trudeau has not closed the door to international action. On the contrary, he acknowledged in a recent speech that the vast frozen areas in question "cannot be protected by Canada alone," that in the long run only international controls will be effective. What Canada is doing is moving in to occupy a vacuum in the hope that disastrous oil spills may be avoided instead of merely being fought over after possibly permanent damage has been done.[38]

And U.S. Senator Mike Gravel of Alaska said, "We should be the first to recognize intelligent innovation on the Canadian side."[39]

The Canadian commitment to seek international consensus on these issues was firm and sincere. Shortly following the transmission of the bills to foreign capitals, Canada made an offer to several countries to engage in informal consultations preparatory to a formal negotiating conference. In late June, Head and Beesley travelled to Moscow, where they engaged Soviet legal and Arctic experts in lengthy conversations. At the outset, the Soviets were adamantly opposed to participation in any kind of international conference, and vehemently so with respect to the kind of conference they suspected the United States was designing. By the end of the talks, however, they were at least willing to consider the possibility. From the Canadian perspective, this was good news, because any conference examining Arctic navigation would be fatally flawed without Soviet involvement. The U.S.S.R. and Canada were entirely agreed that any maritime regime would have to take account of special Arctic circumstances.

The next stop was Stockholm, where the Canadians were told that the Swedish government was much inclined to support both the Canadian legislation and the proposed international conference. The Swedes doubted that adequate preparations for a conference could be concluded in less than six months, however, given their experience with Baltic pollution discussions.

Later in the summer, Head flew to London for discussions with Sir Vincent Evans, the foreign office legal adviser, and a group of legal and technical experts. The British were at first reluctant to accept that any distinction should be made between open water and seas covered with several feet of ice. Their opinion softened late in the day, however, much less as a result of arguments from Head than because of evidence submitted to the meeting by one of their own scientists. The meetings in the three capitals revealed how important it was to engage the full attention of government advisers in the underlying circumstances of the Arctic and the carefully tuned Canadian responses to those circumstances.

As of midsummer, the exercise gave every evidence of success in the international community. A problem remained within Canada, however. The insistence of Fisheries Minister Jack Davis upon an early proclamation of fisheries closing lines, quite independent of the delicate diplomacy with respect to the Arctic, was one that worried Trudeau, Head, and Robertson. On a number of occasions over the course of the next several months, Davis had to be reminded, sometimes forcefully, of the balanced nature of the entire package and the importance of treating these issues functionally, not with the sovereignty bravado that he was wont to employ to his fisheries constituencies.

An American working draft of an Arctic Treaty was submitted to Marcel Cadieux in mid-July. It showed little sensitivity to the Canadian concerns, however. The Canadian response, as was later learned, was paralleled by that of the Soviets when they received U.S. Legal Adviser John Stevenson in Moscow. A Canadian counterdraft was prepared and taken to Washington by Head and Beesley in August. As in previous meetings, the American side was composed of Pentagon representatives, in addition to those from the departments of State, Interior, etc. Canada was proposing that the conference proceed in two phases, the first to be technical in nature to consider the regulations Ottawa was in the midst of drafting, the second to be political to construct the international regime that would enforce them. The Americans, not surprisingly, wished the reverse order to ensure maximum U.S. input into the standards to be set for navigational safety, hull construction, financial responsibility, etc.

Happily, Dr. Robert Uffen, the Canadian government's science adviser, found in discussions with his American counterpart that the U.S. science community favoured a timetable that would permit scientific and technical questions to be addressed and discussed prior to a legal conference. Perhaps those points of view were instrumental in Washington, for a fresh draft treaty, brought to Ottawa in early October, came very close to the Canadian position, and even included a dispute-settlement mechanism that Head had proposed during the Washington talks in August and pursued informally later that month with Stevenson in the course of the annual meeting of the Canadian Bar Association in Halifax, where Stevenson was an invited guest.

This draft was the subject of detailed discussion when Head and Beesley travelled to Washington in November. Head reported to the Americans that an item high on the prime minister's agenda for the discussions scheduled to take place in Moscow later in the month with Soviet leaders was the attendance of the Soviet Union at the proposed Arctic Conference.[40]

By early winter, the innovative Canadian policy seemed clear of most major hurdles, domestic and external. The Arctic Waters Pollution Prevention Act passed through Parliament and was given royal assent on June 26, 1970.[41] Jack Davis's insistence on the proclamation of fisheries closing lines had been successfully stayed; the summer-long carping criticism of the official Opposition was interpreted by the media and the public as just that. (In one remarkable press release during this period, the Conservative spokesperson argued that the government had "pussyfooted," with the consequence that "The American government obviously regards Messrs. Trudeau and Sharp as the mice who can't even roar convincingly."[42]) The UN secretary general had issued a call for a new Law of the Sea Conference, into which could be subsumed the Arctic-pollution considerations, and discussions to this effect began in the General Assembly.

This all came close to unravelling, however, when the cabinet agreed to the fisheries-lines proclamation in mid-December, in spite of the strong contrary position of Trudeau and Sharp. This decision provided the United States with the opening it needed to oppose publicly the fisheries legislation and to suggest that it was a departure from the consultations that had been so congenial and effective hitherto with respect to the Arctic. This move was clearly a major Canadian error, one that Head and Robertson had been deeply concerned about for months. Of all the controversial and highly contentious issues woven through the entire Arctic package, however, this proved to be the only one that could not be contained within the overall strategy. The cabinet demanded action, and it was impolitic to delay further. This knowledge was of little solace, however, in face of the stinging – and justified – State Department statement:

> . . . on December 17, the United Nations General Assembly approved by an overwhelming majority a resolution which scheduled a Law of the Sea Conference for 1973 which will deal with a wide range of oceans issues. . . . Canada . . . was a co-sponsor of that resolution. Moreover, Canada, perhaps more than any other country, played a very important lead role in achieving a commitment by the international community to resolve these issues multilaterally. Therefore, the United States is deeply disappointed and profoundly regrets that Canada has chosen to assert a unilateral claim of jurisdiction over ocean space only one day after the United Nations, with the approval of nearly all member states, including Canada, determined to resolve these problems regarding the law of the sea by international action.[43]

The Soviet Union officially protested to Canada shortly thereafter on similar grounds, adding that it was wrong in the wake of the wise

Arctic policy to move this way on fisheries. This protest did not prevent a Soviet delegation from travelling to Ottawa in February 1971, however, to pursue the discussions opened in Moscow the previous June. Present for this round, as earlier, were O. N. Khlestov, head of the legal division of the Soviet ministry of foreign affairs, and Head and Beesley for Canada. Considerable attention was given to the contents of a draft international convention that could gain the support of the United States and other maritime countries.

By late winter, the attention of all maritime states was turning increasingly to Geneva, where the preparatory committee for the forthcoming 1973 UN Law of the Sea Conference was now under way. The purpose of the conference was to gain international acceptance of a number of issues, either not resolved with the 1958 Conventions or arising since. Among them was the width of the territorial sea, the new concept of extended economic zones for resource exploitation and conservation purposes, and, of course, marine pollution. In the meantime, Canada continued work on the drafting of regulations under the Arctic Waters Pollution Prevention Act and engaged in widespread consultation with interested governments. It continued as well with the preparation of an Arctic Waters treaty, the American proposal that was distinct from the all-inclusive UN exercise; in discussions with the United States and Soviet Union, Canada sought to ensure their involvement. All this amounted to a three-pronged approach for Canada. While it was not expected that each area of activity would necessarily reach fruition, it was important that each be pursued in order that Canadian Arctic interests be fully protected and that Canada's international reputation not be sullied.

Of the three activities, the one that seemed least likely to succeed was the regional Arctic treaty concept launched by the United States. From the outset, the Soviets had been reluctant to participate because they feared their own interests as a coastal state would likely be jeopardized. Canada in good faith had entered into this exercise at the invitation of the United States, and so continued discussions with each of its neighbours. By midsummer 1971, External Affairs, under the direction of Alan Beesley and in consultation with other government departments, had produced a detailed working draft. The Americans were aware, however, that in two heads of government meetings (at Moscow in the spring of 1971 and at Ottawa a few months later),

Premier Alexei Kosygin had expressed to Trudeau a clear preference for a universal approach. In these talks, Trudeau and Kosygin were each concerned that the peculiar climatic circumstances of the Arctic might not be reflected and adequately protected in a regional treaty designed by non-Arctic maritime powers. While Canada was prepared to negotiate in such a forum, however, the U.S.S.R. was not.

By year's end, the UN Law of the Sea Conference exhibited clear and growing support for the Canadian approach to marine-pollution prevention. The open and responsive way in which Canada conducted its regulatory consultations, including provisions for pollution prevention officers with wide discretionary powers, combined with a broader international awareness of the problems associated with ice-infested waters, gave promise that the ultimate UN treaty would enshrine in international law the principles that Canada had proposed in its own Arctic legislation. That did, in fact, happen, with the inclusion of Article 234, the "Arctic" clause, entitled "Ice-Covered Areas."[44]

The Arctic Waters Pollution Prevention Act had turned out to be, as Trudeau had forecast in the spring of 1970, the face of future international law. It had come to be accepted as a progressive, constructive step taken by Canada on behalf of the international community. Moreover, its regulatory apparatus would define the standards for navigation of potentially dangerous bulk cargoes. Shortly thereafter, double-hulled vessels began coming into service, with the encouragement of environmentally sensitive governments and liability conscious marine insurers. Because of the careful negotiations, the Canadian legislation attracted not one protest from other countries when it was proclaimed on August 2, 1972. The UN Law of the Sea Convention was signed in Montego Bay, Jamaica, and opened for ratification on December 10, 1982. Canada would soon be able to withdraw its Arctic amendment to the acceptance of the compulsory jurisdiction of the International Court of Justice, and did so in 1985.

V

This had been a protracted struggle, but one that concluded with a sense of sweet satisfaction. In all the years to come, no other issue would combine quite so dramatically a range of ingredients permitting Canada to be so broadly influential in the international community.

Two nuclear-weapons episodes (described in Chapters Three and Five) aside, no other incident was as profoundly important to humanity as a whole. But in neither of those cases was Canada able to conclude quite so emphatically the policies it launched. Neither did those incidents include infuriating jingoistic pressures of press and opposition that, with respect to the Arctic, took the form of demands for the proclamation of territorial closing lines. In rebuffing those pressures, the Canadian government dealt chauvinism a well-deserved blow. By refusing to accede to the sometimes crude threats of the U.S. navy and its advocates in the U.S. government, it moved the international concept of freedom of the seas decisively forward from protection of navigation to protection of the resource.

At the outset of this exercise, we had no assurance of how it would conclude. Equally, however, we had no doubt as to how we wanted it to conclude. Trudeau had said the following in a speech to the annual meeting of the Canadian Press in April 1970:

> We have told our friends and neighbours that the Canadian step, designed to protect the Arctic waters, will not lead to anarchy; it is not a step which diminishes the international rule of law; it is not a step taken in disregard of the aspirations and interests of other members of the international community. Canadian action is instead an assertion of the importance of the environment, of the sanctity of life on this planet, of the need for the recognition of a principle of clean seas, which is in all respects as vital a principle for the world of today and tomorrow as was the principle of free seas for the world of yesterday.[45]

Many years later, that most highly regarded of all Canadian foreign-policy observers, John Holmes, wrote that the Arctic Waters Pollution Prevention Act "launched the Trudeau administration on its most effective and laudable international enterprise, a leading and highly constructive role in the most important contribution to world order since San Francisco."[46]

CHAPTER THREE

Nuclear Weapons: The Canadian Dilemma

I

As a member of the Pearson government, Trudeau was aware of the prime minister's sense that Canadian foreign policy was in need of close scrutiny and likely of substantial overhaul in order to relate effectively to the changing international scene. Trudeau was aware as well, and supportive, of Pearson's decision to charge Norman Robertson with responsibility for the review exercise. He knew Robertson to be one of the most respected members of the public service and to be among the small cadre of very senior officials in the Department of External Affairs.[1]

What Trudeau did not learn until after he had been sworn in as prime minister was the indifference with which many of Robertson's colleagues greeted this task and the consequent weakness of the final document, in large measure a justification for the maintenance of the status quo. To Pearson and Robertson, men deservedly proud of the quality of their work and the incisiveness of their own thought processes, this product must have been a keen disappointment, particularly in light of its timing. The report was completed in April 1968, on Robertson's deathbed, and delivered to Pearson in the final days before he stepped down from office.[2] It represented the last official contact between these men in an association that had begun decades earlier, when each was a junior member of Canada's fledgling foreign service.[3]

The inadequacy of the report was a major factor in prompting Trudeau to call for a thorough review of foreign policy as part of his election-campaign platform. The rapidly approaching deadline for renewal of Canada's adherence to the North Atlantic Treaty suggested that the overall review begin with an examination of Canada's commitment to NATO, as well as the country's range of interests and representational strengths in Europe. Each of these parallel exercises would be carried out by the Department of External Affairs, and each was expected to conclude within a few months; the first would require extensive involvement of the Department of National Defence. The decision of the Trudeau cabinet to launch the defence review was taken on May 15, 1968, and it called for its completion by mid-August. On July 19, cabinet requested a global foreign-policy review.

In an endeavour to encourage reviews that would be more thorough than a simple revelation of current policies, Trudeau stressed publicly that he wished to see the widest range of options considered. Comments of this sort, however, complemented by the musings and speeches of a number of his new cabinet colleagues, proved to be all too provocative to a broad range of Canadians and were quickly interpreted in alarmist fashion. These alarms increased in frequency when cabinet rejected the August defence review paper on the grounds that it amounted to nothing more than a reaffirmation of current policy. The reviewers were asked to begin again, and to remember that this was a new government, one seeking a range of alternatives in order to best understand Canada's responsibilities and opportunities in a changing world.

As word spread that ministers had rejected a paper advocating the continuation of the status quo, a common assumption came to be voiced again and again, identifying the new government as pacifist and inclined towards a diminishment of international defence responsibilities. The controversy could perhaps have been contained had Trudeau been willing to state unequivocally – and well in advance of completion of the review – that all options were not to be considered. This, on principle, and in deference to a number of his cabinet colleagues, he refused to do. And so the accusations mounted in frequency and in shrillness in an atmosphere of increasing intellectual sterility. Not surprisingly, suspicions intensified, and the threshold of frustration on all sides plummeted, as each review was ever more delayed, dropping many months behind schedule. The tension was evident during Question Period in the House of Commons:

October 18, 1968[4]

Mr. MacLean: ". . . since this statement has been promised by the Prime Minister on several occasions, he might like to make some reply."

Mr. Trudeau: "It is not envisaged that in the immediate future we will have any announcements to make."

November 12, 1968[5]

Mr. Lewis: ". . . can the Prime Minister indicate when the review of foreign policy is likely to be concluded?"

Mr. Trudeau: "Mr. Speaker, I share the hon. member's impatience. At this time I cannot say when the review will be concluded."

November 19, 1968[6]

Mr. Diefenbaker: ". . . does not the Prime Minister think the time has come to give them [the people of Canada] the facts?"

Mr. Trudeau: "Yes, I think the Canadian people have the right to full information. The trouble is that we are in the process of reviewing our policy, and if we were to tell them our policy before reviewing it, there would be little purpose in reviewing it."

February 7, 1969[7]

Mr. Mather: "Does he expect it will be concluded during the current year?"

Mr. Trudeau: "Yes, Mr. Speaker."

The delays were much more than mere irritants. The NATO Defence Planning Committee was scheduled to meet in late May 1969. Were cabinet to have the opportunity to read thoroughly what undoubtedly would be voluminous materials, and debate responsibly the issues and alternatives, a last-minute cabinet paper would surely not be acceptable. Nor would the House of Commons be satisfied with a peremptory timetable. The Standing Committee on External Affairs and National Defence had launched its own hearings, and reasonably expected the government to take its advice into account.

As the dual review processes extended ever further into 1969, Trudeau's impatience was stimulated by his concern that the inquiries appeared to be much more narrow in focus than he had requested – and had assured Parliament and the public they would be. His concern intensified deeply when he met briefly in Europe in January 1969 with members of STAFEUR, the External Affairs task force studying Canadian interests in Europe, among which were the appropriate levels of representation and dedication of resources. These distinguished diplomats were among Canada's most senior. Their collective experience, however, had been gained overwhelmingly in postings to Canadian missions in the United States or to the several European capitals. An influential member of the group was Robert Ford, longtime ambassador in Moscow, who believed deeply that the pre-eminent and continuing threat to Canadian security was an unpredictable and expansionist-inclined Soviet regime. Ford's views were complemented by those of the others, who regarded Western Europe as representing not simply the place of origin of the majority of Canadians but as well a primary marketplace for Canadian exports, a source of cultural richness, and the home of institutions and practices of deep importance to Canada's democratic traditions. There was no doubt in this group that the Soviet Union was inclined to aggressive tendencies; nor was there more than passing thought given to the increasing importance to Canada of the numbers of developing countries, many of them members of the Commonwealth. The latter, it was true, fell outside the group's terms of reference. Equally salient, these countries represented a potential competitor for the government's financial resources that STAFEUR wished dedicated to European activities.

Revealingly, the group gave the impression it was unaware of the fact that Trudeau had flown to Europe straight from a House of Commons and a Canadian public that were deeply troubled by the Nigerian civil war. Indeed no other single issue had so seized and maintained its hold on the public conscience in the first session of the twenty-eighth Parliament. Scarcely a day had passed without questions in the House of Commons; seldom did newspapers and television news programs not contain news and commentary about this deeply felt human tragedy. Yet to the ill-concealed astonishment of Trudeau and Head, the Canadian ambassadors in Europe expressed their opinion that this major African drama was of little more than passing importance to Canada and of inconsequential influence in the web of Canada's external relations. East–West should be the focal point, they argued, the driving force of foreign policy, the primary contender for financial and human resources. Each of us, in contrast, were concerned about the demonstrable needs of the developing countries and the inexorable influence that they would bring to bear upon future generations of Canadians.

This difference of opinion would widen into a chasm in the months and years to come. It would surface publicly in prime ministerial policy speeches, most notably at the Mansion House in London in 1974 and at the plenary session of the Conference on Security and Cooperation in Europe in Helsinki the following year. Throughout successive Trudeau governments, the bulk of the older generation of Canadian diplomats would predictably express their dissent, even in face of a world rapidly changing, and would urge more conventional views. (A major exception was the broadly supported initiative to open linkages with the People's Republic of China, a negotiation which would formally open in Stockholm in February 1969.)[8] The STAFEUR exercise would become intimately connected to the defence review, because of the impassioned support its members proclaimed for a continuation, broadly unaltered, of Canada's role in NATO.

As the months passed, the defence review inevitably became focused almost entirely on NATO. This meant that a comprehensive examination of defence policies would still be necessary, one which would follow the foreign-policy review launched by cabinet in July 1968. In fact, defence issues would remain in play throughout the several Trudeau administrations. The NATO debate would be followed by the NORAD renewal, by a number of major equipment acquisitions (the long-range patrol aircraft, the follow-on fighter aircraft, modern battle tanks, the patrol frigate program), by a range of peace-keeping decisions, by the cruise-missile testing policy, all in addition to the basic defence review. This chapter will address itself to the events that led Canada to withdraw from its nuclear strike role in Europe.

II

The Canadian atomic engagement had begun in earnest in 1943, when Canada joined the United States and Britain as a partner in the Quebec Agreement for nuclear collaboration. From that moment on, Canadian atomic knowledge emerged from the theoretical and the limitations of laboratory experiments into the hitherto unexplored universe of technological application. Few Canadians were then aware of this involvement, so secret was the entire exercise, and little has since been disclosed.[9] The challenge was one of unprecedented quality: an activity that took the participants to the frontiers of scientific knowledge, while all the while promising incalculable strategic importance to the defence of democracy. This activity was one of many Canadian contributions of immense value in the darkest days of the Second World War. Canadian leadership in the field was made manifest in 1945, when the first nuclear reactor outside the United States began to function in Chalk River, Ontario.

In the immediate postwar months, there was little ambivalence on the part of Canadians towards this awesome Pandora's box that had been opened with the assistance of their countrymen. A deep revulsion towards the horror of military applications of atomic explosions combined with a calm confidence in the promised peaceful applications of atomic technology. The Canadian government encountered no opposition in its dual policy: to support enthusiastically the Baruch Plan,[10] and concurrently to encourage research and development in such diverse fields as power generation, medical therapy, and agricultural isotopes. No serious consideration was given to either the development or the acquisition of atomic weapons; in the result, Canada became the first – and for many years remained the only – country that was possessed of both the scientific knowledge and the infrastructure necessary to develop the engineering requirements for the production of weapons, but chose not to do so. It is highly unlikely that any Canadian government at any moment would have retained the confidence of the public had it embarked on a nuclear-engineering and weapons-acquisition policy, as did the British government of Prime Minister Clement Attlee. (Even the latter set forth on this task in complete secrecy and without the support of several key ministers and important industrial actors.)[11]

The Canadian decision in 1948 to accept charter membership in the North Atlantic Treaty Organization would place in question the continuance of these policies. If Canada were not itself an atomic-weapons state, should it anticipate joining forces with allied military units possessing them? Even more to the point, should Canada agree to train its forces to deploy and fire atomic weapons in the discharge of alliance undertakings? The issue was as vitally important as it was unprecedented for those Canadian decision-makers who were transforming Canadian foreign policy from its prewar timidity into a bold, multilateral context. Canada had been a proud and effective contributor to the allied military success from 1939 to 1945, and had later skilfully employed its reputation as an architect of the postwar international community. The country's influence was acknowledged in a number of ways: one of the six non-permanent seats on the first UN Security Council; one of the first nine seats on the International Court of Justice; a Montreal headquarters for the new International Civil Aviation Organization; a permanent seat on the executive board of the International Monetary Fund and the International Bank for Reconstruction and Development (later to be referred to as the World Bank). These were all extraordinarily significant accomplishments for a country that had entered the Second World War with virtually no armed forces, with a population of only eleven million, and with a gross national product (GNP) smaller than that of Argentina. Each recognition, moreover, took the form of a role in the new structure that was designed to ensure a more equitable and peaceful world for future generations.

By 1948, however, the promise of that world had been cast in doubt. The brutal Soviet occupation of Czechoslovakia prompted the wary states of Western Europe to join with the United States and Canada to form a collective defence alliance intended to deter the perceived threat of an apparently aggressive, westward-looking Soviet Union.[12] The physical form of the deterrent quickly became atomic in order to counter the massively larger Soviet land force. Canada had chosen in each of its international institutional memberships to be a dependable, contributing team-player. No less was now expected of it by its NATO partners. Thus did Canada hesitatingly reverse its determined demobilization and undertake to dedicate ground and air elements to be stationed in Europe, as well as air and maritime elements to function from Canadian Atlantic bases. The experience of the immensely successful Second World War British Commonwealth Air Training Plan, situated in Canada, would soon be turned towards the operation of a NATO air-training scheme utilizing refurbished Second World War airports, most of them in the Prairie provinces. Perhaps not surprisingly, in conjunction with a number of its NATO allies, Canada agreed in due course to accept a nuclear role. Its airmen and soldiers were trained to employ gravity nuclear bombs to be fixed to the wings of the newly acquired CF-104s based at Lahr, as well as Honest John surface-to-surface missiles as part of its Mechanized Brigade based at Soest. Canada also accepted a seat on NATO's Nuclear Planning Group.

By the mid-sixties, Canadian NATO forces in Europe were broadly and deeply committed to nuclear war; doctrine, equipment, and training all embraced the NATO nuclear option from its earliest "trip-wire" posture through to the later "flexible-response" scenario. Until 1969, successive Canadian governments supported unhesitatingly NATO policies that were uncompromising in their refusal to rule out the possibility of a first use of nuclear weapons, even as the Canadian public demonstrated its increasing hesitation and sometimes opposition to this role.

During that same period, Canada had entered a second military alliance. The North American Air Defence Agreement (NORAD) was signed on May 12, 1958, with the United States as the sole partner. NORAD was distinct from NATO, premised as it was on the fear that the Soviet Union might launch an airborne (later missile) attack over the Pole, primarily against the United States, but inescapably against Canada as well. From the Canadian perspective, there was little reason to believe that any nuclear attack on American strategic airfields (or missile silos) in the border states would have measurably less impact on major Canadian population centres than would strikes aimed primarily at the Canadian cities themselves.

The decision to equip Canadian interceptor aircraft with nuclear-tipped, air-to-air Genie missiles was therefore not contentious, even though it meant that nuclear weapons would be stored on Canadian soil.[13] With remarkably little public discussion and virtually no opposition, the Canadian military dedication to nuclear weapons and a Canadian role in a nuclear war became a reality, based upon the assumptions of political necessity and military effectiveness. Not until 1963, with the acquisition of a technologically limited ground-to-air missile system called Bomarc, did Canada's nuclear-weapons policy become a controversial public issue, and then with unpredictable consequences.

The decision to acquire Bomarcs was taken by the government of Prime Minister John Diefenbaker as part of a broad-ranging increase in the capability of the two NORAD partners to defend North America against a Soviet bomber attack. In the interval between that decision and the delivery to Canada of the first missiles, the Diefenbaker cabinet announced its unwillingness to permit nuclear warheads to be installed upon them. In a display of public diplomacy that proved to have greater impact upon the Canadian polity than any similar event since President Taft's 1911 encouragement of reciprocity, the Supreme Allied Commander, Europe (a NATO position then occupied by U.S. General Louis B. Norstad), revealed to an Ottawa journalist that the Bomarc was militarily ineffective unless nuclear-tipped, and that this had always been known to the Canadian government.

The revelation, added to the Opposition's criticism that Canada was reneging on a solemn treaty commitment, led to a political firestorm. Diefenbaker's minister of national defence, Douglas Harkness, resigned, precipitating a political crisis that led to the resignation of the Conservative government and the subsequent election of a Liberal minority government led by Pearson. In an early act, the Pearson government agreed to acquire nuclear warheads for the Bomarcs, claiming as it did so that the issue was not so much military capability as it was international credibility. In a striking irony, the Bomarc I missile was replaced by the Bomarc II even prior to the warhead conversion, and soon thereafter was acknowledged to be obsolescent and inappropriate in light of the superpowers' increasing reliance on intercontinental ballistic missiles (ICBMs) – against which the Bomarcs were of no value whatever. They were removed without publicity or remorse.

The Bomarc episode was responsible for a rare public disagreement between Trudeau, then a private citizen in Quebec, and Pearson. When the latter promised that a Liberal government would honour the undertaking to accept nuclear warheads, Trudeau was outraged. In a sarcastic reference to Pearson's recent award of the coveted Nobel Peace Prize, Trudeau categorized him as the "un-frocked prince of peace" in an article in the magazine *Cité Libre*.[14] Though the incident did not deter Pearson from encouraging Trudeau to become a Liberal candidate in the 1965 general election, or appointing him as his parliamentary secretary soon thereafter, it remained alive as a testimonial of one man's deep opposition to nuclear weapons. That opposition would remain in principle, even if modified on occasion in application.

By the mid-sixties, a generation of Canadians had come of age possessed of an attitude towards war quite unlike that of their parents. Stimulated without question by the antiwar movement focused on Vietnam, but encouraged as well by fears of nuclear testing, of nuclear accidents, and of the apocalyptic possibility of a U.S.–U.S.S.R. nuclear exchange, this generation began to question the whole premise of nuclear deterrence. Worries of radioactive fallout from atmospheric nuclear tests – initially in the form of fear of strontium-90 – exceeded any concerns about Soviet pretensions to a global Communist hegemony. In Canada, the Korean War was interpreted quite differently than it was by Americans. The flagrant excesses of McCarthyism, and the apparent timidity of President Dwight Eisenhower to confront this abhorrent phenomenon, only confirmed the opinion of many Canadians that American military pretensions were rooted in domestic circumstances much more than they were in any rational explanation of the international political climate.

Those elements of Canadian foreign policy that evoked much pride among Canadians – imaginative support for the United Nations, including the peace-keeping initiatives of Pearson; an increasingly active involvement in the development processes of newly independent countries; and a dedication to cooperative activities within the expanding Commonwealth – contrasted sharply with the rising military hysteria south of the border. Startling and disturbing as had been the Igor Gouzenko revelations (discussed in Chapter Seven), the experience of the subsequent two decades had not left Canadians fearful of the peril of an international communist menace. More meaningful to them by far was the very real evidence of human-rights violations throughout the Soviet empire and the deeply felt concern of Canadians of Eastern European heritage for the fate of their friends and relatives suffering under communist rule. Appalling as these circumstances were, however, they were not seen as the *causa causans* of a nuclear war. In 1968 and 1969, the United States' decision to deploy antiballistic missiles close to ICBM silos in the northern-plains states agitated many Canadians much more than the alleged Soviet-missile threat that prompted them.

In 1968, Canada continued to be one of only two countries participating in each of the NATO and NORAD alliances, and thus only one of two with military commitments on both sides of the Atlantic, as well as only one of three with armed forces permanently garrisoned out of country. The financial burden was considerable. One major alliance task assigned to Canada was a share in the defence of the "SLOC," the sea lanes of communication eastward across the Atlantic, vital to the resupply of NATO forces in Europe should an outbreak of hostilities with the Warsaw Pact continue for more than a few days and, unlikely as was the possibility, remain non-, or limited, nuclear.

The commitment to keeping open the SLOC assumed the form of antisubmarine warfare, far and away the most expensive form of conventional (i.e., non-nuclear) military activity. Canadian surface vessels and aircraft, utilizing sophisticated electronic detection apparatus, engaged in training exercises with Canadian submarines, all essential for the effective discharge of this role. The Canadian geographic sector of responsibility extended from the Gulf of St. Lawrence northeast to Greenland. For reasons of cost, Canada's Pacific seaboard in these circumstances became dependent for its defence upon the U.S. navy. So, in a different sense, did the high Arctic, so overwhelmingly dedicated were Canada's naval forces to their North Atlantic responsibilities. In the European, North Atlantic, and North American theatres alike, each succeeding generation of weaponry and associated equipment exceeded by severalfold the acquisition and operating costs of its predecessor. Modern warfare was a pricey proposition. A beneficiary of that fact, the burgeoning Canadian defence industry, had already begun to emerge as an influential political actor.[15]

The initial underlying basis for the fundamental Canadian defence policy had been the conviction that the Soviet Union was not merely a restive, unfriendly giant, but was as well intransigent, untrustworthy, unpredictable, and either desperately unstable or demonically self-disciplined. This conviction, by the mid-sixties, was so lacking in credibility among a broad sector of Canadians, including part of the "foreign-policy community" of academics and other observers, that even that highly respected foreign-policy professional, Prime Minister Lester Pearson, felt increasingly required to re-examine the major tenets of Canadian policies in light of changing international – and Canadian – circumstances. This was among the reasons that prompted him to recall to Canada from his Geneva posting the General Agreement on Tariffs and Trade (GATT) delegation Ambassador Norman Robertson, and to give him the task of taking a fresh look at Canadian foreign policy that was mentioned early in this chapter.

As the defence review requested by the Trudeau government progressed, positions within the public service and the armed forces tended to harden. As current policies were explained and justified, some of the very misgivings expressed by the cabinet failed to be addressed. Among those was the obvious fact that Canada's armed forces had become so specialized in pursuit of its NATO and NORAD obligations that – at current and projected resource levels – they were simply incapable of assuming seriously the additional and alternative tasks that the new government expected would be necessary. With the forthcoming decommissioning of HMCS Bonaventure, earlier decided by the Pearson government, the maritime element found itself dedicated overwhelmingly to the North Atlantic, possessing not a single hull capable of navigation in ice-infested waters, and utterly opposed to performing – even contemptuous of – many of the paramilitary roles discharged by the Coast Guard, by fisheries-protection vessels, by the RCMP, by the Ministry of Transport, or by any other of the multiplicity of Canadian "navies."

Canada's land forces were primarily trained and equipped to engage in tank combat on the German plain, an activity entirely alien to peace-keeping or to support of the civil power. The costs associated with heavy armour meant that non-related infantry and support forces had been pared to the bone; the concept of a modern mobile force, capable of rapid deployment and compatible with the discharge of varying tasks in Canada and elsewhere, was a fact in theory only.

In the air, Canadian pilots on operational missions were flying increasingly obsolescent CF-104s in Europe and CF-101s in Canada, while the more modern CF-5s, designed for tactical ground support, were unwanted by NATO and unnecessary anywhere but in Vietnam, the war for which they had been designed. The arthritic Argus was a testament to the skills of mechanics and the stamina of aircrew as it conducted its ASW (antisubmarine warfare) patrols. The Canadian Arctic, for all intents and purposes, was an area of indifference, except for the ever-changing commitments to the detection and interdiction of incoming bombers, and the conduct of sensitive electronic-intelligence activities.

Much as the case could be, and was, made that this state of affairs was the result of woefully inadequate financial support, that argument was wholly non-responsive to a new government determined to freeze defence expenditures and to explore the utilization of the Canadian Armed Forces in novel-but-effective fashion, and certainly in a fashion that would not continue to leave the Pacific and Arctic coasts without any credible defence perimeter. Canada's Armed Forces, supported by successive governments loyal to alliance strategies and requirements, had been virtually transformed into a parody of NATO itself: committed to a conventional response to a massive Warsaw Pact incursion into Western Europe, but quite incapable of doing so without relying quickly on nuclear weapons. The assumption that this worst-case scenario was plausible had been publicly challenged by reputable observers, and as recently as 1967 been questioned by no less a personage than Henry Kissinger. The scenario remained scripture, however, even when touted in outrageous terms by the enthusiastic British minister of defence, Denis Healey, who linked *any* aggression by Warsaw Pact forces into a rapid and seamless web of retaliatory nuclear escalation, quickly reaching the strategic-weapons level.

Official NATO policy in the late sixties argued for conventional containment, but in reality its military formations still dictated employment much more akin to the earlier trip-wire strategy than to the more sophisticated flexible-response strategy then officially in place. Thus the Canadian Air Division, consisting of 108 aircraft, was largely deployed (72 aircraft) in a dual reconnaissance/nuclear strike role, while the Mechanized Brigade, consisting of 60 Second World War Centurion tanks, assorted other armoured vehicles, and supporting artillery, was trained and equipped to launch nuclear ground-to-ground ordinance as well as conventional ballistics. These were professional forces, superbly qualified and highly respected by their peers and by NATO, and sincerely welcomed (with their dependents

and civilian-support elements) by European hosts. The overall military impact of their presence, however, was another matter.
According to the British Institute of Strategic Studies, in a paper
released in this period, the Canadian contribution in Europe (which
included some 10,000 service personnel in all) was part of a total
NATO complement of 3,750 operational combat aircraft, 6,400 tanks,
and 875,000 troops. Thus stated, the Canadian aircraft represented
4 per cent of the tactical aircraft total, while Canadian ground personnel and tanks represented 1.5 per cent of the totals on the north
and central fronts. If these forces performed a significant role, as their
advocates argued, it was surely a political role, an expression of
resolve, much more than a military role. That being the case, those
roles should surely not contain contradictions. Yet such appeared to
the Trudeau government to be the case.

Evidence was found in the STAFEUR report. Small though the force
numbers were, it argued, they were significant, and gave to Canada a
desirable influence within NATO and bilaterally with our European
allies. STAFEUR was forced nevertheless to point out that the benefits
reaped from that influence were difficult to quantify. In the decade of
the sixties, for example, Canadian exports to Europe dropped from
more than a quarter of the Canadian total, to just 16 per cent, of
which more than half went to Britain. The EEC Common
Agriculture Policy not only discouraged entry of Canadian produce
but in addition actively subsidized French grain exports into foreign
markets in competition with Canadian products. To 1969, Canadian
contributions to NATO common infrastructure in Europe totalled
some $175 million, while NATO defence purchases in Canada were in
the order of $1 million. Notwithstanding that the net foreign-
exchange cost to Canada of maintaining armed forces in Europe was
about $120 million per year, and that Canada routinely remitted
both customs duties and sales tax to European suppliers to Canada of
all imports of defence equipment of more than $250,000 in value, all
Canadian exports of defence equipment to Europe were subject to
full duties and tax. Both Britain and the United States, the two other
countries with forces permanently garrisoned out of country, were
relieved of this obligation. Not Canada. This "influence" could be
jeopardized, argued the STAFEUR authors, were Canada to withdraw

from, or substantially diminish, its NATO role. Not surprisingly, this argument failed to impress many ministers.

Later, following the announcement of the Canadian decision to reduce its personnel in Europe, a quite different set of issues was raised, this time by several of the allies. They argued, *inter alia*, that the reduction seriously impaired the strength of NATO, sent compromising signals to the Warsaw Pact (thus weakening the NATO bargaining strength for balanced force reductions), and encouraged advocates of an American withdrawal to press their case. Some of the most impassioned invective came from allies whose force deployments were considerably less than their commitments, and who had remained largely mute as the United States shifted NATO forces out of Europe to meet its needs in Vietnam. Canada, clearly, was expected to perform at a special standard; a compliment perhaps, but self-seeking certainly. Partly in anticipation of this kind of argument, Trudeau had stated to the National Press Club in Washington, D.C., in late March 1969, "We are as pleased as is any country when our views are sought or our assistance required. But we may be excused, I hope, if we fail to take too seriously the suggestion of some of our friends from time to time that our acts or our failure to act in this or that way will have profound international consequences or will lead to wide-scale undesirable results."

III

The defence review process reached its most critical phase in February. A lengthy, well-documented cabinet paper emerged from External Affairs that justified completely the current policies and argued strongly for their retention and continuation. Trudeau understood that the conclusions were carefully drawn and respectfully submitted. Nevertheless, in light of the well-known – and, in his judgement, broadly-supported – argument that changing circumstances required policy revisions, he knew how outraged his more reformist cabinet colleagues would be, and sensed how disappointed a large segment of the Canadian public would be, should the recommendations be accepted without challenge. Almost a year had passed since Prime Minister Pearson had called for a re-examination of policy; months of heated public debate had made the issues familiar to millions of Canadians.

For the new government now to admit that the advocates of change were misguided, that ministers were in error, that public servants were not to be challenged, that the lengthy review process was apparently a charade – this was not a course of action acceptable to Trudeau.

The document was deeply disappointing to be sure, and, in light of the London exchanges with the STAFEUR group a few weeks previous, could be interpreted as a slap in the face to the new government, an assertion of power by a well-established mandarinate. Trudeau chose not to attribute motives to the authors; instead he assessed a failing grade to the document. He informed the lead ministers, Mitchell Sharp and Léo Cadieux, that he would not release the document for cabinet consideration. He asked that it be taken back, that the recommendations be reconsidered in light of the stated government wish to examine alternatives to current policy, that a fresh set of proposals be brought forward, and that heed be paid to the rapidly ticking clock.

It was impossible at this stage to determine which of the parties was most taken aback by what had occurred – a novice prime minister, deeply rooted in the Westminster tradition of policy determination by elected ministers, or a proud Department of External Affairs, not accustomed to being challenged over the advice it proffered. Neither of the principals could anticipate what would happen next, or that stakes would so quickly rise. There was little bureaucratic delay this time round. The department reread its paper, quickly reaffirmed the correctness of its views that past policies were correct and the government's preference for change unwarranted, and repeated its recommendation that the status quo be retained. Canada's NATO roles and commitments, argued officials, should not change.

Trudeau was deeply saddened. In the face of ample evidence that East–West relations were glacially mired, that NATO military policy in his judgement was adventurous and dangerous, and that the Western alliance in the opinion of many observers was in need of imaginative reassessment, he was being told to change nothing. The seeming NATO stranglehold on Canada's foreign policy had been the subject of a number of discussions between Trudeau and Head over the months. This latest incident seemed to each of us to be proof of our hypothesis that, in this area of foreign policy, Canada's instincts for responsible innovations were suffocated by the professional establishments' desire for team acceptance.

But what could be done now? Innocently, but effectively, officials had held onto the ball while the clock ran down. There now remained only a few weeks before the final cabinet decision had to be made. It was too short a time for a review *de novo*, and there was no evident source of credible, alternative advice. To Head, the situation was especially disturbing, for he was aware that many experienced military officers and seasoned diplomats were strong advocates of change. A number of persons from each grouping had earlier expressed to him their support for fresh policies. Now, of course, in light of firm advice to ministers that had been signed off by their superiors, they were silenced in their criticism.

Head was nevertheless confident that his own deep worries about NATO policies were shared by others, many of them with much lengthier and more impressive credentials than his own. When Trudeau asked him in gloomy fashion if anything could be done, Head replied in the positive. There was still time, he volunteered, if not to recast the entire policy memorandum, then to prepare another, one which stated cogently, and hopefully persuasively, the existence and attractiveness of arguments critical, at least, of the nuclear-strike role. If the prime minister authorized him to undertake such a task, he was reasonably certain it could be pursued without attracting attention. He would assemble a small team of specialists, all with considerable experience and unlimited access to necessary data, and would assume responsibility for the final text of a document that offered credible alternatives to some elements of the current policy.

Trudeau asked the names of those Head had in mind. There were three: Hume Wright, a career External Affairs officer, long charged with responsibility for military affairs, now on secondment to the Privy Council Office where he served as assistant secretary to the cabinet responsible for foreign and defence policy; Fred Carpenter, a retired major-general, long serving in NATO-related commands in Europe and a former commandant of the National Defence College of Canada, the country's prestigious military-policy think-tank; and Henri de Puyjalon, assistant secretary to the Treasury Board, long engaged in administration of the spending estimates and financial requirements of the

Canadian Armed Forces. Fired more with desperation than with the expectation of a quality product in light of the shortness of time, Trudeau told Head to proceed.

The four quickly assembled and became acquainted with one another, in some cases for the first time. With Head functioning as chairman, they soon agreed on a program of work, division of responsibilities, and a timetable for completion. To avoid the curiosity of others, an empty suite of offices was utilized, and the title "Non-Group" was adopted as identification. The efforts that followed were intensive – all the more so because each person except Carpenter was still expected to attend to his normal functions. For Head and Wright, this included preparations for the prime minister's forthcoming official visit to Washington, D.C.

In the short time available to it, the non-group chose to examine only the NATO tasks, and then only those in Europe. It addressed issues of flexibility, of rapid deployment, of weaponry, of costs. It made a strong case against the nuclear-strike role. The result did not purport to be an exhaustive study. Its purpose was to illustrate to ministers that responsible alternatives to current Canadian policy did exist. The *Non-Group Report* was delivered to the prime minister a few days prior to the scheduled special weekend meeting of cabinet. After reading it, he chose to circulate it to ministers, in effect throwing down a gauntlet to those who had prepared the official paper. Inevitably, and unfortunately, the two ministers responsible for that paper interpreted it as a reflection on their competence by the prime minister.

On the eve of the weekend cabinet meeting, in the course of a dinner at 24 Sussex Drive in honour of Australian Prime Minister John Gorton, who was in Canada for an informal visit, Mitchell Sharp telephoned Trudeau to inform him that he was considering resigning over the issue. He was persuaded not to, and an agreement was reached that the *Non-Group Report* would not be addressed as a cabinet document. Trudeau called Head into the library for a quick conference. He worried that Sharp's proposal would diminish the effectiveness of the document, but Head was of the opinion that the report had already made its mark. Ministers would have read it and would likely use some of the arguments contained in it as part of a more disciplined discussion of defence policies. The earlier worry that an emotive, divisive, and factually discursive debate would ensue, shedding more heat than light on the issues, was probably diminished. The significant number of ministers who had been voicing criticism of Canada's NATO role would now have the opportunity to coalesce and structure their concerns. And Trudeau could be confident, Head argued, that his public promise would be fulfilled; cabinet would consider a range of options. Coupled with the report of the Standing Committee on External Affairs and National Defence tabled shortly before,[16] ministers were now possessed of ample material to fuel their discussion. The anger earlier expressed by some ministers at what they had regarded as a manipulative official paper was now muted.

The *Non-Group Report* was quickly categorized by officials in Ottawa as so radical as not to deserve attention. Indeed, Sharp and External Affairs expressed opposition a few weeks later, when Head prepared a text for Trudeau's use in the House of Commons defence debate that borrowed language from the report. Among the arguments and recommendations put forward by the non-group were the following:

Physical security from outside threats now, and in the long run, can be secured only by pursuing four goals, simultaneously at first but recognizing that attainment of the last two are the only ultimate solution:

(a) Protection of the credibility of the United States deterrent – the American second-strike capability.

(b) Co-operation in deterring, or in promptly settling, wars of a nature that might, by their location, escalate into nuclear war.

(c) Contribution to international peace forces, and to non-military initiatives which will foster trust and strength in international conflict-resolution procedures and an effective system of world order.

(d) Dedication of an increasing percentage of Canada's GNP to activities which are designed to relieve or remove such traditional causes of war as economic insecurity.

. . .

The North Atlantic Treaty Organization is the product of a Canadian idea. Canada participated in the NATO "three wise men" inquiry.[17] It is unthinkable that a responsible Canadian government would precipitately withdraw from NATO against the genuine wishes of its allies.

It should be regarded as equally irresponsible, however, for Canada to continue in NATO without attempting to make rational many of the inconsistencies in NATO policy which weaken the organization's credibility.

This should be Canada's NATO role: to urge it to make realistic assessments and then to act accordingly, not to continue participating because of the exhilaration of "consultation" or the entreaties of the Europeans. There is no shortage of witnesses who regard NATO as being less than it might." [Quotations were here offered from speeches or articles by Richard Nixon, George Kennan, and Lester Pearson.]

. . .

The promotion of a rational NATO policy, accepted and understood by all members, is a task worthy of Canada. The deployment of Canadian Armed Forces as an effective part of such a rational policy will strengthen the alliance, contribute to our own sense of purpose, and will raise the morale of the CAF. It will also prove to be the key for the flexible employment of Canadian Forces elsewhere: – in Canada, to supplement the civil authorities; – around Canada, to provide an adequate multipurpose maritime coastal shield; – abroad, in peace-keeping roles. This follows because the training, equipment, and structure of our forces will be compatible with those roles as they are not at the present.

These arguments, together with the strongly stated rationale against the nuclear-strike role (its destabilizing influence), had persuaded Trudeau of the worth of the *Non-Group Report* and its value for ministerial attention. In the course of the subsequent cabinet discussion, the paragraphs quoted above appeared to be more persuasive in gaining support for a continuing Canadian NATO involvement among those ministers advocating withdrawal than did the External Affairs status-quo document. How ironic that a paper that had caused a senior minister to consider resignation was instrumental in salvaging the major thrust of his own policy. Sadly, the "flexible-employment" proposal never did materialize, so adamant was the navy in rejecting virtually any role for itself except antisubmarine warfare, and so insistent were the land forces on retaining heavy armour.

This had been an extraordinarily intense week. It began with the important Washington visit, included both an unexpected one-day return to Washington for the state funeral of President Dwight Eisenhower and the visit to Ottawa of Prime Minister Gorton, and concluded with the two-day cabinet meeting. The ensuing April 3 decision clearly established two principles, the first of which should not have been tested: the necessary dominance of ministerial decisions over official advice, and the ability of the new government to move away from previous foreign and defence policies without losing ministers in the process. Of the two basic NATO components decided upon, the press and Opposition seized upon the reduction of the Europe-based forces as the most important. In the view of Trudeau and Head, that element was insignificant compared with the major decision: to retire from the nuclear-strike role. And it left the impression, incorrectly, that the total force commitment to NATO was reduced from ten thousand to five thousand, whereas the reduction was only to forces garrisoned in Europe.

Because of the importance of consulting with NATO allies on the form and timing of role changes and force withdrawals from Europe, the immediate announcement of the cabinet decisions was limited to the minimum revelation of retention of NATO membership. The Prime Minister's Office's April 3, 1969, press release stated: "The government has rejected any suggestion that Canada assume a non-aligned or neutral role in world affairs." It went on to state military priorities agreed upon by cabinet:

(a) the surveillance of our own territory and coast lines, i.e., the protection of our own sovereignty;
(b) the defence of North America in co-operation with United States forces;
(c) the fulfillment of such NATO commitments as may be agreed upon; and
(d) the performance of such international peace-keeping roles as we may, from time to time, assume.

In the course of a press conference that same day, Trudeau stated, "We hope that the NATO forces and the Warsaw Pact countries will gradually reach forms of arms control and arms limitation and greater *détente*, and we will continue to play this role. That is one of the reasons for staying in NATO, because we believe that apart from the military role we can play in it, we can play this political role of trying to orient these defensive pacts towards less and less escalation, or more and more de-escalation."

IV

From the beginning of the review process, the nuclear component of Canada's defence posture had been a critically important element in the overall assessment by both of us. If our NATO role was, in largest part, political (whether or not it reaped any political benefits for Canada in the form of access to markets, influence, or otherwise), then, at a minimum, the military component of that role must not contribute negatively to the always sensitive East–West strategic equation. In our considered judgement, on the basis of scenarios developed by the non-group, the Canadian role was negative. It was of negative value because the CF-104 task was provocative, and because the overall NATO tactical policy was essentially destabilizing. Whatever Canada's likelihood of success in arguing the latter point in NATO councils, we believed, Canada must not actively contribute to this conundrum with the weaponry of its own armed forces. Much more was at stake here than a moral revulsion to nuclear weapons, no matter how deeply felt or arguably sound that revulsion might be.

The 1969 Canadian nuclear-weapons decision was taken on narrowly drawn and sharply focused military lines. The nuclear-strike role of the CF-104 lay at the heart of the decision. That role was therefore addressed and revised with the greatest of reasonable speed. The elimination of the Honest John nuclear weaponry of the Mechanized Brigade would follow (though, ironically, its relinquishment was concluded first). The clearly defensive antibomber weapons systems in Canada were demonstrably less critical, and their replacement therefore less urgent. The wholly undependable and likely dysfunctional Bomarc was, in any event, soon to be removed. The Genie air-to-air missiles carried by the CF-101s would remain until the aircraft were replaced, because a conventional armament conversion would both be exceedingly expensive and would reduce to unacceptable levels the combat effectiveness of this ageing airplane.

The final decision to relinquish nuclear weapons was without question influenced to some degree by the perceived opinion of constituencies respected by the Trudeau cabinet. The process leading to that decision, however, was almost entirely a product of the Prime Minister's Office. That this was so, and that the policy appeared alien to the establishment, was a commentary on how conformist had been the attitude of the official reviewers.

American – and by extension NATO – nuclear policies had, early on, followed two distinct paths. Although it abhorred proliferation, and declared fealty to the principle of balanced arms reductions, the U.S. government's rapid development and deployment of nuclear weapons fell into one or the other of two categories of strategic and tactical. The NATO alliance from the outset had readily concurred that the United States retain sole responsibility for stewardship of the massively powerful warheads that comprised the strategic deterrent. These weapons took the form initially of gravity bombs, carried by aircraft of the Strategic Air Command (SAC) that operated out of airfields in the United States and various other partner countries, not all of them members of NATO, with over-flight, aerial refuelling, and ground-support clearances and services (including storage of nuclear munitions) provided or allowed by cooperating governments.[18] Later, the deterrent increasingly assumed the form of ground- and submarine-launched ballistic missiles. In 1968 and 1969, the "triad" was firmly in place, reflecting U.S. interservice rivalries every bit as much as military doctrine. As the range, accuracy, and explosive force of missiles steadily improved, efforts increased to harden silos, to make submarines run ever more silently, to experiment with mobile ICBM launch systems, and to maintain round-the-clock airborne patrols – all to ensure second-strike capability. Out of this was to evolve the policy entitled "Mutual Assured Destruction," with its aptly lettered acronym MAD, the logic of which never did penetrate any number of U.S. government agencies, including the Post Office, which claimed that it could resume delivering the mail within days of a major Soviet nuclear attack on the United States, if only citizens would kindly remember to notify their letter carriers of forwarding addresses in the event of atomic incineration. The strategic deterrent was often referred to as a nuclear umbrella, protecting friends and allies from Soviet pretensions. The fact that all the SAC bases and silo fields were pretargeted by Soviet missiles and that most of them were located within a few miles of major population centres in such countries as Canada or Spain was said to be consistent with the umbrella concept.

Until France proceeded with its own independent deterrent, the "*force de frappe*," there existed an apparently clear distinction between strategy and tactics. Nuclear weapons in the latter category were often default systems. NATO governments had decided in the early fifties that they were unable to counter the ever growing strength of Warsaw Pact forces by conventional means, in particular, tanks. The absence of political will to sustain standing armies of adequate size, and not incidentally to commit national economies to the cost of maintaining them, led to the decision to threaten nuclear retaliation to break up massive armoured formations, should these appear to be challenging the territorial integrity of Western Europe. Thus had come into being the infamous NATO trip-wire policy. American forces in Europe, and those of its allies willing to undertake this task, began to acquire an ever-broadening arsenal of "tactical" nuclear devices – bombs, missiles, projectiles, and *in situ* mines and explosives. With this European buildup, and with the variety of military applications thus offered, the rigidity of the trip-wire evolved into the more sophisticated flexible-response doctrine that was later formally declared. As did others, Canadian soldiers and airmen trained to function in the dual conventional-nuclear roles. Alliance procedures evolved for the unprecedented challenges this flexibility would extend to the command and control functions. Finally, release techniques were designed to obtain in timely fashion the authorization of the U.S. president, necessary under U.S. law, for the utilization of NATO nuclear weapons, which in every single instance were of U.S. origin.

The nuclear component of the Canadian arsenal in Europe took the form of gravity bombs to be released from the CF-104 aircraft of the Canadian Air Division, and Honest John ground-to-ground missiles for the Mechanized Brigade. An essential element of the flexible-response policy, one retained by NATO to this day, was the threat by

NATO of the "first use" of nuclear weapons, a threat made hollow by the equally adamant Soviet declaration that any NATO use of nuclear weapons against Warsaw Pact forces in Europe would trigger a Soviet strategic strike against North America. By 1968, the elements in place were formidable: "tactical" warheads (including the bombs to be unloaded by the CF-104s) of an explosive power several times the size of the bomb dropped on Hiroshima; nuclear mines in fixed installations at important choke-points, through which any Soviet advances would have to pass; and nuclear infantry weapons so small as to be employed in platoon-sized formations.

All of this made perfect sense, the think-tanks and the military experts solemnly assured political decision-makers. Henry Kissinger in his 1957 seminal work *Nuclear Weapons and Foreign Policy* had likened nuclear ground warfare to that of naval battles, where the occupation and retention of territory was less important than was the destruction of enemy assets.[19] He had since abandoned that theory, but, notwithstanding, extraordinarily sophisticated gaming exercises assembled brilliant minds from universities and staff colleges to examine the range of ploys and counterploys, thrusts and feints, that would be part of nuclear war. Techniques of damage control, human survival, and battlefield discipline were examined and introduced, tested and monitored, but always in simulated circumstances. And on this fact, in the judgement of critics, rested the ultimate sophistry of the entire concept of tactical nuclear warfare.

A vitally important element of the first-use policy was the belief that a nuclear battle could remain "tactical," and so be geographically contained, neither spreading and escalating nor being returned in kind. It was believed, equally, that NATO battlefield forces could sustain a nuclear blow and then respond effectively. This wholly theoretical and unproved assumption appeared to an increasing number of observers as simply not credible.

In the entire history of warfare, no theatre commander had ever come under nuclear attack. In our judgement, it was untenable to assume that even the most disciplined officer would be restrained in his response if faced with the destruction of his entire horizon, and the undoubted loss of much of his command, control, and communication (C³) function. In a region as densely populated as central Europe, the destruction and death toll of any nuclear explosion would extend far beyond the intended military targets. In military jargon, the "collateral" damage would be enormous, creating immense pressures upon the political leadership for nuclear retaliation, even if the generals counselled restraint.

In both military and psychological terms, nuclear weapons were not simply a bigger bang; they represented a major qualitative departure from any form of conflict ever before experienced. This "ultimate" weapon was a step into the unknown, a step twice employed in relatively primitive fashion (a single bomb dropped upon an unprepared civilian population), but it was now being considered in abstract fashion, devoid of ethical, humanistic, and even legal connotations. (Only later would such as Joe Nye and Freeman Dyson painstakingly present ethical arguments.[20]) These theatre weapons were by their very nature destabilizing, quite unlike the desperately sought and largely attained balance of strategic arsenals. The deterrent value of widely dispersed theatre systems on both sides of the Iron Curtain was speculative at best. A far greater influence for stability and calmness, it seemed to us, was the allied policy of locating large numbers of civilian dependents on NATO bases in West Germany, hostages to common sense as well as to the resolve of Canada and the United States not to forsake Europe in the event of a Warsaw Pact invasion. Critics of NATO policies argued that the think-tank distinction between tactical and strategic conflict would in all likelihood quickly disappear following the first detonation of one of these devices of horrendous destructive power. The even more powerful, intercontinental strategic weapons would quickly be launched.

This likelihood was not without proponents in Washington. It had in fact cautioned all U.S. administrations against resorting to nuclear weapons, no matter how grave the crises they faced or how provocative the circumstances. Notwithstanding, the pace of nuclear-weapon deployment would only increase. Robert McNamara declared publicly in later years that there is absolutely no military role for nuclear weapons; their sole rationale is political – as a deterrent against use by others. If that golden rule applied for strategic weapons, possessed of a second-strike capability, how much more so should it be associated with tactical weapons exposed to destruction early on following the onset of hostilities? Indeed, those weapons that took the form of fixed installations on the border between West and East Germany were inexorably locked into a frightening "use them or lose them" circumstance that would be faced in the earliest minutes of any conflict. The application of this logic, we reasoned, essentially neutered NATO's flexible-response doctrine; more particularly, it made intellectually indefensible Canada's nuclear-strike role.

The airborne weapons carried by the CF-104s were questionable for the most telling of reasons: they were essentially destabilizing because, in the eye of the Soviets, they could only be regarded as a first-strike, or at least a first-use, system. They flew from soft target airbases, and thus could not expect to escape incoming, pretargeted ballistic missiles, or bombs from attacking aircraft in surprise circumstances. Because these aircraft operated in dual roles, Soviet radar operators were counted on to understand that, as the aircraft flew eastward at supersonic speeds, they were undertaking reconnaissance, not aggressive, missions. On such questionable assumptions did NATO assume that errors of cataclysmic consequence could be avoided.

Again and again Trudeau had posed this latter conundrum to experts and officials, demanding that the analysis be found faulty. Although the issue of provocation was never adequately joined, officials told Trudeau that his concerns about "softness" had long since been anticipated: that two aircraft of each squadron were constantly held in a state of readiness, loaded with nuclear bombs and locked in a special compound. In the event of an imminent attack, they could be airborne within fifteen minutes of receipt of nuclear-release orders, orders that would originate with the U.S. president and be passed on to the squadron through SACEUR (NATO Supreme Allied Commander, Europe) and then Air Division headquarters. Should tension be on the rise because of deteriorating political circumstances, the numbers of aircraft on this alert status would increase.

These explanations were not plausible in our minds. Unlikely as a surprise attack would be – notwithstanding the old bugaboo of the worst-case scenario on which all NATO policies were based – such an attack would likely damage the aircraft if conventional, and would certainly destroy them and their runways if a nuclear weapon was employed as on an intermediate-range rocket. Alternatively, if tensions had reached the breaking point and some conventional conflict had begun, airborne Canadian aircraft would project a special quality of uncertainty into the minds of Warsaw Pact radar operators: are they or are they not about to attack in a nuclear mode? This uncertainty, in our view, was either exceedingly dangerous or an illustration of sophistry. Combined with his belief that nuclear-weapons usage in Europe could not be kept separate from the usage of strategic weapons, Trudeau became ever more adamant that Canada withdraw from all nuclear roles in Europe. In this respect, and unlike the case of the more general cabinet decision to reduce the number of forces stationed in Europe, there was virtually no dissent among ministers when they were presented with these arguments.

V

The defence policy review paper presented by officials had starkly stated two alternatives: non-alignment or the status quo. On this joinder of issue, the cabinet had been invited to debate. Not surprisingly, neither of those two options was attractive to the majority. In the result, the decisions taken finally by cabinet on April 3, as Trudeau reported to the House of Commons on April 23, reflected the view that ". . . it is necessary and wise to continue to participate in an appropriate way in collective security arrangements with other states in the interests of Canada's national security and in defence of the values we share with our friends."[21] In that same speech, however, after referring to the "revolution of rising expectations of billions of people" in the developing countries, he stated that Canada now had the opportunity to play a new role in the world – "a role which will emphasize the need to devote energies to the reduction of tension and the reversal of the arms race – a role which will acknowledge that humanity is increasingly subject to perils from sources in addition to an east–west conflict centred in Europe. . . ."[22] This latter sentence was a public signal to those at work on the still-proceeding foreign-policy review that the Eurocentric views of the STAFEUR ambassadors were not shared by the prime minister. While in no way discounting the importance of Europe, Trudeau was endeavouring, for the first time in Canada's foreign policy, to elevate the Third World to a position of central concern and major prominence. It was a conviction he would repeat on many occasions.

The defence review exercise had now entered its denouement. Stormy consultations had taken place in the NATO Defence Planning Committee meeting in Brussels on May 25. The minister of national defence, Léo Cadieux, ably defended the Canadian proposal against exceedingly critical comments, for the greater part originating with his British counterpart Denis Healey. The major reason for the British annoyance was not stated by Healey but was well known: Canada had always paid 100 per cent of the costs of its forces in Europe; Britain did not, insisting that 80 per cent of the foreign-exchange costs of its 6th Brigade be paid by the Federal Republic of Germany. If Britain were to replace the Canadian troops (positioned by NATO within the British army of the Rhine), the German government would expect that component to be paid for by Britain on the same terms as those followed by Canada. Cadieux reported later to Trudeau and Head that the outrageousness of some of the allied arguments erased any lingering doubts in his mind about the wisdom of the new policies.

The final decisions with respect to the restructuring of the NATO forces stationed in Europe were revealed to Parliament by Cadieux on September 19. Those forces would consist of five thousand personnel. A mechanized battle-group would be non-nuclear; the air element would forego its nuclear-strike role by January 1972. The latter date was not nearly as soon as was wished, but was the earliest that could be negotiated with Canada's NATO partners.

The tenacity, at times the ferocity, of this debate proved beyond question the essential truth of the proposition that launched the entire exercise a year earlier: that a major element of Canada's foreign policy was driven by its defence policy, even though the very size of defence resources made Canadian alliance participation primarily of political, not military, importance. Further, that that defence policy was overwhelmingly NATO-oriented and not entirely amenable to the illumination of vigorous analysis. The hyperbolic nature of the forecasts of allied and Soviet reaction to any questioning of NATO policies, and the brutality of the verbal assaults upon Canadian ministers by their European counterparts following the decision, revealed the tragic and dangerous lock-step mentality of a world committed to a power struggle between two armed camps and unwilling to pursue seriously any form of dispute-resolution except through the process of logically unsupportable nuclear sabre-rattling.

As frightening as the strategic balance of terror was, much more terrifying should have been the rapid buildup and deployment of theatre, and especially battlefield, nuclear weapons.[23] By 1969, these were in the field in the many thousands, presenting maintenance, storage, and inventory problems, in addition to those associated with their contemplated use. As time went on, these weapons would become designed for increasing ease of transport and deployment; the term "modernization" would in many instances equate with "miniaturization." Their variety of designed use made them the opposite of the stable strategic deterrent; these weapons were destabilizing, because the timing and occasion of their use was part of the tactical surprise so precious to field commanders. Nevertheless, fuelled by ambitious military-industrial communities and by political leaders espousing populist positions, the modernization process took on a momentum of its own and would reach its zenith in the Reagan–Thatcher era of the late eighties. This happened, ironically, notwithstanding the parallel growth in perfection and deployment of the non-nuclear "smart" weapons, which would be revealed to the public during the Gulf War. The ease with which these miniaturized nuclear weapons could be disguised and transported made them, as each of us would argue in the years to come, highly coveted as contraband devices by terrorists and renegade states alike.

Canada's withdrawal from nuclear weaponry, which began in the fall of 1969, was completed in Europe by 1972 and in Canada a decade later, as CF-18s assumed the role of the aged CF-101s. Long before the final disposition, however, as had been anticipated by Trudeau's early comments, resources were increasingly dedicated to Official Development Assistance. Legislation to create the imaginative and precedent-setting International Development Research Centre was introduced in 1969 and given royal assent in May 1970. ODA as a percentage of GNP increased from 0.21 per cent in 1968 (its peak under the Pearson government) to 0.41 per cent in 1970 (on the way to a high of 0.54 per cent in 1978). Even before the conclusion of the defence review, and certainly prior to the final accomplishment of force restructuring, Canada was deeply engaged in novel political and environmental activities in the waters of the Arctic archipelago, as well as in the constitutional restructuring of the Commonwealth to avoid the departure of a number of African states. This was the "world as it is" referred to by Trudeau in his speech to the House of Commons on April 23, 1969. This world, and these activities, demanded resources often markedly different than the traditional military, and certainly without nuclear weapons.[24]

CHAPTER FOUR

Commonwealth Paradoxes

I

The Commonwealth is as enigmatic in concept as its evolution has been unpredictable in practice. The willingness of dozens of former British colonies to seek common cause with one another and with the onetime colonial master is in itself astonishing. That they have done so in the almost total absence of any formal structure or process is less well known but equally unusual. And that a considerable amount of mutual benefit has flowed from these anomalous circumstances is definitely worth noting.

None of the advantages has been gained automatically, however, and certainly not all of the difficulties have been resolved. From our own involvement in a rich range of Commonwealth issues and activities, including incidents as important and perplexing as the Nigerian civil war, the resolution of the Rhodesian question, the Indian nuclear explosion, and the American invasion of Grenada, the informality of relations proved to be invaluable in the search for accommodation or solution. Difficult as it may be to define the Commonwealth or its purpose, in our judgement it is of immense value in itself and is a model for others to emulate. In the beginning, however, the relationship was considerably more stuffy.

Scholars have identified that beginning as the Colonial Conference of 1907, which adopted a resolution offering no hint of the monumental changes it would inspire:[1]

> . . . it will be to the advantage of the Empire if a Conference, to be called the Imperial Conference, is held every four years, at

which questions of common interest may be discussed and considered between His Majesty's Government and His governments of the self-governing Dominions beyond the seas. The Prime Minister of the United Kingdom will be ex-officio President, and the Prime Ministers of the self-governing Dominions ex-officio members of the Conference. . . .

No suggestion here of equality of members, of independence of action, of geographic symmetry. Instead a London-centred, British-chaired "conference," organized within the confines of an imperial attitude and a colonial mentality.

Notwithstanding all that evolved thereafter – the introduction of the term "British Commonwealth" (to be changed still again to the more generic but seemingly anonymous "Commonwealth" in 1948), the brilliant formula permitting the inclusion of the newly independent republics of India and Pakistan, and the decades-long withdrawal of South Africa because of its racist policies – many of the 1907 assumptions remained in place as Trudeau joined other heads of government for the first time in January 1969. The meeting was still in London; the chairman was still the British prime minister; the British occupied two seats at the table (the prime minister and the secretary of state for foreign and commonwealth affairs),[2] while all other countries were allocated one each. To Trudeau, and perhaps even more to Head, who accompanied him, it was not an encouraging arrangement. How much more uncomfortable, they inferred, was this entire exercise for the newly independent members, several of whose leaders had in earlier years been imprisoned by the British on account of their advocacy of independence. Long before that first meeting was over, Trudeau resolved that basic changes were necessary if the immense potential of this grouping was to be realized.

Compared with any other international meetings, these Commonwealth sessions occupied an inordinate amount of time, eight working days from beginning to end.[3] To Trudeau, still in the early months of his first administration and occupied with a heavy schedule of planning and other meetings associated with a new session of Parliament, that period represented a major dedication of precious time. In the weeks leading up to Christmas he was reluctant to make the commitment. There were other factors as well that gave him pause. For one, the agenda promised to be dominated by two issues of African origin, the Rhodesian stalemate and the Nigerian civil war, to each of which he felt Canada could contribute little other than moral suasion. For another, a quite unrealistic expectation had built up on the part of the press and in the House of Commons that his performance should be of Herculean proportions. His disinclination allowed those of his advisers with domestic responsibilities to encourage him to remain at home, sending Mitchell Sharp in his stead, or to participate for only a portion of the scheduled time. In the end, however, he was persuaded that there was much merit in attending.

Gordon Robertson, the secretary to the cabinet, emphasized the historic contribution that Canada had made to the evolution of the Commonwealth, including the secondment of a senior Canadian diplomat, Arnold Smith, to act as its first secretary general. Were Trudeau not to participate, it would mark the first such meeting not attended by a Canadian prime minister and would lead to quite unfounded, but nevertheless embarrassing, questions about the new government's commitment to its Commonwealth obligations, including the Colombo Plan.4 Robertson's views were always taken seriously by Trudeau, for he represented the wisdom and experience that made the senior elements of the Canadian public service one of the finest in the world. Moreover, in the then-anachronistic traditions of the Commonwealth, Robertson's position as secretary to the cabinet made him, rather than the undersecretary of state for external affairs, the key Canadian official in the organization and conduct of these meetings.

Head argued in favour of attendance from a slightly different perspective. The meeting promised, in a single event, to acquaint Trudeau personally with more than two dozen world leaders, a singular opportunity at this early moment of his governance, and one not to be found in any other situation. Head's own travels had brought him into contact with some of these individuals, and he was certain that Trudeau would be challenged and edified in conference debates with Lee Kuan Yew of Singapore and Julius Nyerere of Tanzania in particular, each of them possessed of a keen intellect and a strong personality. Trudeau had met Lee briefly in November in Ottawa when Lee flew in from Vancouver, where he was undertaking an unofficial respite from office at the

University of British Columbia. At an informal dinner at 24 Sussex Drive, to which a number of Canadian academics were invited, the conversation had been vigorous and informative. Lee's encyclopaedic knowledge of Asia and his formidable debating skills made him a brilliant and welcome dinner guest.[5]

The arguments of Robertson and Head proved decisive, and were bolstered by the suggestion from External Affairs that an occasion could be found while in Europe for Trudeau to meet with the members of the STAFEUR group of senior diplomats then engaged in a major element of the foreign- and defence-policy reviews.[6] In the end, Trudeau chose to route his return from London via Rome to permit him to pursue with the Vatican his desire to enter diplomatic relations with the Holy See. With his acceptance of requests from a number of prime ministers, including Indira Gandhi of India and Kenneth Kaunda of Zambia, to meet in London for bilateral discussions, a meaty schedule of activities was in hand, more than justifying the lengthy absence from Ottawa.

The Eurocentric view of the world held by the British assumed a number of forms in the course of the London meeting, none more evident than in Prime Minister Harold Wilson's desire to place within the communiqué a strong denunciation of the brutal 1968 Soviet invasion of Czechoslovakia. To African leaders in particular, still smarting from the unwillingness of successive British governments to deal firmly with Ian Smith's rebellious and unconstitutional unilateral declaration of independence in Rhodesia, this proposal and debate was seen as a perversion of priorities. Tom Mboya, the brilliant young Kenyan (later tragically murdered), one of six ministers sitting in for an absent Jomo Kenyatta, was particularly offended and acerbic in his remarks. More philosophical, but deeply critical nevertheless, was Julius Nyerere.

The London venue for these meetings offered a number of distinct advantages. London was the site of the fledgling Commonwealth Secretariat, permitting technical conference support and physical facilities. This, too, was the site of Buckingham Palace, the residence of Her Majesty the Queen, head of the Commonwealth, presenting opportunity for audiences, receptions, and dinners in magnificent surroundings. Finally, all Commonwealth members were physically represented in London with diplomatic missions, easing considerably the extraordinary volume of complex preparations and communications. Nevertheless, the historic significance of London, formerly centre of the Empire, presented certain psychological and symbolic concerns to many of the most recently independent states. The chairmanship of the meeting was one of these. An added disadvantage in 1969 was the now inadequate size of the conference room in Marlborough House, the beautiful old Commonwealth Secretariat building, in light of the burgeoning numbers of Commonwealth states. So crowded were seating arrangements that participants found it next to impossible to move once everyone was inside.

Not surprisingly, a proposal to introduce a rotating venue quickly gathered momentum in the course of the week, fully supported by the British, who were not unaware of the cost savings to them should others take turns in assuming the responsibilities of hosting meetings.

An immediate informal suggestion proposed Canada as the location of the next meeting, which was scheduled for 1971. Logical as this choice might be, Head was opposed, for he feared that it would set in motion a sequencing of meetings based on the chronology of attainment of independence: first Canada, then Australia, next New Zealand, etc. Such would not only delay for many years a meeting in one of the new member states, it would as well perpetuate an unhealthy ranking system of purported seniority in what was supposed to be an association of equals. Trudeau accepted this argument and undertook that, if Lee Kuan Yew agreed to host the 1971 conference in Singapore, Canada would be willing to assume responsibility for the 1973 session. The meeting supported this formula enthusiastically and so a wholesome and flexible rotation process was introduced, reflecting well the informal functioning of this unusual association.

II

For Canada in the January 1969 London meeting, an issue of considerable complexity was that of the Nigerian civil war. In the strictest of interpretations, this tragedy was a matter internal to Nigeria, and so could not be forced onto the agenda of an international conference without offending long-held principles of comity and behaviour. On the other hand, circumstances in Nigeria had seized the attention of the Canadian public in a phenomenal fashion in the months preceding the conference, placing Trudeau in a position where Canadian domestic politics demanded of him some involvement with the Nigerian delegation while in London. The Nigerians, in turn, were hypersensitive to their government's battered public-relations image, and so were anxious to present their own interpretation of events – but of their own volition.

What emerged was one of those innovative procedural accommodations that distinguish the Commonwealth from other more formal groupings such as the United Nations. "We recognize that many of you may wish to talk with us about issues not appropriate for this meeting," said Chief Obafemi Awolowo, the leader of the Nigerian delegation. "We should be pleased if you would accept our invitation to tea in the salon of Lancaster House next door. There we can chat informally about many things." And there the discussion was pursued, courteously but vigorously, as the representatives of the Federal Military Government defended their interpretation of events in their country following the rebellious statement of Colonel Odumegwu Ojukwu on May 30, 1967, that he was declaring the independence of the oil-rich eastern region of the country, the homeland of the Ibo tribe, calling it "Biafra." A bloody civil war had been in progress since that time and a no-holds-barred public-relations struggle occupied much of the world's media. In this struggle, a brilliant (and very lucrative) campaign, designed and implemented by the Swiss public-relations firm Markpress, outdistanced the flat-footed federal government at every turn, as each of us knew so well. The haunting eyes of starving Ibo children gazed out of television screens worldwide, conveying the impression that they were innocent victims of brutal Nigerian military measures. In fact, it was later determined, these children were in many instances kept hostage by Ojukwu's regime in a savage endeavour to influence world public opinion. That this endeavour was successful, there can be no doubt. In time of war, truth is an early victim.

Head had been in Nigeria in the summer of 1967, when the insurrection was in its early stages. It would pick up ghastly momentum later, with the Biafrans at one stage bombing the capital city, Lagos, in ineffective but terrifying fashion. Because this was a civil war, in a continent understandably adamantly opposed to foreign intervention, the Nigerian government early on had stoutly refused any outside advice, be it from the Organization of African Unity or from the United Nations. In the then-still-rigid rules of international law and the absolute, non-interventionist language of the UN Charter, there was no lawful way for the international community to express its concern, except by denouncing arms flows and by contributing food and medical relief. The latter was organized and delivered in the early months of the war by the International Red Cross. By mid-1968, however, mutual suspicion and recrimination had contributed to an unhealthy tenseness between the Red Cross and the Nigerian government.

The first session of the twenty-eighth Parliament had opened in Ottawa on September 12, 1968. Following the formality of the Speech from the Throne, the House of Commons had settled down to business. The first item,[7] as always, was Question Period, the distinctive Westminster tradition of exposing the ministers of the Crown to oral questions by members of the Opposition. Unlike the British practice, where formal, written notification is required, Canadian ministers are given no hint of the questions to be posed. This, then, was the initial moment when the recently chosen leader of the Progressive Conservative Party, Robert Stanfield, faced the newly elected Trudeau. New actors, a new Parliament, the first question in the first session. That question would surely relate to issues raised in the recently concluded election campaign, or to legislation proposed in the Speech from the Throne, perhaps to such current Canadian concerns as bilingualism or western grain prices. The question was of interest not only to Trudeau, to whom it would be addressed, but as well to Head, whose responsibilities in those early days included briefing the prime minister each day prior to Question Period. It was Head's task to anticipate questions and reduce the element of surprise by giving Trudeau necessary information for a responsive reply. On that first day, Head failed dismally. Stanfield's question caught everyone off guard:[8] "Mr. Speaker, Will the prime minister tell the House what measures the Government of Canada proposes to take . . . to avert what threatens to be one of the great tragedies of modern times?"

From that moment on, the government had been on the defensive *vis-à-vis* Biafra. On one oft-recounted occasion, Trudeau was approached by journalists as he left his East Block office to cross over to the Centre Block on Parliament Hill. What were his intentions about Biafra? he was asked. Sensitive to the issue of separation, and unwilling to acknowledge even anecdotally the existence of a region endeavouring to break away by means of military force, he replied in a classically unhelpful fashion. "Where's Biafra?" Trudeau called out as he sprinted across the lawn. Of that entire group of journalists and others, Trudeau was probably the only one who had actually set foot in the eastern region of Nigeria. Nevertheless, and predictably, the flood-tides were now open. "Incredible," "astonishing ignorance," "callous" were among the criticisms soon levied against him.

For understandably humanistic yet undeniably sectarian reasons, the secessionist cause was taken up with greater vehemence and success in Canada than in perhaps any other country. Led by Protestant church leaders, a number of whom had been missionaries in Eastern Nigeria, the Biafran claims were championed as an issue between Christian Ibos on the one side and non-Christian Yorubas and Moslem Hausas on the other. In fact, little of principle was involved. The war was occasioned by an opportunistic, fanatic soldier seeking to take advantage of historic tribal rivalries.[9] This distinction was seemingly better understood in the United States, where the large African-American community exhibited almost total disinterest and certainly no support for the Ojukwu rebels. Whatever the facts, however, the war took on a life of its own and quickly built up into a major bone of contention for the Canadian government, which steadfastly championed the principles of federalism and of negotiated settlements of grievances. Canadian members of Parliament made private "fact-finding" trips to Biafra; the Standing Committee on External Affairs heard witnesses, including the Commonwealth secretary general; the Canadian media thrashed the Canadian government for its impotence.

A major factor contributing to the frustration shared by millions of persons in many countries, as well as dozens of governments worldwide, was the rigid nature of Article 2 of the UN Charter.[10] This key element in the architecture of the international community, rigidly excluding "domestic jurisdiction" from outside interference, served as a near-absolute barrier to the intervention by the UN or other outsiders in the internal affairs of a state, unless first invited. Civil wars, even those giving rise to allegations of genocide, were no exception. Only in instances where the Security Council was willing to rule that the circumstances amounted to a threat to international peace,[11] could the Article 2 barrier be penetrated and forceful intervention prescribed. That kind of ruling, of course, was subject to the veto of any one of the five permanent members, a fact that had prevented the full Security Council from ever so agreeing.[12]

The firm support of one such permanent member, the United Kingdom, for the government of Nigeria, and its willingness to respond positively to Nigeria's requests for support in the form of weaponry and ammunition, ensured that a veto was a distinct possibility in the event that the Nigerian civil war ever came formally to the attention of the Security Council. It never did, and for reasons other than the potential veto. The overwhelming majority of African states would have been outraged if, at a time when an illegal white minority government in Rhodesia was flouting world public opinion and evading mandatory economic sanctions – without Security Council forceful intervention – a secessionist rebellion in Nigeria would be seized upon.[13] Throughout the entire period of the war, there was not a single proposal to place the issue on the agenda of either the Security Council or the General Assembly. The secretary general did, however, appoint a special representative for relief and humanitarian work.

By late October 1968, Head had become deeply worried that the unrelenting attack by Opposition parties, the media, and a growing number of responsible citizens' groups, and the unwillingness of critics even to entertain the reality of Charter and other international legal restraints, was likely to erode the credibility of the government. By chance, he had witnessed at firsthand in Lagos in the summer of 1967 General Yakubu Gowon, the head of the Federal Military Government, and had been deeply struck by his apparent decency and humility.[14] This was not a man, he had decided, who was capable of inspiring the terrible acts of which he was accused. Gowon, surely, would be amenable to a reasoned overture with respect to improved techniques for delivery of food and other humanitarian relief supplies to those in need on both sides of the front line.

Head proposed to Trudeau that some dramatic, yet responsible, gesture be taken to demonstrate the prime minister's commitment to an early peace. He proposed the appointment of a special emissary to engage Gowon in discussions. His candidate for this sensitive task was John Holmes, a retired Canadian diplomat, then director general of the Canadian Institute of International Affairs, who was properly held in almost reverence by the Canadian foreign-policy community as a result of his balanced and eloquent articles and books. Marc Lalonde supported the proposal, and Trudeau accepted it, but sought the approval of Mitchell Sharp. The latter expressed his agreement with the idea, but subject to the condition that the emissary be someone much closer to the government than was Holmes. His nominee: Ivan Head.

The visit was arranged by the Canadian High Commission in Nigeria. To increase the impact of the initiative, it was decided that it not be made public in advance; that, following Head's return to Canada, Trudeau should consult with the secretary general of the United Nations in an endeavour to design an effective policy; and that only thereafter would a report be made to Parliament. Head met with Gowon in his office in Dodon Barracks in Lagos late in October 1968[15] with a twofold mandate: to assess Gowon's sincerity about bringing the war to a conclusion and to seek some easing of the prohibition against relief flights into rebel-held territory. Head returned to Ottawa with his report on the eve of Trudeau's visit to New York for consultation with U Thant.

At the United Nations, Trudeau sought U Thant's advice, and Head outlined the Lagos conversations. Two days later, on Monday, November 4, Trudeau read the following statement to the House of Commons.[16]

... As an immediate result of the Lagos talks ... General Gowon has agreed to assist in every way possible and to guarantee the safety of daylight Red Cross flights into Uli airstrip from either or both of Lagos and Fernando Po. This means that the daily volume of relief supplies which could be carried into the rebel area could be multiplied several fold. ... General Gowon has placed a single condition on this guarantee, one which I regard and which I am sure all Canadians will regard as eminently reasonable. It is that Colonel Ojukwu will undertake not to employ the Uli airstrip during daylight hours for arms flights.

The "eminently reasonable" was rejected by Ojukwu.

This aberrant and terrible civil war was the beginning of Trudeau's Commonwealth involvement. Head would return to Lagos on two more occasions prior to the conclusion of hostilities in January 1970. On one such trip to Africa,[17] he sought the advice of Tanzanian President Nyerere, who, in an effort to bring the war to a conclusion, had ostentatiously offered diplomatic recognition to Biafra on condition that Ojukwu would agree to negotiate. Ojukwu had adamantly refused, alienating the Tanzanians in the eyes of other African countries and prompting Nyerere to counsel Head that Canada's policy of non-interference was both correct and wise, and should not be altered.[18] Throughout this period, Head spoke frequently with President Nixon's special emissary to Nigeria, another law professor, Clyde Ferguson.[19]

As a result of the January discussions in London, a Commonwealth observer-force, including Canadian Gen. William Milroy, visited the front lines. These experienced observers reported no evidence of the allegations of genocide by federal troops as widely reported in the press. Significantly, the observer team was denied entry into rebel-held territory, and so was unable to verify the allegations of undoubted hardship, although there was no reason to doubt the appalling accounts of widespread suffering and death, especially among children, which heightened our sense of helplessness over the absence of any effective means of legally intervening to conclude hostilities. Sadly, however, Ojukwu never did relent on his refusal to allow daylight relief flights into the Uli airstrip (based on the spurious claim that this was his only airport and that daylight flights, monitored by the Nigerian air force, would reveal its location and make it subject to bombing). On the collapse of the Biafran forces, Ojukwu and his family, complete with his white Mercedes automobile, flew out of the other, "non-existent" rebel airport. The much touted pogrom against Ibos never occurred. Those who had fled federal territory were returned to their government jobs; those whose homes had been occupied in their absence were reimbursed for the rents collected and held in trust on their behalf. Terrible and far-reaching as was the toll of suffering, Trudeau's faith and Head's judgement in the decency of Gowon were borne out. Left unresolved, however, were those difficult issues arising out of the acknowledgement in the UN Charter of the "sovereign equality" of states and the related principle of "non-intervention."[20] Obsolescent and increasingly irrelevant as were the old principles surrounding absolute sovereignty, they were staunchly defended by all the newly independent states and by others, notably the United States and the Soviet Union.

III

Other Commonwealth issues would increasingly demand Canadian attention and Trudeau's involvement. In the summer of 1970, with the Nigerian civil war concluded, a new and potentially more serious issue came over the horizon. Earlier that year, the Labour government of Prime Minister Wilson had been defeated in British general elections, and the Conservative Party, under its newly selected leader Edward Heath, came to power.

While in opposition, one of the Conservative criticisms of Wilson had focused on his decision to suspend performance of an agreement entered into by the Conservative government of Sir Harold Macmillan to supply naval vessels, helicopters, and other military equipment to the Republic of South Africa. The arrangement was known as the "Simonstown Agreement," after the large South African naval base that would benefit from much of the material. The right-wing element of the British Conservative Party, known as "The Monday Club," was outraged by Wilson's suspension of the agreement, arguing that it cast doubts on Britain's willingness to honour its contractual undertakings. A considerable amount of money was involved in the deal, much of it to be earned by British defence contractors.

Encouraged by the Simonstown activists, Prime Minister Heath revealed his intention to unblock the sale. Heath had never travelled in Africa, was largely unfamiliar with the anguish felt by Africans over the apartheid policies of South Africa's white supremacist government, and so likely did not anticipate the outrage quickly expressed by the Commonwealth states in Africa. Why should they remain in an association that included as a member a country so willing to offer military assistance to a mortal enemy? They quickly rallied other developing countries to their point of view.

Early that summer, the foreign ministers of the non–aligned countries,[21] in session in Nairobi preparing for the third summit conference
of their presidents and prime ministers scheduled for Lusaka later in
the summer, not surprisingly took up the cry against Simonstown.
Much rhetoric filled the air, but Heath remained unmoved, even as
threats were made by some about leaving the Commonwealth. One of
those attending this meeting was Shridath Ramphal, the foreign minister of Guyana. Known to his acquaintances as "Sonny," Ramphal
occupied a second role in the Guyanese government, that of attorney
general. In the latter position, he had earlier that year invited Head to
join an international team of law professors to advise the Caribbean
Commonwealth governments on the reform of legal education in the
region.[22] In the course of that exercise the two became fast friends.

Ramphal had been alarmed by the intensity of the non–aligned
reaction. En route home to Georgetown, he stopped over in Canada
privately,[23] and asked to see Head on an urgent basis. Have no doubt,
he warned, Nyerere is not bluffing. He will take Tanzania out of the
Commonwealth if Britain persists, and many others will follow. To
avoid this undesirable course of events, the considerable influence of
Trudeau[24] must be brought to bear on pertinent leaders or the
Singapore Commonwealth Heads of Government Meeting would be
a débâcle: ill-attended and a considerable embarrassment for its host,
Lee Kuan Yew.

Head sought an assessment of this scenario from External Affairs,
but was told the department had little information on which to base a
judgement. He then discussed the warning at length with Trudeau,
who decided that the issue was of such concern that it justified in the
first instance a communication to Heath, expressing Canada's deep
concern and encouraging a postponement of the Simonstown decision
until all points of view had been adequately expressed. Heath
demurred, and over the months it appeared increasingly likely that the
Commonwealth would in all probability lose most of its African
members. Were it to do so, the likelihood of the Asian and Caribbean
states following suit could not be discounted.

By early December, Trudeau decided to seek the counsel of the key
African leaders. He instructed Head to fly to Africa for discussions with
Nyerere and, as well, with Zambian President Kenneth Kaunda, who

had been the foremost African spokesman on these issues over the years. Head left early in the month for Lusaka and Dar es Salaam.

To each African leader, Head's message was the same: your influence will disappear should you walk away from this issue. Only by going to Singapore, where Trudeau will support your case, will you have some leverage on British policy. Kaunda was characteristically gracious in response, but firmly non-committal. It was Nyerere who delivered the reply, one that placed Head in an unexpectedly difficult position. "We're grateful to Canada for its concern," he said, "and accept the merit of your argument. We are so disillusioned by Britain's African policies – Wilson's inability to deal with Rhodesia, Heath's stubbornness about South Africa – that we must have some assurance on basic values if the Commonwealth is to retain our confidence. President Kaunda has drafted a 'Declaration of Principles' which I have agreed to deliver to you. Canada's attitude towards it will determine our attendance at Singapore." With which he handed a document to Head. "Read it and let me know your prime minister's response." Head promised an early reply from Trudeau. "Not good enough" was Nyerere's firm reply. "Mr. Trudeau's letter said you were authorized to speak on his behalf, and I agreed to receive you on that basis. The document is not long; let me know whether, in general, your prime minister will support it."

Head realized that his own credibility, and that of Trudeau, had shrewdly been tested by this extraordinary individual. There was no question of Tanzania's firm commitment to the reversal of South Africa's iniquitous policies, nor of Nyerere's confidence in Trudeau. As a symbol of its revulsion to the Heath policy, Tanzania had withdrawn its high commissioner from Britain and requested Canada to undertake the traditional diplomatic task of acting as "protective power" of Tanzanian interests in Britain. Canada had agreed, and the maple-leaf flag was raised over the Tanzanian chancery and residence in London.

(An unprecedented complementary event had taken place coincidentally. Anticipating the Tanzanian move, Britain asked Canada to become protective power of its interests in Tanzania. By one of those inexplicable circumstances that visit even the most efficient of foreign offices, Canada agreed. Canada now found itself in the wholly unusual circumstance of representing Tanzania to Britain, and Britain to Tanzania. In an extraordinary tribute to Canadian integrity, both countries urged that this unlikely arrangement continue. And so it came to pass that while Head was in Dar es Salaam on this mission, the maple-leaf flag flew over British properties in Tanzania.

(By coincidence, the distinguished British diplomat Malcolm MacDonald, former British commissioner general in Southeast Asia, son of the late prime minister Ramsay MacDonald, was visiting Dar and residing in the official British residence, from which the British ambassador, in accord with diplomatic practice, had withdrawn and returned to Britain. "Would Head accept a dinner invitation to this Canadian property if the British provided the meal?" MacDonald asked with an impish grin. Canada placed greater weight on substance than on form, replied Head, and the two thus dined tête-à-tête, recalling happy days in Singapore and Malaya, where each had spent several years in the service of their countries.)

Now, as Nyerere focused his piercing gaze upon him, Head swallowed hard, read the short document carefully, recognized immediately that arms transfers of the Simonstown sort were wholly incompatible with it, and declared that it certainly deserved Canadian support. "Still not good enough," said Nyerere. "Will Trudeau support it?"

"I will encourage him to do so" was Head's reply.

Nyerere persisted. "President Kaunda and I need more than that if we are to retain the confidence of our cabinet colleagues should we travel to Singapore."

There was no alternative if the mission was to succeed. "My prime minister will support it," Head volunteered. He then added, "He will do so with enthusiasm, for it is a remarkable document."

"Agreed, then," responded Nyerere with a chuckle. "President Kaunda and I will attend, as will President Obote of Uganda and the Government of Kenya."[25]

A few days later, in Ottawa, Prime Minister Heath dropped by on an informal, "getting-to-know-you" kind of visit, which is one of the strengths of the Commonwealth way of doing things. Over coffee at the British residence, the question of the Singapore Conference was touched upon. Did Trudeau have any sense of how the issues would play? As a matter of fact, yes. "Ivan Head has just returned from Africa, and is here to relate to you the position that African leaders will take. What I wish to inform you, however, is that the African presidents will present to the conference a paper entitled a 'Declaration of Commonwealth Principles,' which they intend as a constitutional document. I have a copy for you here. Let me add that Canada will argue strongly for its acceptance."

Heath had been caught off guard. He had not the slightest knowledge of the recent Head mission, and so turned quickly to the document. As he read it, his demeanour changed visibly. "If this is the price of continued African membership, it may spell the end of British involvement," he stated with force.

"Please consider the consequences of that kind of response," replied Trudeau. "Britain's reputation is at stake in the eyes of the developing countries."

Heath would promise nothing. The language that Heath found offensive related to the provision of assistance to regimes that practise racial discrimination. He insisted that decisions of this sort belonged to Britain to make. This section was the heart of the declaration, and so would become the focus of intense negotiation in the following weeks.

And so the issue was joined. The question did not possess the drama of a major threat to the peace, but in Trudeau's eyes it was of almost the same importance. Was the Commonwealth to be an association of equals, with a mutuality of respect for the basic values of humankind? If so, the declaration, or words equivalent to it, acceptable to the newly independent members, was essential.

The debate would be epic. Round two took place in New Delhi the following month, where Heath and Trudeau were breaking their long journey to Singapore. Prime Minister Indira Gandhi shrewdly organized her official hospitality to leave room for the two to meet. Arrangements were made for a small dinner at the British high commissioner's residence, following an early-evening concert of Indian dance and music. The dinner was attended by only three others on each side (Head and his counterpart from 10 Downing Street, Robert Armstrong – later to become cabinet secretary – among them).[26] The exchange that evening was as forceful as any that Head had ever witnessed, but led only to a draw.

Round three occupied the full eight days of the Singapore Conference, where it dominated the agenda both inside and outside the conference room. Members of the Canadian delegation performed a superb professional role in gaining the confidence, and the measure, of the other delegates. Ralph Collins, John Hadwen, Tom Carter, Michel Dupuy, Don Cornett,[27] and others assisted Head in negotiating language, briefing Trudeau, and drafting and redrafting elements of the proposed declaration. The Canadians worked very closely with key members of developing-country delegations, of which the most influential was without doubt Sonny Ramphal of Guyana. In one unsuccessful endeavour to break the impasse, the heads of government met privately without any ministers, staff members, or record keepers. This session continued for an entire morning before the exhausted principals chose to recess for lunch without achieving any progress.

The issue of arms to South Africa had been subsumed by this time into something even larger – the security of the Indian Ocean. Alarmed by a decision of the U.S. government to build a major nuclear-submarine communication base on the British island of Diego Garcia (some two thousand kilometres east of the Seychelles), Prime Minister Sirimavo Bandaranaike of Ceylon was proposing to the conference that the Indian Ocean be declared a nuclear-free zone, arguing that Commonwealth territories in the ocean not be utilized by either superpower. The British rejected this view as naïve, notwithstanding the fact that it was supported by India, Pakistan, and Mauritius. President Kaunda did his best to keep the Indian Ocean and the South African cases separate but was not successful. Britain saw an armed, militantly anti-communist South Africa as a bolster of peace in the region. (The apartheid governments of that country sought to influence public opinion in NATO countries by newspaper advertisements proclaiming the strength of their anti-communist ideology and even suggesting on occasion that South Africa qualified for recognition as an "out of region" associate.) Australian Prime Minister John Gorton in his public statements supported Diego Garcia as being in the national interest of Australia, because of alleged U.S.S.R. naval activity in the area; in his private statements, he argued that Simonstown likely was as well, and for the same reason.

The culmination of the debate on a declaration occurred in a final, unscheduled, lengthy morning session in a lounge off the conference room, where a half-dozen leaders, attended by Head and one or two others, valiantly sought honourable accommodation. Trudeau championed the declaration. The British position was ably negotiated by Foreign Minister (former prime minister) Sir Alex Douglas Home, who had deftly persuaded Heath to soften his stand. Because these conferences proceeded by consensus, it was vital that no major dissenters emerge. In this respect, Gorton was wholly unpredictable, as he vacillated back and forth. Singapore Prime Minister Lee Kuan Yew at one point threatened to call the conference back into session, there to force the issue, but was persuaded to continue the now-very-lengthy recess.

At last, early in the afternoon, language was agreed upon, and the relieved-but-weary protagonists left for a much delayed lunch, on the understanding that the accepted declaration would be typed and presented to the plenary by Lee for acceptance without debate. The two of us returned to the delegation hotel, where we gingerly lunched together, worried that something might go amiss in these critical final minutes.

Our hearts were in our mouths following our return to the conference when the foreign minister of India, Sardar Swaran Singh (the leader of the delegation in the absence of Prime Minister Gandhi), demanded the floor. "What in heaven's name does he have in mind?" Trudeau whispered. In elaborate language, Singh drew to the attention of the meeting that the Commonwealth declaration, which he claimed India had been instrumental in formulating, was now ready for acceptance, and he urged its support. As he took his seat, it was difficult to find a straight face in the room. Of all delegations, none had been more disinterested than India in the debate, nor less active. In the desire to close this contentious chapter, however, India's claim to credit was not challenged.

The spirit of the original Kaunda draft remained intact throughout this lengthy period. Joined were two principles of equal merit: one, that Commonwealth members should not offer their support to racism or those engaged in it; and, two, that the Commonwealth was an association of independent states, each pursuing policies in its own interests. The resolution of these principles as they applied to Simonstown was accommodated to the satisfaction of all in the following language:

We recognize racial prejudice as a dangerous sickness threatening the healthy development of the human race and racial discrimination as an . . . unmitigated evil of society. Each of us will vigorously combat this evil within our own nation. No country will afford to regimes which practise racial discrimination assistance which in its own judgement directly contributes to the pursuit or consolidation of this evil policy. . . .

The words "in its own judgement" were the cement of agreement. Lest readers too hastily assume that these provided Britain with a loophole through which to parade its disregard of African and Canadian concern, it must be noted that Britain proceeded to remove from the Simonstown transaction the naval vessels that were regarded by Presidents Kaunda and Nyerere as particularly offensive.

No delegation was more jubilant over this outcome than the Canadian, for none had invested more of its negotiating efforts and stature. As the Canadian aircraft taxied towards the runway to begin the return journey, we embraced in the aisle before sitting down. As we admitted to one another, our elation could have lifted the airplane without benefit of the jet engines. In closing the conference, Chairman Lee selected Trudeau, of all leaders present, to receive praise for his "outstanding contribution. . . . Mr. Trudeau, of Caucasian stock, prime minister of a country with the highest per capita income of any Commonwealth country, had felt that the stature of man himself would be diminished if Commonwealth countries were to treat their fellow humans the way white South Africans were doing."

This intense period of vigorous, principled debate served to create a warm bond of mutual trust and affection between Trudeau and Heath. It was Heath who expressed support for Canada's desire to issue its own ambassadorial credentials, without the signature of Queen Elizabeth II (a practice that Her Majesty was reluctant to abandon, even in favour of the Governor General, as is now done); Heath exhibited his considerable sense of decorum by accepting Trudeau's invitation to attend the state funeral of former prime minister Lester Pearson on December 31, 1972; Trudeau was the sole foreign leader to telegraph congratulations to Heath on the occasion of Britain's successful entry into the European Community in 1971. And, a year following Singapore, when Britain was wrestling with the mechanisms to determine the constitution of a legitimately independent Rhodesia, Heath sought Trudeau's assistance. At question was the efficacy of the oft-stated but never tested principle of "NIBMAR": "No Independence Before Majority African Rule." Was this principle endorsed by the African majority, or was it only a slogan of the African political élite? The answer to that question would, of course, influence the form and speed of the independence process.

In an endeavour to determine the issue, Heath had appointed a commission to test Rhodesian public opinion, chaired by a British law lord, Baron Edward Pearce. That choice of chair unleashed a storm of protest throughout Africa. Even before the commission left for Africa, inaccurate interpretations of an earlier House of Lords judgment in which Lord Pearce had participated were offered as evidence of his insensitivity to racial issues. Heath, in Ottawa in December 1971 for an informal visit, raised this conundrum with Trudeau over tea at 24 Sussex Drive. He was convinced that Pearce was a man of integrity and that the Africans' outbursts (complete with threats about withdrawal of Commonwealth membership) were without merit. Acknowledging that his own credibility was still challenged in Africa, he asked Trudeau if Head would undertake a journey to stress Britain's honourable intentions to African leaders.

Trudeau wryly commented on the full circle that had been taken from Head's trip the previous December. Both men laughed, and called Head into the living room, where instructions were given to him. Head proposed calling on two East African leaders, Kaunda and Nyerere, and two in the west, Gowon of Nigeria and Busia of Ghana. Before his departure in early January, however, Prime Minister K. A. Busia had been deposed in a military *coup d'État* and the visit to Accra was dropped from the list.

The message delivered in each capital was the same: don't jump to conclusions, wait for the commission's report; to your surprise it may strengthen your case for NIBMAR. With some reluctance, each agreed. The outcome was just that. Pearce found overwhelming support for NIBMAR in Rhodesia, and the constitutional handover to an independent state (quickly named Zimbabwe) proceeded on that basis. No further complaints were heard from African Commonwealth leaders as they joyously participated in the birth of the new state.

IV

One of the innovations in Commonwealth practices encouraged by Trudeau at the Singapore meeting was the dedication of attention to the issue of governance. "There is no university course or other substitute which teaches one to be a president or a prime minister," said Trudeau, as he encouraged his peers to dedicate part of each conference to an executive session "permitting us to share our governance experience with one another." The Commonwealth heads of government meeting had become the largest, permanent, floating summit in the world, to paraphrase the Broadway song.[28] It would be a shame, explained Trudeau, if this opportunity to exchange information, to assess governance techniques, to learn from one another, were not seized. To ensure that candour would be exercised, and diffidence minimized – participating in these sessions, after all, would be the prime ministers of newly independent countries, as well as those from well-established states – the decision was taken to exclude all but heads of delegations. No officials. Most important, no ministers.

And so began the world's most advanced seminar in the practice of government; one in which every participant was both a practitioner and a student; one in which theory was eschewed in favour of actual experience. Reflective of the Westminster system of parliamentary government utilized in one variation or another by the overwhelming majority of Commonwealth members, Trudeau's first questions to his peers were, "How do you manage your cabinet agenda? How do you ensure both openness of debate and some efficiency in the procedures utilized?" The format was ideal, and the participants enthusiastic. The first full test was at the 1973 Ottawa meeting, where it was regarded as a considerable success. A complementary activity, also agreed on at Singapore, was the creation of periodic meetings of senior officials, in most instances cabinet secretaries. These sessions were intended to be much more technical than those involving heads of government, and proved so to be. The first of the meetings was organized and chaired by Gordon Robertson, Canada's veteran cabinet secretary. It took place in Ottawa in October 1972.

Any meeting of government leaders, especially large meetings, can quickly lose any pretence of intimacy, and can fail even to reflect the primary interests of the participants, as well-meaning but always cautious public servants design the agenda and prepare the briefing materials. One of the results is the reading of formal speeches. In the absence of well-understood rules and a chairperson insistent upon their observance, these often lengthy interventions prevent the lively exchanges and clarifications so attractive to self-confident leaders. In earlier years Commonwealth meetings did not merely reflect intimacy, they were intimate: half a dozen leaders seated around a fireplace. By 1969, however, the numbers involved did not simply overwhelm the size of the room, they overwhelmed any effort to preserve the cut and thrust of informal debate. By 1971, the problem had increased. There were new delegations to be accommodated, forcing a seating arrangement so spacious that the immense oval-table system resembled a racetrack, with extensive tropical floral arrangements placed here and there on the floor in the vast hollow core. Comfort was present in large measure, but intimacy certainly was not. Even neighbours at the table found that whispers one to another were quite inaudible.

Spaciousness spawned still another problem: the number of persons in the room. Chairs multiplied, as ministers and officials took up their vigil behind their leaders. Because some African presidents in particular, either out of prudence or as a form of educational reward, chose to include in their delegations every political rival, entire cabinets came to be arrayed behind some leaders. Tragically, one "head" at Singapore erred in the composition of his delegation: Milton Obote, president of Uganda. In course of Obote's absence, Idi Amin, who had been left behind in Kampala, seized power, with the savage consequences that later marked him as one of the most infamous villains of modern times. Not much could be done at Commonwealth conferences to fend off *coups d'État* (these meetings were not, after all, the equivalent of the Olympic Games of ancient times),[29] but a number of alternatives were available to return the meetings to their original purposes. Agreement was reached at Singapore on Trudeau's proposal to place "procedure" on the agenda of the Ottawa meeting of senior officials.

As the August 1973 Ottawa Summit approached, Trudeau seized upon still another variant from traditional practices. The task of preparing the meeting agenda properly lay within the jurisdiction of the Commonwealth secretary general, Arnold Smith. How, though, should the chairman allocate time to the agenda issues? (At Singapore, considerable annoyance was expressed informally by a number of prime ministers that African issues were so dominant.) What would be the response of heads to the radical changes in procedure agreed upon by senior officials? (Among them were more numerous "executive" sessions, drastically reduced numbers of persons permitted into the meeting room, a prohibition on the reading of any speech, the use of the intervening weekend for an informal country "getaway" for all heads of government – as distinct from the earlier British practice of country-house invitations extended by certain cabinet ministers to selected presidents and prime ministers). New procedures could be, and should be, constructive and wholesome, as should a consensual agenda. They could also be the occasion for obstructionist performances by recalcitrant delegations, however, a very real possibility in a period when not all member countries held in respect either democratic principles or Robert's Rules of Order, and when seven new leaders had taken office since Singapore.[30] Some direct communications with presidents and prime ministers were in order, Trudeau decided. Nothing that would infringe upon the jurisdiction of the secretary general, of course, but something different from the sterility of letters drafted and read more often than not by bureaucratic intermediaries.

Thus began an unprecedented odyssey. In the spring of 1973, Head would visit each one of the other thirty-one Commonwealth capitals (Ottawa was number thirty-two) and engage in face-to-face discussions with twenty-nine presidents and prime ministers.[31] "I want to know what is on the mind of each one of them," Trudeau instructed Head. The resulting records of these discussions proved to be of considerable assistance to Trudeau in his role as chair and in the bilateral discussions arranged with each president and prime minister. Indeed the result was so advantageous that Trudeau would later utilize this practice in preparing for the 1981 G-7 meeting hosted by Canada. In this latter instance, however, Trudeau called on the other six leaders himself.

In the weeks leading up to the Ottawa meeting, the Canadian and some Commonwealth presses began speculating that Idi Amin would show up. In their meeting in Kampala, Amin had told Head he would like to do so. The mere possibility posed a security nightmare for the host government, as well as causing much anguish on the part of some Opposition critics, none more so than MP Gus Mitges, who questioned Trudeau in the House of Commons.[32] The obvious contradiction of Conservative policies seemed to be of no concern to that party or to the press: that Canada should unilaterally defy Nigerian sovereignty for delivery of food to the rebels during that country's civil war, but should exercise its own sovereignty to deny entry to the president of a Commonwealth country desirous of attending an international conference.

In the end, and notwithstanding all sorts of hints and alarms, Amin never came. He did send as his representative, however, his brilliant young acting foreign minister, Paul Etiang, with instructions to read to the meeting a lengthy statement prepared by Amin. Thus arose a dilemma for Trudeau. To allow such a presentation would breach the new rules of procedure. To deny Etiang the opportunity to speak, however, could easily place him in jeopardy on his return to Kampala, where Amin's despotic and bloody practices were becoming more frequent. To resolve the problem, the meeting accepted Trudeau's proposal that the microphones be turned off, that Etiang be instructed to read in a low voice and with as much speed as possible, and that heads of government concentrate on private business. Once again the flexibility of the Commonwealth permitted common sense to prevail.

The meeting itself did what was expected of it. Debate was truly debate; minds met, even if not always in agreement. Trudeau's opening remarks to the conference had obviously reflected the attitude of the other heads of government:

No member of the Commonwealth is so powerful or so self-sufficient as to be able to act independently of the opinion or the assistance of others. At these gatherings of Heads of Government, we are able to ensure that we understand one another's problems and aspirations. This is the significance of this association. I am not, at this meeting, in search of a new role for the Commonwealth, or indeed of any role. The Commonwealth is for many of its members a special window on the world. Over the years its importance will grow largely because it has no specific role, but emphasizes instead the value of the human relationship.

The nature of these meetings does not lend itself to the resolution of any crisis or major problem. By looking to the future, however, we can identify those issues which, if left unattended, might develop into crisis proportions.

Care and circumstance combined to ensure that crisis was not part of the Ottawa event. The Rhodesia agenda item revealed some progress, Britain's accession to the European Community had been accompanied by the Lomé arrangements to ease the impact on African and Caribbean states, drama failed to surface, notwithstanding continuous rumours and alarms in a press dedicated to the search for confrontation and excitement in what was a businesslike meeting. These sessions cannot be likened, after all, to the UN Security Council. But that does not diminish their value. Reporting on the meeting, veteran British journalist and Commonwealth observer Derek Ingram wrote:[33]

There were no "stars," no victories, no defeats. This is not what a Commonwealth conference is about, and these meetings will only become fully valuable when Presidents and Prime Ministers stop trying to use their role for domestic purposes. At Ottawa, there was a marked change for the better. The message is getting through. There was much less playing to the gallery, though it still did happen from time to time.

A good number of the reforms introduced at Ottawa proved to be so attractive and resilient that they were pursued in largest measure at each of the succeeding heads of government meetings attended by Trudeau.[34] None of those meetings exhibited the tensions of Singapore, evidence perhaps of the healthy catharsis that was associated with that event. Not all meetings were equally productive; not all reflected the organic chemistry of mature leaders genuinely striving to understand one another. Occasionally, a person such as Dom Mintoff of Malta would endeavour through rudeness to gain support of unacceptable proposals. The considerable personal warmth and charm exhibited by Prime Ministers Edward Heath and James Callaghan would give way to the aloofness and ill-concealed disdain exhibited by

Margaret Thatcher towards the concerns of many of Britain's former colonies. The humour and eloquence of Errol Barrow of Barbados and Michael Manley of Jamaica rightly earned them reputations as formidable debaters. The dignity of Seretse Khama of Botswana and Ratu Mara of Fiji elevated the impact of their always pertinent remarks. Burgeoning friendships were in some instances terminated by premature death, as with Tun Abdul Razak of Malaysia and Norman Kirk of New Zealand, or electoral defeat, as with Sirimavo Bandaranaike of Sri Lanka. In a delightfully large number of instances, respect and affection combined with future events to permit enduring relationships and collaboration. Either or both of us would find ourselves constructively engaging in international commissions, inquiries, and conferences in future years with many of these Commonwealth personalities: Lee, Obasanjo, Nyerere, Kaunda, Heath, Callaghan, Fraser, and Manley.

V

The 1975 Kingston Conference differed in two respects from its forerunners. First, it was jointly hosted by four of the then-five Commonwealth Caribbean member states,[35] the prime ministers of which had requested Head to meet with them in Jamaica during one of their planning sessions to share Canada's preparatory experience for the 1973 meeting. Second, it was the first meeting attended by Sonny Ramphal in his new role as secretary general, having succeeded Arnold Smith following the latter's two pioneering and successful terms as the first holder of that office. Kingston was the occasion as well to pursue the resolution of one of the most serious single differences that ever arose between Canada and a fellow Commonwealth state.

In May of 1974, India had detonated underground what it termed a "peaceful" nuclear explosion (PNE). Because of the long-standing cooperation between Canadian and Indian nuclear scientists, and the formal-assistance agreements in effect between Atomic Energy of Canada Limited and India's Atomic Energy Commission, there was widespread suspicion that India had surreptitiously employed plutonium (a by-product of the irradiation of uranium fuel rods) from one of the three nuclear reactors acquired or constructed under the Canada–India program, two of them large power-generating facilities, RAPP I and II.[36]

The most likely such candidate was a small research reactor called NRX in Canada and CIRUS in India. This facility was protected by safeguards monitored by the UN International Atomic Energy Agency (IAEA), but they were of a less stringent sort than became the standard with the conclusion of the nuclear Non-Proliferation Treaty in 1970. (In 1975, Head seized the occasion to remind Henry Kissinger forcefully – following Kissinger's public criticism of Canada's allegedly inadequate safeguard system – that CIRUS stood for "Canada India Reactor United States," because the United States had earlier supplied the heavy-water employed as a moderator and coolant in the small reactor and had asked that its name be added to the device as a means of public recognition. Had the Americans been as vigilant then as they now claimed to be in hindsight, Head argued, they could have insisted on much more rigorous safeguards. Kissinger ruefully agreed. He never repeated the unfair accusation; nor, however, did he ever publicly withdraw it.)

Nuclear explosions are the product of lengthy and complicated preparations. Seldom, therefore, do they occur without the spread of some preliminary suspicion that plans are afoot. Canada had become concerned more than three years earlier, in the course of negotiations with India and the IAEA, for a satisfactory safeguard agreement to cover the heavy-water necessary for the then-soon-to-be commissioned RAPP I power reactor.

The negotiations were complicated for a number of reasons quite distinct from technical issues. One, the long-standing Canada–India nuclear-cooperation agreement provided only for "first-generation" pursuit of plutonium (then the international standard), whereas the signatories to the new NPT had agreed upon a much tougher criterion – pursuit (monitoring) of plutonium through its several irradiation, or enrichment, cycles (generations). As a non-signatory to the NPT, India refused on principle to accept this higher level of intrusion into its domestic nuclear affairs. Canada on the other hand, found itself in conflict: bound by its earlier agreement with India, subject to its undertakings under the 1970 NPT. Two, Canada would not be able to supply all the heavy-water necessary, and so arrangements had been made for the United States to supply the balance. Any safeguard regime would require U.S. agreement, as it would that of the IAEA, which would bear the responsibility of monitoring it. Three, current and potential commercial contracts of considerable value to the Canadian nuclear industry would be put at risk if these negotiations broke down and the bilateral cooperation program was terminated.

India had long-championed the moral right of developing countries to pursue their own destinies, including all peaceful applications of nuclear materials. In theory, this would embrace "peaceful" nuclear explosions, because these were provided for in the NPT. Concurrently, India adamantly refused to adhere to the NPT, because of what it called the double standard of nuclear-weapons states. The NPT, India pointed out correctly, had two goals: preventing the spread of nuclear weapons to states not in possession of them, and the nuclear disarmament of those that did. In the seventies, the goal of general and complete disarmament was as distant as ever. India therefore denounced the demands for "horizontal" non-proliferation by those who were not committed to "vertical" non-proliferation. "On what moral ground can the possessors of nuclear weapons deny them to others while all the while building up their own inventories?"

The protracted and sluggish Canada–India–IAEA negotiations were much on the minds of Trudeau and Head as they prepared for their January 1971 stopover in New Delhi en route to the Singapore Commonwealth Conference. In his discussions with Prime Minister Gandhi, Trudeau endeavoured to extract from her an unequivocal commitment to refrain from testing a nuclear explosive. The best he was able to obtain was a stout denial that India had any intention of developing or testing a nuclear explosive device. It was a denial strongly corroborated by Canadian High Commissioner James George. Head remained quite unconvinced, however, resting his doubts on the entirely theoretical supposition that India's nuclear strategy seemed to be to keep all of its options open, and not constrain itself by any bilateral or multilateral undertakings.

In the months that followed, the cabinet wrestled with this thorny problem. Canada was doubly engaged. As an adherent to all the relevant international nuclear conventions – the 1963 Limited Nuclear Test Ban Treaty, the 1967 Outer Space Treaty, the 1970 Non-Proliferation Treaty, and the 1971 Seabed Arms Control Treaty – Canada was a strong proponent of nuclear-weapon containment and elimination. (A point emphasized in the 1969 decision to withdraw from a NATO nuclear-strike role discussed in Chapter Three.) Secondly, as the supplier to India of nuclear technology and materials, Canada was a major author of India's nuclear capabilities. How best could Canada contribute to the closing of India's options: by reneging on its very clear legal obligations to India (which carried with them some considerable influence) or by softening the application of the new and considerably more sophisticated NPT safeguard standards? There was precedent for the latter course. The United States had found itself in a similar dilemma, also with respect to India, and had chosen a middle route – to increase the standard of safeguards for the Tarapur reactor, built with American assistance, but not as high as the NPT contemplated.

These were issues of intense moral, as well as political and legal, importance, and were treated as such by the government. In the course of 1971, a Canada–India–IAEA Trilateral Safeguards Agreement was negotiated, but with an enforcement period consistent with the earlier cooperation agreement, an agreement that the United States supported through its provision of heavy-water to RAPP I. An element in this complicated process was an exchange of correspondence between Trudeau and Gandhi.

In his September letter, Trudeau stated explicitly that the use of any Canadian-supplied material, equipment, or facilities in India, be it from RAPP I or II, or CIRUS, or fissionable material from these reactors, for the development of a nuclear explosive device would inevitably place in jeopardy the nuclear cooperation arrangements. In her reply, Gandhi reiterated India's commitment to the development and application of nuclear energy for peaceful purposes. Pointedly, she did not rule out explosions, saying only that she regarded it unnecessary to interpret the binding legal obligations between the two countries in a particular way based on the development of a hypothetical contingency.

It was against this intensely negotiated, highly emotional background that news of the May 1974 explosion reached Ottawa. There was a widespread and bitter sense of betrayal.

Ed Ritchie, the superbly competent undersecretary of state for external affairs, hastily summoned senior Canadian officials to an emergency Sunday-morning meeting in the Operations Room of the East Block. A memorandum for cabinet was speedily prepared, revealing all that could be learned of events preceding the explosion and recommending both a strong expression of censure on the part of the government and an immediate suspension of the bilateral nuclear-cooperation agreement, consistent with Trudeau's 1971 letter to Gandhi. Because the explosion occurred in the midst of the 1974 federal-election campaign, not all ministers were in Ottawa. Those that were quickly responded to Trudeau's call and, at a special meeting the following day, enacted the recommendations.

Thereafter, endeavours to learn more of the circumstances as well as of India's intentions proved much less than successful, whether pursued through scientific or formal diplomatic channels. India denied any impropriety, and particularly the utilization of any Canadian assistance or the diversion of plutonium from any of the three Canadian-designed reactors. Accompanying these denials were the familiar assertions of the right of developing countries to choose their own policies, free from interference by the North, assertions quickly applauded and repeated by a number of other non-aligned states, with the predictable exceptions of Pakistan and China, who warned of the dangers of Indian militarism.

Whether or not the fissionable material came from one of the Canadian reactors (for sound scientific reasons CIRUS was most suspect, but proof of diversion of spent fuel has never surfaced), there now loomed a fresh international challenge. By this time, India's nuclear facilities included two additional power reactors, MAPP I and II,[37] designed and constructed entirely without outside assistance, one about to be commissioned, the other under construction. Neither was subject to any form of international safeguard or monitoring regime. Isolating India from the influence of other members of the nuclear community could produce the opposite effect of what was intended.

Concurrent with the Indian denials of breach of faith was the oft-repeated assertion that this test explosion was entirely peaceful in nature, not at all intended for military purposes. Not unexpectedly, the international community was not convinced. There was no denial of the extraordinary scientific and, even more, technological accomplishment for which India was to be credited. Equally, however, there was the need for verifiable assurances that the vast Indian nuclear program was, as claimed, peaceful, and would remain so.

The precedential nature of the explosion was terrifying. This was the

first demonstration of explosive competence beyond the five acknowledged weapons states – Britain, China, France, the Soviet Union, and
the United States. At stake was not simply the effectiveness of the
formal non-proliferation regime, but as well the likelihood that there
could be any containment of the several "near-nuclears" (Pakistan among
them, which had also benefited from a peaceful nuclear-cooperation
agreement with Canada) and the even larger number of other states
with nuclear pretensions. Throughout, India contended that it was the
victim of discrimination.

At the Kingston Commonwealth Conference, Gandhi would argue
that "white men possessed the bomb, and yellow men, why not brown
men as well?" Trudeau replied forcefully that that false logic would
extend nuclear weapons to black men, too, like Julius Nyerere or
Michael Manley, and to Inuit and Amerindians and Gypsies – anyone
who could claim some racial distinctiveness. Nuclear weapons were
evil, he argued, capable of untold human tragedy; every effort should
be extended to their reduction and elimination, not to their increase.
In response to Gandhi's argument that the test was in any event for
peaceful purposes, Trudeau asserted that there were no peaceful applications of nuclear explosive technology, notwithstanding the occasional
claim to the contrary by uninformed or self-interested Americans and
Soviets.[38] To the astonishment of the meeting, Guyanese Prime
Minister Forbes Burnham spoke in support of Gandhi, asking how one
could generate electrical energy from nuclear sources if one didn't
explode. This revelation of ignorance about the realities of nuclear
explosions strengthened Head's long-held concern that no government
leader anywhere in the world had ever witnessed an atmospheric
explosion; none, therefore, could do more than speculate about the
enormous destructive capacity of nuclear weapons.

The plenary sessions of heads of government was far from the only
arena for Canada–India nuclear discussions. Immediately following
the federal election the previous July, Trudeau had instructed Head to
open a high-level channel with the Indian government in the hope
that some negotiated solution could be found to this dangerous
impasse. Willy-nilly, Canada was a major contributor to India's nuclear
prowess, and Canada, Trudeau insisted, must assume some responsibility for gaining acceptable assurances of peaceful intent. Canada's high

commissioner in India, then Jack Maybee, had reported that the Indians would be pleased to open formal discussion, and had nominated as their lead spokesperson Kewal Singh, the foreign secretary (equivalent to a Canadian deputy minister). In December, preparations were in place, and Head, accompanied by Michel Dupuy of the Department of External Affairs, proceeded to New Delhi early in January. Thus began a lengthy series of exceedingly intense, often technical, always courteous negotiations between Head and Singh. Twice the venue was New Delhi; in the interim the two met in Kingston, Ottawa, London, and New York, seeking a form of undertaking by India that would satisfy Canada and an international community looking over its shoulder. Occasionally the two prime ministers would join in, either face-to-face as in Kingston, or by receiving the negotiators during their presence in New Delhi or Ottawa.

Negotiations were difficult for several reasons, and an agreement that was finally reached – subject to cabinet approval – was ultimately rejected by the same Canadian cabinet ministers that had earlier agreed upon less extensive undertakings than Head and Dupuy brought back in the spring of 1976. The reasons were complex. Within the Department of External Affairs, there existed a strong anti-India feeling, rooted in the unhappy experience of many foreign-service officers who had served on the three Indochina International Commissions for Supervision and Control under India's chairmanship. (The third ICSC member was Poland in each of the three commissions for Cambodia, Laos, and Vietnam.) Rightly or wrongly, a number of senior officials – Dupuy not among them – distrusted their Indian counterparts. Canada's nuclear regulatory agency, the Atomic Energy Control Board, was still another factor. For reasons never stated openly, it was critical of the AECL India program, and less than enthusiastic about resolving this particular impasse. A third factor was the attitude of several cabinet ministers who remained either outraged or deeply disappointed at what they regarded as duplicity on the part of the Indians. In the outcome, the negotiated agreement, which would have placed a cocoon of verifiable international safeguards around the entire Indian nuclear program, including the two wholly indigenous Madras reactors, was turned down by cabinet – to Head's dismay and Trudeau's chagrin.[39]

Whether by virtue of the arguments raised and the facts presented by the Canadian side during the protracted negotiations, or as a result of as yet-unknown circumstances, the May 1974 test has never been repeated. Twenty years later, India remains the only nuclear power that has chosen to abandon its test series; the only state to have exploded only once. The explosive clock was not turned back – no clock can be – but it has remained frozen for more than two decades, some solace to each of us.

VI

Still another Commonwealth event of note, one entirely unlike any other, was the U.S. invasion of Grenada, ostensibly to protect the lives of a few dozen American youths enrolled in a commercially operated medical school at a far end of the tiny island. Coming as it did only weeks after the Soviet downing of a Korean airliner, this act seized the attention of the world, for it thrust the Commonwealth Caribbean squarely into the spotlight of the East–West Cold War struggle.

American animosity towards any activity in the Caribbean that did not reflect its own rigidly anti-communist ideology, followed in some instances by overbearing pressure, had long troubled Trudeau. The socialist government of Michael Manley of Jamaica had been grievously destabilized through American interventions undertaken during the Nixon and Ford administrations, ostensibly because Manley had invited a few Cuban engineers to Jamaica to replicate and demonstrate the hugely successful micro-hydro installations of Cuban design and use. On one such occasion,[40] Head expressed concern to Henry Kissinger but was assured there was no official U.S. involvement. Disturbed nevertheless, and anxious to let the Americans know how upsetting to Canadians were the consequences of these events, Trudeau raised the issue with Gerald Ford during a dinner cruise on the presidential yacht *Sequoia* in the course of a visit to Washington, D.C., in June 1976. The president repeated Kissinger's denial of any U.S. government interventions.

Years later, the avowedly anti-communist Ronald Reagan had come to power. A sequence of unsettling events had wracked the government of tiny Grenada (133 square miles in area with a population of

100,000) almost since it had gained independence under the demonstrably erratic, increasingly bizarre, and often thug-like leadership of Eric Gairy. On March 13, 1979, Maurice Bishop and a handful of followers staged a comic-opera and almost entirely bloodless *coup d'État*. They installed themselves as an avowedly Marxist "Peoples Revolutionary Government," determined to steer Grenada onto a socialist course and seeking support in doing so from the Soviet Union and Cuba. In due course, this government was recognized by most states, including the nearby Commonwealth countries, who found Bishop's policies as deeply distasteful as the *coup* itself. These neighbours grew ever more suspicious of the purposes intended for the immensely increased Grenadian defence forces (from 50 to more than 2,000) in a region of the world that prided itself on civility and friendly relations. The new Reagan administration publicly criticized the Bishop regime as a Cuban satellite that was building up its air and port facilities in a menacing fashion. When, therefore, the regime fell into disarray, with Bishop and some of his followers arrested and then massacred by their militant associates on October 19, 1983, alarm bells rang in neighbouring islands.

An emergency meeting of the regional organization CARICOM (Caribbean Community) took place in Trinidad, during which several members encouraged the employment of economic sanctions, if necessary, to restore order in Grenada, where a twenty-four-hour curfew had been imposed. Thereafter, the Organization of Eastern Caribbean States met in Barbados, which was not a member, and a confused sequence of events began, which led to a decision by the U.S. government to invade the tiny island. The Commonwealth leaders most supportive of U.S. military intervention were Tom Adams of Barbados, Eugenie Charles of Dominica, and Edward Seaga of Jamaica. (Jamaica was geographically far distant from Grenada. The closest country, Trinidad, adamantly refused to support or participate in such a measure.)

Accounts of who encouraged who, when and where, remain controversial to this day.[41] What is clear, however, is that, notwithstanding the lengthy and unquestioned presence in the region of British and Canadian interests and of the strong Commonwealth precedents for consultation, neither Prime Minister Thatcher nor Trudeau was informed of what was afoot. (Charles would say later that she had intended to speak to Trudeau, but couldn't find his telephone number. Seaga would telephone to apologize.) Wholly unaware of what was being hatched up, Canada had instructed its senior diplomat in the region, Larry Smith, to fly into Grenada to assess the situation, inquire into the welfare of any Canadians there, and assist in any evacuations if he deemed this advisable. Smith made arrangements to do so, and was actually en route when his aircraft was turned back to Barbados. The U.S. invasion was under way.

Trudeau was deeply distressed about this overwhelming use of American force against a minute Commonwealth state, launched on the basis of evidence that was far from persuasive and in the absence of any serious endeavour to seek a negotiated resolution. The ghastly events that had taken place in Fort Rupert prison were indefensible and demanded punishment, as did the authoritarian government need to be repressed and replaced. A military invasion unauthorized by international law was not, however, an acceptable means. In the House of Commons he expressed himself in these terms on October 16 in response to efforts by Progressive Conservative spokesmen to suggest that the Liberal government was untrustworthy in the eyes of the invaders, and for that reason had not been consulted:[42]

> . . . it seems to me that the reason invoked by the United States and the other Caribbean nations involved is that they wanted a different sort of Government there. It was not so much a question of protecting nationals as it was of ensuring a Government which was compatible with their views as to how a Government should operate. If there is no further explanation than that, I think we would quite clearly say the actions were unjustified.

Prime Minister Thatcher was equally critical and was quoted by the London *Times* on October 31, 1983, as saying that Western countries did not use force "to walk into other peoples' countries. . . . You have to be absolutely certain . . . that there is no other choice, no other way."

At the meeting of Commonwealth heads of government in New Delhi a month following the *coup* and invasion, the Grenada incidents were the subject of heated debate. Trudeau was far from alone in his criticism of this kind of action. He was fully supportive of some steps to enhance the special security needs of small island states, the subject of a study which the secretary general was asked to undertake, but deeply disturbed at the extreme response to the Grenadian crisis and the manner in which it was handled. The final conference communiqué revealed, in carefully couched language, the divisions.

> Commonwealth leaders discussed recent events in Grenada which have caused such deep disquiet among them and in the wider international community. . . . They reaffirmed their commitment to the principles of independence, sovereignty, and territorial integrity and called for the strict observance of these principles.

President Reagan had announced that one of the factors that stimulated the U.S. invasion had been the alleged presence on Grenada of Cuban military construction crews, who were building a runway capable of accommodating Soviet combat aircraft. Such activity had been confirmed by U.S. intelligence, he said, and constituted a threat to the security of the United States. This particular allegation of Grenada's intentions bemused the government of Canada, which was funding the construction of a modern airport terminal at the end of that runway as a stimulus to the potential tourist industry of this beautiful little island. For reasons known only to themselves, the Cuban runway workers proved to have access to small-calibre weapons and displayed some skill in using them against the attacking American forces.

Following the invasion and the subsequent withdrawal of the U.S. troops, and the restoration of a constitutional government, the airport facilities were completed and formally opened. The dedication ceremonies were attended by Canadian High Commissioner Noble Power, representing Canada. A handsome bronze plaque, mounted in an immense boulder at the passenger entrance, gave credit to Canada's involvement, complete with a replica of the Canadian maple-leaf flag. The size of the boulder and the dominance of its location made it impossible for any incoming passenger not to notice. One such person would be President Reagan, who planned

to come in 1984 in celebration of the triumphant exercise of the previous year. Travelling with him, as always, would be a large contingent
of journalists, not all of them true believers in the virtues of the invasion. The plaque would unquestionably seize the attention of each of
them, and just possibly reactivate the military runway controversy.
Shortly before Reagan's arrival it certainly came under scrutiny by the
president's advance team. By the time Reagan arrived, it had disappeared. In one of those major mysteries that occasionally intersperse
the hum-drum of international relations, its subsequent whereabouts
have never been ascertained.

VII

The Grenada episode was the single occasion in a decade and a half of
Commonwealth involvement by Trudeau when some fellow prime
ministers chose to seek outside counsel and military support without
first exploring a consensual agreement. It was a dark period and a far
cry from the cooperative spirit of the Singapore Declaration of
Principles. It was particularly dark because of the willingness of the
actors to move so quickly to armed force, and to do so without adequately exploring alternatives, or seeking the understanding and
support of all neighbouring Commonwealth countries. This incident
apart, the Commonwealth norm of easy, candid, frequent meetings and
communications, most often in informal circumstances, increasingly
appealed to Trudeau as a model for intergovernmental relations.

The Commonwealth was pervasive. Trudeau's first official trip
outside of Canada, and his first to an international conference, had
been the January 1969 Commonwealth heads of government
meeting. His first extended overseas tour included a number of
Commonwealth countries – New Zealand, Australia, Malaysia, and
Singapore. His final foreign initiative – the activity following the
destruction of Korean Airlines flight 007 in August 1983 – included a
Commonwealth flavour.[43] The heads of government meeting in New
Delhi that year encouraged him to travel to Beijing for consultation
with Chinese leaders.

As with members of any such disparate a group, there was an
uneven willingness among Commonwealth leaders and senior officials

to utilize and benefit from the opportunities for informality. Those benefits – in the form of access to information, of a better understanding of complex situations or differing points of view, of the exercise of influence, of camaraderie – were simply not prevalent in other multilateral associations. Notwithstanding – perhaps because of – an extraordinarily broad range of cultural, geographic, historic, and economic circumstances, these men and women of the Commonwealth found themselves able to identify concerns, join issues, exchange views, learn from one another, agree and disagree, and to do so most often without rancour, almost always with some sense of mutual advantage. In this forum none was allowed to dominate, none to masquerade successfully behind the disguise of anonymous underlings. There was a purity about the Commonwealth process that quickly revealed the quality and the honesty of players and positions. The filters introduced at the 1973 Ottawa heads of government meeting enhanced even further the clarity of the product. The rules of encounter denied subterfuge, exposed fuzziness, contributed to lucidity, and increased the likelihood of accurate perceptions. Some individuals appeared to be overwhelmed by this environment; others, for their own reasons, would on occasion react with disdain. Each category, in the period 1969 to 1984, was in a distinct minority. For every Desai, there was a Bandaranaike or a Barrow; for each Thatcher, there was a Callaghan or a Kirk.

The Commonwealth conferences (and all of the circumstances and procedures associated with them) came to be employed by Trudeau as a standard against which to measure other multilateral fora. Could a comparable association of francophone states be created? Perhaps. (And so was encouraged L'Agence de coopération culturelle et technique.) Why can't we talk to one another directly, rather than read speeches at one another? he asked his peers at a NATO summit. (The astonishment and opposition this question provoked led to his criticism some years later that NATO gatherings at that level were primarily symbolic and ceremonial, occasions for the pro forma endorsement of positions and undertakings already reached among officials or military officers. This did not mean that they were without value, just that they were other than advertised, and certainly much less than their potential offered.)

Over the years, Trudeau and Head became increasingly convinced that the world in many instances was a far different place than was assumed by conventional wisdom; that the abundance of risks and opportunities could not adequately be assessed or addressed without a recognition of this fact; and that every opportunity should be seized to explore and test in disciplined fashion the experiences, perceptions, and proposals of those with distinct points of view. Comfortable as was association with familiarity, it did not satisfy the need to broaden knowledge and understanding. If Barbara Ward was correct,[44] and we sensed she was, the global human and physical circumstance was not only considerably different from what orthodox opinion believed it to be, it was changing with a bewildering and unprecedented rapidity. Predictable reactions and linear projections were no longer intellectually defensible, even though in many instances they may have been politically acceptable. Each of us shared a sense of foreboding that facts signalling future events were often ignored or misunderstood, as historians could catalogue litanies of errors in the past. In the absence of crystal balls, it was best to seek every useful occasion to obtain the broadest and most honest forecasts available. The Commonwealth setting suited these purposes admirably, and deserved Canada's dedicated support.

CHAPTER FIVE

North–South Dimensions

I

The UN Charter was very clear in establishing the priorities of the post-Second World War era. Three of the four elements contained in the Charter preamble quickly became familiar concepts to UN supporters in the countries of the North: peace, human rights, international justice. The fourth element, of critical importance to the burgeoning populations of the countries of the South, attracted less attention, even though its language was crystal clear. That element, in the words of the Charter, was the promotion of "social progress and better standards of life in larger freedom." For the billions of persons living in the often impoverished areas of the world, many in countries that were just emerging from long periods of colonial status, this principle was seen as a beacon of hope. The goals of the leaders of the independence movements, after all, extended well beyond the bare bones of political freedom. Visionaries such as Mahatma Gandhi had been vigorous advocates of a reduction of the great disparities in living standards that separated the well-to-do from the impoverished. The better-off countries agreed. At San Francisco they pledged "to employ international machinery for the promotion of the economic and social advancement of all peoples."

In the decades to follow, no design fault in the architecture of the international community would become more rancorous or less effectively addressed than this one which separated the wealthy in the North from the poverty-stricken in the South. Overwhelmed initially by the drama of newfound independence, screened later, ever more massively, by the shadow of the Cold War, the North–South chasm would deepen and broaden. Evidence could be found in living standards, in terms of trade, in social attitudes, and in political behaviour. The early, often naïve, assumptions that political independence would lead to economic benefit were soon dispelled by a range of realities. The frequently genuine but generally tentative efforts of the industrialized countries to assist the less advanced states in their development efforts proved all too often to be inadequate, and in some instances were seen by the South as neo-imperialist in character, as an effort to perpetuate economic dependency.

Most tragic of all, these mostly poor countries found themselves increasingly characterized by the superpowers as bit players in the East–West confrontation, to be either wooed or intimidated in the global quest for strategic military advantage. Ever so frequently, these superpower activities assumed the character of comic opera. Nascent independence struggles in the remaining colonies, or local political activities overwhelmingly related to domestic circumstances, would be seized upon by one or other of the Soviet Union or the United States as evidence of ideological affinity to their planetary pretensions. Embassies would be opened, counselling offered, and aid – often in the form of weapons – would flow. Protestations that these "friendly" activities were part of the battle for "the hearts and minds" of peoples gained little credence with those who found themselves as objects of solicitation. In largest number, the ordinary folk of these countries were preoccupied with the daily chores associated with economic subsistence. "Better standards of life in larger freedom" would remain for most as an illusion that mocked their aspirations for lives of some dignity.

By the late sixties, each of us had been exposed to the realities of circumstances in the developing countries: Trudeau in the course of his backpacking through the Middle East, Asia, and Africa; Head as a junior foreign-service officer in Southeast Asia and then while engaging in scholarly research in West and East Africa. We both had been struck by the resourcefulness and dignity of rural dwellers everywhere; we were offended by the greed and political chicanery often evident on the part of some businessmen and government officials in these regions, encouraged in many instances by favour-seekers from abroad. We came to understand how difficult it was for the new governments to alter lines of communication and trading patterns that had been entrenched over the centuries by colonial or hegemonic powers. And we were alternately bemused or saddened by the wiles of those governments in developing countries that sought to influence the policies of either the United States or the Soviet Union through promises of fealty to the principles of capitalism or socialism.

Long before the 1968 federal election, the axes of the two mighty dynamics, East–West and North–South, were defiantly in place. There was no doubt, however, as to which of the two was dominant. In the North, the common vocabulary of international observers reflected the simpleminded categorization of good guys, bad guys, and the rest. The industrialized democracies became, naturally enough in the minds of their citizens, "The First World." The communist states of the Soviet Union, China, and Eastern Europe were called "The Second World." All others, the developing and often newly independent countries of Africa, Asia, Latin America, and the Caribbean, were "The Third World."[1]

The governments of this "Third World," on the other hand, in initially elevated but fatally flawed fashion, sought some means of distancing themselves from each of the major adversarial camps and their former colonial masters. Encouraged by three of the most charismatic of their leaders – Nehru of India, Nasser of Egypt, and Tito of Yugoslavia – they joined together in what they called "The Non-Aligned" movement.[2] Predictably, their denials of association with either East or West and their increasingly shrill protestations of purity attracted anger and derision from each of the armed camps. Not surprisingly, those engaged in the full fury of ideological combat could feel only contempt for non-believers. At the height of the Cold War, one's mortal adversary inspired much more respect than either the non-aligned or the traditionally neutral. When Cuba proclaimed itself to be one of the adherents of the non-aligned theology, and was warmly embraced by the other celebrants, any remaining vestige of credibility of the movement in the eyes of either superpower disappeared.

And thus did confusion reign in the minds of even the most sympathetic members of publics in the North. "Newly independent" was an identifiable characteristic. "Developing" (which added the long-independent Latin American nations to the first category)[3] was more difficult to comprehend, but exhibited some integrity. "Non-aligned" was something else. When a state, as so many did, claimed membership in all three categories simultaneously, eyes tended to glaze. Little wonder, therefore, that the derogatory but all-embracing phrase "Third World" quickly gained universal usage. Only in the aftermath of the demise of the Soviet Union has favour grown for the geographically inaccurate, but politically benign, term "the South" as a catchment for those countries – of whatever age, of wherever geographic location, and whatever political leaning – that can properly be described as possessed of "developing" economies. These countries range (in 1995) from the extremely wealthy in terms of per capita income, such as Kuwait, to the desperately poor, such as Mali. They are developing, in the view of the World Bank, because their economies are neither mature nor industrialized.

Over the years, Canada's ties with the South had varied considerably. They varied from region to region yet were far from intimate with any. As early as the eighteenth century, a brisk trade in salt-cod and tropical products (sugar, rum) had emerged between the British colonies in Atlantic Canada and some of the islands of the Caribbean. Canadian missionaries in places as distant as China or central Africa would acquaint the faithful at home with the plight of their foreign flocks. Tentatively, but unenthusiastically, some Canadian businesses probed the commercial potential of these alien societies, but in general regarded them primarily as markets for resource-based commodities such as flour or lumber.

Elements of the Canadian Armed Forces had served in a number of thitherto exotic locations in the course of the Second World War and returned with tales of excitement and adventure. Against this limited background, the broad-based willingness of Canadian society in the post-Second World War period to participate as an active member of the international community, including the price to be paid as a measure of doing so, has been nothing short of remarkable. Such an extended engagement is less explicable than was Canada's decision to respond positively to the appeal of Britain to come to its assistance in each of 1914 and 1939. In the result, it may well be said that this dedication to positive and constructive internationalism has not only identified Canada's image in the eyes of the world, it has in large measure focused and shaped our national character, while all the while projecting it outward. If so, Canadians owe an immense debt of gratitude to a relatively small number of superbly competent public servants who contributed far more than their numbers would suggest to both the architecture of the new international community and to the policies of a Canada feeling its way in a world of unprecedented change. One of the participants in that era is also one of its finest chroniclers. In his two-volume study, *The Shaping of Peace*,[4] John Holmes describes vividly these events and identifies the Canadian participants. It is a sound record of a proud period of Canadian history.

If international citizenship meant the assumption of new responsibilities towards these distant societies, Canadians signalled that they would not be opposed. The government of Prime Minister Louis St. Laurent had moved decisively to be included as a charter member of the Colombo Plan, the world's first North–South economic assistance program.[5] The modest government machinery administering these activities was located initially in the Department of Trade and Commerce. Called the External Aid Office, it was led for much of its existence by a person of legendary energy and dedication, Nick Cavell.[6] Later, the Canadian government saw the need to place this aspect of Canada's foreign relations on a more secure footing, and so, in 1968, it created the Canadian International Development Agency, which reported to the secretary of state for external affairs. In order to accept the government's invitation to become CIDA's first president, Maurice Strong agreed to leave his powerful and lucrative private-sector position as president of Power Corporation; thus was launched the international public career of one of Canada's most accomplished citizens.

Understanding as Trudeau was in 1968 of the plight of the developing countries, and fully supportive of Canada's still-diminutive development-assistance program,[7] he was nonetheless surprised at Head's proposal that he dedicate his first prime ministerial speech to North–South issues.[8] He did not demur, however, and delivered a text that emphasized the importance of these relations, arguing that assistance to the developing countries was not charity but in Canada's long-term interests.

The social, economic and political betterment of any man anywhere is ultimately reflected in this country. If at the same time our consciences – our humanitarian instincts – are served, as they are and as they should be, then so much the better. Unquestionably the concept of international assistance is appealing because it is one of the most uplifting endeavours in which man has ever engaged. But we must never forget that in this process Canadians are beneficiaries as well as benefactors.

From that earliest, pre-electoral moment onward, Head would continue to insist that the nations of the South deserved a place of priority in Canada's foreign-policy panoply. He reasoned that much more was at stake here than issues of humanitarianism, important as they were. In his judgement, social instability would lead to political turbulence and the rise of international tensions. He was less worried about the spectre of communism than he was about uncertainty, unpredictability, and turmoil in societies that deserved better, and in economic markets that were often frail at best. Trudeau agreed with him that, if solemn international treaty undertakings such as the UN Charter were deserving of respect, if non-confrontational mechanisms for the settlement of disputes were meritorious, if human dignity and welfare were worthy goals, the immensely complex developmental challenge deserved sustained attention.

Any effective restructuring of the international community demanded much more than the delivery of aid, however. New patterns of trade and new forms of human relationships would be necessary. Old, well-established privileges would be challenged. All this required a bold approach and a sophisticated understanding on the part of the publics of the industrialized countries. It demanded as well a clearer perception of North–South relations than had always been evident.

Canadian government attitudes towards development assistance were, in the fifties, remarkably narrow. When, in early 1951, the St. Laurent cabinet decided to make $25 million available to the Colombo Plan, it simultaneously stipulated that $10 million to $15 million of that sum be employed for the purchase of Canadian wheat. Later in that decade, Prime Minister John Diefenbaker would state the policy in the clearest of terms in the course of a 1958 tour of Asia. Speaking at a press conference in Colombo, he expressed the hope – "if not the expectation" – that Colombo Plan countries would take a substantial part of Canada's increased aid in the form of Canadian wheat. Basil Robinson, a foreign-service officer who accompanied Diefenbaker on his seven-week world tour, would write later, "These statements sounded peculiar alongside his equally emphatic agreement that aid was best when given without strings attached."9

To the surprise of both of us, attitudes even more introverted than these remained deeply entrenched in the Canadian bureaucracy in the late sixties. Shortly into his mandate as president of CIDA, Maurice Strong sought routine cabinet approval for an admittedly novel but scarcely earth-shattering activity – support for the work of the International Rice Research Institute at Los Banos, Philippines. IRRI had been founded some years earlier by the Rockefeller Foundation as part of its campaign to assist developing countries to increase their own food production.10 The application of modern methods of agricultural research and plant breeding, combined with innovative demonstration programs to acquaint local farmers with planting, tilling, and harvesting techniques, had been brilliantly successful. New varieties of high-yield rice promised substantial increases in production of this staple food item. Now IRRI proposed to extend the benefits of its program to other countries in the region, and an international consortium of donors had been formed to provide the necessary support. This was an early incident in what later became known as the "green revolution" in Asia.

Attractive as all this appeared from a developmental perspective, it was seen by the Canadian Department of Agriculture as potential competition for prairie grain-growers. The department reasoned that Southeast Asia could become a rich market for Canadian wheat if local rice supplies were unable to feed the growing populations. These narrow arguments carried the day; at a cabinet committee stage, approval for the project was denied. Strong could scarcely believe such a rationale, and turned to Head for assistance. Head, in turn, alerted Trudeau, who instantly recognized the shortsightedness of the department's position. The decision was overturned by ministers at the earliest opportunity. The fifties concept of assistance was finally curtailed, but certainly not abolished.

II

There was a good deal of admirable high-purpose, as well as much undetected naïveté, in the early development-assistance activities. At the grass-roots level, the youth of the North responded with enthusiasm to invitations to apply their skills abroad. U.S. President John Kennedy's Peace Corps was widely seen as a symbol of the new age of dedication and idealism. Within Canada, a much more modest but exceedingly effective operation called Canadian University Service Overseas (CUSO) had been created in 1961 as a non-governmental organization, and later became heavily funded by CIDA.[11] Recent graduates spent two or so years in one of several developing countries, most often as teachers in rural schools, and generally almost entirely without local Canadian support (unlike the Peace Corps, which had an elaborate infrastructure attached to U.S. embassies abroad). They created immense goodwill for Canada, gained a sense of purpose for themselves and an understanding of the challenges facing societies in the developing countries, and did so for little more than expenses and a modest honorarium.[12]

It was not long, however, before a number of developing countries made clear that they needed in addition persons with professional skills. CUSO and WUS (World University Services) responded by recruiting more technically experienced volunteers, and CIDA greatly enlarged its practice of contracting with Canadian "experts" in response to specific requests. These latter persons, understandably, expected fees comparable to their reputation and, in many instances, housing, schooling, and other prerequisites to compensate as much as possible for their absence from the familiar circumstances of life in Canada. As the years went by, some of these living arrangements gained an unfortunate reputation in the developing countries. Often the CIDA project arrangements with those countries would place responsibility for the provision of acceptable housing on the host government, a heavy burden, and in some instances an unseemly one. Julius Nyerere raised the issue with Head on one occasion, much more in sorrow than anger. "We deeply appreciate the contribution of the Canadian experts," he said, "but Canada's insistence that we provide them with housing far more luxurious than the highest Tanzanian standard leads to cynicism among many in my country."

Over the years, the quite justifiable employment by CIDA of qualified Canadian engineers, technicians, scientists, and consultants created within Canada a cadre of internationally experienced professionals. They contributed to the higher reputation of Canada abroad because of their competence and the remarkable Canadian hallmark of decency. In many instances they also proved to be the bridgehead for Canadian business activities in developing countries. Canadian consulting engineers, for example, are highly regarded in many countries and have built up a number of successful business operations.

Similar expectations for the follow-on business successes of Canadian firms awarded CIDA contracts have been more limited. Extraordinary advantages were available in these public-funded contracts in foreign countries. They offered largely risk-free opportunities to set down roots, gain experience and contacts, adjust to local circumstances, and build local reputations. Not surprisingly, a good many Canadian companies have engaged in a considerable number of CIDA-financed business over the years. They have produced credible results on the ground and in their own financial circumstances. Sadly, however, few business enterprises have been inclined or able to seek business contracts abroad on their own merit wholly within the marketplace, without CIDA support. Those that have, not surprisingly, have done very well. They are in a distinct minority, however, considerably outnumbered by those that gained overseas experience under the umbrella of Canadian government contracts, but which remain unwilling to assume the risks entailed in a purely commercial transaction.

This illustration is only one of many thrown up by Canadian developmental assistance experience. The earliest anticipation on the part of development theorists and practitioners alike that "foreign aid," properly designed and implemented, could stimulate economic growth and social strengthening has proved over the years to be far too optimistic. Theories of "rising tides" and "trickle-down" benefits were simply no match for the pervasive and deep-seated incidence of poverty in so many countries. The analogy of the successes of the Marshall Plan [13] in Western Europe following the Second World War quickly proved false, because of the widely disparate circumstances faced by governments of industrialized countries recovering from wartime damage on the one hand, and, on the other, those of developing countries with virtually no industrial or managerial experience. Nevertheless, for many years, all too many supporters of Official Development Assistance (ODA) would publicly recite the brilliant results of the Marshall Plan as incentive for widespread support of programs in developing countries.

Still other weaknesses in the development-assistance structure were taking hold in these early years and, understandably or not, failed to be recognized or, in some instances, rectified. One, certainly, was the increase in size of the ODA "establishment." This was the natural consequence of a number of factors. One of these was the rapid growth of the ODA budget. Discharging its 1968 election commitments and responding to the clearly expressed public mood of the time, the Trudeau government had introduced reduction in budgetary expenditures in every major sector but two: regional economic expansion and ODA. A second reason for staff buildups was the human inclination to put additional persons to work to overcome the perceived sluggishness of developmental results. More Canadian design, more Canadian management, more Canadian monitoring was the response. A third factor was a consequence of the practice of "Canadian content" in ODA projects, particularly in major infrastructure activities and food aid. A whole new bureaucracy was required in order to obtain the supplies and ensure that all geographic regions of Canada had a fair chance of participating.

The international-development effort was far more complex, of course, than the direct transfer of goods and services from North to South on a bilateral basis. Within the UN system was a complex array of institutions and processes seized of these issues. These included in the first instance such specialized agencies as the World Health Organization and the Food and Agriculture Organization, whose mandates were global in scope but which found themselves increasingly devoted to problems of particular interest to the developing countries, and operations, of which the UN Development Program is intended to be the principal administrator and coordinator, designed for the exclusive purpose of channelling technical assistance to the South. A separate group of institutions, specialized in monetary and financial activities, directed much or all of their attention to issues vital to the developing countries. The World Bank, the International Monetary Fund, and several regional-development banks fell into this category.

In 1964, developing countries had championed the creation of still-another apparatus, the UN Conference on Trade and Development, to deal with some aspects of the critically important field of international commerce, one that had remained inadequately addressed when the United States and the United Kingdom led the opposition to the creation of an international trade institution as part of the Bretton Woods grouping.[14]

This panoply of international activity dedicated to development-related issues demanded oversight and policy direction from several Canadian government departments, principally those with mandates in the fields of finance, trade, and external affairs. In the result, a considerable amount of ministerial time was employed in the many policy discussions, made all the more complex because of the realization that "development" was inexact and ill-understood. Nonetheless, the countries of the North – with differing degrees of enthusiasm, admittedly – accepted various shares of responsibility in the international effort to reduce the stunning disparities in standards of living between certain categories of countries, and within many. These disparities, and the obvious inequities they represented, prompted a fundamental difference of opinion among ministers, members of the government, and certain officials with respect to the most appropriate Canadian policy in response.

Of the two categories, one (a distinct minority) held that, because these disparities were in large measure a reflection of the fundamentally skewed nature of the international trading system, Canadian policy should be directed to its rectification. The case can be simply stated. The great empires of centuries past had been built on the premise of role allocations: (i) the sourcing in the colonies of low-value raw materials and the processing of them into high-value manufactured products in the cosmopolitan power, and (ii) the protection of the colonial markets against the entry of any value-added goods, except those of the cosmopolitan power. Such an arrangement depended upon a vertical economic structure that dictated plantation agriculture, resource exploitation, and the virtual absence of diversification in either products or trading relationships. Efficient as these arrangements may have been in terms of productivity, and immensely profitable for the monopoly companies and the colonial powers, they were of minimal lasting benefit to the colonies. Few local workers were trained to perform other than the simplest of tasks, and virtually none were groomed to occupy managerial positions in either industry or government. As a consequence, at independence, there was a dearth of persons reasonably prepared to assume positions of responsibility. The twin inadequacies of institutional capacity and human competence, combined with trading patterns designed to perpetuate a dependency relationship, would be among the most debilitating and enduring of all challenges facing these countries.

To tackle these systemic flaws in effective fashion, argued this school of thought, what was needed were major alterations in the rules of commerce, in the architecture of the international economic infrastructure, and in the terms of trade. Without those fundamental adjustments, the structural weaknesses and problems would remain: the foreign-exchange earnings of an entire country (such as Malawi or Jamaica) would ride the roller coaster of commodity price fluctuations of one (tea) or two (sugar and bauxite) products; and the routing of telephone calls or mail between adjacent cities such as Accra and Lomé (distance: 185 kilometres) would proceed via London and Paris (total distance: 10,400 kilometres). In such circumstances, the obstacles to a rationalization of production and marketing are so formidable as to be overwhelming.

Equally formidable, of course, is the task of reforming such a system. And especially so, perhaps, for a country such as Canada, which is both vulnerable as a commodity producer to the vicissitudes of world markets, yet is a beneficiary as an industrial power of the relatively stable and high prices of manufactured goods. Better then, said the second category of ministers and others, that Canada's interventions be useful and defensible, but less heroic. Rather than enter into the highly charged and uncertain sector of structural change, let us engage in a transfer of skills and other assistance that will be visible both to Canadians and to the citizens of the recipient countries, and which will be understood by Canadians to be a sharing of their own well-being. In this way we will be acting in a humanitarian and constructive fashion, but not engaging in major policy struggles with those dominant powers supportive of the status quo, powers which in some instances are Canada's major trading partners.

In 1968, Trudeau signalled clearly his own sense of these issues. Aid, as necessary as it was, must be understood as only an intermediate step at best; trade and self-reliance must become an essential goal for developing countries if they are to reduce their debilitating economic dependence on the powerful industrialized states. That was a central point in his 1968 University of Alberta speech:[15]

> As Canadians we must realize that international cooperation, particularly in the field of economic assistance, in order to remain effective, must take on a new form. From the present pattern of commodity and food assistance, of gifts of manufactured goods and loans of money, we must, in response to the economic needs of the developing countries turn more and more to preferential trading arrangements. The two United Nations Conferences on Trade and Development have made clear that economic aid, in order to be effective, must increasingly take the form of trade. . . .

This dynamic would ebb and flow over the years, pitting the two points of view in sometimes open dispute. In 1975, at a time when the North–South divide was most bitter and threatening of interests on both sides, Trudeau was encouraged by Head to seize the opportunity of an address to a prestigious audience assembled by the Lord Mayor of London in the Mansion House to present his arguments.[16] The opposition of the Department of External Affairs on this occasion approached bitterness, so determined was it that Canadian policy pursue in singleminded fashion an enhanced economic relationship with the countries of the North, even if to the disadvantage of the South, and that the speech reflect that priority. It was on that occasion that Trudeau said:

> The role of leadership today is to encourage the embrace of a global ethic. An ethic that abhors the present imbalance in the basic human condition – an imbalance in access to health care, to a nutritious diet, to shelter, to education. An ethic that extends to all men, to all space, and through all time. An ethic that is based on confidence in one's fellow man. Confidence that with imagination and discipline the operation of the present world economic

structure can be revised to reflect more accurately the needs of today and tomorrow. Confidence that these factors which have the effect of discriminating against the developing countries can be removed from the world's trading and monetary systems. Confidence that we can create a trading order which is truly universal and not confined to or favouring groups defined along geographic or linguistic or ideological or religious or any other lines. Confidence that access to liquidity for trade and for development will not be restricted by factors other than those accepted by all as necessary in order to contribute to the health of the entire world system.

III

The transformation of fragile (often artificially composed) states, bereft of adequate numbers of educated and technically competent citizens, into robust, competitive, social and economic units was a challenge much more formidable than anyone at the time would concede. Woefully, as Lee Kuan Yew would point out to critics in the North, the training ground for colonial citizens with a penchant for a political future was the local penitentiary. Not all colonial regimes were equally repressive or historically shortsighted, of course. Nevertheless, not many countries upon independence could count on more than a few dozen citizens with any depth of experience in the hands-on tasks of governance. As a result, unrealistically high expectations and simplistic proposals for problem-solving permeated the developing world. An understandable, but nevertheless immature, habit of shifting blame to others became a prominent characteristic within the G-77 movement. It was not a universal attribute; Lee and Julius Nyerere, as two examples, were unremittingly critical of the inequities of the international system, but were equally insistent within their own societies that in the final analysis countries such as Singapore or Tanzania had to look to themselves for the betterment of their own futures. Events would reveal, however, that more than motivation and self-discipline were necessary for success. One of the key variables, fluctuating from continent to continent and country to country, was the structure of economies.

In all too many instances, states were wholly dependent for export earnings upon a single resource commodity – tea, copper, sisal, sugar – and found themselves bound almost inextricably into a web of dependencies with the former colonial power or with the dominant foreign investor. Telecommunications linkages, ocean freight tariffs and protocols, access to financial services and to industrial technologies – all were often beyond the power and the ability of the developing country to alter or renegotiate.

These circumstances were not intended, in our judgement, to penalize and subdue the developing countries, yet again and again this was the effect. Terms of trade that were favourable to the sophisticated industrialized countries, familiar commercial arrangements, and dedicated agricultural or resource-extraction practices were a formidable combination. When these were reinforced by local élites who benefited from their special relationship with the overseas power, local governments often decided that their policy options were limited to two: the introduction of revolutionary, socialist regimes, intended to break the yoke of the seemingly "predatory" foreign power; or the negotiation of profitable arrangements that guaranteed rich rewards for government insiders willing to corrupt themselves in return for private riches. Whichever the choice, the governments of the developing countries found themselves subsequently in even less tenable circumstances as they wrestled with the challenges of economic and social development.

Socialism and the nationalization of foreign-owned assets provoked retaliation of sometimes brutal proportions on the part of the affected countries.[17] Complicity in shady payoffs, on the other hand, simply confirmed the opinion of the self-righteous critics making the payments that these countries were not to be taken seriously. Seldom was adequate heed paid to the fact that the industrialized countries of the North had required several centuries, and in many instances the propitious presence of overseas colonies, to transform themselves from agricultural societies into modern diversified industrial powers and that in the process none of them demonstrated impeccable democratic or human-rights practices. In that long process of maturation, the introduction of increasingly sophisticated educational systems, the installation of widespread infrastructure, the accretion of experience and managerial skills, often took place in economic environments that guaranteed protected markets for the industrial goods produced. Much of the early wealth of Britain can be traced to the profitable combination of low-cost fibres from overseas colonies on the one hand and, on the other, monopoly markets for the textiles manufactured from them. "Value added" is the economist's term.

As the industrialized countries in cynical fashion increasingly raised tariff and non-tariff barriers against the entry of such goods from the developing countries in the post-Second World War years, the message was not lost on the latter. The rules were set by the powerful; all of the rhetoric to the contrary, including UN Charter provisions, were simply techniques to assuage the consciences of the North. They changed nothing.

More was involved, of course, than a simple power struggle in which the South was woefully unprepared to compete advantageously. The elements of a mid-twentieth-century economy were complex and difficult to replicate in alien environments, no matter how conscientious the effort. The list of challenges requiring simultaneous attention was long. As important as any other was the need to transform agricultural practices in order to meet the food and nutritional demands of growing populations. Those practices in some instances were traditional, in others they consisted of plantation-type techniques for the production of export crops. In both instances, the obstacles were a combination of market, social, and technical elements.

In agriculture, as in industry, access to – and understanding of – modern technology was a necessary ingredient for success. Yet technology and the knowledge necessary for its utilization were increasingly the products of private-sector initiatives. In the seventies and eighties, more so than at any previous time in human endeavour, knowledge was becoming a private "good," with a hefty price tag upon it in the form of royalties or licensing agreements. "Intellectual property" was the term given to this burgeoning concept; patents and copyrights became an increasingly active element in international business, as well as in international relations. A dedicated UN agency was created to address the issues arising from these practices,[18] and international negotiations increased for the inclusion of protection for intellectual property in trading regimes.[19] In an increasingly technology-dominated marketplace, developing countries found themselves more and more incapable of producing, acquiring, or utilizing the new forms of knowledge so essential to their agricultural practices, the health of their populations, and the competitiveness of their manufacturing sectors.

The plight of the peoples in the developing countries, each of us firmly believed, should not be regarded as circumstances isolated from the interests of Canadians. Without question, these human beings were entitled to lives of dignity and reasonable expectations of a better economic and social future. The sharing with them of some portion of Canada's immense good fortune was a natural instinct, one which had been reflected in the generosity of individual Canadians for many decades through church and other appeals. Humanitarian assistance for the victims of natural disasters and other misfortunes was both decent and unexceptional. Much more was involved here, however, than humanitarian linkages, and much more was demanded of the industrialized countries than marginal transfers of resources in the form of capital assets or technical training. International development was at once more complex than the delivery of "foreign aid" and more demanding of thoughtful responses than charitable mind-sets provided. Ironically, in a period of expansive economies in the OECD countries, there was both a greater degree of public support for development-assistance activities and a disinclination to come to grips with some of the most perplexing and stubborn elements confounding meaningful achievement.

The disinclination was found on both sides of the North–South divide, even if stimulated by differing circumstances. In the North, there was an unwillingness to acknowledge the increased dependencies of the industrialized countries upon the nations of the South. The international community was rapidly becoming more complex and interlinked. Any number of information and technical systems, upon which the North leaned heavily – weather forecasting, air-traffic control, maritime navigational rules, communicable-disease regulations, agriculture quarantines, the interdiction of terrorists, food-export inspections, etc. – were operable only with the cooperation of *all* states, North and South alike. The economies of all countries of the North depended heavily, none more so than Canada, upon the health of their export trade. Increasingly, the rapidly growing countries of the South promised to be important trading partners – indeed, already were in Canada's case. By 1980, the developing countries were buying more from Canada than were Japan and all the members of the European Community combined. On their side of the axis, developing countries had demonstrated all too frequently their disruptive influence on the international agenda when their own disputes flared into the awareness of the countries of the North, demanding the political attention of the Security Council, attracting humanitarian interventions, generating outward flows of refugees and capital, and threatening commercial and investment interests.

In these and other respects, what seemed to us to be incontrovertible evidence of the extent of the North's vulnerability was simply not accepted by the OECD countries generally (or by many of Trudeau's cabinet colleagues) as deserving of the responses we felt necessary. The prevailing attitude was often one of lip service without addressing squarely the major underlying deficiencies in the international system. Clearly, it seemed, declarations of good intent and the provision of marginal funding were wholly incapable of resolving the fundamental problems. All the while, disparities between rich and poor increased among countries, as well as within them, and the temper of the international community displayed a marked fractiousness along North–South lines. There was no guarantee that the necessary majority of countries of the South would agree to support the law of the sea proposals (critically important to Canada) simply because the North told them it was in everyone's interest to do so, or that adequate attention would be paid to increasingly serious international environmental issues (as at the 1970 Stockholm Environmental Conference), or that there would be effective progress in eliminating trade irritants.

Within Canada and within the government, understanding of and support for North–South was unquestionably far more sophisticated and widespread than, for example, in the United States, yet the "comfort zone" of policy initiatives fell short of the imaginative activities pursued by the Nordic countries and the Netherlands – even in certain instances by Australia and New Zealand. We admired immensely the outspoken advocacy and political courage in these respects of leaders such as Prime Minister Olaf Palme of Sweden, former chancellor Willy Brandt of West Germany, and Development Ministers Jan Pronk of the Netherlands and Judith Hart of Britain, even though we disagreed on occasion on certain issues. Again and again, however, cabinet and caucus reaction to events and proposals seemed to us to be episodic and shortsighted. Certainly, as already stated, ODA as a percentage of Canadian GNP rose steadily, even during a period of economic difficulties and budgetary restraints.[20] Considerable excitement surrounded the creation of the innovative International Development Research Centre (IDRC – of which more later) and unqualified support was forthcoming for the Aga Khan's request of Trudeau that Canada permit the entry of thousands of East Asians of the Ismaili faith forced out of East Africa following the *coup d'État* of Idi Amin in Uganda, this latter in the midst of a difficult election campaign in 1972 in which one of the most contentious issues centred on alleged unemployment-insurance frauds and distribution of welfare burdens.[21]

These were important initiatives, of which Trudeau was very proud, and perhaps the most that could be accomplished during this turbulent political period. There was a keen awareness on the part of each of us that responsible leadership must not permit rhetoric to reach well beyond performance. Thus, in speeches within Canada and without, there was a conscious endeavour to maintain a defensible linkage between the desirable and the possible. Thus the Mansion House sentence:[22] "We know in our hearts what has to be done if we have not yet found in our minds the way it can be done."

There was as well a sadness that the principle of open markets and recognition of comparative advantage could not be further advanced. Not surprisingly, the initial industrial endeavours of a number of developing countries fell into the relatively low-technology sectors of textiles, clothing, and footwear. In these areas of activity, countries such as Bangladesh and Barbados were demonstrating their ability to produce goods of a quality and an acceptability to the Canadian market, a market that was voracious in its demand for lower-cost goods, both at the low end (snowsuits and running shoes, for example, so necessary for lower-income families) and the high end (custom-manufactured items in Hong Kong and China, commissioned by the burgeoning Canadian couturier fashion industry). A necessary realization, however, no matter how sadly accepted, was the fact that the very factor which made textiles, clothing, and footwear an attractive entry point for industrial activity in the South – low levels of labour skills, absence of alternative economic opportunities – made these same activities an economic and social necessity in some regions of Canada. Thus, notwithstanding the penetrating and persuasive research of such entities as the Textile and Clothing Board, which demonstrated the overall cost to the Canadian economy – and particularly to the low-income population – of Canada's protectionist policies, the socio-economic-political realities of depressed regions within Canada and of special-interest groups proved dominant. Not all elements of these Canadian industries were to demonstrate insights and efficiencies in modernizing their production, inventory, and marketing techniques to compete effectively with low-cost imports.

The two of us worried deeply, and discussed frequently, the obvious paradox: Canada, an enlightened, advanced industrial power, seemed incapable of managing the adjustments necessary to give the developing countries a leg up on their industrial development, and Canada a boost into the increasingly high-tech age of manufacturing. In the result, we acknowledge fully the critical observations of such commentators as Harvard professor Glenn P. Jenkins that the cost to the Canadian economy of the import quotas and tariffs in 1979 was some $467,402,000; that the bilateral quotas "voluntarily" accepted by certain developing countries cost the poorer households in Canada over three times as much, relative to their income, as they cost the high-income households. As Jenkins wrote:

> . . . the pure economic waste generated by this policy per year is equal to over $14,000 per additional man-years of employment created. Considering that the average annual wage in the clothing sector was less than $10,000, this policy of protectionism is both extremely inefficient and costly to Canada.[23]

The obvious alternative, of buying out these inefficient industries and retraining or otherwise compensating the affected workers, was simply not politically acceptable to government supporters in the regions principally involved – certain parts of Quebec and southern Ontario – nor, for reasons never understood to us, to elements within such government departments as Finance and Industry, Trade and Commerce. Thus, continued Canadian support was extended to the vexatious and morally reprehensible Multi-Fibre Arrangement,[24] which came to a belated demise only in late 1993 with the successful conclusion of the Uruguay Round of the General Agreement on Tariffs and Trade (GATT).

IV

Without question, the single most tumultuous sequence of events on the North–South axis throughout the period from 1968 to 1984 was the invocation by the Organization of Petroleum Exporting Countries (OPEC) of successive – and massive – price increases, as well as supply restrictions of crude oil. The justification for the pricing action was that it was a long-overdue "adjustment," to relate the value of oil to the energy equivalents in other fuels such as coal. But the supply interruptions were seen as demonstrably naked endeavours by some OPEC members to influence the foreign policies of consumer nations, forcing them to relinquish relations with the state of Israel.

The harsh reaction of the oil-consuming nations of the North to these acts cannot be overstated; that the major influence in the design of these policies was a group of Arab states led by Saudi Arabia added to the inflammatory denunciations that came from many. For the first time ever, a group of developing countries had demonstrated its ability to create an effective cartel and to wield economic power in an effective fashion to the disadvantage of the industrialized states. These events were hailed in many parts of the South as a long-overdue reversal of the historic power relationship that had always favoured the North.

It is not simply the industrialized powers that consume oil, however. The non-oil-producing developing countries, far and away the majority of the countries of the South, faced massive deficits in their foreign-exchange accounts as they endeavoured to grapple with this new economic burden. The Northern countries most capable of adjustment pursued a variety of policies. Japan, wholly vulnerable to offshore sources of virtually all its resource requirements, quietly and capably made a number of fundamental changes with respect to sources of supply and to conservation practices. Certain European countries raised fuel prices dramatically to encourage conservation, and entered into novel cooperative arrangements with one another in order to share supply shortfalls. Canada launched a number of programs to encourage conservation, to share the burden of the unprecedented price hikes between the consuming and the producing provinces (to the outrage of the latter),[25] and took steps to ensure that supply deficiencies did not deprive certain isolated U.S. communities of heating fuel. In the United States, the principal reactions seemed to be hysteria in the streets (with automobiles lining up for blocks to refuel in the fear that supplies would disappear for lengthy periods – which happened almost nowhere) and expressions of outrage by most business and government spokespersons. Apart from the introduction of a mandatory fifty-five-mile-per-hour speed limit on major highways, virtually no permanent modifications were made in the gluttonous oil-consumption habits of Americans; the country's retail gasoline prices remained (as they still do) at a fraction of the levels in Europe, Japan, or Canada.

The influence of the OPEC actions upon the tenor and temperament of North–South relations was overwhelming. Emboldened by this reversal of fortunes, if only in a single restricted sector, the G-77 group of developing countries demanded new rounds of negotiations with, and widespread concessions from, the North. Two special sessions of the UN General Assembly took place in a bitter atmosphere, as the South, led by Algeria, made demands for a "New International Economic Order." A range of novel instruments and regimes was called for, fixing the prices of a number of commodities within arbitrary ranges, all to be placed within the cocoon of a "common fund," which would act as a buffering mechanism against major price shifts up and down.

To these proposals, the United States was for the most part openly hostile, viewing them as departures from pure market principles – which they were. Canada, on the other hand, as both an exporter and importer of a number of resource-based commodities, was sympathetic to the purpose, if not the particular techniques, of policies to introduce some pricing stability into the often volatile market swings of certain commodities. The government encouraged "producer-consumer" agreements of a kind that had long existed, and occasionally succeeded, in certain instances,[26] and which had been introduced by the European Economic Community in a particular format called "Stabex,"[27] to protect the exports of former colonies in

Africa, the Caribbean, and the Pacific against violent price – and therefore income – fluctuations.

But within the Canadian government, there was a deep division among officials about the realism of anything related to the common fund and its attendant "basket" of several dozen commodities. The economic departments contended, with some merit, that the scheme was unworkable and should not therefore be countenanced. Head and External Affairs persuaded Trudeau, however, that the principle be given an opportunity to be tested under appropriate safeguards, not dismissed out of hand. And so instructions were sent to the Canadian delegation at UNCTAD IV (the fourth UN Conference on Trade and Development) in Nairobi in 1976 to vote in favour of the measure. That decision and the Nairobi outcome eased considerably the state of tension along the North–South divide. In the years that followed, the common-fund proposals proved virtually impossible of operation and the issue quietly subsided.

The OPEC actions had a number of other impacts on the international scene as well, some of them evident to this day. An immediate result was a flood of oil revenues suddenly directed to producers not able to absorb or employ them, and these countries chose to place the huge sums surplus to their requirements in banking institutions not prepared to handle them. In an endeavour to keep the money in circulation, large loans on attractive terms were offered to many developing countries. Liquidity in these volumes is not without peril, however. It was not long before international economic circumstances changed dramatically, and interest rates shot up to record levels; a number of heavily indebted countries then found themselves incapable of servicing their debts (in some instances because the loan proceeds had been used unwisely or corruptly). When Mexico announced in 1982 its inability to make scheduled interest payments on its massive debt, the international banking community realized that it was gripped by a major debt crisis.

Canadian chartered banks as well as the Canadian government were affected. An early instance of the latter was a request by Jamaica that Canada offer it balance-of-payments credits to support its currency. This kind of assistance was not at all unknown in the world; Britain had been given similar help by Canada in the early post-Second World

War period and, later, by the International Monetary Fund (IMF). Nevertheless, the request was a first for Canada because of its North–South character.

The cabinet approved this new variation of development assistance in 1975, even though there were some misgivings about certain of Prime Minister Michael Manley's economic policies. Quite quickly as well, Canada was called upon to participate in a sweeping range of World Bank and IMF measures designed to assist the developing countries, or certain especially vulnerable groups of them, against the vagaries of international financial and monetary circumstances. Early on, Donald Macdonald, then minister of finance, was elected the first chair of the newly created "Interim Committee" of the IMF, a committee that oversaw certain immediate measures to ease the plight of the oil-consuming developing countries. Sadly, the plight remains at the time of writing, and the "interim" committee continues in existence.

V

One of the fora created at the outset of the 1974 pressures to reconstitute the "North–South Dialogue" was the Conference on International Economic Cooperation, sited in Paris, and designed to function at the ministerial level. The two co-chairs selected by their peers were Canada, representing the countries of the North, and Venezuela, representing the South. Allan MacEachen, then secretary of state for external affairs, and Perez Guerero, his Venezuelan counterpart, ably directed this months-long exercise. On a day-to-day basis, the senior Canadian official in charge was Michel Dupuy, a senior foreign-service officer, who ensured that we were each kept informed of the twists and turns of the negotiations, and so were able to offer direction and advice.

Still another indirect outcome of the ferment of activity triggered by the OPEC decisions, and the tragic balance-of-payment circumstances in which many countries found themselves, was the creation of an Independent Commission on International Development Issues, composed of a number of distinguished persons from North and South (including one Canadian, Joe Morris of the Canadian Labour Congress) and chaired by former West German chancellor Willy Brandt. In some respects, this commission was a successor to the earlier commission appointed by the World Bank and chaired by Lester Pearson. In two years of research and hearings, the Brandt Commission was able to document many of the concerns that had seized each of us about the interdependence of countries North and South: the rapid destruction of forest cover as a result of fuel-wood and pasture demands; the linkage in the South of political instability to economic decline; and the increasing economic dependence of the countries of the North upon the markets of the countries of the South. The combination of these several elements, said Brandt, made development "the greatest challenge to mankind for the remainder of this century."[28]

One of the Brandt Commission's specific recommendations was the convening of a North–South summit to discuss such urgent issues as access to technology, resource transfers, energy development, and a global food program. Mexican President Lopez Portillo proposed that such a summit take place in his country, and invited Chancellor Bruno Kreisky of Austria to co-chair it with him. (Kreisky had long been a sensitive proponent of North–South cooperation. He and Trudeau had been the only two leaders of the thirty-three participating in the 1975 Helsinki Conference on Security and Cooperation in Europe who made specific reference to the needs of the developing countries in their speeches to the plenary session.) Canada was one of a small number of countries asked to co-sponsor the summit, which Trudeau agreed to do, and was an active participant in the intense preparations for it. Shortly prior to the summit, held in Cancún in 1981, Kreisky's health failed, and he was forced to withdraw. The countries of the North invited Trudeau to replace him.

The meeting was the first of its kind to involve the newly elected U.S. President Ronald Reagan, and proved – partly as a result – to be a tumultuous and far from successful event. The profound ignorance of Reagan about circumstances in the developing countries, and his naïve belief in the ability of free-market mechanisms to solve all problems everywhere, was a depressant. Nevertheless, an honourable compromise was reached among many of the leaders present – Reagan, Thatcher, Nyerere, and Gandhi among them – but was scuttled by the others on the advice of Kreisky's foreign minister, Willibald Pahr. A golden opportunity for real North–South progress was lost, cascading the relationship into the depths of Northern indifference for years thereafter.

The failure to reach consensus was particularly troubling to Trudeau. In anticipation of Cancún, in his role as chairman of the Ottawa G-7 Summit earlier in the summer, he had organized the agenda to permit more time to be dedicated to North–South issues than at any previous summit (a full half-day). The section of the summit communiqué that addressed relations with the developing countries was the longest of any. The tone of those paragraphs was understanding of the plight and the aspirations of those countries. In substance, undertakings were made with respect to ODA levels, energy cooperation, food security, and the resource levels of the international financial institutions. Because six of the seven Ottawa Summit participants would be present at Cancún, and because of the warm comments directed to the communiqué by such major developing countries as India and Mexico, Trudeau was hopeful that the Cancún outcome would be positive. Alas, it was not to be.

Also in anticipation of Cancún, a special Canadian parliamentary activity had been launched. The House of Commons struck a Special Committee on North–South Relations, chaired by Herb Breau of New Brunswick, and composed of extraordinary MPs from all sides of the House, including Doug Roche and Bob Ogle. Head, by then at IDRC, was one of the witnesses called before the committee. He chose the occasion to argue for developmental activities on the basis of "opportunity cost," the cost to the North if it failed adequately to invest in the South. The committee report was an exceptional document and was well received by the House of Commons when tabled.[29] It was of considerable help to Trudeau and the Canadian delegation at the Cancún Summit, but could not by itself break the deadlock. Post-Cancún, the "North–South Dialogue" assumed the form of a stony silence, vestiges of which remain to the time of writing.

From 1968 to 1984, the North–South policy landscape changed constantly. Issues inherent to the North–South relationship occupied a major portion of the agenda at virtually every international summit – Commonwealth, G-7, bilateral; few government departments were not engaged in one way or another with programs or projects involving the developing countries; the Canadian ODA budget, measured as a percentage of GNP, topped out at 0.54 per cent in 1978; CIDA, the fledgling agency created in 1968, was by 1984 a major bureaucratic organization. Major advances had been made in Canadian refugee and immigration policy; Canadian companies were encouraged in various ways to invest in and engage with developing countries as an example to the timid; technology transfers, direct investment, and employment creation could all be linked with profitable business activity throughout the South, if only shrewd management and sound practices were pursued (as they were, by the extraordinary husband-and-wife team of Tom and Sonja Bata);[30] the earlier successes of non-governmental organizations such as CUSO were replicated by others such as Canada World Youth; Canadian involvement in the immensely successful Consultative Group on International Agricultural Research drew on the abundant skills and knowledge of such Canadians as Fred Bentley, Omond Solandt, Bill Tossell, and Robert McGinnis; Canadian concessional lending in support of development projects began to give way to grants, and a Generalized Preferential Tariff system was introduced to benefit developing countries; Petro-Canada spun off a subsidiary to assist developing countries in their own research for energy sources; Gérard Pelletier, in his role as Canadian ambassador to the United Nations in New York, played a continuing, sensitive role in the search for effective policies.

All this and more. Yet North–South disparities continued to grow in a number of regions; discouraging, sometimes abhorrent, practices sprung up or continued in countries where Canada had only limited influence (as in Chile, where the excesses of the Pinochet regime were overlooked by outsiders – some of them Canadian – who emphasized the benefits of a capitalist system); the apartheid evils of minority regimes in Africa showed little evidence of decaying, indeed were stoutly supported as bulwarks of anti-communism by some Canadians; the complications of an increasingly global economy seemingly made the crafting of an effective code of conduct for transnational corporations more difficult; the political exigencies of "Canadian content" in assistance projects, reminiscent as this was of the primitive early attitudes of Canadian governments of the fifties, resisted most efforts to reform them. Perhaps as disappointing to us as any single factor involving Canadians was our failure – despite any number of speeches or interviews – to raise the consciousness level of the public with respect to the vital importance to Canadian interests of North–South issues.

Not that the period was without signal successes. Perhaps the most illustrious was the creation and the performance of the International Development Research Centre, conceived by Maurice Strong and supported strongly by Prime Minister Pearson, who became the chairman of the first board of governors following his retirement from elected office. IDRC was created by Act of Parliament in 1970 as an organization funded by, but independent of, government. Its policies were set by an international board, drawn from South as well as North. Its function was to support applied scientific research in the developing countries in a range of disciplines. The first board, encouraged by the centre's brilliant initial president, David Hopper, chose to emphasize research chosen by and pursued by scientists from developing countries in their own institutions, thus ensuring that the work was responsive to local needs and supportive of the enhancement of the capabilities of those scientists and institutions.

In accord with the IDRC Act of Parliament, the centre's president was selected by the board. When Hopper left to join the World Bank as a vice-president in 1977, the board struck a search committee chaired by Sir John Crawford, vice-chancellor of Australian National University. Many months and dozens of candidates later, the board reached a decision. Head was offered the position and took up office in March 1978. During his term, IDRC was chosen by the American honours-science organization Sigma Xi as "the organization best preparing society for the next century" and given the first of the newly created "XXI Century Awards." Later, one of China's eight state councillors, Dr. Song Jian, would proclaim to a Chinese national television audience that IDRC represented the "world's finest model of effective international cooperation."

The centre was a superb example of what could be done when all political parties agreed. Some of the research projects supported by IDRC were of major significance; its governors and staff enjoyed the highest of reputations. There are many examples. Of the governors, Sadako Ogata of Japan would become the UN high commissioner for refugees, and M. G. K. Menon of India the elected chairman of the International Council of Scientific Unions; of the staff, Jacques Diouf of Senegal would be elected by governments as director general of the UN Food and Agriculture Organization, and Pierre Sané became president of Amnesty International.

In retrospect, no category of foreign-related activities throughout the several Trudeau administrations from 1968 to 1984 appeared to us as more important, or generated more sustained interest and effort, than that of North–South. Canada was neither able, nor inclined, to engage in massive military involvement within the East–West alliances. What it could do, however, and do effectively, was to act intelligently, imaginatively, and forcefully along the much more complex – and in the long-term more important – axis of North–South. Consciously dedicating priorities and resources in that direction did not, of course, gain many enthusiasts in the Pentagon or in the widespread web of defence industries, and certainly prompted the contempt of Prime Minister Thatcher, who chided Trudeau at every meeting about his "soft-headed" attitude towards developing countries "who only had themselves to blame" for their economic sluggishness. What this emphasis did do, however, was to implant firmly in the minds of millions of persons within the developing regions that Canada was sensitive to their plight, was supportive of their struggles to enhance human dignity, and was deserving in return of cooperation at the United Nations and elsewhere in the quest for an improved international community. In sum, our belief in the vital importance of the North–South dynamic to Canada was matched by our insistence that Canada's performance in this respect reflected well the decency and purpose of the greatest proportion of Canadians. In turn, we believe, that performance was influential in the shaping of our image as a people in the eyes of Canadians, as well as by the majority of humankind.

Did Canada's policies and efforts in the period from 1968 to 1984 reasonably or adequately reflect the importance we attached to North–South issues? Reasonably? – we think so in light of all factors and competitive pressures. Adequately? – obviously not when one assesses the extent of the needs. In terms of endeavouring to understand better the issues and problems, and creating constructive relationships with leaders of developing countries, prime ministerial trips to countries of the South more than balanced journeys to the industrialized neighbours of the North. Such travel was undoubtedly facilitated by the

utilization of long-range Canadian Armed Forces jet aircraft not available to earlier office-holders, but it demanded a continuing dedication
both by Trudeau, who was told throughout by his political advisers that
such destinations were not electorally "useful," and by Head, who
encountered, much more often than not, attitudes ranging from disinterest to antipathy on the part of many Ottawa-based senior officials in
the public service. A systemic adjustment for the better was the gradual
increase in numbers of the most senior External Affairs officers
appointed as heads of mission in developing countries (in contrast to
the situation in 1968, where the pattern heavily favoured Europe;
appointments such as Escott Reid to New Delhi being rare exceptions). The volume of policy initiatives, many of them of constructive
effect, increased immeasurably. Finally, there was a constancy of dedication to North–South issues, even if action was not always possible,
and – so important in a democracy – an unflagging attempt to emphasize their importance to the Canadian public in the form both of
speeches and of actions.

⊰⊱

CHAPTER SIX

The Neighbourhood

I

Urban dwellers everywhere are familiar with neighbourhood change: change in character, change in dimension. The departure of long-familiar families and their replacement with newcomers changes dramatically the once-intimate character of a residential street. The construction of a commercial mall suddenly alters shopping and recreational habits, often extending the perimeter of the neighbourhood well beyond its former limits. In such instances, adaptation is necessary.

Neighbourhoods within the international community undergo similar transformations, demanding sometimes major attitudinal and policy adjustments on the part of national governments. In 1968, Canada's neighbourhood was quite firmly composed of the United States and the countries of Western Europe. "The North Atlantic Community" was real. It was based on historic, cultural, commercial, and security considerations. Other regions of the world may well have been neighbourhoods, but they were not ours.

In this process of identification of community, distance and geographic features often bear little weight. Viewed on a polar projection, for example, Canada was strategically positioned between the two great nuclear-armed adversaries: the United States and the Soviet Union. Little matter; in 1968, the U.S.S.R. was not a "neighbour." Equally, oceans could be seen as barriers or links, depending on attitude and past experience. The North Pacific fell into the first category; the North Atlantic was in the second.

To each of us, these familiar assumptions had outlived their usefulness by 1968 and were now hindrances to an understanding of the

new realities. In an era of ballistic missiles, of satellite-based communications systems, and of rapidly burgeoning societies and populations, the concept of "neighbourhood" was in a state of rapid flux.
The Canadian economy and society were each increasingly influenced
by actors in Asia; Canadian security and the physical environment of
the Canadian Arctic were both dependent upon the policies and practices of the Soviet giant over the Pole. That other grouping of states
south of the Rio Grande, part of our Western Hemisphere, with
whom Canada had enjoyed a range of linkages over many decades –
but not of a coherent or sustained nature – was unquestionably
deserving of a fresh look. While Canada's intimacy with the United
States remained firm, indeed became even more embracing in the
decade of the seventies, the neighbourhood we inherited in 1968 was
not what it had been. Adjustments were necessary. Throughout,
however, the proximity and immense importance of the United States
guaranteed that this neighbour could never be overlooked or under-
estimated. Canadian foreign relations were destined in large measure
to be Canadian–American relations.

Extending well beyond the power of any ideology or government
in office in either country, Canadian foreign policy had long been
dominated by the United States. This had been the case in selective circumstances since 1776, and in almost universal fashion since 1945. The
phenomenon was not a matter to be dismissed as good or bad, it was a
fact of life that all Canadian governments accepted, or suffered if they
did not. "Living with Uncle," John Holmes has wryly termed it.[1]

Nevertheless, if Canadian foreign-policy-making begins, of necessity, with a consideration of the United States, it does not follow that
that country should be the determinant of Canadian decisions. On this
point we were insistent, as had been all Canadian governments over
time. The challenge, of course, was the design of policies that would
be effective, over the longer run, in the protection and promotion of
Canadian interests. It was a challenge of growing complexity, as
American influences became increasingly evident within and without
Canada. From 1968 to 1984, there was never the slightest doubt in
Trudeau's mind that this segment of Canada's neighbourhood
demanded attention more than any other.

So pervasive by 1968 was American influence upon Canada, sometimes directly, sometimes obliquely, that the government deemed it would be most accurately reflected in the 1970 foreign-policy review by including references to the United States throughout the several studies, rather than dedicating a single volume to the relationship. To have done the latter, as was considered, could not possibly have conveyed the universal nature of the United States' presence and the penetrating effect of its policies and activities. The first volume of *Foreign Policy for Canadians* early on referred to the Canada–U.S. relationship as one of "two inescapable realities, both crucial to Canada's continuing existence."[2] The first of the realities was internal, "the multifaceted problem of maintaining national unity." The second reality was external,

> the complex problem of living distinct from but in harmony with the world's most powerful and dynamic nation, the United States. . . . It is probably no exaggeration to suggest that Canada's relations almost anywhere in the world touch in one way or another on those of its large neighbour.[3]

Again and again in that first volume, as in each of the three regional volumes, were references made to the United States. How should Canada manage its complex relations with its powerful neighbour?

> The key to Canada's continuing freedom to develop according to its own perceptions will be the judicious use of Canadian sovereignty whenever Canada's aims and interests are placed in jeopardy – whether in relation to territorial claims, foreign ownership, cultural distinction, or energy and resource management.[4]

The sustenance of Canada's distinct identity, salient to its national purpose, would succeed or fail largely as a consequence of Canada's management of its relations with the United States. That was a central theme of the foreign-policy review.

Throughout the decade and a half that Trudeau was prime minister, the vicissitudes of U.S. policy consequent upon the administrations of five different presidents[5] would demand our constant care and attention, ranging from sympathetic understanding and support to firm defence of Canadian interest. For each of us, the experience was invigorating without exception. This was partly the result of the fact that we both, as graduate students at Harvard, and in countless other associations, were cognizant of the dynamism and the accomplishments of American society. We both admired and were deeply influenced by the ideas and the written work of figures as ranging in scope as Jefferson, Thoreau, Whitman, and Roscoe Pound. Although voiced on behalf of all Canadians, Trudeau's words to the joint session of the U.S. Congress in 1977 were a personal testimonial, one which never wavered even in the most difficult periods of strained relations: "The warmth of your welcome reinforces what I have always known: that a Canadian in the United States is among friends."

Canada, we fully recognized, owed much to the presence of our neighbour to the south. In asymmetric fashion, we believed, the United States owed much to the presence of its pacific and responsible neighbour to the north. Recognition of that latter indebtedness did not come automatically to those in power in Washington, however. One of the reasons for this, one buried in the American psyche and quite beyond any sustained influence by Canada (or other outside powers for that matter), is the deep-seated commitment to certain abstract principles that burn fiercely within American breasts and that lend themselves readily to selective interpretation or inconsistent application in order to support this or that current U.S. interest. The willingness of successive U.S. administrations to trumpet the righteousness of these principles while embracing or denouncing foreign governments, international institutions, or transnational activities is likely no worse nor more persistent than is found in any other large power. But the enduring assumption by Americans that they are possessed of an unassailable superiority is. That assumption, sometimes based on moral principle, at others upon the flimsiest of pretences, or premised on shamefully revisionist recollections of history, and generally clothed in the peculiarly American belief in some variant of "manifest destiny," can create an impermeable canopy for U.S. policies. Depending on the circumstances, foreign governments react with bemusement, frustration, or fury at their impotence to penetrate the membrane and gain meaningful modifications. Happily, the decency and common sense of the vast majority of Americans act as a gyroscope to modulate excesses over time. No other society in the world is so dedicated to transparency and self-criticism. Nevertheless, this valuable counterbalance offers faint recompense for those caught in the sometimes turbulent fluctuations of immediate U.S. policy decisions.

Another factor of a double-edged sort with which Canadian policymakers must contend is the oft-voiced American assumption that Canadians – and by extension Canada – are "just like us": disposed towards orderliness, constancy, the peaceful resolution of disputes, and pursuing a range of shared values – as Canadians indeed are – but always possessed as well of identical interpretations of events, and common views with respect to preferred responses – which Canadians are not. This American assumption is much more problematic than its most common manifestations: overlooking or misinterpreting Canadian interest (as in certain of President Richard Nixon's economic policies), or taking for granted Canadian acquiescence in U.S. initiatives (as in President Jimmy Carter's fierce posture towards the Soviet Union). Worrisome as those instances are, however, the greater danger constantly present is the possibility that some of the most cherished and fundamental precepts of the Canadian identity become vulnerable to serious erosion. (President Ronald Reagan's hostility towards domestic social and economic pluralism and his proclivity to international unilateralism are examples of this danger.) Each of us became frequent witnesses to exhibitions of astonishment and genuine sadness on the part of Americans who were absorbed with the assumption of "sameness." Ours was not, of course, the first government to be so treated. This was a phenomenon familiar to generations of Canadians.

Other, more visible factors associated with the United States – the overwhelming dimensions of its size and influence, and the constitutional division of powers between legislative and executive branches – were more readily understandable, and so amenable to rational policy decisions by Canada and other powers, than were either of the two attributes just discussed. Whatever the issue or the policy, however, one constant element in the bilateral relationship was the courteous and respectful demeanour of American representatives in their dealings with us and our associates. With the single exception of some members of the Reagan administration, we were always impressed with the professionalism of U.S. negotiators, and touched by their genuine friendliness, even in the most spirited and difficult of circumstances. In these personal, albeit official, relationships, the constant factor was a recognition of a shared goal: the genuine desire to be – and to be seen as – a good neighbour.

Recognizing and assessing the mix of the several U.S. policy determinants is constantly required in the design and implementation of foreign policies by all non-American members of the international community. For Canada, however, the challenge is much the greater, because of the extent and intimacy of our linkages: in 1968, 80.7 per cent of foreign direct investment in Canada was of U.S. origin; 67.9 per cent of Canadian exports were sold in the United States; the number of border-crossings was the highest in the world; American films dominated all those screened in Canadian theatres; a network of pipelines, power grids, and transportation routes crisscrossed the border, ranging in scope from the St. Lawrence Seaway to tiny intercommunity roads; the burden of continental defence was shared in exemplary, mutually advantageous fashion; a natural environment of immense geographic scope and a multitude of peculiar atmospheric and topographic circumstances was recognized as demanding common stewardship; and daily activities of governments, business, and individuals were conducted within the framework of one of the world's most intense networks of bilateral treaties and formal international agreements, more than 120 in number (which would almost double by 1984), and hundreds of less formal but very important protocols and conventions.

As between any set of neighbours, however, intimacy of contact and frequency of encounters does not guarantee constancy of agreement. Not surprisingly, the flavour of the relationship and the intensity of purpose of the national actors fluctuate from year to year and from one U.S. administration to another. In some instances, a major element of the bilateral relationship would demand attention, in others the focus would be on the broader setting of one or more of our several multilateral connections. Always, however, one knew it was unwise to assume that any U.S. administration would or could keep these two categories distinct. A Canadian government not understanding of U.S. ambitions or anguish (even paranoia) about events in far-away places could seriously mislead itself about likely U.S. responses to even the most local of Canadian–American issues.

The lesson to be learned was that the United States is not simply a neighbouring country, as New Zealand, for example, could view Australia, or as Argentina regards Brazil.

Much more important in the Canadian–American relationship than the simple size differential (population, economy, power) is the fact that the United States is a global actor with security, economic, social, and cultural aspirations that tend to be open-ended. As Allan Gotlieb would often say later during his term as Canadian ambassador in Washington, "The United States is not simply a country, it is a civilization." Such being the case, Canada's management of its relationship must assume a degree of complexity quite unlike any other. Many of Canada's international initiatives in the period from 1968 to 1984, for example, affected the United States because of its global outreach. A number of those instances are described not in this chapter but in those sections of the text dedicated to the initiatives themselves, such as Arctic jurisdiction (Chapter Two), NATO nuclear policies (Chapter Three), or the recognition of the People's Republic of China (Chapter Seven).

Still another, and not-to-be-underestimated, element in the management of Canadian–American relations reflects the fact that cross-border contacts involve a cast of millions, performing on a stage as broad as the continent itself. The interests and desires of some of these actors are in certain instances much more in harmony North–South across the border than East–West within either country. Regional groupings of governors and premiers pursue their own agendas; large corporations or groups of commercial interests communicate, meet, and transact business virtually without heed to national policy-makers; countless numbers of private citizens regard nationals on the other side of the border not as foreigners but as fellow members of this or that alumni organization, religious affiliation, trade association, or service club, as personal friends or extended family members. This multiplicity of activity influences policy-makers in each country, but always the weight of the influence is most deeply felt in Canada as a direct manifestation of simple arithmetic. Ten to one is the ratio: the difference in populations, in GNPs, in size of the public accounts.

No single formula could possibly embrace the range of circumstances that defines this dynamic, organic relationship, and certainly not in the period that extended from 1968 to 1984. Each new presidency ensured that focus or emphasis would change, on occasion leading to crisis, on others – and almost as unsettling – leading to indifference. In this relationship John Holmes's commonsense advice was wise: "The first principle to accept is that crisis is normal and more often than not, therefore, no crisis."[6] A continuing element of immense influence upon the Canadian–American relationship in this period, yet one over which Canada had virtually no influence, was the circumstance of U.S. relations with others. The mood of any given administration would be coloured intensely by the state of the Cold War, by the performance of the world economy, or by almost any condition that the intensely xenophobic and highly emotional nature of American society could deem to be detrimental to its interests. Then would nationalist sensitivity demand policies or actions that would often affect Canada, even if unintentionally, simply because of the complexity of our bilateral involvement.

The ever-present background to the great majority of U.S. policies and practices, and particularly so during the Cold War period, was the nebulous concept of national security. A crosscurrent of Canadian–American relations in the period from 1968 to 1984 therefore bore the influence of security concerns as interpreted by one or more of the numerous U.S. agencies bearing some share of the overall security responsibility. These perspectives could be either reassuring or irritating, depending on circumstance and agency. Whichever, however, a Canadian government quickly gained full sense not just of the intensity with which Americans viewed security, but of their dedication to what they regarded as their ultimate responsibility for the worldwide protection of freedom. Whether one agreed with this or that tactic or strategy, one developed considerable respect for the seriousness and the professionalism of most American actors. Even on those occasions, and there were several, where Canadian interpretations of events or Canadian choices of policy were at odds with the pronounced preferences of the U.S. administration, seldom was there displayed to either Trudeau or Head anything but courteous consideration of the Canadian position. Indeed, this respect extended throughout the entire sixteen years and across the whole spectrum of relations. It was regarded by us as an invaluable element in the relationship, a benefit to be stewarded jealously. Neither of us can recall a single instance in which we were told that a Canadian posture or decision on bilateral issue "A" would influence the American policy or practice on bilateral issue "B."

Both governments designed their policies responsibly, which meant taking into account the interests of the other, and both negotiated their positions with spirit. On occasion, each would utilize appropriate multilateral fora, such as the United Nations or NATO, to develop support for their proposals. Not always, of course, could full agreement be reached. Throughout, however, and this during the height of Henry Kissinger's widely touted practice of "linkage," Canada was consistently dealt with honourably and openly, issue by issue. More than any other single feature, we regarded this practice as firm evidence of the solid footing and unique relationship between the two countries. It was a precious asset, much envied by others.

Falling within the national-security perimeter in one form or another, quite obviously, were such issues involving Canada as the testing of antiballistic missiles by the United States, and the Canadian decision to withdraw from the nuclear-strike role in NATO (Nixon administration); the renewal of the NORAD agreement, and the Conference on Security and Cooperation in Europe (Ford administration); human rights, the Panama Canal negotiations, and the boycott of the Moscow Summer Olympic Games (Carter administration); and the Mackenzie River Valley testing of cruise missiles and the Trudeau "peace initiative" (Reagan administration). The broad interpretation of national security by the United States lent a special flavour to any number of other issues and activities, however, among them: Canadian claims to maritime jurisdiction in the Arctic; energy, including the dedication of stored crude-oil production as strategic reserves; the diplomatic recognition of the People's Republic of China; civilian air traffic between Canada and Cuba; the regulation of Canadian foreign investment; Canadian immigration policy; Canadian mineral production, including oil and gas policies; and even, far-fetched though it seemed to us then – and now – some of Canada's development-assistance programs.

In each of these instances, and in the many others that seemed always to be on the minds of one or other of the plethora of U.S. agencies with which the Canadian government had continuing relations, Canadian interests and points of view were as a rule weighed seriously and occasionally reflected in final U.S. decisions.

Not without reason, the relationship between Canadian prime ministers and American presidents tends both to colour and to reflect the
quality of the intergovernmental relationship, and this notwithstanding
the highly influential foreign-relations role played by the U.S.
Congress. In the sixteen years from 1968 to 1984, Trudeau met with
his American counterparts on more than twenty-five separate official
occasions, ranging from bilateral visits to major multilateral conferences. With the single exception of President Lyndon Johnson, whose
administration was nearing an end at the time of the 1968 Canadian
election, Trudeau had ample opportunity to form an opinion of each
of the presidents. (Even in hindsight, however, it is not possible to categorize this or that presidency as "friendlier," or "more understanding,"
or "easier to get along with." Elephants are elephants, whatever their
political colouring.) Yet there is no doubt that the administration that
demanded intense attention of us – both because of new U.S. policy
directions and fresh Canadian policy initiatives – was that of President
Nixon. Relations with the Nixon administration began prior to the
presidential inauguration, in the transition-team phase, and all because
of a myth.

II

THE NIXON YEARS – 1969-1974

One of the imponderable circumstances faced by any political administration is the body of conventional wisdom held dear by the electorate. Whether in simple error, or based largely on myth, such public
perceptions have the power to influence both policy and the acceptance ratings of those who formulate it. One such example of mis-
founded perception quickly confronted us in 1968. It related to the
historical practice of state visits between Canadian prime ministers and
American presidents. For some reason there was abroad in Canada the
belief that, among the very earliest official visitors to Washington,
D.C., following the inauguration of a new American president was
always the Canadian prime minister. Were this practice not to be honoured by President Richard Nixon, so went the myth, it would be a
clear signal of the disinterest, or worse the dislike, of the new president
for his Canadian counterpart. The belief bore no relation to the fact

that only once had a Canadian prime minister been among the first White House guests, when Prime Minister John Diefenbaker called on President John Kennedy in February 1961. Not surprisingly, therefore, Trudeau was persuaded by his domestic advisers that an early visit was a political requirement.

In due course, instructions were given to Ambassador Ed Ritchie in Washington to indicate to the State Department and to the Nixon transition team how welcome would be an invitation for a visit early in the new term. Canada was not alone in seeking this honour. On occasion the ensuing courtship took on the tenor of high drama among the several contestants for the initial invitation in the Washington diplomatic corps. To the new U.S. administration, the hints and pleadings more likely gave the impression of either low comedy or persistent nuisance. Such, on occasion, sadly, is the realistic cut and thrust of diplomatic activity and priority. In this particular instance, the desirability of an early visit was seen to be as important by External Affairs and the Canadian bureaucracy generally as it was by the press and public opinion.

Happily from all points of view, a proposal for a highly acceptable date was forthcoming and quickly accepted – March 24 to 25, 1969, little more than two months following the inauguration (on January 20) of the first Republican president since Dwight Eisenhower. As symbolic as the invitation itself was the form in which it was tendered: a personal telephone call from Nixon to Trudeau on February 20, 1969.

Preparations for the visit recognized the overwhelming importance of two separate elements in the Washington program. The first, of course, was the fixing and the discharge of a discussion that reflected accurately, out of the myriad aspects of the Canadian–American relationship, those of greatest importance to Canada. These discussions, of course, would take place for the most part in confidence. The second activity was the opportunity presented to Trudeau to project an image of a government and a people that would appeal to the broad and influential American public (including the Congress) as being responsible and credible. The occasion for this second ingredient of the program centred on a speech to be delivered to those gathered in the world's most prestigious media forum – the Washington National Press Club.

As briefing papers were assembled by External Affairs from the several government departments with responsibilities influenced by the American relationship (and there were few departments that fell outside this category), Head quickly recognized a continuation of the practices that had proved so cumbersome at the January meeting of Commonwealth heads of government: selectivity of topics tended to give way to inclusiveness; in-depth materials were displaced in the requirement to reduce bulk; and conciseness demanded that explanations and arguments be so abbreviated as to lose their flavour. For a prime minister who demanded a thoroughness of analysis and an assemblage of logical process, these techniques would not, Head knew, be persuasive. Especially was this so because many of the issues deserving of consideration contained sizeable political elements. The proposed deployment of antiballistic missiles was one such, the continuing entry into Canada of young Americans avoiding the Vietnam draft was another. Of immense importance to Western Canada were questions of Canadian oil exports and the hazy American concept of a continental energy policy.

What was required for Trudeau's purposes were materials supplementary to the package of traditional briefing books and "talking points" organized by External Affairs. Thus arose the practice of additional memoranda, these prepared by Head following consultations with Trudeau, that endeavoured to contain information, reflect points of view, and propose interventions from the perspective, not of an adviser, but of a principal. These were intended to offer Trudeau the opportunities for flexibility, debate, range, and exercise of personal attributes that official documents, no matter how skilfully prepared, could not. These memoranda were much more than "colour"; they often proposed priorities, additional subjects for discussion, and information not in the several departments' briefs. These memoranda never displaced the others; they were always used as a fine-tuning, intended by Head to strengthen the comparative advantages held by Trudeau as he entered into bilateral discussions with other leaders. As the years went by, and as the occasions increased for the two of us to prepare for such meetings, the sophistication of this process increased. In March 1969, however, this aspect of documentation remained relatively rudimentary. From the outset, however, Head's materials endeavoured to describe in depth the other principal. Nixon was not an easy subject.

Nixon has been caricatured so intensely, and often so well, that it is difficult even now to capture the essence of the man. As is so well known, he was not at ease with other people. Less well known is the fact (certainly in Trudeau's relations with him) that he was genuine in his wish to be gracious to those who were his guests. Nevertheless, one sensed that he was often preoccupied with other issues. On first meeting him, therefore, it was natural to assume that his apparent distance of demeanour was a reflection on those in his immediate presence. Over time, and in a range of differing situations, it became clear that this impression of withdrawal was simply one part of a multifaceted personality. He was a reflective man, perhaps worried more than was healthy about tactics rather than about broader concepts. Yet the latter clearly inspired him, and it was here that his worth was evident. Part of his complexity undoubtedly derived from the often contradictory concurrence of roles Americans expect their presidents to play. As an example, the Nixon that greeted Trudeau at the portico of the White House that wet spring day in 1969 was a parody: his face was covered with a coat of grotesque orange makeup applied for an earlier TV interview and kept on because of the presence of press cameras attending our visit. (On a later visit to Washington, in 1971, we were part of a network program being filmed, "A Day in the Life of the President.")

The business segment of the visit was relatively brief, as is most always the case with bilateral meetings with American presidents, and consisted on this occasion of two portions: a private conversation between Nixon and Trudeau in the Oval Office, followed by a somewhat longer session in the Cabinet Room, where ministers and officials were gathered. The purposes of the visit were straightforward: to be confident that the new administration was fully aware of Canada's perspective on salient bilateral issues; to exchange points of view on current international events; and to gain some measure of the quality and the personalities of the major actors on the American side. For these reasons, a number of ministers and senior officials accompanied Trudeau. The discussions revealed no surprises, nor were any expected.

The second major element of the visit, the address to the National Press Club, was only slightly less important than the official discussions. This, after all, was the opportunity to reveal, in unfiltered fashion, both the tone and the character of the still-new Canadian government. In the United States, where the press played such an influential role both on public perceptions and upon official policies and activities, this unofficial dimension of the visit could not be regarded with indifference.

A major reason for the importance that all actors attached to the role of the American media is found in the United States' constitutional division of powers. The source of much of the legislation that would be of immense impact upon Canadian interests lay within the two chambers of Congress, beyond reach of Trudeau on this visit. That same legislative branch, with all its seemingly labyrinthian committee structure, was also the source of impressive influence upon the executive branch, from which policy flowed and in which regulatory powers resided. The media was the most constant, and often the most influential, information bridge between the White House and Capitol Hill. To gain access to this bridging mechanism, and particularly to its most potent elements – the *New York Times*, the *Washington Post*, and the three major television networks – was a prize sought by all players on the Washington scene. Once obtained, that access deserved extraordinary preparation and care. Much more than governments, which by nature must be attentive and courteous, the press could be fickle – and particularly so towards those who appear to be courting it. Trudeau had long since chosen not to be one of that category.

This was to be the first Canadian foreign-policy speech since the U.S. election, and for that reason, too, it had to be right. Quite properly it would lead to careful examination in Canada. External Affairs followed the custom of many years and assumed initial responsibility for the text. Not surprisingly, because diplomats must by nature be cautious, the proffered draft revealed little that couldn't be found in an article in a very conservative academic journal. Alarmed that the incomparable opportunity of addressing such an influential audience was in danger of being wasted, Marc Lalonde telephoned Head mid-afternoon the day before our departure for Washington. "Start from scratch," he said. "Don't even look at what has been submitted."

By the next afternoon, Head's fresh draft was ready, and it bore no relationship to the department's efforts. Shortly following arrival in Washington, Trudeau, Lalonde, and Head, in the presence of Ambassador Ed Ritchie, fine-tuned the document. The speech chose to emphasize that Canada should not be misunderstood if it stood up for its own interests, objecting on occasion to unconscionable – even if unconscious – acts by the United States. That part of the message was tempered by humour: "Living next to you is in some ways like sleeping with an elephant. No matter how friendly and even-tempered is the beast, one is affected by every twitch and grunt."

Another element in the message was designed to dispel any nervousness should Canada initiate any departures in the design of its foreign policies, as in the overture to the People's Republic of China. The current foreign-policy review, Trudeau pointed out, "is not an excuse to prove our independence; that independence needs no proving. Nor is it an exercise intended to illustrate to the United States our potential for irritation. We have no desire, and no surplus energy, for that kind of activity."

The message appeared to be clearly understood in Washington. The humour drove the point home that Canada should be understood to be a junior partner, but a partner nevertheless, one not to be overlooked or overridden. It was in Canada, not in the United States – and certainly not in the Nixon administration – that Canada was characterized in diminutive fashion within the elephant metaphor. In cartoon and editorial content of Canadian newspapers the imagery was changed to portray a Canadian mouse in bed with the American elephant. This may have reflected the subconscious attitude of Canadian journalists who rarely found their material reproduced in American publications, in grotesque contrast to the reverse practice. It was not then and never subsequently viewed by either of us as an accurate impression of the Canadian–American relationship.

The 1969 visit placed into fresh context the broad-ranging, often animated, and seemingly pervasive relationship between the two administrations. In the years that followed, there would be incidents of intense disagreement as well as occasions for unprecedented cooperation. Trudeau and Nixon would meet face-to-face on five subsequent occasions: in official bilateral sessions of varying formality in Washington and Ottawa and on *ad hoc* ceremonial occasions, such as the funerals of former presidents Dwight Eisenhower and Georges Pompidou or the anniversary of the St. Lawrence Seaway. There were as well a number of telephone conversations, but not nearly so frequently as apparently became the practice much later between Prime Minister Brian Mulroney and President George Bush. The reason was twofold. One, neither Trudeau nor Nixon was attracted to small talk, preferring to concentrate their attention on substance, and to communicate with one another through channels appropriate for the purpose. Two, the increasing reliance by Nixon on his national security adviser, Henry Kissinger, and the latter's ever-increasing role as the White House intermediary, made necessary the creation of a suitably tailored counterpart role within the Prime Minister's Office (a function that was soon replicated in many other foreign capitals, so necessary was it to be able to utilize the communications channel chosen by Nixon, which became increasingly active as Kissinger's influence increased). In Canada, the role fell to Head as the member of the Trudeau team able to speak directly and instantly to and for the prime minister on foreign-relations issues. In the years that followed, telephone calls and visits between Head and Kissinger, and between Head and Kissinger's surrogates, Generals Alexander Haig and Brent Scowcroft, were often employed. That same channel continued, even increasing in frequency, during the Ford and Carter administrations, between Head and Scowcroft in the first instance and with Zbigniew Brzezinski in the second.

The telephone conversations that occurred between Trudeau and Nixon were not always occasions for serious diplomatic discussion. One touching example took place on Christmas Day 1971, when the president called personally to offer his congratulations upon the birth of Justin.[7] The message was deeply appreciated, was gracious and warm in content, and was much more reflective of the personal relationship between the two men than anything the public press and some contemporary historians have chosen to emphasize.

Not surprisingly, a major atmospheric element in Canadian–American relations throughout the Nixon years was the brooding presence of the Vietnam War. There were not in Canada the same social disruptions as in the United States, but there was an overwhelming abhorrence of this dreadful experience and, on occasion, repugnance to U.S. acts (principally the bombing of North Vietnam). Canada was not a belligerent in Vietnam, but it was present as a member of the International Commission for Supervision and Control and did have views to which it felt a responsibility on occasion to give voice. On a day-by-day basis, however, Trudeau was far from disposed to offer criticism from the sidelines. Nor were he or his ministers driven by any ambition to be architects of a peace, as some in the Pearson cabinet had aspired to be. Barbaric, devastating, poisonous of human and international relations as were so many aspects of this conflict, there was no possibility of any effective third-party influence. The Nixon administration would brook no interference, countenance no criticisms, and entertain no suggestions. The principals in this tragedy refused absolutely to share their fate with any outsider. If effectiveness was to be a measure of Canadian foreign policy, Vietnam, sadly, offered no opportunity for influence.

Yet in a surreal way, Canada was a participant; not in the conflict, of course, but as part of the woefully hollow international inspection mechanism established by the 1954 Indochina Conference in Geneva.[8] This role, as events unfolded, gave to Canada an opportunity to contribute to an honourable conclusion of hostilities, and the withdrawal of American forces. The role was interpreted quite differently by Canada, however, than it was by the United States. As an unheralded chapter in the dismal history of the Vietnam War, this sequence of events led, first, to considerable disappointment, and eventually to a very real sense of annoyance. Neither reaction proved to be of the slightest significance to Nixon or Kissinger. The events in question related to the composition and terms of reference of the proposed International Commission for Control and Supervision in Vietnam. This was the new machinery that Kissinger hailed with a flourish as successor to the old ICSC and as guarantor of the honour of his negotiated settlement with the North Vietnamese authorities.[9]

Prior to 1973, Canada had been a hardworking and dedicated member of each of the three Indochina International Commissions for Supervision and Control established by the Geneva Conference, one each for Cambodia, Laos, and Vietnam. These were thankless assignments, draining on Canadian diplomatic and military personnel and often hazardous in the extreme,[10] the source of sometimes immense strain on bilateral relations between Canada and the two other commission members, India and Poland, and the cause on occasion for bitter criticism of Canadian activities by journalists and other critics.[11] A prime cause of Canadian frustration over the years arose from the fuzzy and generally toothless jurisdiction given the commissions by the international accords that established them. Again and

again, in instances which appeared to the Canadians to be clear infractions of the truce by one side or another, or in debates over the need
for the commissions to inspect and report, Canada would be over-
ruled by the other two commission members on grounds that were
difficult to accept.

Canada's concerns in these respects were widely known and broadly
shared. The Canadian commissioners and their teams, after all, were
highly regarded,[12] as were Canadian peace-keepers in a number of UN
assignments. In situations ranging from the physically most dangerous to
the diplomatically most delicate, Canadian peace-keepers had for many
years performed with distinction and honour. Almost always had they
contributed to some resolution of the issues in dispute or, at least, to
some suspension in hostilities. This had been the case in the Middle East
(UNEF), in the Congo (ONUC), in Kashmir (UNMOGIP), and in Cyprus
(UNFICYP). The clear exception was Indochina, an admittedly different
kind of assignment. Nevertheless, if – as was to be hoped – there was
to be some form of armistice agreement and if – as was contemplated
– there was to be a role for an armistice observation commission (a
credible whistle-blower, authorized to travel freely and probe deeply),
then Canada was prepared to help.

As the Kissinger–Le Duc Tho negotiations in Paris appeared to be
nearing conclusion, work began in Ottawa on the design of processes
and mechanisms that would be effective for a postwar commission.
This was a serious exercise, one launched at the initiative of Ed
Ritchie, then undersecretary of state for external affairs, one that drew
heavily upon the unparalleled experience of Canadians, and one that
was both known to the U.S. government and, seemingly, enthusiastically welcomed by it. Ritchie saw this endeavour as an effective
utilization of Canadian comparative advantage, as a constructive contribution to the cessation of a war that had caused untold hardship and
death to countless numbers of Vietnamese and tens of thousands of
American service personnel, that had created deep divisions within
American society and had brought immense grief to three U.S. administrations, causing the retirement of one president, Lyndon Johnson.
Trudeau concurred entirely, and encouraged the exercise to proceed so
long as it was transparent and the United States was kept informed.

These instructions were faithfully adhered to, and by late 1972, a fleshed-out proposal was handed to the State Department, one that included a draft document establishing a commission and detailed protocols setting out its authority and operating procedures. The task, we all believed, had been carried out not simply in good faith but with considerable skill and insight based on eighteen years of field experience. It was an experience that preceded by many years any U.S. involvement in Vietnam. What Kissinger and his immediate advisers thought of the documents, however, we were never to know. At his epic press conference of January 24, 1973, Kissinger unveiled a supervisory mechanism replete with structural weaknesses and deeply flawed processes, one which bore no evidence of any study of the Canadian document.

It was at the same press conference that the membership of the new Vietnam Commission was revealed, one that included Canada as a member.[13] The question of Canadian participation, at least, had been the subject of intense discussions within Ottawa and between Ottawa and Washington. The formal request to Canada had been made late in the course of the 1972 Canadian election campaign. One of Trudeau's concerns, one communicated to the Americans formally by Mitchell Sharp in his discussions with Secretary of State William Rogers and to Kissinger by Head on the occasion of a private breakfast meeting between the two in the White House in mid-November, was the ability of the commission – indeed of Canada – to play an effective role. So doubtful was Head in these respects that he opposed any Canadian participation in the new exercise, even though he recognized the importance of a mechanism that would permit the United States to withdraw its combat personnel and recover its prisoners of war. Without such a mechanism, there could be no guarantee that the war had really concluded. In question, however, was whether the Kissinger–Le Duc Tho mechanism was adequate for the task.

Quite apart from the deep disappointment which we all felt about the non-acceptance of Canada's proposals, most particularly by Ritchie and those in External Affairs and in National Defence who had toiled so assiduously on this project, the circumstance of extending our presence in Vietnam presented a major quandary for Canada. At the heart of the issue was something much more serious: involvement in an exercise so significantly flawed that, in the judgement of the Canadian experts, it bore no chance of success. On the one hand, Canada had no wish to play the role of spoiler; on the other, it was not prepared to be a public dupe. Thus was the decision taken to participate for an initial period of only sixty days. Were our fears to be proved groundless in that period, we would extend our term. In the meantime, Canada would conduct itself with dignity and professionalism.

Michel Gauvin, former ambassador to Ethiopia and to Greece and one with a distinguished Second World War combat record in the Canadian Army, was given the assignment as Canadian commissioner. His instructions: to make it work if such could honourably be done. His advice, as the 60-day limit approached: the flaws discerned earlier in the much-touted Kissinger document were indeed fatal to its success. With that, Canada announced it would withdraw following a period of 90 more days (later extended to 120), an announcement, we later learned, which prompted Nixon to utter his famous expletive into the White House tapes.

The withdrawal in midsummer of 1973 ended more than nineteen years continuous Canadian presence in Vietnam, a period twice the length of the post-Second World War occupation of Indochina by France and several years longer than the U.S. military presence. This was the longest, and certainly the single most unhappy, offshore contribution ever made by Canada to the international community.[14] Canada was eventually replaced by Iran on the new commission, an exercise that later collapsed totally as the North Vietnamese occupied Saigon, forcing the Americans to withdraw fully.

If security-related issues were the most frequently experienced of American preoccupations throughout the long period of Nixon's presidency, those of an economic character were far and away of the most vital concern to Canada. Never, after all, in the entire period from 1968 to 1984, did Canadian military intelligence perceive or anticipate any credible threat to Canadian territorial integrity on the part of Soviet forces. By contrast, the ever-present influence of the dynamic U.S. economy was undeniable and seemingly inescapable. That influence had long been present within the country but assumed a qualitatively different character during the Second World War when Canada transformed itself from a predominantly agricultural and resource-extractive society into a modern, industrialized power, overwhelmingly due to sizeable transfers of capital, technology, and skills from American sources. These transfers continued and increased in the postwar period, and were complemented by the attractiveness and availability of the burgeoning U.S. domestic market. For producers of a broad spectrum of goods, whether "raw," such as natural gas, or "finished," such as automobiles or furniture, this combination of inputs and markets became the essential formula for economic growth.

In these circumstances, the Canada–U.S. border tended to dissolve. So, too, inexorably, did the traditional levers of Canadian economic policy-makers. By the early sixties, alarms began to sound about the diminishment of Canadian economic sovereignty. Within the Liberal Party the issue was most dramatically joined by two of Prime Minister Pearson's ministers, Walter Gordon in support of nationalist policies and Mitchell Sharp as the advocate of openness. The debate was far from resolved in 1968, by which time it was increasingly clear that the U.S. private sector tended increasingly to regard the now-considerable trade-and-investment flows as transcorporate rather than as international. A "special relationship" had evolved between the two governments in recognition of these distinctive circumstances. Special or not, however, the relationship was not – could not – be equal, and thus was introduced an element of Canadian vulnerability that could not be overlooked by even the most outspoken champions of unfettered access. Just how vulnerable Canada had become, we were to learn quickly and without warning.

On August 15, 1971, Nixon chose a nationwide television address to announce to the American public – and the world – his bold catalogue of unilateral acts designed to protect the declining U.S. dollar against his perception of unfair practices by some countries. There was not the slightest doubt that the primary target of his wrath was Japan, which had been hugely successful in penetrating the rich U.S. market with its superbly crafted automobiles and brilliantly designed electronics products. Japanese policies and practices could not be overlooked, said Nixon, because "Japan is America's largest trading partner." The enormity of Nixon's misperception could not be overstated: in 1970, U.S. exports to Canada exceeded by a considerable margin not only U.S. sales to Japan but the total of U.S. exports to Japan, France, the United Kingdom, and the Federal Republic of Germany *combined*. This flagrant ignorance on the part of the American administration simply confirmed what Canadian governments had worried about for years – the apparent fact that the United States took Canada for granted. Much more serious than perceptions, however, important as they are for obvious reasons, would be the devastating effects on the Canadian economy and standard of living if these announced practices were to be carried out. They included import surcharges and special assistance to export-producing American firms. An added U.S. misconception related to currency exchange rates. Central to Nixon's concerns were the practices of several OECD countries to maintain artificial exchange rates. Not so Canada, however, which had allowed its dollar to float since June 1970.

Thus was launched full-blown and without notice the first major crisis in Canadian–American relations during the period of Trudeau's government. Adding to the sense of drama at this time was the fact that Trudeau was absent from Canada, holidaying in the Adriatic. Acting as prime minister was Mitchell Sharp, who immediately called together the ministers who were most directly involved, including Jean-Luc Pepin (Industry, Trade and Commerce) and Edgar Benson (Finance). The initial assumption (one which was primarily the view of the deputy minister of finance, Simon Reisman) was that the United States had simply erred, and thus had departed from the "special relationship" that had long served as an umbrella sheltering Canada from the stormiest of tempests arising out of shifts in U.S. trade, monetary, and fiscal policies. That assumption proved to be grievously in error, as was the officials' advice on the means to restore the status quo (to remind Washington that Canada is "different"). At high-level meetings hastily arranged in Washington in the next few days, Sharp and Benson were bluntly informed by the combative U.S. secretary of the treasury, John Connally,[15] that there had been no error. The president intended to do exactly what he had done; any errors in the ranking of U.S. trading partners was an insignificant oversight. The ministers and their deputies were stunned. Until that moment this issue had been a matter of serious concern in Ottawa; it now suddenly escalated to one of considerable alarm.

Sharp asked Head to come to his Centre Block office. Would Head support Sharp's advice to Trudeau to return immediately to Ottawa to take charge of the Canadian response? Head said yes without hesitation, and Sharp telephoned Trudeau. Two days later, Head met Trudeau at the ramp of the Canadian Pacific Airlines flight as it landed at Dorval airport in Montreal and briefed him on the most recent developments as they flew together to Ottawa on a small government airplane.

Events in the next few weeks revealed that the situation was indeed of critical proportions, and that many more countries than Canada were seriously affected. Notwithstanding that serious criticism was clearly and repeatedly conveyed to Washington from several world capitals, supported by carefully prepared arguments that the Connally initiatives represented major departures from previous American practice, and – much more seriously – from solemn American undertakings to its trading partners, the Nixon administration refused to budge. In this period, too, legislation was presented to the Congress and a range of regulations for its implementation were proclaimed. The impact upon Canadian exports and upon Canadian markets was severe – and was expected to worsen.

In mid-September, word reached Ottawa that Nixon was communicating with selected trading partners, proposing meetings at the head of government level to discuss what the press had termed "Nixonomics." No such invitation had been received in Ottawa, and formal inquiries through the embassy in Washington (where Marcel Cadieux was now ambassador) gave no hint as to whether one could be expected. Marc Lalonde convinced Trudeau that one must be sought, and urgently. Head was in New York City at the time, participating in a conference at New York University that had been convened by Professor Thomas Franck, a Canadian scholar in charge of international legal studies there. Lalonde called Head to instruct him to do his best to persuade Kissinger of the importance of the issue. Head telephoned Kissinger and received a response that was much more forthcoming than he had hoped: yes, the issue was certainly deserving of a meeting between Nixon and Trudeau; yes, it was unconscionable that a relationship as important as that which linked Canada and the United States should be subject to the dominance of the Treasury Department; yes, Kissinger would gladly intervene and ensure that an invitation would be issued. And Kissinger followed through (as he would do in every future instance when he gave an undertaking to Head).

The meeting took place in Washington on December 6, 1971. As in the first visit to Washington in March 1969, two sessions ensued at the White House: one in the Cabinet Room, the other in the Oval Office. The variation on this occasion, however, and one that would set a precedent for subsequent meetings between Nixon and Trudeau, was the presence in the Oval Office of two others: Kissinger and Head. While senior ministers and officials from both sides argued heatedly down the hall, Trudeau and Nixon were able quietly and without rancour to resolve the impasse to the complete satisfaction of each. The surcharge would be lifted against Canadian exports, and no further demands would be made with respect to the value of the Canadian dollar. At the conclusion of the meeting, Head and Kissinger met in the latter's office to agree upon the terms of any public announcements. Each understood the need not to disclose any details of the arrangement until the United States had successfully concluded similar discussions with its other major trading partners. This entirely reasonable condition nevertheless presented Trudeau with a major predicament at his press conference the following morning: how to convince sceptical Canadian journalists that the meeting with the president really did represent a breakthrough in the sticky impasse. In the absence of any details, or confirmation from the White House, Trudeau's assertions to this effect, not surprisingly, were mocked by the press as hyperbole on the part of a politician under attack within his domestic political constituency.

That evening would be a relaxed one for the Canadians. Nixon offered a small black-tie dinner for the principals on both sides. In informal fashion, he called on those members of his cabinet who were in attendance to voice one by one their impressions of the Canadian–American relationship. The first to speak was Vice-President Spiro Agnew, widely believed at the time to be in deep political trouble. Agnew's opening remarks about his political future were so subtle and so humorous that he had the entire table whooping with laughter.[16] The evening was a warm conclusion to a particularly testing period for Trudeau. An illuminating element was the instruction that Kissinger gave privately to Head that afternoon: Secretary Connally and Trudeau must not be permitted to speak to one another in the absence of others, for this could lead to Connally upsetting the careful – and still undisclosed to Connally – arrangements set in place that afternoon. For that reason, too, Kissinger had ensured that Trudeau and Connally would not be seated next to one another at dinner. "Should Connally approach Trudeau over cocktails, we must gather round" was Kissinger's admonition to Head.

There would follow any number of other economic disputes between the two countries during the Nixon presidency, not all of them by any means resolved so satisfactorily or, in some cases, resolved at all. One particularly difficult issue festered throughout 1972. It was really a lingering element of the 1971 crisis, revived during the Nixon visit to Ottawa in April 1972. Canada's argument, as voiced by Trudeau to Nixon in December 1971, was that the immense volume of trade between the two countries was essentially in balance. Indeed, when "invisibles" (items such as royalties, dividends, insurance premiums, tourism, licence fees) were added to the "merchandise" figure, the total "current account" revealed an historic imbalance in favour of the United States. This demonstrable fact had impressed Nixon but not Connally, who was determined to root out any examples of advantages, preferences, or "unfair" practices drawn to his attention. One such, in his view, was the 1965 Canada–U.S. Auto Pact, which contained a safeguard provision to assure a "fair-share" for Canada in each of three sectors: assembly plants, parts manufacturing, and R&D. Discussions to modify this protection took place between Jean-Luc Pepin and Connally, then with the latter's successor, George Shultz, and were referred to in numerous exchanges between Kissinger and Head, all in an endeavour to reach a trade "package" acceptable to both countries. The issue only subsided with the departure from Washington of Nixon. In the meantime, any number of other trade irritants – ranging from tourist duty-free allowances through citrus imports and defence procurements – were satisfactorily resolved.

Nixon's address to a joint session of Parliament during his 1972 visit to Ottawa marked the welcome conclusion of the old "special" economic relationship between the two countries that was so endearing to some Canadian ministers and to some of the most senior public servants. In Trudeau's eyes, however, such a relationship gave to Canada a diminutive role, one which placed it permanently in the position of a supplicant. For that reason Head had suggested in a lengthy letter to Kissinger in March that Nixon's speech should be employed by the president as an opportunity to fix a clear milestone in relations between the countries, one as symbolic as Secretary of State Frank Knox's 1911 denial of U.S. annexation pretensions or President Franklin Roosevelt's 1938 Queen's University statement that the "United States will not stand idly by if domination of Canadian soil is threatened. . . ." Head expressed the hope that the president would declare that Canadian independence clearly extended to its own determination of its economic policies, free from U.S. interference. That message featured prominently in Nixon's address. His reference to "separate identities" was well received in Ottawa, and broadly welcomed throughout Canada.

III

THE FORD YEARS – 1974-1976

By late 1974, Canada's U.S. neighbourhood was unquestionably understood on both sides of the border as one shared by two quite distinct entities. Future differences of opinion would certainly arise, and some seemingly insoluble difficulties (such as energy) would continue. In other sectors, however, considerable progress had been made: the UN Law of the Sea Conference was well on the way to enshrining Canada's Arctic requirements, thus fully legitimizing the pioneering steps taken in the Arctic Waters Pollution Prevention Act; in an era of détente, Canada's rational and persistent approach to East–West issues was gaining increased approval within NATO, where Canada's efforts to raise the nuclear threshold, and its involvement in the Conference on Security and Cooperation in Europe negotiations, were both respected; the running sore of Vietnam had been reduced in size with some useful assistance by Canada; some real progress had been attained in terms of Great Lakes and boundary-waters environmental practices, including a major treaty, The Great Lakes Water Quality Agreement. No major shadows threatened to darken the first meeting with the new U.S. President, Gerald Ford, and none appeared.

The visit was proposed as official but informal and took place in Washington in early December. By that time Ford had done much to ease the trauma and close the wounds in American society opened by the resignation of Nixon. One of his first acts upon acceding to office had been to appoint Kissinger as secretary of state, thus assuring Americans and others that U.S. foreign policy would not be subject to any sudden shifts or reversals. Prior to his choice by Nixon as his vice-president, replacing Spiro Agnew, Ford had been a veteran of Congress, where his openness and gregariousness had made him many friends. The personal attitudes of decency and guilelessness so associated with him proved invaluable in dispelling the by-then much-criticized aura of an "imperial" presidency that had surrounded Nixon. Those characteristics made him an easy person to meet and to like; Gerald Ford was the least pretentious of men.

On the occasion of that first Ford–Trudeau encounter, the White House discussions were entirely congenial, the initial stage in the development of a warm friendship between Ford and Trudeau, which extends to this day. Because the Nixon penchant for secretiveness was not part of Ford's personality, the numbers present in the Oval Office were more reflective of international practice. Kissinger was there, of course, in his new role as secretary of state, which permitted the new Canadian secretary of state for external affairs, Allan MacEachen, to be present. Continuing the practice of previous years, the national security adviser, now Brent Scowcroft, participated, as did Head, who knew Scowcroft well in his earlier role as Kissinger's deputy at the National Security Council (NSC). It was a good beginning to what later proved to be a brief presidency.

Trudeau would see Ford on a number of occasions during that abbreviated term, including the 1975 Helsinki Conference on Security and Cooperation in Europe, a NATO Summit in Brussels and the Puerto Rico Economic Summit (later to be called the G-7) that same year, and a brief meeting in June 1976 as a prelude to the American bicentennial celebrations. On each of these occasions Ford proved to be well informed about matters of concern to Canada and – of even greater importance – genuinely desirous of accommodating differences in a mutually acceptable fashion. In those instances when reconciliation was not possible, the president left us with the impression that he was as disappointed as we were, and equally as desirous of containing any infection, lest other aspects of the relationship become contaminated. Unlike the case during the Nixon presidency, the bulk of Canadian–American contacts at the head of government level took place in the context of multilateral, not bilateral, activities.

Warm relations with leading legislators continued in this period as well. An official visit to Washington was primarily an event involving the executive branch of the U.S. government: the president, one or more of his cabinet, and selected senior officials. Generally, however, a courtesy call upon congressional leaders was possible, as had been the case during Trudeau's first visit in 1969. On that occasion, on the initiative of the experienced Ambassador Ed Ritchie, a lunch was arranged with the members of the Senate Foreign Relations Committee and the House Foreign Affairs Committee. It was a worthwhile event, which facilitated subsequent contacts.

Since then, Head and a ranking member of the Senate committee, Republican Charles "Mac" Mathias of Maryland, had found themselves together at a number of international conferences, and a warm relationship had evolved. Mathias proved on many occasions to be a helpful sounding board and source of wise advice. While preparing for the visit to Washington to call upon President Ford, Head telephoned Mathias to inquire if senators and congressmen would be interested in meeting Trudeau on the occasion of his first call upon President Ford, but in less formal circumstances than earlier. The reply was enthusiastic, and a breakfast meeting was quickly organized by Senator Mike Mansfield of Montana, chairman of the Senate committee.

The initial reaction of the new Canadian ambassador, Marcel Cadieux, was far from positive. A diplomat of the classical school, Cadieux was worried that the Congress was not an appropriate branch of the government for prime ministers to court. The event proved to be so buoyant, however, and so effective in ventilating and correcting flawed interpretations of Canadian policy, that he candidly reversed his opinion. As a complement to the success of the White House meeting, the session rounded out a most worthwhile trip, emphasizing the informal – yet exceedingly important and pervasive – nature of the American–Canadian relationship.

Ford did not bring to the White House the wealth of foreign-policy experience of his predecessor, and to his credit did not claim otherwise. What he did contribute to the presidency was a refreshing transparency of purpose and a demonstrable affability. He projected an image – never overturned – of one who regarded conspiracies as alien to his very nature. Communications with Trudeau were frequent, those between Scowcroft and Head even more so. On issues where there was a commonality of interest – as in the preparations for the Western Economic Summit at Dorado Beach, Puerto Rico – the relationship was comfortable and productive; in those instances where there was a sharp division of opinion – Taiwanese pretensions prior to the Montreal Olympics, as the obvious example – the differences were narrowly defined and purposely contained. The Olympics issue was much more an American domestic political imperative than it was a reflection of bilateral differences. This became evident in 1980 when the United States accepted for the Lake Placid Winter Olympics a formula virtually identical to that which was employed by Canada in 1976 – and which was then the object of such fierce criticism.

In the summer of 1976, however, no hint came from Washington that U.S. "principles" were about to reverse themselves. Then, encouraged by the somewhat pompous assertions of the International Olympic Committee that its purpose was to keep politics out of sport, and reflective of the still-powerful influence within the United States of supporters of the Kuomintang government of "Nationalist China" and its pretensions to be the sole legitimate government of the mainland, the Ford fury was every bit as expressive as anything originating from Nixon, as he asserted that ". . . the games have now been totally corrupted by a politicization that reduces this international sports contest to a mocking of the Olympic ideal and to a mere sideshow in the ideological wars."[17]

For our part, we had no desire or interest in offending the IOC. We had considerable interest, however, in honouring the integrity of our own China policy, which included a refusal to take sides in the intense dispute respecting the extent of Chinese territorial sovereignty.

By 1976, the question of who represented China in the United Nations had long since been resolved in favour of the government in Beijing, largely on initiatives taken in the wake of the Canadian–Chinese recognition formula reached in 1970. In any number of other multilateral bodies and organizations, the same reality was recognized. Not so, however, in the esoteric world of the Olympic

Games, where the National Olympic Committee in Taipei continued to be accepted by the IOC as the legitimate representative of the Republic of China.

Within the IOC, the question of the participation of the People's Republic of China had been the subject of contradictory and inconsistent rulings since the early fifties. In 1959, a decision was taken to remove the Republic of China as an eligible Olympic member, giving the Taiwanese the opportunity to reapply as Taiwan. Accordingly, Taiwan had competed in the 1960 Rome Olympics as "Formosa." This decision prompted intense criticism from the U.S. government, however. It called the act one of political discrimination brought about by Communist pressure. In subsequent games, Taiwan competed as the Republic of China. In 1975, the People's Republic of China applied for admission in the IOC and asked that the Republic of China be excluded. The committee's inability to decide on this issue led to delays in the decision right up to the time of the Montreal Games. As a result, Taiwan continued to enjoy the support of the IOC in its bid to compete at Montreal as the Republic of China. This had the not-unexpected effect of attracting vigorous protests from Beijing, protests addressed to the international community in its broadest sense, to the IOC, and to the host state of Canada.

Any Canadian efforts to placate the Beijing government by arguing that this was a matter solely within the jurisdiction of the "apolitical" IOC would clearly be of little impact. Beijing opposed the entry into Canada of the Taiwan team, and encouraged the Canadian government to deny the necessary visas, an act that would clearly violate solemn undertakings to the IOC and would, moreover, destroy the balance inherent in the 1970 formula. It was a step that Trudeau would not consider. Neither, however, was he prepared to permit any government to do damage to Canada's foreign-policy interests by utilizing Canadian territory to masquerade as an entity it was not. Thus was taken the decision – after efforts at persuasion had failed – to insist that Taiwan not hold itself out to be China, something it clearly was not. Taiwan, Trudeau said, could call itself anything it wanted, so long as the name was not in flagrant violation of international comity.

Shortly following a meeting in which Lord Killanin, the president of the IOC, withdrew his earlier threats to remove the IOC sanction

from the Montreal Games over this issue, Trudeau spoke to the House
of Commons:[18]

> . . . it is not our policy nor our practice to bar any athletes from
> the games. We welcome the athletes from Taiwan. We hope they
> will compete. We do not discriminate on the basis of sex, race or,
> indeed, national origin. All we are saying . . . is that we will not
> let athletes come into Canada under false representations and to
> pretend that they represent a country, China, that they do not
> represent.

To those in the United States still possessed of the illogical and
unreal spectre of hegemonic international communism, and those (not
all) in the IOC that believed their privileged position need not relate to
international practice or to ordinary comity, Canada's stance was vehemently criticized. As events transpired, Taiwan chose not to participate.
Three and a half years later, at the Lake Placid Winter Olympics in
New York State, the Canadian formula was repeated with scarcely a
whimper of protest from the U.S. government. There, as at Montreal,
Taiwan was denied the right to participate as the Republic of China.
In the result, the Taiwan team returned home.

The 1976 inclusion of Canada as an economic summit participant
was in tenor and performance far more important than the Olympic
furore, for this was international acknowledgement of Canada's
enhanced stature. In some respects it was a further step in the long road
that commenced with Canada's engagement in the 1919 Versailles
Peace Conference, and which included such recognition as our time-
to-time election to the Security Council. In another respect, however,
it was qualitatively different. Head employed a sports analogy in his
characterization of the occasion. "For the first time, Canada had been
accepted as a permanent player in the major leagues," he said. That
acceptance was by no means universally tendered, however, nor
greeted within the Canadian government with equal enthusiasm.

There had flourished for many years a regular consultative mechanism, shared by the five largest market economies (Britain, France, the
Federal Republic of Germany, Japan, and the United States) and
referred to as the G-5. The group had come into being as a recognition

of common concerns among the five in economic and monetary matters. Opportunities for frequent consultations are clearly valuable to governments. Thus these five had taken advantage of such regular events as the annual meetings of the World Bank and the International Monetary Fund for their finance ministers to caucus separately on issues of particular interest. The practice was well known throughout the international community, and occasioned grumbles only in instances where smaller countries believed their interests were somehow being affected without their knowledge.

This informal and obvious grouping of interests changed dramatically in 1975 when France decided to act as host to a "World Economic Summit," a meeting of presidents and prime ministers of the G-5, and included Italy. This was an unusual step, the convocation of an international conference by a single country on its own initiative while tightly controlling the list of invitees. When word of this "international economic summit" first circulated, low-key representations were made to each of the G-5 states inquiring on what basis Canada (which at the time had a GNP larger than that of Italy) was not included.

As it turned out, there proved to be considerable support for the inclusion of Canada. In early October the *New York Times* reported that Washington was discussing publicly a conference of seven countries (the G-5 plus Canada and Italy). The Federal Republic of Germany and Britain each intervened with France to this effect (Foreign Minister James Callaghan raised the question personally in conversations with his French counterpart, Jean Victor Sauvagnargues). The Japanese stated they had no objection to Canada's involvement. The French stuck to their original plans, however, and no invitation was issued to Canada.

Whether this decision was intended as an affront to Canada, perhaps a continuation of the Gaullist campaign of diminishment that began with General Charles de Gaulle's 1967 remarks in Montreal, no one could be sure. President Valéry Giscard d'Estaing wrote to Trudeau following the Rambouillet meeting in very warm terms, explaining that one additional invitation had been extended to Italy as a friendly gesture to a neighbour which was then chairman of the European Community, not as a matter of precedent. This explanation was not entirely satisfactory to the other G-5 members, however, who had reasons of their own to support Canadian involvement. The United

States and Japan were desirous of more non-European participation; Germany and Britain sought to dilute somewhat the French attempts at primacy (to the extent that Chancellor Helmut Schmidt told President Giscard d'Estaing that he would not attend any future meeting of this kind unless Canada participated).

Throughout this episode, Trudeau insisted that Canada not play the role of a demandeur. He rejected wholly advice from External Affairs officials that Canada remonstrate with France, either before or after the summit. He was content that Canada's eligibility had been recognized by many, and that the point had been well made that no self-selected group of countries should purport to be representative of others in a "World Economic Summit." He was critical of the department, therefore, when some senior officials employed in public statements the very kind of language to which he objected. This sort of whining he regarded as undignified and counterproductive.

The following spring the Americans proposed the convening of a second summit, and made it clear that Canada would participate as a full partner.[19] President Ford selected late June as the date and Dorado Beach, Puerto Rico, as the location. With the full expectation that these meetings would be continuing events, some formal preparatory process took shape. Heads of government and two ministers (generally agreed to be Finance and Foreign Affairs) would be at the table. None others of any rank would be in the room, with the exception of a single note-taker from each country, who would be seated well away from the principals. The intention was to encourage a free exchange of views in an environment that permitted candour. A preliminary meeting at the official level took place in Washington to assist in setting the agenda. Thus arose the practice of personal representatives, later to be dubbed "sherpas." On the first occasion, Head represented the prime minister, Peter Towe represented the secretary of state for external affairs, and William Hood represented the minister of finance.[20]

These summit meetings quickly gained a cachet of their own, and gradually began straying far from the economic agenda that had prompted them in the first instance. Thus, to our concern, did they assume the character of a "directoire," a grouping assuming for itself the personality of some representative body, which it surely was not, and addressing crisis issues rather than considering future trends. The

merit of such regular consultations, however, with the attendant
opportunity for heads of government to speak to one another in relatively intimate circumstances, could not be denied. In practice, as could
be expected, the quality and sharpness of focus of the discussions
varied with the cast of leaders in attendance and the individual in the
chair. At the Dorado Beach Summit, however, the quality was uni-
formly high.

In the United States, the year 1976 was the bicentennial of the
American Declaration of Independence. The event would not pass
unnoticed in Canadian–American relations. Many months prior to
July 4, Lorraine Monk, the brilliant director of the still-photography
division of the National Film Board of Canada, had chosen to commission a volume of photographs celebrating the Canadian–American
friendship, one to be released as a Canadian contribution to the bicentennial celebrations. She seized on an idea earlier proposed by Sydney
Newman, who, during his term as chair of the NFB, had proposed pho-
tographing the border. Working with a team of talented Canadian
photographers, and associates such as Professor Charles Haines of
Carleton University's department of English, a magnificent large-
format volume was produced, entitled *Between Friends/Entre Amis*,[21]
and Head inquired of his U.S. counterpart, Brent Scowcroft, if
Trudeau, Monk, and a few collaborators could "drop by" the White
House to present a specially cased volume to President Ford. On
June 16, in a brief but exceedingly cordial reception, the gift was
placed in the president's hands, and the production team was introduced. Later, Trudeau and Head were Ford's guests for an evening
dinner cruise on the presidential yacht *Sequoia*. In the course of an
early-summer evening, the atmosphere on board reflected in every
respect the warmth of the relationship as expressed by Trudeau in his
foreword to the picture book:

Over hundreds of years we have worked and played together,
laughed and mourned together, fought side by side against
common enemies. Our two peoples have helped each other repair
the havoc of natural disasters, inspired and applauded each other,

opened our hearts and our homes to each other as to valued and welcome friends. . . . The true nature of our international relationship . . . is revealed by the fact that it is defined not by our differences, but by our capacity and eagerness to resolve them.

Ford did not come to Canada during his term in office but his secretary of state did. In the fall of 1975, while he still held the separate position of national security adviser, Kissinger flew in for a brief visit, tightly orchestrated by his Canadian host Allan MacEachen. There were talks with Trudeau, a small lunch at 24 Sussex Drive, and an introduction to the House of Commons, where Head had escorted Kissinger following the lunch and sat with him and his wife, Nancy, in the gallery as members of Parliament noisily paid tribute to this distinguished visitor. The previous evening a gala dinner had been offered by the secretary of state for external affairs.

Still another senior visitor in this period was James Schlesinger, in his capacity as secretary of defence, a role in which he pursued a policy of raising the nuclear threshold in Europe, where Canada's earlier withdrawal from a nuclear-strike role had attracted his interest.

Ford's tenure did not permit him to introduce any major departures in U.S. foreign policy. He continued to pursue the broad goals of détente introduced by his predecessor, and so had journeyed to Vladivostok for a celebrated meeting with Leonid Brezhnev officially to launch the SALT II process in 1974.[22] Yielding to pressures from his supporters, he had shuffled his cabinet in major fashion in late 1975. Among other changes, Secretary of State Henry Kissinger was asked to relinquish his second role as national security adviser; his deputy, Brent Scowcroft, assumed this function (as he would again in 1988 at the request of President George Bush, clear acknowledgement of the merit of this unassuming, highly disciplined man). Those "irritants" in Canadian–American relations that were present in the final months of the Nixon administration would remain as issues throughout Ford's tenure and into the term of President Jimmy Carter: border television, fisheries management, natural-gas exports and pipelines, the extent of direct American investment in Canada, the pricing of agricultural commodities, and civil aviation agreements. In some instances, the aggrieved party was the United States; in others, Canada. The range of issues, and their complexity, reflected the extensive inter-engagement of Canadians and Americans. Each demanded special attention and focused efforts. They deserved consideration, moreover, within the broad context of the bilateral relationship, which is to say that neither government should fail to bear in mind (as if Canada ever could!) that the two nations had achieved a degree of interpenetration and inter-dependence unlike that experienced by any other pair of countries. Canada insisted that this singular state of affairs not be interpreted by the United States as subservience or as a guarantee of automatic concurrence. The demise of the old "special" relationship, with its overtones of paternalism, meant that Canada was less restrained in its selection of economic policies, but equally that it was more accountable to the Canadian electorate as it did so.

Overall, the governance challenge appeared to us to be primarily one of maintaining the tone and the equilibrium of the relationship, thus permitting appropriate weight to be given to individual issues as they arose. We had rejected the proposal promoted by Robert Stanfield and the Progressive Conservative Party in the course of the 1974 federal election for the creation of a standing Canada–U.S. board or commission, with jurisdiction to oversee the relationship, because we recognized Canada's inability to maintain a rough balance in staff work and agenda priorities across the vast spectrum of activities should such a mechanism be instituted. The resources that the United States would be able to bring to bear would be far in excess of those on the Canadian side. The issue was not one of the equality of the partners; it was one of the disparity in numbers – "depth," in sports parlance – between nations, with a ten-to-one population and wealth ratio. There was really no parallel between this suggested all-encompassing level and such narrowly focused permanent bodies as the International Joint Commission.[23] There was still another ground for our concern. In our judgement, the bilateral relationship was in many instances influenced deeply by the involvement of the two countries – sometimes harmoniously, sometimes not – in a rich fabric of multilateral relationships involving other countries. That broader dimension should not be overlooked, as might be the case in a panel restricted to bilateral issues. If all of this was to be reflected adequately, a much more sensitive and flexible mechanism was required than a bureaucratic structure prone to rigidity and non-responsive to nuance and adjustment.

IV
THE CARTER YEARS — 1977-1981

The election of Jimmy Carter as the thirty-ninth president in November 1976 provided an opportunity to consider alternatives to previous practices. In the days immediately following the election, Head discussed the merits of various governance techniques with Zbigniew Brzezinski, the likely Carter appointee as national security adviser, when the two met in Georgia. Brzezinski was well acquainted with Canada. He had been raised in Montreal,[24] and educated at McGill before settling in the United States and creating an enviable reputation as an Eastern European scholar and analyst at Columbia University. He needed no encouragement to acknowledge the importance to the United States of a sound and sustainable relationship between the two countries. The outcome of the discussions was an agreement to encourage early and frequent communications between Carter and Trudeau, and to emphasize at this level the need to concentrate on the overall state of relations — the "management of the relationship," they called it. Thus Trudeau was invited to come to Washington as one of the earliest visitors following the inauguration.[25]

Brzezinski would not be the only senior member of the Carter administration with a long familiarity with Canada and Canadians. Elected as vice-president was Walter Mondale, the veteran U.S. senator from Minnesota, who had long demonstrated a knowledgeable interest in Canada, most recently with particular attention to the energy needs of his northern state. The two of us had first met Mondale in March 1969, on the occasion of Trudeau's visit to Washington, at which time Ambassador Ed Ritchie had included him on his guest list for a dinner in the Canadian residence. In the intervening years, Head and Mondale were often in touch, utilizing such opportunities as their joint membership in the Atlantic Conference[26] to meet and exchange views. It had been Head that Mondale contacted in 1975, for example, during a period of deep concern about secure supplies of petroleum and natural gas, when he was seeking appointments in Ottawa with Trudeau and other ministers and officials. The visit had been opposed by External Affairs on the ground that the Ford government would interpret it as hostile to the Republican administration. Not only was such apprehension alien to the United States' own practice of welcoming visits

from senior members of political oppositions, it was as well a misread-
ing of the political mood in Washington, as events proved. Mondale's
visit to Ottawa in mid-February was low-key and useful all round. He
met with Trudeau and others of his choice, dined privately with Head,
and generated a considerable amount of goodwill in the process with
absolutely no fallout on official Canadian–American relations. The visit
proved to be a valuable dress rehearsal for Mondale's return to Canada
as vice-president in early 1978.

The election of Jimmy Carter as president brought to an end a
period of eight years of Republican tenure in the White House. Many
years had passed since a person so fresh to federal politics had been
elected president. In Washington there was considerable excitement
about the arrival of this "newcomer" and his promises of change. In
foreign-policy terms there were two elements of major interest to
Canada. One of these was Carter's declared intention to pursue a
"moral" foreign policy, an element of which would be his insistence on
a good human-rights record as a condition of friendly relations; the
other was the personal attention he pledged to the thorny issue of
nuclear proliferation. Each would be the subject of discussion between
Carter and Trudeau during the official visit to Washington in February
1977, as would Carter's pledge that he wished to replace "balance of
power" policies with a politics based upon world order, a concept that
he likely gained from Brzezinski.

It was a meeting quite unlike any that Trudeau had experienced
with other presidents. One reason, of course, was the newness of Carter
and many of his associates. Some, such as Mondale and Secretary of
State Cyrus Vance, had previous Washington experience (indeed Vance
had long since gained considerable respect as an international negotiator, and in the process made the acquaintance of a large number of
non-Americans, including Head), but many had not. In the result, considerable deference was extended to Trudeau as an experienced statesman. A second reason for the tone of the meeting was the quite
extraordinary command of detail evidenced by the president. His
knowledge of his brief did much to reassure us that he was equipped,
and intended, to be America's chief executive officer. Critics would
later argue that Carter's very penchant for detail was his weakness, for
this would undermine his ability to concentrate on strategy and to

pursue a steady course towards clearly defined objectives. Whatever the merit of this criticism, it was not one that would often cause difficulties for Canada during the Carter presidency. A notable exception was the important Canada–U.S. Fisheries Treaty, which failed in the senate because of inadequate attention from the White House.

The final factor that distinguished this meeting from those preceding it was the deep and sincere courtesy of Carter. This personal trait was far different from the sometimes awkwardness of Nixon; different, too, from the friendly informality of Ford (and entirely distinct from the garrulous charm of his successor, Ronald Reagan). Carter was genuinely courtly, one whose mannerisms were at once friendly and proper, conveying forcefully the deep human convictions of the man.

The team supporting Trudeau on the visit included a new player: Don Jamieson, who had succeeded Allan MacEachen as secretary of state for external affairs.

An important element in the visit's program had unexpectedly fallen into place the previous November. On the occasion of one of the biennial sessions of the Atlantic Conference, Head had spent considerable time, as always, with Senator Charles Mathias and Senator Adlai Stevenson III, of Illinois, a Carter supporter. Mathias disclosed to Head his view of the value to both countries were Trudeau to address a joint session of the Congress. "I can't guarantee that it can be arranged," said Mathias. "Quite frankly, there was such a spate of simply dreadful performances by invited dignitaries that senators and congressmen are now inclined to allow the practice to die. No invitations have been extended for quite some time." The senator was confident, however, that there would be enthusiasm were Trudeau to agree.

The task fell to Head to persuade Trudeau to do so. When it was revealed that no Canadian prime minister had ever before been granted this honour, that task became even more daunting.[27] Trudeau's senior advisers Gordon Robertson and Jim Coutts quickly joined Head as advocates in support of the event, and were successful in their persuasion. Mathias on this occasion, as on so many others, proved to be both friendly and influential. Shortly following the official invitation from the White House for a visit to take place in the weeks immediately following the inauguration in 1977, there issued an invitation from the Speakers of the two Chambers of Congress. The momentum then

under way in Quebec for some variant of separation had led to a
massive increase of interest in the United States about the future stability of Canada. The speech responded to that interest and linked
Canada's experience with the expectations of the international community, and particularly the developing countries, where cooperation,
understanding, and tolerance were necessary if a "new world order"[28]
were to be constructed. As Trudeau would say on this topic:

> Both English-speaking and French-speaking Canadians will have
> to become more aware of the richness that diversity brings and less
> irritated by the problems it presents. . . . I am immodest enough to
> suggest that a failure of this always-varied, often-illustrious
> Canadian social experiment would create shock waves of disbelief
> among those all over the world who are committed to the propo-
> sition that among man's noblest endeavours are those communi-
> ties in which persons of diverse origins live, love, work and find
> mutual benefit. . . . Increasingly, the welfare and human dignity of
> others will be the measurement of our own condition. I share
> with President Carter his belief that in this activity we will
> achieve success.

   The drafting of the speech attracted considerable interest in Ottawa.
Coutts and Robertson made suggestions. The overall design, and the
text itself, however, were the product of Head, who engaged extensively with Trudeau in doing so.
   Trudeau and Carter would meet frequently during the latter's
administration. In early May 1977, a regular meeting of the G-7
Economic Summit took place in London at the invitation of British
Prime Minister James Callaghan, and was followed immediately by a
heads of government session of NATO.[29] The London venue for the
former event was chosen to provide one element in the extensive celebrations of the twenty-fifth anniversary of the reign of Queen Elizabeth
II, which included, a month later, a meeting of the Commonwealth
heads of government. London was in a festive mood that spring, with
lamp standards and shop-windows festooned in royal regalia.
   As Callaghan was calling the Economic Summit to order in a pan-
elled conference room at 10 Downing Street, Japanese Prime Minister

Takeo Fukuda, the most elderly of the heads of government, suddenly spoke out, "I've been in this room before! This was the site of the 1936 London Naval Conference which I attended. I was a junior member of the Japanese delegation." This unexpected intervention lent a light-hearted air to the opening moments; it served as well as an organic linkage with a preceding era, when diplomacy failed to overcome the forces of nationalism, isolationism, and deception. The memory of those earlier shortcomings, and the massive extent of the tragedies that were their consequence, served as a background to the stimulating discussions around the small table.[30] A measure of the changed circumstances prevailing in the international community forty years later was the inclusion on the agenda of the 1977 meeting of the economic plight of the developing countries. Canada's role as co-chair of the Conference on International Economic Cooperation, the then-principal forum for North–South discussions, gave to us a particular incentive to ensure that the importance of this critically important aspect of international relations be fully accepted by all seven governments. Trudeau was partially successful in his championing of this recognition, as the communiqué reveals.

A most important contribution to confidence-building and stability, one reflected as such at the NATO meeting, had been the impetus that Carter gave to non-proliferation measures and his support of the London Nuclear Suppliers' Club. At London in previous weeks, a number of states, including Canada and – significantly – the Soviet Union, had agreed upon a detailed "trigger" list of components necessary for the construction of nuclear explosive devices, and agreed that an embargo should be placed upon their sale. This demonstration of practical cooperation, one which led to close and continuing consultations over the years, was a significant advance in this esoteric and perilous sector. Carter's interest was shaped by his experience as a former U.S. naval officer who had served as an engineer aboard nuclear-powered and armed submarines. He was the first nuclear-age NATO leader with a firsthand technical awareness of these awesome weapons.

Subsequently, during the later annual sessions of the G-7, and at the splendid ceremonies in Washington on the occasion of the execution of the Panama Canal Treaty in September 1977, Trudeau and Carter would meet and consult on bilateral as well as multilateral issues. Into the former category fell, early on, a shock wave emanating from Carter's much-heralded attack on the "three-martini" business lunch. As part of his package to reduce income-tax benefits for business entertainment, the president had curtailed tax deductions for out-of-country conferences and conventions. Because Canadian cities, most particularly Montreal, were favourite destinations for private-sector and professional organizations, the "Convention Expenses" issue quickly became a highly visible irritant and the subject of serious Canadian interventions with U.S. authorities at all levels until its demise. During their bilateral discussions at the time of the Panama Canal Treaty celebrations, Trudeau and Carter reviewed that issue, as well as that of the festering worry over the Garrison River diversion in North Dakota. The diversion proposal was under study by the International Joint Commission, but it was important that Carter realize how importantly Canada regarded this cross-border river activity.

Another difficulty in this period, one with much more serious overtones, related to the long-standing efforts of both countries to negotiate mutually successful and effective arrangements for the management of fisheries on the Atlantic and Pacific coasts, and the fixing of contested maritime boundaries. Sharing of the marine resources, and concern about conservation, had stimulated a complicated series of negotiations, which had been given impetus in July 1977 by each country's appointment of special negotiators with mandates to discuss these thorny and complex problems. Canada's negotiator was Marcel Cadieux, one of Canada's most senior and experienced diplomats, one knowledgeable about the applicable principles of international law. His term as ambassador to the United States had acquainted him with his American counterpart, Lloyd Cutler.[31]

One of the major negotiating difficulties was the asymmetric interests of each country on the two coasts. Principles, quotas, and formulae appropriate for one ocean tended to be the reverse for the other. This gave fishing interests, highly vocal in each country, the opportunity to complain that their government had not protected them as well in the Atlantic as in the Pacific, or vice versa. The two governments had wisely accepted the global outcome, however, and signed a major treaty. In Canada, discussions between the federal government and the several coastal provinces had led to the acceptance by the latter of the final document. Indeed, these provinces had been significant participants throughout the entire negotiating process. Canada would have no difficulty in ratifying the treaty.

In the United States, however, where treaties must pass through the Senate before the executive can ratify and proclaim them, a major stumbling block appeared. The powerful Atlantic-fisheries lobby sought and gained the support of Rhode Island Senator Claiborne Pell, maintaining that the U.S. government had caved in to Canadian pressure on the East Coast. In one of those frustrating examples of the American governmental system that can be so disturbing to other countries, Pell was able to block the necessary consent resolution. The weight of the Carter administration had not been brought to bear in a timely fashion because of competing domestic concerns. In the result, the ratification vote was denied and the treaty virtually collapsed.[32]

The secretary of state for external affairs, Mark MacGuigan, a former international law professor, was deeply hurt by the symbolism of this incident. In a speech in the United States he warned his American audience that this kind of performance destabilized international confidence in the good faith of the U.S. government. If a treaty carefully negotiated and solemnly signed with duly authorized officials is then rejected by American constitutional processes, he argued, how can foreign governments ever know when to trust the word of the U.S. government? It was a damning indictment, all the more so because of the calm and scholarly nature of its author. As MacGuigan knew, the argument would fall on deaf ears in the United States, where the prerogatives of the senate had much earlier produced the Connally amendment (the so-called "self-judging" amendment) to the American acceptance of the compulsory jurisdiction of the International Court of Justice.

The Fisheries Treaty episode was an unfortunate chapter in the history of Canada's relations with the United States. It was a clear example of the perils and challenges inherent in one's association with this powerful and complex country. It was a far cry from such examples of friendship and cooperation in this period as the official visit of Vice-President Mondale in early 1978, a visit all the more significant because of Carter's unprecedented assignment to his vice-president of substantive, as distinct from the normal ceremonial, responsibilities.

Mondale wished to visit Ottawa – where his official host would be the Speaker of the Senate,33 the Hon. Renaude Lapointe – and as well Alberta, where he would be able to pursue discussions relative to his continuing interest in energy matters. In Ottawa he met with Trudeau and several ministers. For the Alberta segment, Premier Peter Lougheed had extended a gracious invitation and provided warm hospitality. The visit came close to cancellation at the last moment because of the death of the elderly Hubert Humphrey a few days before. Humphrey was a much-loved public figure, and had been Mondale's mentor and predecessor as U.S. senator from Minnesota. The funeral in Minneapolis attracted large numbers of dignitaries from Washington, including the vice-president, who flew out in one of the presidential "Air Force One" airplanes. Mondale then came straight to Ottawa on a smaller air force passenger jet that he employed to fly to Edmonton, accompanied by Head. The Mondale visit followed shortly the successful conclusion of negotiations with the United States over the controversial (domestically and internationally) Alaska Highway natural-gas pipeline, a project subject to factors that far exceeded the ability of any Canadian government effectively to influence them.

Mondale's trip proved to be the final White House-level visit to Canada of the Carter administration. Carter never found time to accept the open invitation extended to him by Trudeau in 1977, thus becoming the first full-term president since Herbert Hoover not to have come officially to Ottawa. Meetings between the two thereafter were always in multilateral circumstances, though telephone calls allowed Trudeau and Carter to consult regularly and to keep relations on a productive track.

Peter Towe had succeeded Jake Warren as Canadian ambassador to Washington when the latter elected to retire following a lengthy and distinguished career in the Canadian public service. For Towe, who took up his position in July 1977, this was the third tour of duty at the Washington Embassy during his life as a foreign-service officer. He was superbly equipped by training and experience for this assignment. Major progress was made during this period in the complex, extremely important UN Law of the Sea Conference, allowing a treaty to be readied for signature in late 1980. In the bilateral negotiations conducted by Cadieux and Cutler, agreement had been reached on the procedures to be followed to settle major segments of the extensive Canada–U.S. maritime boundary.[34]

In East–West circumstances, the promising ease in tensions had ceased, and the mood deteriorated markedly as Soviet forces entered Afghanistan in late 1979. Carter, encouraged by Brzezinski, announced that, in retaliation, the United States would boycott the Moscow Olympics, scheduled later in the year, and urged NATO members to follow suit. At the same time he barred U.S. grain exports to the U.S.S.R. Carter brought the full weight of his office to bear in his efforts to punish the Soviets for their Afghanistan policy in a concerted international fashion. The Joe Clark government then in office in Ottawa chose to follow the Olympics boycott, but would not institute a grain embargo. Instead, and wisely, it undertook not to increase Canadian exports to take advantage of the shortfall from U.S. sources.

The two issues were far from dormant as Trudeau returned to office following the February 1980 election. Without question, the Soviet invasion, and the wholly unacceptable pretext on which it was based, demanded an unequivocal censure by the international community. Because of the U.S.S.R. veto in the Security Council, that censure would require a mechanism other than the United Nations. In selecting it, there were two principles demanding adherence. The first was the international norm of equivalence, or proportionality. The second was Trudeau's strong penchant for effectiveness.

The Soviets were seeking the broad international exposure and acclaim that an event of the magnitude of the Olympics brings. It would be inconsistent to criticize the U.S.S.R. for its presence in Afghanistan, while simultaneously participating in an activity that projected an image of civility and sportsmanship. Equally, the International Olympic Committee plea that athletics and politics were separate could no more be supported by Trudeau than it could by the Soviets, who had long-employed international sporting competitions as a lever of political influence. Nevertheless, Trudeau was convinced that an Olympics boycott would have no effect whatever on U.S.S.R. actions in Afghanistan. As well, the employment of boycotts *per se* left a sour taste in the mouths of Canadians. The efforts of African and Caribbean countries to influence the policies of New Zealand by staying away from the 1976 Montreal Olympics, and threatening to do the same at the 1978 Commonwealth Games in Edmonton, were so recent as still to rankle. Were boycotts of international sporting events to become an accepted practice, any future event could be held hostage for any number of grievances, or on the basis of simple reciprocity – as was to happen in 1984 when the Soviet Union refused to participate in the Los Angeles Summer Olympics. Finally, the hopes and dreams of dozens upon dozens of young Canadian athletes who had trained for years for this moment would be dashed, in many instances irreconcilably, were Canada to agree to the boycott. For these reasons, Trudeau refused to join the boycott until the Canadian Olympic athletes met and endorsed the continuation of the Clark policy.

Head played no role in this decision. He had relinquished his role as special adviser to the prime minister in the spring of 1978, as he had indicated was his wish a year earlier. While he and Trudeau remained frequently in touch, his new duties as president of the International Development Research Centre, an organization governed by an international board, were inconsistent with any day-to-day involvement in the broad spectrum of Canadian foreign policy.

It was in the interlude between the 1979 and 1980 elections, when the Conservatives formed the government, that the ultimate agony of the Carter administration was played out in faraway Tehran. The exiled Shah, in refuge in Mexico, had sought temporary access to the United States for emergency medical treatment not available in Mexico. When his needs were corroborated by U.S. physicians, a humanitarian Carter agreed to his entry. The incident was seized upon by an opportunistic Ayatollah Khomeini to arouse immense anti-American hysteria in Iran. In flagrant breach of one of the basic principles of international law and comity, militant Iranian mobs seized the U.S. Embassy and embarked upon a lengthy occupation designed to humiliate a president for whom considerable antipathy was already felt as a result of the courageous American efforts to conclude the long state of war between Egypt and Israel, efforts which would lead to the successful Camp David accord later that year. The American personnel held hostage in this barbaric act were released only following the inauguration of Ronald Reagan, who had made much of Carter's apparent ineffectiveness during the 1980 election campaign.

The hostage-taking provided the occasion for a risky, heroic series

of acts by Canadian Ambassador Kenneth Taylor, his wife, Pat, and staff
members of the Canadian Embassy in Tehran. Surreptitiously, and at
great danger to themselves, they provided refuge in the Canadian residence to six American diplomats until arrangements could be concluded to spirit them out of Iran under cover of Canadian diplomatic
documentation. The exercise was kept a closely held secret by Prime
Minister Joe Clark and senior officials for fear that it might be detected by the Iranians. Its success brought immense goodwill to Canada
from an American public deeply dispirited, a celebrity status to Taylor
unprecedented in the normally anonymous world inhabited by diplomats, and much acclaim – properly – to Clark for authorizing the effort
to evacuate the Americans and ensure the safety of the Canadians
involved.

The final year of Carter's presidency gave him little opportunity for
attention to other than his political future. Back in office following the
1980 Canadian federal election, Trudeau would meet Carter only once
more, at the G-7 Summit in Italy that summer.

V

THE REAGAN YEARS – 1981-1984

Of the several dozen heads of government whom Trudeau came to
know in the period from 1968 to 1984, none had a more engaging
manner than Ronald Reagan. None, however, was less willing to participate in intellectual debate or address himself to facts outside his
immediate personal experience. Reagan's ideological rigidity would
melt away with a smile when he encountered personally any proponent of the evils against which he thundered so relentlessly in his
speeches and his Saturday radio programs. Liberals, socialists, even
communists, when once possessed of an individual human face were
accepted as friends with whom Reagan's charm would function as a
disarming elixir.

He was at the same time the most personable and the most imper-
sonal of men. The strongest objections taken to one of his policy proposals, or the most vigorous advocacy of a position inimical to his own
ideology, would be answered with a smile, a nod, and often a fascinating but quite irrelevant anecdote. Face-to-face, it was next to impossible

to join issue with Reagan. He gave the impression of being constitutionally incapable of personal animosity or of firm adherence to any concept, no matter how simple. The first attribute made him a very likeable person, the second a most frustrating one, because it was seemingly impossible to tell that he had thoroughly grasped a subject. One gathered the impression that his well-known and repeated denunciations of this or that practice so distrusted by the right wing of the Republican Party were nothing more than brilliant repetitions of a familiar script supplied to him by someone else. Guileless and decent, he was the friendliest and most honest of men. As a functioning head of government, however, it was hard to conceive of someone less able to understand issues and take responsible decisions. He projected an image of being an instrument of others; persons who never let him stray from their sight. Reagan performed the public role of president superbly and, seemingly, effortlessly.

Two constants of the Reagan administration were the antithesis of Canada's fundamental values and long-pursued policies. Either of them was perilous to an independent Canada; together they represented the most formidable assault – albeit indirectly – on Canadian interests by any U.S. government since that of Taft.[35] The first took the form of Reagan's indifference to domestic pluralism and his apparent belief that minority communities were either anomalous or best helped by governmental abstention. To a Canada in which all political parties were dedicated to the principle of sharing, and to the utilization of public regulatory mechanisms to guard against abuses by privileged or powerful groups or individuals, the simplistic Republican image was both anathema and symbol of a dangerous alternative, because of its attractiveness to vested interests.

The second of the Reagan era constants took the form of a blatant antipathy to multilateralism in the international community. This attitude did not translate into isolationism, as in pre-Second World War days, but was quite the opposite. The United States was the richest and the most militarily powerful country in the world, and would utilize its power to preserve and enhance that position. So long as multilateral fora such as NATO served American interests, they would enjoy U.S. support. Should any appear not to be doing so, as the Republican nationalists often felt was the case with the United Nations, there would be opposition or outright disengagement. For Canada, especially, but as well for dozens of other medium-sized and small countries dependent upon functioning international regimes to moderate excesses by the giants, this attitude created profound disquiet. The wholly unidimensional characterization of the Soviet Union as an "evil empire" was regarded as a threat to peace and to conflict resolution by many of Reagan's contemporaries – though not, most emphatically, by Prime Minister Margaret Thatcher. Reagan's singleminded determination to combat communism in the Western Hemisphere, even through the support of the most brutal of military dictatorships, caused anguish to all who were committed to poverty alleviation and dedicated to the concept of human rights.

A third constant, one with a potential to reduce considerably the effective control by Canadians of their own economy, was the unfettered support offered by the Reagan administration to the interests of U.S. business. The results of this policy were seen in any number of foreign-policy decisions. Early examples included the shameful criticism of the UN World Health Organization's campaign to encourage breast-feeding in preference to commercial infant formula, and the denunciation of the Law of the Sea Convention, largely because of its enlightened provisions that declared the minerals lying beneath the seabed beyond the limits of national jurisdiction to be "the common heritage of mankind." An example of more immediate impact on Canada was the reaction of the United States to those elements of the National Energy Program that were interpreted by the U.S. oil industry to be detrimental to their interests. The sensitivity of U.S. companies that dominated the Canadian industry, and the automatic way in which the White House supported their allegations of injury, only stiffened Trudeau's resolve to emphasize Canada's own interests and its standards of conduct, which met every international norm for fairness and responsiveness. In much more militant fashion than any of the Nixon initiatives, however, Reagan and his associates interpreted "fairness" as "socialism," detestable in their vision of an unhindered, unregulated private sector.

In the day-to-day hurly-burly of Canadian–American relationships, Reagan on the whole seemed neither less nor more aware of their complexity than any of his predecessors, with the exception of Carter.

In personal terms, Trudeau and Reagan enjoyed an entirely friendly involvement with one another, but one which, to Trudeau, was superficial substantively. He found that access to the ear or the person of Reagan was readily and courteously obtained; the value of that access, however, was always questionable. The two met on four separate occasions early in Reagan's presidency. The president reversed the long tradition of Canadians making the first visit; he came to Ottawa officially in mid-March 1981, and returned in July to attend the G-7 Economic Summit. The bilateral visit was reciprocated by Trudeau in Washington, D.C., in July. The other encounter was of a different kind, a meeting in Grand Rapids, Michigan, in September, on the occasion of the inauguration of the Gerald Ford Library. In this instance, on Trudeau's suggestion, he and Reagan met over breakfast with Mexican President Lopez Portillo to discuss issues common to the three North American countries.

There was no doubting the influence that Reagan brought to the annual G-7 gathering. From the first of the meetings, engaging all seven members (at Dorado Beach, Puerto Rico, in 1976), the intensity of the sessions and the dominance of the heads of government had never diminished. These get-togethers appealed to Trudeau as stimulating and highly useful, for they provided an opportunity for in-depth debates among the seven in an atmosphere of candour and relative informality not available elsewhere on a regular and frequent basis. The presence of two ministers per country around the table had never been other than a useful backstopping to the discussions conducted by heads of government – and of considerable value for ministerial-level contacts and discussions outside the principal sessions. Gradually the media had grown fascinated with the meetings, to the extent that expectations had emerged that were wholly unrelated to the purpose of the meetings, but this was secondary, even though it created a distorted lens for public awareness. Increasingly as well, the utilization of personal representatives or "sherpas" for between-meeting consultations and meeting preparations was eroding the spontaneity and genuineness of the gatherings themselves. Nevertheless, the participation of persons of the thoughtfulness of James Callaghan or Valéry Giscard d'Estaing, and the discipline of such as Helmut Schmidt or Margaret Thatcher, ensured that the central purpose of the annual conferences would not be diluted. Issues were ventilated thoroughly and debated vigorously. Policies were better understood and collaboration more likely to be obtained.

This all changed dramatically at the 1981 summit, the first attended by Reagan. The host was Canada, the site was Château Montebello in the Laurentian region of Quebec just downriver from Ottawa. The concerns of the American advance team for this meeting were focused almost entirely on process and physical arrangements: frequent rotation of U.S. cabinet secretaries as the agenda proceeded, opportunities for many more coffee breaks (with the access of officials to leaders that this permitted), extraordinary concern about media involvement. From that meeting on, the incisiveness of Carter was replaced with the affability of Reagan. The difference was profound, especially as Thatcher chose increasingly to align herself with the rigid and ideological economic and Cold War attitudes of Reagan. The occasions when Thatcher criticized Reagan, or was less than enthusiastic in supporting his initiatives, were rare. One such, the U.S. invasion of Grenada, has already been discussed in Chapter Four.

Throughout this entire period, Trudeau never doubted the innate sincerity of Reagan. There was not the slightest suggestion in his make-up of hypocrisy or meanness of spirit. It was to this basic person that Trudeau appealed as tensions increased so rapidly and dangerously following the destruction by the Soviet air force of Korean Airlines flight 007 on September 1, 1983. Never in the months that followed did Trudeau encounter any unwillingness on the part of Reagan to receive the information that he conveyed to him or his proposals as they were presented. Derision, even denunciation, as expected, emanated from some of the ideologues and showboats in the Republican administration. Typically, however, these outbursts seemed not to disturb the president. That the hard-liners did not emerge as victorious is a tribute to the underlying humanism and optimistic demeanour of Reagan, as was evident in the final resolution of this crisis, a face-to-face meeting in Geneva in 1985 with General Secretary Mikhail Gorbachev. Much of the responsibility for the perilous sequence of events that followed the destruction of the civilian airliner rests necessarily on Reagan's thoughtless reactions and unsophisticated instincts. Much of the credit for the favourable outcome is surely his as well, however. Trudeau's endeavours to contribute positively to this outcome are described in Chapter Eight.

As 1984 began, the immediate neighbourhood had not changed so much as had the casts of characters on either side of the border. The recommendations of the Royal Commission on Economic Union and Development Prospects for Canada, chaired by Donald S. Macdonald, would set in train changes of immense purport when seized upon by the government of Prime Minister Brian Mulroney. The broader neighbourhood – across the Arctic and on the other side of the Pacific – was undergoing massive transformations, much of it either hidden from view or beyond the public's attention because of the drama of the Cold War and the hyperbole of the Reagan administration. Head's involvement by now was almost wholly absorbed in the broad North–South perspective of developing and industrialized countries through his engagement at IDRC. As he and Trudeau gazed south across the Canada–U.S. border, they realized that those in Congress who had responded so warmly to Trudeau's 1977 encouragement of a mutual rededication "to a global ethic of confidence in our fellow men" had largely been succeeded by persons with a quite distinctive outlook.[36]

This American view of the world catered to simplicity, passed off as old-fashioned values, and a "might is right" attitude that was pre-Hobbesian in its fierceness. To those who believed deeply, as we did, that the future of the human species would be overwhelmingly influenced by the attitudes and actions of the four-fifths of humankind who lived in the developing regions, the Reagan mindset was more than disturbing, it appeared to be seriously flawed and downright dangerous. In this respect, were the Reagan blindness to the reality of the human condition to prevail, the future well-being of Canadians as well as Americans would be placed in grievous jeopardy. That the immediate neighbourhood could not remove itself from the world beyond was our message from 1968 to 1984, and our even stronger belief today.

CHAPTER SEVEN

The Second World

I

In any catalogue of influential events of the twentieth century, the Communist Revolution of 1917 will likely rank as the most significant, though surely not the most constructive or the most enduring. The responses prompted by the promise of communism reverberate still. The energies marshalled and expended for and against the Communist ideology, and the postures assumed and acts undertaken by governments and individuals, were evident at one time or another in every region of the world.

Unlike the fascist dictatorships that were cataclysmic in their impact, but that were – after all – modern variations of a theme of dominance and advantage long familiar in human affairs, communism in its theories represented hope for the masses. It did not depend upon the personality of a single figure, but was founded upon intellectual premises as well considered and well articulated as those of any competing political philosophy. However distorted the theories of Engels and Marx became in their application by ruthless disciples, and however fallacious were some of their assumptions, this ideology properly commanded – and still commands – the respect of millions. Karl Marx reflected, albeit in revolutionary rhetoric, the same concerns about disparity of wealth and power and human dignity that have occupied social commentators from Socrates to Rawls. Tragically for tens of millions, however, Marx's concepts and admonitions were more often than not dishonestly seized and cruelly perverted by opportunistic practitioners all too prepared to rationalize their acts. Equally tragically, the underlying circumstances that gave rise to the fervour of the "masses" were misread and denied

by the nations of the West, an error which led to the East–West struggle that so shaped much of this century. Apprehension about that misunderstanding had been voiced by Professor Harold Laski of the
London School of Economics in the interwar period. "There was no
doubt in Laski's mind that unless an intellectual bridge was built
between the dogmatism of conservative capitalism and the collectiviz-
ing trends of the age, there would be a catastrophic age of terror and
revolutionary violence."[1] (The accuracy of that insight was a major
stimulus to each of us decades later as we surveyed an analogous circumstance: the growing gulf of indifference and misunderstanding in
the North at events in the South, issues addressed in Chapter Five.)

The post-Second World War competition prompted by the use of
communist militarism and expansionism gave birth to activities noble
and heinous, productive and wasteful, illuminating and dismal. In
many instances the balances and the verities are still far from certain.
Such were the consequences of the secretiveness and the fearfulness
that were so pervasive for so long, and which echo still in some places.
Among the ironies of this period was the selectivity employed by many
of those inspired by George Kennan as they responded to the pre-
science of his warnings about the Soviet Union, but disregarded his
plea for proportionality. Among the major errors that followed, as
recited by McGeorge Bundy, national security adviser to Presidents
Kennedy and Johnson, was the mistaken assumption by the United
States in 1950 of the existence of a global communist hegemony, and
the stupendous dedication of effort and expenditure that ensued in
order to counter the perceived but non-existent (in that form) threat.

In a struggle of such proportions, Canada could not be unaffected,
nor was it. The revelations of Igor Gouzenko in September 1945 were
interpreted as corroboration of the dishonesty and the power of a
threatening Soviet Union.[2] Canadians were among the first in the West
to be subject to the hysteria and disablement that followed, just as a
Canadian at the United Nations was among the first to receive the
verbal wrath of the intransigent and zealous Soviet government.[3]
Alarmed and uncertain, Canada abandoned for the time being its dedication to "common" security as anticipated in the fledgling United
Nations, and became one of the first advocates of a "collective" security system in the form of NATO. In subsequent years, as the Cold War

engendered ever more passionate reactions in the United States, Canada and Canadians seldom exhibited the same extremes in rhetoric or in policy. Notwithstanding the zeal exhibited by the counsel engaged in the royal commission inquiry into the allegations of Gouzenko,[4] Canada was never a participant in such excesses as the U.S. congressional hearings dominated by Senator Joseph McCarthy. Tragically, however, the poison of those hearings and the convictions of those embroiled in the murky worlds of espionage and counter-espionage crossed into this country and damaged irreparably the reputations and the lives of several Canadians.[5]

In circumstances of such vehemence, it was difficult for any Canadian government to define for itself an effective role that sought some insight into Soviet behaviour. As a member of NATO, Canada was privy to a good deal of intelligence about Soviet – and, by extension, Chinese and Cuban – nefarious activity. Canada was, as well, subject to the discipline of alliance undertakings and, often, attitudes. No postwar prime minister was prepared to undertake any major departures from orthodox alliance priorities, yet neither were any of them content to accept a monolithic interpretation of events. Limited commercial transactions in non-strategic goods were not regarded as inimical to the West's security and so, with the U.S.S.R. and the People's Republic of China, sales of wheat were negotiated and pursued. Yet in the mainstream of political contact, there was a deliberate reluctance to take any step that might be interpreted as conferring legitimacy upon the acts of the Soviet government.[6] This diffidence was partly a reflection of alliance attitudes, but partly as well a recognition of the strong feelings of Canadians of Eastern European origin who had watched with justifiable horror the occupation of their homelands and the reduction of their remaining relatives and neighbours to conditions of near slavery.

Canada's attitudes towards communism and the socialist countries reflected in part Canada's own experience. Canadian governments of all political persuasions had understood and supported the relevance and benefits of a mixed economy. State ownership of productive assets did not bring forth the kind of hypocritical response seen in American politicians of the postwar period. Canadians, too, understood the anguish and the anger that led to the 1919 Winnipeg General Strike and the 1949 Asbestos Strike, and were overwhelmingly supportive of government programs designed to transfer wealth from the better-off to the needy on both an individual and a regional scale. Finally, perhaps because they were more generally tolerant than their neighbours to the South, perhaps because they were more phlegmatic in their observations of human conduct, Canadians accepted a wide diversity of political parties; in vivid contrast to the United States, the Communist Party was not branded a criminal organization in Canada (any more than it was in most European countries).

In 1968, there remained considerable support for Prime Minister John Diefenbaker's refusal to join the U.S. economic embargo of Cuba, support not shaken by the 1962 missile crisis. There was a mood that ranged between scepticism and cynicism of the American "domino theory" of events in Southeast Asia; pride in the heroic contributions of Canadian servicemen and -women in the Korean conflict did not extend to the advocacy of any similar intervention in Vietnam, even though armed forces from Australia and New Zealand were there. There was evidence, too, that the common sense of Canadians was offended by the U.S.-led campaign in the United Nations to deny the reality of the People's Republic of China. Canadian visitors to the Soviet Union returned with horror stories, but ones related more to the backwardness and inefficiencies they encountered than to fears of a threatening military competence. Latent uncertainties and a real anger had erupted, however, as Soviet tanks crushed the Prague Spring earlier in the year, and the brutality of the Brezhnev Doctrine became evident.

Against this background of events and attitudes, each of us in 1968 believed that the time had come to face squarely the isolation of China, and to explore the possibilities of easing tensions in Canada's relationship with the Soviet Union. Each course of activity, we knew, would attract some form of criticism from the U.S. government, but each, we believed, represented the views of most Canadians (including the majority of the Canadian foreign-policy community), as well as being in the best interests of the world as a whole. The intention to seek a formula for recognition of the People's Republic of China was revealed in the foreign-policy paper released during the 1968 election.[7] Concerns about the intransigence of NATO policies towards the Soviet Union grew deeper in the course of the defence-policy review discussed in Chapter Three.

Any remaining beliefs in a communist hegemony should surely have evaporated following the tumultuous schism between China and the Soviet Union in the late sixties and the increase in tension between them over Soviet support for North Vietnam. A not-to-be-overlooked hazard for Canada, therefore, was the potential animosity of one or other of these countries as Canada sought to ease relations with both simultaneously. (Nor was this a theoretical concern. A factor that detracted from the hoped-for success of the visit to China by French President Georges Pompidou in 1973 was China's criticism of France's dedication to a policy of détente.) Nevertheless, a continuation of previous Canadian policies seemed to us not to reflect the opportunity at hand for constructive change, and happily there was little reluctance in cabinet to innovation. It was in Canada's interest, and seen to be consistent with Canadian traditions, to seek a more orderly state of world affairs, where tensions could be relieved and conflicts resolved through structured, non-violent means. Communication was the first step, more complex with respect to China, where there was no diplomatic presence, than with the Soviet Union, where Canada had a functioning embassy under the direction of the veteran and highly respected ambassador, Robert Ford.

II

Unlike any of his predecessors, or any member of his cabinet for that matter, Trudeau had travelled through China and had gained distinct impressions of circumstances there, some of which were recounted in the book which he and longtime friend Jacques Hébert wrote following his most recent trip in 1960.[8] In China, as in his private visit to the Soviet Union in 1952, Trudeau was struck by the sense of pride of many of those whom he met. Each society, no matter how extensive its shortcomings, was entitled, he believed, to be treated with courtesy and the respect demanded by international diplomatic protocol. If Canada were to be at all influential in the relations with either of these giant countries, it would be as a result of reason, not the flexing of any imagined muscle. Communications and exchanges, therefore, would have to be correct.

With respect to China, that was easier said than done. In 1968, the

People's Republic remained so withdrawn as a result of its own policies, and so isolated as a consequence of the policies of others, that the
apparently straightforward task of delivering a message to senior
Chinese authorities was a complicated challenge. It was literally easier
for a private citizen to obtain a visa to visit China than it was for most
governments to pass an official document through one of the few
channels open to them. The universal "post office" later to be available
to all governments – diplomatic missions at the United Nations – was
in 1968 still non-existent for the People's Republic of China. The Cold
War standoff between East and West denied membership to a number
of independent states on both sides of the divide created by suspicion:
the two Germanys, the two Koreas, the two Vietnams, and the People's
Republic of China.

Of these countries, the People's Republic of China was a special
case. In 1945, at San Francisco, the UN Charter was signed by the then-
government of China, the Kuomintang regime of Chiang Kai-shek.
China became a member of the General Assembly, as did all the fifty-
one Charter signatories. In addition, because of its wartime role, it
was named as a permanent member of the Security Council, entitled
to a veto on all important matters. For more than a decade, however,
a civil war had been raging between Chiang's Nationalists and Mao
Tse-tung's Communists. By 1949, the Communists were victorious,
and Mao proclaimed his party to be the legitimate government of
China; the defeated Nationalists fled to the island of Taiwan. From
this tiny offshore base, Chiang claimed to be the legitimate governor
of all China.

In similar contested circumstances, the international community has
long pursued an impartial policy of recognition of the effective government, irrespective of the willingness of any individual country to
enter into diplomatic relations with it. This practice, Mao had every
reason to expect, would lead in a reasonable period to the recognition
of his government as legitimate, and, by a similar process, to permit it
to occupy the seat of China in the United Nations. Alas, in one of the
strangest ironies of history, that was not to happen. In 1968, twenty
years following the revolution, the Beijing government was still ostra-
cized by many members of the international community, and denied
acceptance by the United Nations.

The standoff was influenced deeply by the insistence of each Chinese government, Nationalist and Communist, that it was the government of all China – mainland and offshore islands alike. Each vigorously resisted any suggestion that there existed two Chinas, with two governments, each worthy of independent recognition. It had been this assertion by Beijing that it was the sole legitimate representative of all China, including Taiwan, that caused such concern in the United States. There, the virulent opposition to communism was reinforced by the fear that, at some point, the Mao regime would invade Taiwan and endeavour to annex it by force.

In this dispute, Canada was not willing to take sides. After twenty years of Kuomintang government, no matter how dictatorial and brutal, there was no question in our minds that it was effectively in place in Taiwan. If Canada were to enter into diplomatic relations with the People's Republic, therefore, this seemingly intractable situation would have to be resolved, or at least sidestepped. In 1968, there was no acceptable formula at hand, but Trudeau felt the effort to find one was justified. With a mainland population representing one-quarter of the human race, and the potential to be an immense influence in international affairs, it was not in anyone's interest that this anomaly continue. The Chinese were a dignified, accomplished race. To fail to recognize the undoubted successes of the communist regime would be foolhardy.

Not all Canadians agreed. There was opposition by some to the extension of any legitimacy to the Communists, associated in some instances with a fear that a People's Republic Embassy in Ottawa would be the centre of espionage and other clandestine activities detrimental to Canadian interests. A champion of this anti-communism school by 1968 was John Diefenbaker. He purported to speak on behalf of those in Taiwan who resisted Mao and his followers and who extolled the free-enterprise system there, which was already proving profitable to some Canadian businesses. Within the sizeable Canadian Chinese community, largely of Cantonese origin, allegiance ran strongly in favour of continued ties with Taiwan. "Continued," because the Chinese Embassy in Ottawa represented the Nationalist Government of Chiang Kai-shek. Should some agreement be reached with the Beijing government, ties with Taiwan would undoubtedly be severed, and that embassy closed. The opposition of these groups was understandable, but was far from influential in deterring the government or in gaining widespread public support for their position.

In the absence of any obvious channel of communication, External Affairs recommended that the first message expressing a desire to discuss the possibility of mutual recognition be delivered through the People's Republic Embassy in Stockholm.[9] In mid-February 1969 – following some toing and froing – Canadian Ambassador Arthur Andrew, a senior and highly regarded career foreign-service officer,[10] met officially with the People's Republic chargé d'affaires to inform him of Canada's desire to begin discussions with respect to recognition. Some six weeks later, the Chinese indicated they were prepared to talk, and suggested that Stockholm be the venue. The first fully substantive meeting took place on May 20. For the purpose of the negotiations, a team of China "experts" would fly out as required from Ottawa. The leader of this group was John Fraser, a Chinese linguist.

Over the course of the next year and a half, the discussions proceeded at a desultory pace, with no indication by the Chinese that they were at all anxious about the time or the form of the outcome. Trudeau understood the Chinese psyche well enough to realize that no pressure to hasten the process would be of the slightest effect. Because of the innovative nature of the negotiations,[11] considerable interest was taken in them both within and without Canada. Canada's friends requested that they be kept informed through diplomatic channels. In the House of Commons, the government was called upon frequently by Diefenbaker and others to explain what was going on. Very early on in the negotiations, in response to a question from Robert Stanfield, Trudeau offered the rationale with respect to the extent of territorial sovereignty that was finally accepted by the Chinese. On May 30, 1969, he said:[12]

> ... recognition of the government does not necessarily mean the recognition of all its territorial claims. . . . I think that if a country wishes to recognize Canada we would not demand that it recognize, for example, our sovereignty in the Arctic.

Two months later, Mitchell Sharp repeated this explanation in the House:[13]

> We have not asked and do not ask the Government of the P.R.C. to endorse the position of the Government of Canada on our territorial limits as a condition to agreement to establish diplomatic relations. To do so might cast doubts on the extent of our sovereignty. We do not think it would be appropriate, nor would it be in accordance with international usage, that Canada should be asked to endorse the position of the Government of the P.R.C. on the extent of its territorial sovereignty. To challenge that position would, of course, also be inappropriate.

Some fifteen months later, on October 10, in the course of the seventeenth meeting, this rationale would emerge in the joint statement revealing the agreement to establish diplomatic relations.[14] "The Chinese Government reaffirms that Taiwan is an inalienable part of the territory of the People's Republic of China. The Canadian Government takes note of this position of the Chinese Government."

Steps began immediately to appoint ambassadors and staff, and to pursue the multitude of tasks inherent in the establishment of new embassies. For each country, these were time-consuming and often frustrating tasks, yet on the Canadian side, certainly, undertaken with a considerable sense of adventure. Canada's first ambassador was Ralph Collins, chosen because of his seniority (as assistant undersecretary of state for external affairs, who had served as Canadian ambassador in South Africa) and his Chinese experience and linguistic competence. Collins was one of several senior foreign-service officers who had been children of Canadian missionaries and who possessed an invaluable fluency in Mandarin. Two such others would follow him in the normal rotation: John Small and Arthur Menzies.

Ralph Collins had been the department's nominee for the Beijing post, and was enthusiastically endorsed by Trudeau. He had served in China as a professional diplomat during the Second World War as a staff member in the Canadian Legation headed by Gen. Victor Odlum. At that time, in Chungching, he had honed his language skills and understanding of the Chinese culture. Collins had been the senior External

Affairs officer in the Canadian delegations to the London and
Singapore Commonwealth Conferences and had proved to be an astute
adviser, as well as one possessed of a wealth of experience and a
delightful, dry sense of humour. He would interpret with balance and
insight the complex and closely held Chinese scene, as well as be a
stout defender of Canada's position and interests. As expected, Collins
quickly established the contacts in the Chinese government necessary
for his mission, and gained the respect of all he met.

The Chinese had acknowledged the importance they attached to
their first new embassy in the West in more than twenty years by
appointing one of their most senior officials, Huang Hua, who would
later become foreign minister. In Ottawa, Huang conducted himself
with courtesy and dignity, and did much to dispel the still-existent suspicions of covert activities held by some. In the course of his tour of
duty, and on many occasions later in New York, Beijing, and elsewhere,
Huang gained the respect and the friendship of each of us. Neither
country could have chosen their first emissary better; the contributions
of these two were seminal to the functioning relationship that developed between Canada and China.

Three years had passed since Canada announced its intention to
seek diplomatic relations with the People's Republic. In that interval
the foreign-policy review had been concluded, referring to the China
exercise in the following terms:[15]

It is evident that there can be no lasting peace or stability in the
Pacific or in the world without the cooperation and participation
of China. Achieving this participation and cooperation will be a
slow and difficult process, given the ideological limitations that
govern Chinese foreign policy combined with their almost total
lack of historical experience in dealing with other countries on an
equal basis. Nor has China's isolation been entirely self-imposed.
The importance for world peace and stability of ending this isolation is so great that the Government decided to enter into negotiations with Peking for the establishment of diplomatic relations
in the hope that Canada would be able to make a contribution
towards bringing China into a more constructive relationship
with the world community.

By early 1971, the earlier American opposition to the Canadian initiative had long since evaporated and, unknown to the world, President Nixon was preparing for his own dramatic reversal of U.S. policy. Much to our satisfaction, the Canadian formula, or variations of it, were serving as the means for the opening of diplomatic relations between China and a number of other countries. At the United Nations, the vexing "credentials" question was resolved, permitting a People's Republic representative to take the place of China in the General Assembly and the Security Council in the autumn of 1971. Long before the triumphant Nixon visit, the twenty-two-year-old American-led isolation of China had been overcome. To our immense pride, the honourable means of doing so had been considerably stimulated and assisted through Canadian efforts.

This was demonstrative evidence of the effectiveness of Canadian foreign policy; the accomplishment was to the undoubted advantage of Canada but, more importantly, to the entire international community. A China open to the world would be subject to the same diplomatic persuasion as other countries, and could be expected over time to adjust its political, economic, and social practices to bring them into harmony with international norms. Of equal importance, this ancient civilization was given the opportunity to share its accomplishments with others, and to reap the recognition it deserved for uniting a disparate population and setting in motion policies to deliver health care and education to hundreds of millions of persons who had never been exposed to either since the Sun Yat-sen revolution of 1911.

Pleased as we were by all this, the Canadian perhaps more joyous than any other was Chester Ronning, a retired foreign-service officer who had been a tireless advocate of Canadian recognition for many years. Like Ralph Collins, Ronning was a missionary child born in China and a Chinese speaker. He had served as Canadian chargé d'affaires in the Canadian Legation in Nanking in the interval following the Second World War, and there had established a warm relationship with a rising young Chinese official, Huang Hua. He would in all likelihood have been named ambassador at that point had Canada elevated the status of the mission, as was considered following the assumption of power by the Communist government. But Canada had hesitated, unlike Britain and France, and soon faced the impasse of the

Korean War, where Chinese troops intervened to turn back the UN forces as they approached the Chinese border. The legation was closed, and Ronning returned to Canada.

Chester Ronning's next foreign posting was as Canadian ambassador to Norway, where he was a great favourite because of his own Nordic background.[16] It was in Oslo that Trudeau first met him and became exposed to his wisdom and charm. Head's involvement with Ronning began somewhat later, when King Gordon introduced the two at the University of Alberta. Ronning had retired to Camrose, but travelled widely, including in China, and was a popular public speaker. Tall, with a shock of white hair and an attractive twinkle in his eye, Ronning was an engaging person. He was possessed of a sparkling sense of humour and a passionate dedication for justice. The marriage of one of his daughters to Seymour Topping, a journalist of the *New York Times*, gave Ronning entrée to the editorial board of the United States' most influential newspaper. Almost single-handedly, he was successful in encouraging the *Times* to advocate an American opening to China, a prodigious accomplishment in a period of fierce U.S. opposition to the Mao regime.[17]

In Alberta, and later in Ottawa, Ronning would confer frequently with Head, almost always discussing China. In the course of the later conversations, following recognition, Ronning emphasized the importance that the Chinese would attach to an official visit from the prime minister of Canada. "Do not delay pursuing an invitation," he advised, "to do so would be interpreted as indifference or lack of deep respect." The moment to act would present itself in unexpected circumstances. It would take the form of a tour of Canada by Chinese table-tennis players, in a sense a mirror image of the tour of China by American players in 1971.

The table-tennis demonstration in the early spring of 1972 was treated by the Chinese and all others with the solemnity of a formal diplomatic event. Accompanying the team were several senior Chinese government representatives. Head was one of the Canadian guests witnessing the extraordinary skill of the players, while engaging in the simultaneous serious discussions that the Chinese clearly desired, as if repeated protestations of the friendship between our respective peoples was the purpose of the occasion. Slowly, the conversation became more focused, and Head was told how welcome Prime Minister Trudeau would be were he to visit China. In the cautious, obscurantist style employed by Chinese diplomats of the period, this could only be interpreted as an important signal. Head replied that he was confident the prime minister would accept a renewed invitation to visit were one officially to be forthcoming. Quickly this response was translated for the recently arrived Chinese ambassador, Yao Kuang, a non-English speaker who had succeeded Huang Hua following the latter's appointment as Chinese representative to the United Nations. The ambassador's agitation suggested strongly that this exchange had been a major objective of the table-tennis tour.

Shortly thereafter a formal invitation arrived in Ottawa, and was formally accepted. No thought could be given immediately to a date, because of the imminence of the 1972 election. In the months thereafter, a time convenient to Trudeau was chosen – October 1973 – long enough following the Ottawa Commonwealth heads of government meeting in August to permit the necessary priorities to be settled and briefing books to be prepared. As was customary, responsibility for organizing the trip and assembling the accompanying members of the delegation fell to Head. The task of selecting such delegations was never easy because of Trudeau's insistence that the total number, including himself, never exceed twenty-one without his express consent. Certain functions demanded obvious inclusions – an RCMP security liaison officer (two if Margaret Trudeau was travelling, as she did to China); a PMO press-office contingent of five to respond to the needs of accompanying journalists; two secretaries to deal with meeting notes, communiqués, and the like; interpreters; a senior member of Parliament; and representatives of the government departments most involved. (These latter were necessarily chosen on the basis of their intimate knowledge of the issues, not their seniority.)

This trip, more than any previous one, whetted the desires of public servants and PMO staffers, yet the limit of twenty-one remained firm. There was simply no room for non-essential persons of any kind in the official party. Journalists were every bit as desirous of travelling on this occasion, and their swollen number, plus an extra-large aircrew in view of the lengthy trip, resulted in a very full airplane. A special passenger, carried as a courtesy to the Chinese, was their recently arrived ambassador, Chang Wen-chin.

A consensus was quickly reached that the visit should acknowledge the immense reputation enjoyed in China by the legendary Norman Bethune. Health-care and medical services would be an important element of the discussions, and should feature in the selection of gifts, an aspect of any visit that is held in high regard by Asian societies as a symbol of seriousness, as is the composition of the delegation. Included in the party, therefore, was the deputy minister of national health and welfare, Dr. Maurice Leclerc, who was formerly dean of medicine at the University of Sherbrooke. Some pioneering surgical instruments, designed by Bethune during his days as a clinician and medical researcher in Quebec, were located and mounted on handsome display plaques; a modern, Canadian-manufactured operating table was taken as well. The Bethune mementoes were well received. The operating table, intended to impress the Chinese with the prowess of Canadian suppliers, proved to be a bad choice. This glittering example of high technology, dependent upon a steady supply of electrical power for hydraulic and other functions, was simply far in excess of the rudimentary standards of Chinese surgical wards in the early seventies. High-technology it may have been; appropriate technology it certainly was not. It was destined to be stored for an indefinite period.

Yet another issue challenged us, one which grew out of all proportion to its importance and, in the way of the world, threatened to assume the image of a symbol by which the success of the visit would be measured within Canada. The issue was a panda bear.

Two prominent visitors to China had recently returned home with pairs of rare pandas, which quickly became the most popular features of the London and Washington zoos. If Britain and the United States were so favoured, then surely so would be Canada! That speculation quickly launched an outburst of public-relations campaigning made possible by the fact that, in Canada, unlike the other two countries, there was no zoo in the capital city. Quickly did the contenders step forward: Toronto, Granby, Calgary – the list lengthened by the day, supported by local newspaper campaigns. Were all the candidates to be rewarded, the scant supply of this endangered species would clearly be inadequate. Perhaps sensing this, the Chinese never did offer us one of these attractive creatures. We decided to be prepared, however, and so took along with us a pair of beavers – Canada's most identifiable, though certainly not endangered, animals – to be offered as a possible exchange.[18] These were accepted with grace by the Chinese, but with no evidence of the excitement that pandas would have elicited among Canadians.

The list of topics that we wished to discuss with the Chinese was of formidable length, one that would challenge the time available for formal exchanges – and especially so because of the need for translation, always a time-consuming exercise. Health-related issues were high on the list, among them the possibility of entering into some form of arrangement that would permit formal exchanges of experts to explore the reciprocal advantages of modern and traditional preventive and therapeutic techniques, as well as science and technology matters generally.[19] Family reunification was important to many Canadians – most particularly, perhaps, to those still favouring Taiwan – whose relatives in China were not able to obtain exit visas. Commercial ties would be discussed, seeking to ensure the continued availability of China to Canadian wheat, potash, and sulphur, but examining as well the opportunities available to penetrate this vast potential market with value-added Canadian export goods and services. We sought information and assurances about a range of Chinese political and social activities of interest to Canadians, including freedom of religious practice and choice of educational opportunity. The Chinese interpretation of several international situations was of interest to us: the Vietnam War; the law of the sea negotiations just under way; nuclear proliferation; and China's views of the Soviet Union and its policies.[20]

As much of interest to us as the actual responses to Trudeau's questions, or the voluntary Chinese interventions, was the tone and style of the Chinese interlocutor. This was Premier Chou En-lai, known to us almost intimately before the trip from all that had been written or said of him. In 1973, few international figures were so well known. Unlike the often-mysterious, and now-ailing, Mao Tse-tung, Chou appeared much more transparent to the Occidental mind. His exposure to the outside world had been considerably more extensive than had Mao's, and rich descriptive accounts were available from knowledgeable observers of his travels, his student experiences, his encounters with other heads of government and diplomats. Long before we met him face-to-face, we were aware of his reputation for dignity, for courtesy, for sagacity. Never before or after had either of us experienced quite the same sense of anticipation at meeting a foreign leader. On our arrival at Beijing airport, as we gazed out the windows from the front cabin, we watched this slim, ageing figure approach the door of the aircraft almost shyly, pausing there in order to lead the Canadian official party to the waiting motorcade through a formation of hundreds upon hundreds of gaily dressed Chinese dancers waving pennants and flourishing garlands. Chou spoke English diffidently, French with more confidence, but utilized Chinese on all formal occasions. He was an exemplary host.

In the formal conversations the two sides sat opposite one another across a narrow table, nine to a side, Trudeau opposite Chou and, as was our practice, Head to his immediate left and the Canadian Ambassador John Small next to him on his right. The other members of the party, including MP Charles Caccia and Trudeau's principal secretary Martin O'Connell, stretched out on either side. The composition of the Chinese delegation represented all the complexity of the ugly and confusing Cultural Revolution, still raging throughout the country. Wang Hong-wen, later to be identified as one of the hated "Gang of Four," was at the table; so was the pixie-like Deng Xiao-ping, then enjoying the second of his remarkable series of political incarnations. There also was the urbane and fluently English-speaking Chinese ambassador to Canada, Chang Wen-chin, who had replaced Yao Kuang shortly prior to our departure for China, an intended signal from Beijing of the renewed seriousness with which the People's Republic government viewed the bilateral relationship. On the Canadian side, Trudeau would on occasion turn to one or other of the officials to provide some detail or to respond to the specifics requested in one of Chou's questions. A number of these persons had travelled with him on other official visits, and he had considerable confidence in them: Bob Joyce, Tom Burns, Frank Petrie, Michel Dupuy.[21]

For the Chinese, only Chou En-lai spoke. Behind Chou, however, was a second rank of officials. One of these was his talented interpreter, Nancy Tang, whose effortless idiomatic vocabulary and North American speech inflections revealed her education at the University of

California. The others, clearly, were the experts, as distinct from the political figures at the table. Each had volumes of material – tables, texts, maps – which at appropriate moments would be passed forward to Chou for his reference. Assuming that these persons were all members of his personal staff, Head asked him on one occasion when they were standing alone chatting how many persons were employed in the Chinese equivalent of the Prime Minister's Office. Given the size of the population and the central nature of the government, he expected a figure in the high hundreds at the very least. "Two and a half" was Chou's response. "The half is a loyal adviser too elderly to work full days, but too useful to retire fully."

The banquet offered by Canada to respond formally to the Chinese hospitality – important for protocol – took place in one of the salons of the immense Great Hall of the People on Tiananmen Square. The date was extraordinarily propitious: October 13. It was the third anniversary of the agreement to enter into diplomatic relations. It was as well thirteen years to the day following Trudeau's last visit to China. The seriousness of this occasion called for a formal exchange of toasts, really of short speeches. Translating for Trudeau this evening, as at the Chinese banquet two nights earlier, was a young woman from Kapuskasing, Ontario, now a foreign-service officer, by the name of Gilliane Lapointe. Her extraordinary fluency in Mandarin drew praise from the Chinese and made us all extremely proud of her.

In the course of the visit, each of us had ample opportunity to converse casually and at length with Chou – in pauses at formal functions, while seated with him at the numerous banquets in the Great Hall of the People or elsewhere, or while travelling, for he accompanied the Canadian party by rail from Beijing to Luoyang in the first stage of the elaborate itinerary carefully put in place by our hosts. Our firm impression was of a simple person, deeply committed to the communist cause, but not at all with the aim of achieving personal power, one who was almost deferential to all those around him, whether Chinese villagers or foreign guests, a decent human being who attracted respect because of his person, not his position. (Three years later, on the occasion of Chou's death, the spontaneous and widespread outpouring of grief on the part of masses of Chinese citizens nationwide amply confirmed to us the sense of reverence which we had observed in those about him in the dark days of 1973.)

That year there still existed an aura of mystery that permeated this extraordinary society, a mystery that had only gathered strength over the centuries since Marco Polo brought back his tales of wonder and his descriptions of incomprehensible accomplishment. For us, part of the mystery took the form of the involvement in our visit of the mythical Chairman Mao. Would the "Great Helmsman" request that Trudeau be presented to him? No promises had been made, and understandably. As Premier Chou En-lai was the official host, Mao as head of state was not bound in protocol to make an appearance. Second, as everyone knew, he was ill; the extent of his condition was referred to in every rumour that swirled around our ears. All this notwithstanding, there was a sense on the part of the entire Canadian party that a measure of the trip – perhaps even of the bilateral relationship itself – took the form of a face-to-face meeting. As the days in Beijing passed one by one without any reference to an audience with Mao, the tension grew. And then it happened, as inscrutably as can happen only in China. A quiet word by Chou in Trudeau's ear late one afternoon; a limousine ride through the Forbidden City; a private meeting with the chairman in his home, in the presence of only a handful of others – all Chinese: Nancy Tang, Chou, and Wang.

Photographs were taken through the curious but effective wide-angled camera lenses employed by the Chinese,[22] and there ensued a fascinating if not stimulating conversation of approximately thirty minutes that revealed Mao to be knowledgeable of Canada to an unexpected degree. He was patently unwell, however, and tired quickly. It was clear to Trudeau that Mao remained leader, but only symbolically. The vital, intellectual force of the Chinese government rested in Chou En-lai, the loyal yet moderating lieutenant who represented the aspirations and commanded the affections of the vast majority of the Chinese people.

In the meticulous Chinese fashion, every hour of each day was scheduled with activity: in the evenings, formal banquets in the Great Hall of the People; a patriotic performance of the Peking Opera; the overnight train journey to Luoyang, where Chou strolled with the party through the magnificent Longmen caves; the motorcade to nearby Chengchow (Zhengzhou) to view the archaeological discoveries; the flight south to Guilin (the first group of foreigners to be allowed to travel there since the revolution); and a boat trip on the scenic Li River. Prior to our departure from Beijing, Chou surprised us with a very special lunch at the Summer Palace. Present among the Chinese was, as expected, Deng Xiao-ping. Invited unexpectedly as special guests were several Canadians visiting China at that time: Arthur Erickson, Paul and Eileen Lin, Chester Ronning, and Moshe Safdie. Our food was served on exquisite porcelain dinnerware that had belonged to the Dowager Empress.

In Luoyang, the Communist Party practice of elevating the local party secretary was observed. This gentleman acted as host at the official lunch, moving Chou En-lai to second place in the Chinese protocol list and seating him between Trudeau and Head. As the party drove through the countryside and the city streets of the interior, thousands of Chinese lined the sides of the roads, staring at these strangers as though we were aliens from outer space. For many of them, who had likely never before seen Occidentals, we might as well have been just that. From the absence of automobiles in Beijing to the practice of human-drawn produce carts in the country, China showed itself to be clearly a country of modest means. We were a break in the daily monotony. Chou did not accompany Trudeau south; that task was assumed by Deng Xiao-ping, an indication of his high ranking in the mysterious power structure.

As we transferred to our own aircraft at Guangzhou preparatory to the long flight home, we began our assessment of the success of the visit. In Trudeau's statement to the House of Commons on our return, he described the basic posture he assumed in the formal talks:[23]

I said . . . that in my belief, the true measurement of national greatness was found not in military might or in political hegemony but in the willingness of a country to recognize the importance of individual welfare, human dignity and a sense of personal accomplishment and fulfillment.

Later in that same address, in an endeavour to place in perspective the emergence of this great nation into full membership in the international community, he said:[24]

It has not been the vastness of the Pacific that has acted as a barrier between Canada and China. The gulf has been found all too often in the minds of those of us who are unwilling to recognize the magnitude of one of the most significant revolutions in the history of the world and the extension of basic human amenities to hundreds of millions of persons to whom they had been denied for millennia.

In sum, we were reasonably certain that the Chinese leadership understood and appreciated the distinctiveness of Canada and its policies. No criticism was made of our earlier decision to withdraw from the nuclear-strike role in NATO or the reduction in number of Canadian forces stationed there, as France had been rebuked for its apparent easing of military pressures on the Soviet Union's European flank. Appreciation was voiced of Canada's supervisory commission role in Indochina and, certainly, for its support of the People's Republic claim to the Chinese seat at the United Nations. No special relationship was tendered, nor had one been sought. It was clear that the self-confidence and resolve of this proud people would be the critical factors in its choice of its own future. Seek good relations with other countries, China certainly would; function in the international community in a non-hegemonic fashion, we were reasonably certain; follow its own independent timetable according to its own self-interest, we had no doubt. This immense society, never before effectively governed in a unified fashion, so desperately poor that a daily concern was the potential impact of starvation and plague and tempest, was seized with problems of a kind and a strength virtually unknown in Canada. For decades to come, its primary efforts would be to raise the standard of living of its people and to create some sense of nationhood; a daunting task even for a people as disciplined and resourceful as the Chinese.

On the eve of an unknown succession in leadership, all this represented a challenge of heroic proportions, yet with no hero in sight and no apparent appetite in the people for another Mao. For all China's seeming fragility, however, the two of us shared in common the unshakeable belief that this country would in future become one of the two or three most influential in the world. For that reason it must not be allowed to assume that it was without friends, or without responsibility to the international community at large. Canada's influence, as always, was limited, but it should continue to be exerted with that future in mind.

As is the diplomatic practice, Trudeau had extended an invitation to Chou En-lai to visit Canada and, as was the practice, the invitation was accepted without a date being set. The return visit of a Chinese prime minister to Canada would not occur until 1984, however. In the interval, Mao Tse-tung died, and the cataclysmic aftermath of his passing, in the form of the Gang of Four, erupted and was resolved. Chou's own death, and the spontaneous, widespread outpouring of grief on the part of ordinary Chinese – contrary to the Creon-like insistence of the authorities – contributed to the passage from the Mao era into the untested waters of a collective leadership. Deng Xiao-ping, who had disappeared once again in the Gang of Four era, re-emerged, even though shyly at first, remaining until the time of writing as the linkage to the magic of Chou. Zhao Zi-yang emerged as premier in 1980, and it was he who responded to the much earlier invitation. His 1984 visit was not spectacular, but was important nevertheless, and provided the occasion for Zhao and Trudeau to renew acquaintance. They had met in Chengdu in 1979 when Trudeau was in China on a private visit, one which would include Tibet.

Chinese premiers are not in the custom of travelling widely or frequently, but Zhao was nevertheless at ease in his role. By now, much of the earlier nervousness of the Chinese with respect to Taiwan had subsided. The world overwhelmingly regarded the People's Republic as the sole legitimate government of China; Taiwan was seen for what it was, a harsh dictatorship with a burgeoning economy based on capitalist principles. In Canada we expected no hostility to the visit from any source and experienced none.[25] China continued, after all, to be one of Canada's most important wheat purchasers and was slowly developing as a reliable supplier of low-cost manufactured goods suitable for the Canadian market. Zhao appealed to those who met him as relaxed and comfortable in his office, more outgoing in his manner than had been the preceding generation and less hesitant in his embrace of the unfamiliar. This reaching out would prove to be his undoing in 1989 as he sought to form a bond with the rebellious students in Tiananmen Square.

Still another dimension to the Canada–China relationship took form in the eighties. China in its pride had studiously refused to accept any foreign aid as it steadfastly pursued its own development agenda. Some help, often in the form of turnkey construction projects, was delivered by the Chinese to other developing countries, but nothing was sought or accepted in return. A quite unexpected departure from this practice had suddenly taken place in the late seventies, when a decision was made to seek technical development assistance from multilateral, but not bilateral, organizations. The UN Development Program (UNDP) was duly consulted and so, to Head's surprised delight, was the International Development Research Centre (IDRC). Assistance was requested of IDRC in the form of specialized computer information systems to organize libraries and research archives. Head was willing to respond positively, but only if the Chinese agreed to transfer to other developing countries, through the IDRC mechanism if appropriate, agricultural and health-care techniques that the Chinese had perfected. Written exchanges on these points continued until 1980, when a formal negotiation took place in Beijing and a Memorandum of Understanding was signed. Leery of the tentacles of the Chinese bureaucracy, Head proposed that the Chinese nominate as their cooperating agency their major scientific body.

And so the agreement was signed with the State Science and Technology Commission (SSTC), whose chairman was Vice-Premier and State Councillor Fang Yi. At a formal reception in the Great Hall of the People, Fang assured Head that IDRC's scientist-to-scientist methodology would be respected without interference. And so it was, even increasing in intimacy when Fang was succeeded as commissioner by State Councillor Song Jian. The senior levels of persons supervising this arrangement guaranteed the absence of the kind of bureaucratic intricacies that would befall all bilateral programs, including CIDA's, when they were later introduced under the aegis of a ministry – one giant step junior to the powerful commissions. In terms of scale, the IDRC activities were a fraction of the size of those of CIDA, but of extraordinary influence. In recognition of that influence, the state council approved the conferring upon Head in 1990 of an honorary university doctorate degree, one of only thirty-one conferred in the almost half-century since the 1949 revolution to non-Chinese, and the only one to a Canadian.

Trudeau would return to China once more as prime minister, in 1984, as part of his peace initiative. The courtesy and seriousness with which he was received were as pronounced as on the first visit in 1973. Premier Zhao Zi-yang greeted him as an old friend and offered his full support to the proposal to reduce nuclear tension. Deng Xiao-ping received him for substantive discussions.

In the period between 1968 and 1984, there occurred no major reverses or crises in Canadian–Chinese relations. (Tensions over such issues as the Montreal Olympics, and seemingly endless frustration relating to the construction of embassy premises in Beijing, were part of the sometimes unpleasant but not unexpected nature of international life.) There were several reasons for this. For one, the relationship was in its early stages, and so had not developed an intense network of linkages that were subject to tension and severance. That same newness meant that, for the most part, there was no baggage of historic claim and counterclaim, of imagery to be overcome, or reputations to be righted.[26] Finally, Canada dealt with China on a bilateral basis, not through the mechanism of a multilateral military structure, and so was not caught up in the crosscurrents so associated with alliance policies. Canada's relations with the Soviet Union in the same period were, by contrast, subject to each of these three categories of circumstance, and, not surprisingly, the Canada–U.S.S.R. bilateral record in that same sixteen-year period reflected considerably more turbulence, as it had in the decades prior to 1968. Yet the difficulties, when they came, were increasingly negotiated satisfactorily, and the cooperation led to meaningful advantage.

III

Canada's relationship with the Soviet Union over the years, while certainly more eventful than that with China, nevertheless tended to be episodic rather than constant or predictable. Some of those episodes had bordered on the bizarre, as with the extraordinary expedition of Vilhjalmur Stefansson, who in 1921 journeyed deeply into the Arctic wilderness to lay claim for Canada to Wrangel Island, eight hundred kilometres northwest of Nome, Alaska, and unquestionably within the Soviet sector. (The "claim" had not been authorized by the Canadian government, and quickly led to denunciations from the Soviet Union and a comic-opera sequence of statements in the House of Commons by ministers first supporting the claim, then rejecting it.[27])

In a little-acknowledged episode, some four thousand Canadian soldiers were sent to Archangel, Murmansk, and Vladivostok as participants in the ill-advised and unsuccessful Siberian expedition of the British government in the winter of 1918-19. The expedition's aim was to assist the Russian government in its resistance against the Bolshevist forces.[28] Later, during the Second World War, Canadian seamen were among those heroic forces who defied Nazi submarines as they transported desperately needed supplies into the Soviet Arctic port of Murmansk. Extraordinary acts, all of them, unknown in their entirety to most Canadians and Soviets alike.

By 1968, the Canadian image of the Soviet Union was shaped almost entirely by harsh events and equally harsh allegations, even though moderated by the warming breezes of détente: the fearful threat of Soviet military aggression, either in the form of an advance into Western Europe or a nuclear attack upon North America; the horrifying accounts of Stalin's internal excesses, as revealed in Khrushchev's remarkable accounts to the Soviet parliament and in Solzhenitsyn's chilling novels; persecutions of Jews and Ukrainian dissidents, of considerable distress to large numbers of Canadians; and the still-reverberating echoes of Gouzenko's accounts of Soviet perfidy. This did not create a picture of an attractive neighbour. A neighbour, nevertheless, it was, and one that Trudeau was determined to assess and deal with in a realistic fashion.

The first opportunity to do so occurred in the course of the defence-policy review, as described earlier. The second, and partly coincidental, occasion took the form of the foreign-policy review. In *Foreign Policy for Canadians*, the government spoke of the Soviet Union in the following language:[29]

Canada . . . has a substantial, and growing, interest in developing its relations with the Communist countries of Eastern Europe, not only because of the benefits of increased trade, scientific and technological cooperation and cultural exchanges with those countries but also because of the contribution it can thus make to détente. The prospects for such cooperation are particularly good with the Soviet Union, with which Canada shares the experience of being an Arctic country. There is no doubt that the improved climate of East–West relations and the accompanying growth in East–West contacts and exchanges have enhanced the practical opportunities for Canada to pursue those objectives.

An early occasion to speak direct to the Soviet leadership about issues of this kind presented itself even prior to the completion of the review process. Andrei Gromyko, the veteran foreign minister, had accepted with alacrity an invitation to visit Ottawa that was extended to him by Mitchell Sharp, and arranged a trip in conjunction with his attendance at a session of the UN General Assembly in early autumn 1969. Shortly following his participation in the "leaders'" debate and the round of consultations so valuable to foreign ministers on this annual occasion, he flew up to Ottawa. It was the first-ever visit to Canada by a Soviet official of his rank, a vivid reflection of the low level of attention paid to the bilateral relationship by each country.[30] Gromyko's reputation as a hard-line survivor had been well earned, beginning with his long apprenticeship as a career diplomat. By 1969, he had been in his challenging position of foreign minister for twelve years, serving Nikita Khrushchev and Leonid Brezhnev. He was one of the grand masters of the international diplomatic game, representing the interests of the U.S.S.R. so ably that he and his country had become indistinguishable in the eyes of outside observers.[31]

In Ottawa, Gromyko was at his charming best; a gracious, witty guest, who was able to defend the position of the U.S.S.R. effectively and effortlessly. His principal interlocutor was of course his counterpart, Mitchell Sharp, but his discussions with Trudeau were much more than a courtesy. They explored together the international scene, as well as the state of bilateral relations. They agreed that more effort was required on the part of each government if stereotypes were to be erased and some progress recorded in the reduction of irritants and the recording of benefits. Trudeau was much impressed by Gromyko. He found him an attractive personality, one of obvious intelligence, who spoke his mind forcefully, yet without giving offence. There was no evidence of posturing or of ideological cant in his remarks; no small talk either, of the kind that diplomats must practise on occasion simply in order to maintain lines of communication when there is nothing substantive that can be said. One welcome message that Gromyko conveyed was an invitation to Trudeau from Prime Minister Alexei Kosygin: "Please come at your early convenience." A date attractive to both leaders was shortly thereafter identified and preparations for the visit began.

Trade was one of the few existing bilateral activities, and so it commanded attention in our preparations for the trip. Trade Minister Jean-Luc Pepin had been to Moscow earlier in the year and had concluded an agreement on cooperation in the industrial applications of science and technology. Trudeau would encourage the Soviets to think more broadly. He would take with him as a gift to his host that ubiquitous Canadian engineering marvel, a Bombardier snowmobile.

As with China, wheat was a major Canadian export item. Canada's desire was to maintain its markets for non-manufactured goods such as wheat, and to increase sales of value-added products. The Soviet economy was in a better position to absorb items of this nature than was China's; equally, it was able to produce goods that the Soviets wished to sell to Canada in light of the bilateral balance-of-payments deficit in the current account between the two countries. These Soviet manufactured items generally found little favour among Canadian consumers, however, for – apart from staples such as vodka or caviar – they tended either to be of unattractive design or undependable quality. A nation dedicated to serving heavy industry and the needs of a powerful military machine was not the most flexible of trading partners.

Nevertheless, there were opportunities on both sides, and the attention given to the trade issues by the leaders would have some modest results. A Calgary entrepreneur by the name of Bruce Nodwell, who had developed heavy-duty, all-terrain tracked vehicles, suitable for muskeg and snow, had established a firm foothold and made a number of sales.[32] The Soviets would in due course enlarge their Canadian customer base for their superb machine tools, and would successfully bid for custom-made turbine blades on a large hydro-electric project. Later, the Lada would appear in Canadian streets – to mixed reviews – as a low-price, no-frills family automobile.

An aspect of the relationship that gripped the imagination of both countries, and that offered some mutual advantage if cooperative arrangements could be designed, was the fact that each country had a massive Arctic land mass and coastline. No other countries in the world were so experienced with the challenges posed by conditions of extreme cold and harsh terrain. There was an abundance of experience to be shared, and scientific cooperation to be pursued. In the Soviet Union, unlike Canada, some large population concentrations had located inside the Arctic Circle, and we wished to visit one or more as a stimulus to the acquisition of construction techniques for large structures, pipelines, and other transportation systems. Additionally, the Arctic was increasingly proving to be an area very sensitive to pollution. The controversy surrounding the voyages of the *Manhattan* through the Northwest Passage emphasized the need to quickly arouse the interest and the support of the international community in order to minimize the increasing risks to which the environment, worldwide, was being exposed. In this respect, the Soviet Union would be a critically important player (as discussed in greater detail in Chapter Two), and it was our intent on this trip to encourage interest in this subject, to which the U.S.S.R. had long been indifferent.

A much more sensitive issue was that of family reunification. In the Ukraine particularly, but scattered more broadly among Jewish communities, there were numerous individuals who wished to emigrate in order to join their relatives already in Canada. These linkages were barred by the refusal of the Soviet authorities to issue passports or exit visas. A list of many of these persons had been compiled in cooperation with the Canadian Embassy in Moscow, where the ambassador and his staff sought to engage their release from the grip of the xenophobic Soviet system. This human-relations element in Canada's relationship with the U.S.S.R. was the lens through which many Canadians viewed the giant authoritarian state. As witnesses to the importance with which Canada viewed this issue, the official party would include in it three members of Parliament: Barney Danson, parliamentary secretary to the prime minister; Dr. Stanley Haidasz; and Walter Deakon.

An aspect of humanitarianism that would be welcomed, we knew, was the cultural dimension. Any opportunity for enriching exchange visits of musicians or other performing artists would be endorsed and pursued. In both countries, visits of orchestras or dance companies, because of the quality of performance promised, would be seized upon by local audiences. And, to sports fans, the same was true for athletic and sporting competitions. The Soviets had taken up hockey with a passion, and were now powerful competitors in a sport once dominated by Canada.

Thus, we were convinced that there existed ample dimensions of peaceful activity that was of interest to broad constituencies. We wished to concentrate on this kind of human accomplishment – productive, scientific, artistic, and athletic – as a mechanism to create a more normal relationship. The great unknown in the NATO–Warsaw Pact standoff was the "intent" of the Soviet leadership. Since it was possessed of a massive military machine, prudence demanded a credible defence in the absence of some assurance that the armed might would not be employed for offensive purposes. In these circumstances, any success in better understanding the Soviet attitude and engaging the Soviets in normal, non-military, activities would be of benefit to all countries. Particularly would this be the case in environmental issues.

The trip was scheduled for October 1970. Detailed preparations would not get under way, however, until well into the new year. The major Arctic Waters Pollution Prevention Bill had first to be attended to in the cabinet and in Parliament, and the first major overseas trip – around the Pacific Rim, culminating in Japan for the world exposition at Osaka in May – was completed. Head would travel to Moscow in June, as events turned out, not as a precursor for Trudeau's trip but as a step in the negotiating process relating to the Arctic environment.

The international climate during the summer and fall of 1970 offered encouraging evidence of a reduction in East–West tensions. West German Chancellor Willy Brandt had met with his East German counterpart, Willi Stoph, in March, the first-ever German summit. The U.S.A.–U.S.S.R. Strategic Arms Limitation Talks (SALT) began in Vienna. Canada and the Soviet Union concluded an agreement resolving maritime incidents between fishing ships of the two countries in the Pacific Ocean. By late September, all necessary trip arrangements were concluded: the briefing books were prepared, the delegation members selected, the itinerary approved. Then, to the horror of Canadians, on October 5, FLQ terrorists kidnapped the British trade commissioner, James Cross, in Montreal. On October 11, Quebec Minister of Labour Pierre Laporte was abducted. The infamous

October Crisis was upon us. There could be no thought of the prime minister being absent from the country during this tragic and dangerous period. With apologies, the Soviets were informed that the trip must be postponed.

In due course, a new date of May 1971 was set. By the time it rolled around, a number of developments had occurred. Most important to Canadians, the ordeal of the FLQ had passed, but not before the cowardly murder of Pierre Laporte. Cross was released unharmed in return for an agreement to allow the kidnappers to flee to Cuba. At Singapore in January, the Commonwealth heads of government had resolved the impasse over British plans to sell weapons to the Republic of South Africa as part of a debate that extended to security in the Indian Ocean, a subject Trudeau wished to pursue in Moscow with Premier Kosygin. The process of détente continued, as the United States and the Soviet Union concluded a treaty banning nuclear weapons from the ocean floor, while the SALT negotiations continued with good progress. East Pakistan declared its independence, leading to a sequence of events that would include another India–Pakistan war before Bangladesh emerged and several millions of East Bengali refugees returned, after fleeing to India. Of a more immediate nature, but with an impact on the trip, Trudeau married Margaret Sinclair. The Soviets graciously extended their invitation to include her. The trip would be the first of many in which Margaret would participate.

In Moscow, following our arrival on May 17, a courtesy call was paid upon Soviet President Nikolai Podgorny. Formal talks took place with Premier Alexei Kosygin[33] and, separately, with General Secretary Leonid Brezhnev. On each of these occasions, Andrei Gromyko participated. There could not have been a greater contrast between two men than Brezhnev and Kosygin. Although they were approximately the same age (in 1971 Brezhnev was sixty-five, Kosygin, sixty-seven), and obviously close political allies, Brezhnev was clearly dominant in appearance and in mannerisms. His thick black eyebrows were formidable, his neck and wrists were of the size, and suggested the power, of a wrestler. He was a heavy smoker and restlessly toyed with his cigarette lighter while talking, turning it over and over in his huge hands. Kosygin was retiring by contrast, quiet-voiced and with soft eyes. His fatherly demeanour and appearance were emphasized even further in the presence of his charming daughter, Mrs. L. A. Gvishiani, the wife of one of the Soviet Union's better-known scientists. As a widower, Kosygin would rely on his daughter to accompany him to appropriate state functions.

Acting as interpreter throughout the trip was the legendary Victor Sukhodryev, who had performed the same function for Nikita Khrushchev. In the Kremlin conference rooms, he sat at one end of a long table, with delegations down either side, the two principals closest to him. Sukhodryev's command of English and Russian was such that he could even translate jokes from either language, normally an impossible task. He would draw on aphorisms or slang to convey with accuracy the point made, and relied on casual conversations wherever he travelled to ensure his familiarity with current idioms. Because he was also a senior diplomat, with responsibility for Western European and North American affairs, he brought considerable substantive knowledge to the table, permitting him to be incisive and accurate when technical terminology was employed and obscure references made. He would also act as the formal note-taker for meetings, guaranteeing to the Soviets an almost verbatim record of a formal encounter.

Discussions between heads of government tend to be formal by their very nature. Discussions with a senior Soviet are exceedingly so. This is not a reflection of individual personalities, but of the stolid, careful form of communication practised by Communist representatives. The likelihood in these circumstances of departing from the agreed agenda, or of coming unexpectedly to an unanticipated accord, is simply not possible. Negotiations in these circumstances are a painstaking, sequential affair that generally address only the margins. The then-recently concluded eight-year struggle in the United Nations to reach agreement on principles of "Friendly Relations and Cooperation Among States"[34] was fresh in our minds as an example of the challenge facing those negotiating with ideologically inflexible Soviets. Much of what we wanted to achieve in writing as an outcome of the Moscow discussions had been prenegotiated by officials prior to our departure from Ottawa. Thus the formal protocol on consultations, which was executed with considerable flourish while in Moscow, was the product of an earlier process. Other issues, particularly those which demanded a concession, or an undertaking of a novel sort – the question of reunification of families was a good example – would be reflected in the final communiqué. (Trudeau had handed to Brezhnev a list of more than one hundred persons desirous of leaving.) In the U.S.S.R., the production of such a document demanded arduous negotiations of many hours in length until both sides were agreed that it reflected accurately what the leaders had agreed to in the meeting. The Canadian officials, led by Undersecretary of State Ed Ritchie, and including Russian-speaking veterans such as Robert Ford, Marshall Crowe, Peter Roberts, and Pierre Trottier, understood that the venting of frustration in such instances was of no value whatever. Toe-to-toe slogging was required, word by word, sentence by sentence.

A most valuable outcome of the meetings was the conclusion of the protocol calling for regular high-level consultations. This was an acknowledgement by the Soviet Union, never before made, that Canada was a power worthy of recognition on its own merit, not one to be regarded as an appendage of the United States, as had been the Soviet inclination previously. This document was intended as a political extension or counterpart to the agreement signed earlier in the year by Jean-Luc Pepin, which related to cooperation in the industrial application of science and technology and which had established six working groups, each in a separate industrial sector, as an incentive to some progress.

Aware of the repugnance with which some in Canada regarded any kind of political relationship with the Soviet Union, we endeavoured to describe with accuracy the setting of the protocol. Trudeau would refer to it in the following words in the House of Commons on our return:[35]

The relations between Canada and the Soviet Union in the post-war years have not all been of a wholesome or a desirable nature. I harbour no naive belief that as a result of this protocol our two countries will find themselves suddenly in a relationship which will reflect nothing but sweetness and tender feelings. As I stated in my speech in the Kremlin, there remain many fundamental differences between us; differences relating to deep-seated concerns springing from historic, geographic, ideological, economic, social and military factors.

Those differences could not be used as an excuse for making no effort to overcome them, however. The protocol was one means for the two countries to begin to understand one another better.

The extensive land mass of the Soviet Union was borne home to us as we set out from Moscow to pursue the itinerary agreed upon by us. First to Kiev, as recognition of the major contribution made to Canada by generations of persons of Ukrainian origin; then twenty-eight hundred kilometres east to Tashkent in Uzbekistan, before turning north for a seven-hour flight to Norilsk, three hundred kilometres north of the Arctic Circle, before flying west over the Kara and Barents seas to Murmansk; then turning south to Leningrad, the last port of call.

By comparison with Canadian communities in the Arctic such as Inuvik, Norilsk was an engineering marvel. With a population of 167,000 at the time, it was the U.S.S.R.'s second-largest Arctic metropolis (Murmansk was the largest; population 310,000), located in a rich mining area and joined to the seaport of Dudinka by railroad. What was in the thirties a Stalinist forced-labour camp was now a modern city with broad streets and boulevards, profusions of solid masonry buildings six and more storeys in height, and modern recreation facilities. We were there in late May, when the midnight sun brought illumination around the clock to this snow-swept, frigid community. On the streets we were greeted by throngs of friendly persons of all ages, beseeching us to trade maple-leaf pins for one of the variety of badges portraying this bustling region. Here, clearly, Soviet ingenuity had overcome the daunting problems associated with construction and operations in a hostile climate and year-round frozen soils. It was here that the reality of polar distances and navigation sank in upon us. At Norilsk we were closer to the most northerly Canadian community (Alert, on Ellesmere Island) than we were to Tashkent, our previous Soviet stop. Geographic neighbours, indeed!

Murmansk was the home port of the *Lenin*, one of the giant nuclear-powered icebreakers used by the Soviets to keep open their major Arctic shipping routes. We toured this immense Finnish-built vessel as part of our inspection of one of the world's largest naval bases and distant fishing fleets.[36] In Leningrad, the home of Premier Kosygin, we viewed stunning contrasts: the exquisite Czarist palaces, and the mind-numbing expanse of Piskarevskoe Cemetery, where more than six hundred thousand Leningraders lie in common graves, victims of the infamous nine-hundred-day Nazi siege of the city.

The long flight home from Leningrad to Ottawa was not a relaxing one for either of us. We had received word while in the U.S.S.R. that the tabling in the House of Commons by Mitchell Sharp of the protocol on consultations had prompted the Progressive Conservatives to demand that the protocol be debated in Parliament. When the House Leader refused to dedicate the time necessary for such a debate, the Conservatives chose to utilize one of their allotted days under Standing Order 86 for this purpose. Because the day they chose coincided with our arrival home, and because Trudeau's engagement in the debate was seen as essential, there was no alternative but to get off the airplane after eleven hours of flying and head for Parliament. We therefore used the long flight to prepare the text of the remarks Trudeau would deliver immediately following our landing. Included in the statement were references to the subjects discussed in the broad-ranging talks, a description of the environment into which the protocol was placed, and a reminder that, in the foreign-policy review, the government had declared its intention actively to seek opportunities to further Canadian interests (of which peace is foremost) and not to wait passively for events to occur that would demand defensive responses. Trudeau repeated what he had asserted in the Kremlin to the Soviet leaders, his unwavering belief that "the foremost goals of every government must be the attainment of social justice, fundamental human rights, and the dignity and worth of all human beings."[37]

Prior to departure from the Soviet Union, Trudeau had extended an invitation to Premier Kosygin to come to Canada. No date was set, but in the normal routine of international exchanges the following year was a likely time. In the course of the summer, however, Head became concerned by the suggestions of the Soviet ambassador that further forms of agreement quickly now be considered as evidence of the momentum of the relationship. Head did not want the Soviets to assume that Canada's interest in stabilizing and strengthening the relationship was other than sincere. Equally, however, he knew how unwise would be any successive proclamations of good faith and cooperation if circumstances did not merit them. How best, then, for

Canada to manage this dynamic in a balanced, honourable fashion, one that could be seen as both open and responsible? Why not propose to Moscow an early date for the return visit, he suggested to Trudeau, a date so early that there could be no possibility of new agreements being seriously advanced by the Soviets.

The novelty of the idea appealed immediately to Trudeau, and Head discussed it with Mitchell Sharp and Ed Ritchie, who both found it attractive. Robert Ford, always concerned about how the Americans interpreted any Canadian initiative, was far from enthusiastic, but had no basis for objecting. And so an autumn date was proposed and agreed upon by the Soviets. The visit would be utilized as an occasion to review progress, not to launch major new initiatives, and to acquaint Premier Kosygin with the diversity, accomplishments, and individuality of Canada. This permitted a much simpler agenda than that of the spring visit to Moscow.

In the five-month interval between visits, a succession of events occupied our attention, some of them discussed earlier. The most important for Canada was, of course, President Richard Nixon's economic measures, including the controversial import surcharge intended to alleviate the American balance-of-payments crisis. The passing of an earlier era was marked in three communist countries: in the U.S.S.R., Nikita Khrushchev died; in China, Lin Piao was killed in a mysterious airplane crash as he sought to flee the country; in Yugoslavia, Leonid Brezhnev and Marshal Tito signed a declaration confirming Yugoslav independence.

The Kosygin visit in October 1971 would be the first ever to Canada by a Soviet head of government, and each of us was determined that it be employed as far as possible to dissolve old stereotypes, which so distort the realities of opportunity and risk that are the stuff of international relations. For the formal segments in Ottawa, only brief thought was given to an address to a joint session of Parliament. In some quarters such an event would be regarded as conferring too much honour. Conversely, it was a platform that could prove very sterile when a foreign-language speaker was involved. In its place, Head proposed to Trudeau that Kosygin be invited to appear before a parliamentary committee, most appropriately the Standing Committee on External Affairs and National Defence, where there would be opportunity for questions and answers, a much more accurate demon-stration of Canadian democratic practice than the largely symbolic practice of a speech to a joint session of Parliament. Trudeau thought the idea intriguing, but wondered whether a foreign head of govern-ment would voluntarily submit himself to such an activity. He spoke about it to the chairman of the House committee, Ian Wahn, who enthusiastically endorsed the proposal. Thus an invitation to that effect was dispatched to Moscow. Much to our pleasure, it was accepted. The Kosygin appearance in the House went a long way to dispel the dark image of evil Soviet leaders so popular in the public mind. He responded with candour and openness to difficult questions about Soviet society and foreign policy. He acted at all times with dignity and courtesy, as did the Canadian MPs who questioned him. It was an extraordinary exercise, one that would be utilized as a precedent a dozen years later when Mikhail Gorbachev would visit Canada as Soviet minister of agriculture.

While Kosygin was in Ottawa, however, a most unfortunate inci-dent occurred. Following the first round of formal discussions in the Centre Block on October 18, Trudeau escorted Kosygin to the main entrance under the Peace Tower, where a motorcade was drawn up to carry the members of the Soviet party to the Château Laurier, where they were staying. Trudeau, Kosygin, and Head paused in the archway of the building, while Trudeau described the major buildings that comprise Parliament Hill. The East Block, Kosygin was told, was the oldest. There is Canada's original cabinet room, and the office occu-pied by Sir John A. Macdonald and successive prime ministers. "May we walk over and see the interior?" asked Kosygin. Of course, was the reply. As Head turned to inform the RCMP escort of the change in plans, Trudeau and Kosygin descended the steps and began to walk along the driveway. For whatever organizational reason, the security personnel followed just behind. Suddenly, from the crowd of onlook-ers gathered below, there burst a man who flung himself on Kosygin's back. In a moment, the assailant was accosted and placed under arrest.[38] Kosygin announced he was uninjured and wished to continue. It was an unnerving moment for all.

The itinerary outside Ottawa had been planned carefully to acquaint the Soviets with as much of the country as could be reasonably seen within the confines of a limited visit. First, Kosygin travelled to Montreal, where tours of Canadian industrial plants complemented those he had made in the Ottawa region. Then, he proceeded by air to Vancouver, where a highlight was a professional hockey game between the Vancouver Canucks and the Montreal Canadiens. Then, he flew to Edmonton, with its large Ukrainian population, and, finally, to Toronto for visits to the Pickering nuclear-generating plant and the Ontario Science Centre. In Toronto, members of the Jewish and Eastern European communities engaged in well-organized, noisy, and lengthy demonstrations. They left no doubt in the Soviet party's minds that, in Canada, activities of this kind – if peaceful – were part of our demo-cratic heritage. More upset than the Soviets about these events were Head and other members of the Canadian accompanying party, who were kept awake most of the night by the chanting of young Jewish protesters outside the hotel.

Not long after the departure of the Kosygin party from Canada (to Cuba), President Nixon announced publicly his intention to visit Moscow the following year. It was a move that pleased each of us, both because of its potential for reducing superpower tensions and because it was confirmation that Canadian international initiatives, if taken responsibly and openly, might possibly be of some influence in paving the way for positive steps by others. One could not expect any acknowledgement to this effect from a superpower, and certainly not from one led by persons with the egos of Nixon and Kissinger, but there was considerable satisfaction, nevertheless, among those many members of the Canadian foreign-policy community who were not mesmerized with immobility and shadow-watching, characteristics not entirely absent among some of their colleagues.

IV

In the course of the Moscow discussions with Brezhnev and Kosygin, a considerable portion of the discussions was devoted to multinational issues, prominent among them the environment and international peace and security. In the ensuing years, these topics would continue to absorb the attention and energies of the two countries in fresh fora. The longtime Soviet initiative for a

Conference on Security and Cooperation in Europe (CSCE) would be accepted by NATO members, but subject to the condition that issues of importance to the West as well as to the East be included, and that preconference negotiations ensure there be an overall outcome of mutual benefit. In separate negotiations, the NATO concept of confidence-building measures would be advanced in the guise of formal discussions with respect to "mutual and balanced force reductions (MBFR)." Coincidentally, Canada's desire to ensure that its Arctic environmental concerns be addressed by an international conference not dominated by shipping states would be met by the commencement in 1973 of the formal UN Law of the Sea Conference. A contributing factor to the commencement of this latter exercise was the objection of the Soviet Union to a much more restrictive type of conference, confined to a small number of nations, as had been proposed by the United States.[39]

The MBFR talks quickly took on many of the characteristics inherent in the old East–West standoffs. The site chosen for the negotiations was Vienna. The major participants, including Canada, named ambassadors and opened missions dedicated to this activity. Year followed year without breakthroughs. Canada was not qualified to be a major player in MBFR. The principals were clearly the United States and the Soviet Union, and it would be their views that would dominate, though Canada would contribute as best as it could to a satisfactory outcome.

CSCE, by contrast, gave to Canada the opportunity to perform much more effectively, contributing policy-relevant concepts, solid staff work, and negotiating skills in the quest for structures and processes that would function beneficially in the cause of peace. It was a challenge that roused the interest of the professionals in External Affairs. Undersecretary Ed Ritchie had a talent-rich department from which to draw participants; Michael Shenstone and Tom Delworth, successively, would lead the Canadian efforts. In keeping with Canada's experience, officials had proposed to Mitchell Sharp that Canada endeavour to extend the scope of the discussions to include non-security issues. Freedom of movement of peoples and ideas was put forward as a concept that would be promoted by Canada in concert with such like-minded partners as Denmark.

Sharp found the proposal highly attractive and encountered no difficulty in gaining the support of his cabinet colleagues. With tenacity and considerable proficiency, the department's officers engaged in a multi-year undertaking, which was successful in lending to CSCE an exceedingly important dimension. The "third basket," as the Canadian and Danish proposals were called, addressed a bundle of humanitarian concepts.[40] The Final Act of CSCE, signed at Helsinki on August 1, 1975, thus contained a major segment entitled "Cooperation in Humanitarian and Other Fields." It was this segment that gave rise to the "Helsinki Watch" movement, monitoring human rights behind the then-Iron Curtain.

The Helsinki Conference was a major international event attended by the heads of government of thirty-three European states, plus the United States and Canada. In the course of the multilateral discussions, there were numerous occasions for bilateral contacts. Prior to our departure for Finland, we were informed by Canadian Fisheries officials that the Soviets were continuing to fish beyond their quotas in the Atlantic Ocean off Newfoundland, notwithstanding Premier Kosygin's assurance to Trudeau in Moscow the previous year that Soviet fishing fleets would adhere to the agreed catch limits. Canada's efforts to discipline the Soviets by denying them port facilities in the Atlantic provinces had not deterred the overfishing, but had damaged the Canadian companies that normally pursued the profitable business of provisioning these vessels while in port and catering to the shore-leave pursuits of the Soviet crews. In Moscow, Kosygin had readily agreed to Trudeau's proposal that the issue be reopened at a later date if Canada continued to feel aggrieved. So it was that, in the Conference Hall in Helsinki, Trudeau approached Leonid Brezhnev and Andrei Gromyko, urging that the issue be settled satisfactorily once and for all. Agreed, said the always-decisive Brezhnev, picking up a red telephone from his desk, "Let us instruct our staffs to resolve it before we leave Helsinki." Brezhnev then appointed Victor Sukhodryev as his representative; Trudeau named Head.

What followed in the course of the next two days was the most brutal, yet in some ways most satisfying, conflict-resolution exercise in which Head had ever been engaged. Sukhodryev was for these purposes not the amiable interpreter but the defender of Soviet interests.

The progression of his arguments was taken from the classical hard-line U.S.S.R. school of international relations. Initial Phase: (i) blustering denials of any wrongdoing, combined with accusations that the issue was conceived for politically provocative reasons; (ii) rejection of the evidence of Soviet overfishing as fabricated; and (iii) countercharges that, if there is damage to the fish stock, it is the result of greed and mismanagement by the Canadian industry and government. Second Phase: (i) explanations that the Soviet North Atlantic Fishing Fleet (headquartered in Murmansk) is an autonomous authority not subject to direction from Moscow; and (ii) excuses that the Soviet delegation in Helsinki (accommodated on a Soviet vessel tied up in the harbour) has no immediate means of communicating with Murmansk. Third Phase: (i) admission of surprised finding that individual captains had indeed overfished contrary to their clear orders; and (ii) acknowledgement that the North Atlantic fleet was more aggressive than either the North Pacific or Black Sea fleets. Final Phase: (i) announcement that General Secretary Brezhnev has attended personally to this unusual situation and taken appropriate action; and (ii) assurances that the Soviet leadership will not allow the Canadian complaints to upset the trend towards satisfactory relations between the two countries.

Had there not been convincing Canadian evidence of Soviet infractions, or the novel circumstance of an undertaking by Brezhnev to Trudeau to get to the bottom of the issue during the CSCE meetings, the result would have been much different. Head's own insistent stance in the course of the negotiations left not the slightest shadow over the genuinely easy-going relationship that had developed over the years between him and Sukhodryev. Two years later they would travel together to Tbilisi. On their return to Moscow, Sukhodryev would entertain Head at a dinner party in his apartment with friends and family, complete with photographs and a tour of the premises – a rare occurrence in the labyrinthian private lives of senior Communist officials in that period.

V

Throughout the Cold War, Canada and the United States had taken a number of steps in Arctic Canada to offset the possibility of a Soviet attack over the Pole. The Distant Early Warning (DEW) Line of radar stations across the Arctic coast from Alaska to Baffin Island, built in the fifties, complemented the earlier and more southerly Pinetree and Mid-Canada lines. The DEW Line was designed to permit the early detection of any Soviet bombers and assist in their interception by fighter aircraft. Later, as intercontinental ballistic missiles came into service, the DEW Line was supplemented by a Ballistic Missile Early Warning System (BMEWS). Both systems were operated by the North American Air Defence Command (NORAD), which also kept track of the increasing number of orbiting space vehicles used for communication, navigation, and intelligence purposes by several countries. Late in 1977, the U.S. Space Command, located at NORAD, detected the increasingly erratic behaviour of one such satellite, *Cosmos 954*, as its nuclear-power source (fuelled with enriched uranium-235) began to fail. This was a Soviet naval reconnaissance satellite in a near-polar orbit that brought it out of the Southeast Atlantic and across a strip of North America a couple of times each day. Quite by coincidence, Trudeau was briefed by NORAD officers during Christmas week when he visited NORAD headquarters near Colorado Springs in conjunction with a skiing vacation at Vail as a guest of former president Gerald Ford. *Cosmos 954* was one of the many pieces of space debris drawn to Trudeau's attention.

By early January, it was clear that *Cosmos 954* was close to complete decay and would soon plunge into the atmosphere. Where this would happen could not be predicted accurately, nor could the extent of the debris that would strike the earth's surface be calculated. It was possible, however, that the dense reactor core on board would not disintegrate entirely, raising concerns about radioactive materials scattering on impact. In the possible event that that point would be in the Canadian north, a Canadian team, supported by specially equipped U.S. personnel, was prepared to rush to the site to gather any remaining materials and so minimize damage to humans, wildlife, and watersheds.

Shortly after 7:00 A.M. on the morning of January 23, 1978, Head was informed by Zbigniew Brzezinski that 954 was down in the Northwest Territories. Brzezinski recited the exact location in degrees and minutes of latitude and longitude. The first Soviet space vehicle to land in Canada had come from the South, not the North! Brzezinski was telephoning from the White House, which had just received the exact location of impact from NORAD headquarters in Colorado. Head quickly passed this information to the duty officers at National Defence headquarters and External Affairs, as corroboration of the signal that would have been sent through the NORAD chain of command to Ottawa. He then telephoned Trudeau at 24 Sussex Drive as he was rising.

Shortly thereafter, President Jimmy Carter telephoned Trudeau directly to extend the formal offer of U.S. assistance in the task of search and retrieval. It was an offer that had been made previously through official channels, and one that Trudeau now accepted with thanks. At this stage the extent and nature of damage were wholly unknown. With daylight, the track of the debris began to be identified and the costly cleanup process instituted. Material was scattered from a point west of Baker Lake across to the eastern end of Great Slave Lake. The United States, as a major space power, had long been prepared for emergencies of this sort. *Cosmos 954* was one of seventeen such Soviet satellites; there were twenty-two American satellites with radioactive materials. The United States had a second interest in this exercise, however, one that could conceivably conflict with Canada's treaty obligations. Following the primary recovery mission, the United States wished to analyse the debris in an endeavour to gain insights into the sophistication of Soviet space and nuclear technologies. Yet the space vehicle, or what was left of it, remained the property of the Soviet Union under international law.

In the short period since the advent of the space age, several important international treaties relating to satellites had been negotiated and adhered to by a significant number of states. One of these recited the undertakings of the parties not to place into orbit weapons of mass destruction; it also established the principle of international legal liability for states launching objects into outer space.[41] A second, more relevant, treaty was entitled "Convention on International Liability for

Damage Caused by Space Objects."[42] Article II of this treaty reads, "A launching State shall be absolutely liable to pay compensation for damage caused by its space object on the surface of the earth or to aircraft in flight." A third treaty requires subjacent states to return to the launching state whatever comes down.[43] The rights and responsibilities spelled out in these three "pioneer" space conventions were binding on each of Canada, the United States, and the Soviet Union. We were determined that the principles not be undermined through expediency or abstinence.

In those first hours of excited decision-taking, it would be important to adhere to the still-nascent, but nevertheless explicit, rules that had been painstakingly worked out to govern rights and responsibilities in the event of space vehicles plunging to earth. This crash represented the first instance of a satellite descending upon the territory of a state other than the one that launched it. What Canada did in these circumstances would be a precedent for the future. To those dedicated to a functioning international legal order, this represented a rare opportunity to demonstrate care. Accordingly, following hurried early-morning meetings on Parliament Hill with Trudeau and the minister of national defence, Barney Danson,[44] Head telephoned the Soviet ambassador to inform him of the location of the impact and of the operations now under way. He asked whether the U.S.S.R. wished to participate in the cleanup and otherwise assume responsibility for this event. The ambassador's initial reply was to the effect that he had no instructions from Moscow and so was in no position to confirm that the wreckage was of Soviet origin, a position that would not change for more than twenty-four hours.

During the evening of Wednesday, January 25, the Soviet ambassador telephoned Head to inform him that a message for the prime minister had now been received from the "Soviet leadership."[45] The message conveyed three points: (i) a conviction that *Cosmos 954* was designed so as to prevent any damage upon re-entry into the earth's atmosphere; (ii) an explanation that Soviet experts had predicted the failed satellite would fall into the Bering Sea, and for that reason no advance warning had been made to Canada; and (iii) an offer of assistance in the location and recovery of debris. This latter offer was never carried through, however, nor was any demand made upon Canada for the immediate surrender of anything recovered. Thus the examination of debris by the Atomic Energy Control Board of Canada and by the U.S. Department of Energy never became an issue. With this message, however, the important matter of ownership was established, necessary for any Canadian claim for compensation.

The satellite, fortunately, had come down far from any human settlements. The cleanup was completed with despatch, effectively removing any hazard to the environment. The legal claim proceeded much less speedily, however, with the Soviets initially denying any liability. In due course, a claim was forwarded through diplomatic channels, as provided for in Article IX of the space-object liability convention. The compensation demanded was for $6 million, and a full settlement of $3 million was made in April 1981. Thus was concluded the world's first nuclear space crisis. We remain confident that throughout the hurly-burly of a challenging and potentially dangerous series of events, the Canadian response was responsible and constructive. The Canadian Armed Forces and the scientific personnel in the field exercised their skills in a professional manner; those seized of the policy implications kept their attention focused on the future. A previously untested international legal regime was honoured and important precedents established for the future.[46]

Quite by coincidence, in the company of several of his regular canoe companions, Trudeau was paddling the Hanbury–Thelon River system in the Northwest Territories (midway between Baker Lake and Great Slave Lake) the following year, when an abandoned cabin was spotted near the river bank. Stopping to investigate, the party found evidence of a hasty departure – scholarly books scattered about, cooking utensils and bedrolls left behind. On their return to Southern Canada, Trudeau and his companions were told that several scientists had located there in the wilderness in the winter of 1977-78 only to have their solitude shattered by helicopters arriving to evacuate them and take them to a decontamination centre. Unknown to them, their cabin was directly in the track of the debris from *Cosmos 954*! They were not harmed, but chose not to return.

The Soviet ambassador at the time of the *Cosmos* incident was Alexander Yakovlev. He had taken up his post in Ottawa in 1973 and had quickly distinguished himself from his competent, but orthodox, predecessors.[47] He was a decorated veteran of the Second World War, and highly educated. He had obtained a Ph.D. from Columbia University many years previously, but had allowed his English to become quite rusty in the interim. Yakovlev possessed an infectious sense of humour, which well complemented his sound intellect and grasp of world events. He remained in his post for ten years, becoming dean of the diplomatic corps by the time of his departure. In that period, each of us came to know him well, and admired him as a person of considerable character. On several occasions, Trudeau lunched with him either at 24 Sussex Drive or at the Soviet residence.[48] Yakovlev and his wife, Nina, were frequent dinner guests at Head's residence, spending their final evening in Canada there prior to returning to Moscow.

Yakovlev was extraordinarily adroit and effective in his role as ambassador. He interpreted astutely the political scene in each of Canada and the Soviet Union and so was able to contribute to a constructive working relationship. He had encouraged Eugene Whelan to invite to Canada the latter's Soviet counterpart, an up-and-coming politician by the name of Mikhail Gorbachev, whom he knew to be a protégé of General Secretary Yuri Andropov. That trip was an eye-opener for Gorbachev. It was his first visit to North America. Accompanied by Whelan and Yakovlev, he toured a number of farms and agricultural facilities in Ontario and Alberta. In Ottawa, he and Trudeau met for what would be the first of many encounters.

Yakovlev's sense of balance and history were nowhere more in evidence during his tour in Ottawa than in February 1978, when the Government of Canada, on the strong recommendation of the RCMP, named thirteen Soviet diplomats as *persona non grata*, and demanded that they leave Canada immediately for abusing their diplomatic privilege by attempting to suborn a Mounted Police officer.[49] This decision could have been a serious blow to the reputation and career of the ambassador, and could have precipitated a frigid period in the bilateral relationship, were the U.S.S.R. to respond in its traditional fashion by insisting on a reciprocal removal of an equivalent number of members of the Canadian Embassy in Moscow.[50] It was to minimize this boomerang effect that Head immediately set to work.

The Soviet activities were serious in their own right, but they were as well deeply troubling because they were clearly inconsistent with the declared intentions of the Soviet leadership and Ambassador Yakovlev to pursue a relationship of respect and trust. Either those protestations were deliberately deceptive, or the espionage activities had been carried out independently of political direction. Difficult as it was for citizens of a democratic society to accept the second interpretation, it was our inclination to do so, as a contribution to the containment of any backlash. The wisdom of that decision was borne out within the following days, when Yakovlev handed over to Head documentary evidence received from Moscow establishing vividly how an RCMP Security Service officer in a Western European country was then engaged in an equally unsuccessful and doubly illegal attempt to bribe and suborn a Soviet agent. This exercise, we were to learn from an embarrassed RCMP commissioner, had been authorized by the officer's superiors, but had not been revealed to either the commissioner or the responsible minister, and for good reason: it was entirely prohibited by both government and RCMP policies. It was thus illegal in Canada, and illegal in the country where it was happening. Deceptive practices were clearly not confined to communist states, a fact that would seize us with apprehension following the destruction of a Korean airliner in 1983. We gained a new appreciation of John LeCarré's celebrated phrase, "looking-glass war."

When told of the government's findings, Yakovlev was almost in mourning, denying to Head the possibility that some, at least, of those accused could possibly be guilty. (There was no way, in an ordinary espionage operation, that the ambassador would know who on his staff were engaged in illegal activities.) He and Head were each anxious to preserve some modicum of the warmer relationship and range of co-operation that had been carefully nurtured in recent years. In order to do this, Yakovlev asked for the opportunity to see one or other of us as necessary without delay, as he deftly began to pick his way through the minefield ahead. And so it happened. Head would take the ambassador's telephone calls at all hours, and receive him in his Langevin Block office on the weekend. Trudeau was available at 24 Sussex Drive without notice, so confident were we both that Yakovlev would not abuse the privilege. Nor did he, though he did grumble ruefully to Trudeau on one occasion as he was about to step into his limousine that he found it ironical that the Canadian government had issued licence plates to his car (based on chronological seniority of diplomatic missions in Ottawa) with the number CD 007. Even in this dark moment, he was able to chuckle.

In the end, with much handholding and calm nerves prevailing, Yakovlev was able to convince his Moscow superiors that the interests of each country would best be served by no retaliation. Neither, to our considerable relief, was the RCMP operation in Europe used by the Soviets to embarrass Canada publicly – as any accusations at that time would surely have done in light of the recent findings of the Macdonald Royal Commission into RCMP activities. To our knowledge, this was the first time anywhere that such a benign outcome occurred. We did not gloat over this considerable achievement, but reflected sorrowfully on the rigidity of attitudes that still prevailed in the murky worlds occupied by spies and counter-spies. We were grateful that a person of the strength of character and human quality of Sasha Yakovlev was the Soviet ambassador at the time.[51]

The fact that this incident came shortly following the *Cosmos 954* saga meant that the uproar among Opposition members of Parliament was intense and prolonged. The furore was at its silliest when a Progressive Conservative MP sought to link the two events, asking whether the United States had shot down the Soviet satellite and whether the diplomats were expelled because they knew of the shooting down.[52]

Trudeau would see Yakovlev in Moscow in February 1984, while he was attending the funeral of Yuri Andropov. On that occasion he met for the first time Andropov's successor, the ill-fated Konstantin Chernenko, and pursued with him the issue of nuclear tensions discussed more fully in Chapter Eight. Within a year there would be new leadership in both Canada and the Soviet Union. In five years there would be dramatic events in the Soviet Union and in China that could not have been predicted, events that in themselves raised troubling questions about the future. Each instance emphasized how little the outside world understood these societies that were so different from our own, and how vulnerable in the nuclear age are all states to abrupt upheavals in such influential nations as these two. By 1984, much remained to be understood about each, as major social and economic transformations continued. From our perspective, Professor Harold Laski's plea for an intellectual bridge retained every bit of its validity and its vigour, as it still does at the time of our writing these words. Canada cannot play the role of managing engineer in the construction of that bridge, but is surely capable of contributing to the architecture of the design. To do any less would be a mark of irresponsibility, as it would have been had we not endeavoured, beginning in 1968, to engage these two mighty nations in a more rational and orderly relationship, one that recognized their immense potential as participants in a more sane and humanistic world community.

—— ✠ ——

CHAPTER EIGHT

Hits and Misses

I

History — the recorded sequence of events that are the product of human activity — is a function of perspective. In the compilation of that record, there is no guarantee that the accounts of either spectators or participants are accurate. Thucydides warned that "eyewitnesses of the same occurrence gave different accounts of them as they remembered."[1] Participants, on the other hand, may be overwhelmed in the turbulence of the action, and confused about cause and effect. Nor should this be surprising if we recall Winston Churchill's observation, earlier quoted, that "History is just one damn thing after another." The challenge to discern and to assess becomes more difficult in the recounting when not just events, but policies, are recalled and re-examined. Where the results of any given policy were not as anticipated or desired, did the fault lie in the design of the policy or in the mechanics of implementation? There is not always a clear distinction between the two.

The goal of policy, be it domestic or foreign, is to lend some purpose and coherence to activity; to anticipate and shape when possible, to discipline response when not. In the period from 1968 to 1984, the design of foreign policy and the conduct of foreign relations were not always in harmony. Nor were outcomes always as desired. The chronicler is satisfied simply so to observe and record; the theoretician endeavours to discern patterns; the practitioner was striving to remain on course. This chapter is illustrative of the always bumpy nature of that course as we encountered "one damn thing after another" in our design and pursuit of several goals-oriented policies.

II
THE THIRD OPTION

Diversification has been the golden rule of every economic planner since the dawn of organized human activity. The balancing of risk is as familiar to the peasant farmer on the terraced slopes of the Andes as it is to the portfolio manager of a Toronto-based investment fund. The rule is universal in its application: exposure to meteorological conditions, to market forces, to the influence of a single powerful actor (be it government or purchaser), should wherever possible be diminished through the diversity of resources and activities. The wisdom of the rule is self-evident; the means of honouring it, however, are not always obvious. From the late eighteenth century onward, Canadian economic circumstances illuminated the importance of the rule, and demonstrated its elusiveness in practice. Most of the resources for Canadian investment capital, and most of the markets for Canadian products, have for centuries been outside of Canada: initially British, more latterly American. Following the Second World War, the importance of the United States to the Canadian economy increased dramatically. By 1968, 22.6 per cent of Canadian goods and services were exported (measured as a percentage of GDP), two-thirds of those to the United States. At the same time 36 per cent of Canadian capital requirements came from foreign sources, four-fifths of those from the United States.

It had been the concern of many in Canada that this dual dependency was depriving the Canadian government of the means to manage the domestic economy. This in turn inspired the debate over economic nationalism referred to in Chapter Six. Each side in this honourable intellectual struggle recognized the merit of the other's arguments. There was no dispute, therefore, over the perils that would follow should the Canadian government be deprived of many of its effective levers of economic control. In that event, both fiscal and monetary policies would be driven by decisions taken elsewhere, be it on Wall Street or in Washington, D.C. Nor was there any dispute about the vulnerability of Canadian living standards should Canadian productivity and competitiveness decline, or Canadian savings erode, within the comfort of a protectionist environment. Where the two sides joined issue was in their differing visions of how these undesirable

circumstances could most effectively be thwarted. A necessary ingredient in the policy proposals of each was the diversification of Canadian
markets for both capital and goods.

This debate was by no means singularly Canadian. It surfaced then,
and continues still, on all continents, and assumes varying forms in
reflection of local conditions. In Latin America, the brilliant Argentine
economist Raoul Prebisch formulated his doctrine that world markets
for non-manufactured goods tend to be highly inelastic in regard to
pricing, while those for manufactured products are the reverse. That
being so, argued Prebisch, the industrializing economies of Latin
America should pursue import-substitution policies, manufacturing
domestically the products demanded by their own growing populations, and so capture the value-added profit element that had been
escaping abroad. Sound as the theoretical base for the Prebisch doctrine was, it failed to anticipate the rapidly increasing factor of new
technologies, most of them of foreign origin and often available only
in packages dependent on open economies. The protectionist policies
of many Latin American countries thus became particularly vulnerable
to the economic crises of the eighties, exacerbated as they were by
heavy foreign debt-loads.

In Japan, and in Europe, policies dependent on markets of scale
were introduced. The vitality of Japanese technological prowess and
the quality controls of its industrial sector contributed to brilliant performances worldwide by Japanese manufacturers and financial institutions. In Europe, the gradual dissolution of economic barriers, which
began years earlier with the creation of the Coal and Steel Community,
continued, leading inevitably to the realization of Jean Monnet's vision
of a European Union. Not even the United States, far and away the
world's largest economy in this period, could escape these upheavals.
To the frequent disdain of those who controlled traditional industrial
practices, manufacturing techniques were altered radically. The new
success stories were found in the high-technology electronics and aero-
space industries that began obtaining their components from all parts
of the globe, making foreign markets more accessible as they did so.

Canada alone among the industrialized countries in the seventies
was isolated from these trends. With an economy a fraction of the size
of those of the United States, Europe, or Japan, Canada exhibited

unfavourable structural characteristics of major proportions. The country could not likely ever shed itself of its dependency upon foreign-export markets and upon foreign sources of capital and technology. Unlike the smaller European nations, however, or even the dynamic states of Southeast Asia, geography prevented it from associating with an assemblage of other states in order to reduce risk and to enjoy the efficiencies of scale. Canada's sole neighbour was the giant to its south, and, since 1911,[2] the Canadian body politic had been firm in its resistance to formal economic continentalism. For better or worse, Canada's geographic and historic relationship with the United States demanded artful political policies equally as much as rational economic management. This balance, long familiar to Canadian statesmen, scholars, and business leaders, had been commented upon in the foreign-policy review,[3] but became dramatically evident to all Canadians with the startling imposition by the United States in August 1971 of Draconian protectionist policies, aimed primarily at Japan, but of greatest injury to Canada. One benefit of this paroxysm of anguish was the opportunity it presented to the Canadian government to examine fresh policy alternatives. And so the call went out to ministers and officials alike for techniques that would permit the diminishment of Canada's economic dependence upon the United States. Risk-reduction through portfolio and market diversification was the goal of the exercise.

No one doubted the immensity of the challenge. The benefits and sheer convenience of access to American markets by Canadians were the envy of countries all over the world. Propinquity, tastes, familiar business practices, and transportation infrastructure all contributed to the wisdom of individual business decisions; cumulatively, however, those decisions and practices had led to the vulnerability now so evident. The senior economic ministers – Edgar Benson of Finance and Jean-Luc Pepin of Industry, Trade and Commerce – undertook to explore with Secretary of State for External Affairs Mitchell Sharp the design of an alternative policy.

There was no one more experienced for this task than Sharp, the veteran of the nationalism debate within the Pearson government of the previous decade. He well understood both the need for, and the elusiveness of, diversification of export markets. He remained disappointed at the reluctance of Canadian business to follow the openings into Latin America that he had revealed to them in his provocative forays through that region shortly following the 1968 election, but understood that U.S. shareholder control of many large Canadian companies dictated the tightening, not the loosening, of continental integration. Two additional, and increasingly negative, consequences of this practical integration were the consolidation of R&D activity within American parent companies and the denial to Canadian subsidiaries of the right to compete with the parent for foreign markets. These were elements of the branch-plant syndrome that so troubled many Canadians.

Because the composition of this problem contained so many ingredients peculiar to Canada's relations with the United States, so would any attractive policy proposals feature that relationship. Thus emerged the "Third Option" policy in 1972.[4] It was written not in response to criticisms alleging omissions in Foreign Policy for Canadians, but was overwhelmingly generated by the events of August 1971. It was entitled "Canada–U.S. Relations: Options for the Future," and began:

> In the review of Canadian foreign policy which the Canadian Government published in 1970 under the title Foreign Policy for Canadians, the challenge of "living distinct from, but in harmony with, the world's most powerful and dynamic nation, the United States" was described as one of two "inescapable realities, both crucial to Canada's continuing existence" in the context of which Canadian policy needs – domestic and external – must be assessed. The other was the "multi-faceted problem of maintaining national unity."

The paper quickly posed the issue:[5]

> ... the fundamental question for Canada is whether and to what extent interdependence with the United States impairs the reality of Canada's independence. How strong has the continental pull become? Can it be resisted and controlled and, if so, at what price?

Three broad courses of action were examined: one, to continue on the same route as heretofore; second, to become even closer to the United States; third,

> Canada can pursue a comprehensive long-term strategy to develop and strengthen the Canadian economy and other aspects of its national life, and in the process to reduce the present Canadian vulnerability.

The government chose the third option.

Two distinct, largely parallel, diversification strategies were apparent, one necessarily of a longer term than the other. The first, clearly, entailed the strengthening of Canadian trade relations with the major industrialized democracies of Europe and Japan. The second, which appealed to each of us as even more necessary and more promising over time, was the cultivation of markets in the developing countries of the South. This latter endeavour was an element in Canada's overall North–South strategy as discussed in Chapter Five.

It was to External Affairs that the government turned for strategies with respect to Europe and Japan. What was wanted were proposals that would offer fresh stimuli to relations that had been carefully tended for years but showed few signs of innovative vitality. Discussions with the European Community, for example, had been congenial and extended for some time, with formal visits between Ottawa and the European Commission,[6] but with no evidence that improvements were desirable or possible. John Halstead and Michel Dupuy, two senior officials in External Affairs who had considerable experience in European and economic affairs respectively, responded to the challenge. Much to the bemusement of their colleagues in Finance, and, particularly, in Industry, Trade and Commerce, these men proposed an innovative, formal relationship with the European Economic Community, which would be described in a general economic and trade treaty. Flexibility and room for adaptation to new circumstances were the novel elements in their conception. They called the new formula a "contractual link."

Halstead and Dupuy understood well that the European Commission, in its policy formulations, recognized the importance of maintaining and enhancing relations with all major trading countries. It was not in the interests of Europe, any more than of Canada, either to withdraw behind its borders or to concentrate exclusively on the United States. Yet Europe was still far from becoming a single entity, and so negotiations towards any new arrangements would require discussions not just with the commission but with all member states. That number was in course of expanding from six to nine.

Cabinet endorsed the proposal in broad fashion late in 1973, and Canadian heads of mission to the nine EEC member countries and to the community itself began the preliminary explorations required. An official visit to Ottawa in November 1973 by Sir Christopher Soames, the EEC vice-president for external relations, gave Trudeau a welcome opportunity to explore the concept in depth. Soames was British and a dedicated European. He was well aware of the goodwill that had been engendered by Trudeau's congratulatory message to Prime Minister Heath on the occasion of Britain's entry into the community.[7] He gave every indication of willingness to recommend a positive European response to the imaginative Canadian initiative.

The concept was purposely undetailed in order to allow it to expand and mature over time. It was this fluidity, however, that prompted Robert Stanfield in his role as Leader of the Opposition to categorize reports about it as "a bag of fog."[8] As in all instances involving novel policy initiatives, a delicate balance was demanded in assessing the chances for success. This balance seemed again to elude us, as public expectations rose and fell and as press interpretations varied widely. The Stanfield comment, for example, was made in response to an endeavour by Trudeau to explain to the House of Commons both the nature of the contractual-link exercise and the then-state of play:[9]

There is a degree of novelty to this exercise. The Community, understandably, is as yet far from certain of the shape it will assume, or the powers it will possess in years to come. . . . [Yet] There was a significant meeting of minds both on the conception of this new relationship and on the initial steps to set the process in motion.

Early on, a consensus developed among those developing the new policy that the personal involvement of Trudeau was necessary if the vision and the extent of the concept were to reach the ears of the European leaders whose support was required. The novelty of what was being proposed ruled out the employment of a written form of communication. Visits to the European capitals were recommended to Trudeau by Mitchell Sharp. Any such visits could not be confined, of course, simply to the contractual-link proposal, but would necessarily embrace the range of bilateral considerations that occupied the attention of the respective governments. This fact demanded considerable preparation for each country. Second, the desirability of joining several European capitals into a single trip made scheduling a complicated challenge.

Between 1968 and 1974, Trudeau had been in Europe on four official occasions. The first was to participate in the January 1969 Commonwealth heads of government meeting in London (with a brief extension to Rome and the Vatican). The second took the form of the visit to the Soviet Union in the spring of 1971. The third was an informal, working visit to Britain in December 1972, of the kind long favoured by Canadian and British prime ministers, for discussions with Prime Minister Heath and Her Majesty the Queen.[10] The fourth was a brief trip to Paris in 1974 to attend the funeral of President Georges Pompidou. The obvious next country to visit on an official basis, in light of Canadian history, trade, and cultural interests, was of course France. But the Gaullist governments of that period had exhibited no particular desire to receive Trudeau in light of his outspoken criticism of France's encouragement of Quebec separatist elements, and Trudeau was reluctant to travel elsewhere in Europe until the French connection was made.[11] The opportunity would not arise until the June 1974 federal election, when the decisive return of the Liberal government with an overall majority in the House of Commons signalled to Paris that federalism in Canada under Trudeau's leadership was resilient and enduring. In that election, sixty-two of the seventy-four Quebec seats returned Liberal members. Now was an invitation extended, and now could the quest for the contractual link get under way in earnest.

In October 1974, the European tour began with the splendour of an official visit to France, involving formal discussions with French Premier Jacques Chirac, and President Valéry Giscard d'Estaing. There was no evidence of strained relations. Cautious, but by no means negative, encouragement was offered for the creation of the novel linkage. Then on to Belgium for a formal bilateral visit, as well as consultations at the Brussels headquarters of the EEC. Belgium Prime Minister Leo Tindemans received Trudeau hospitably as expected and declared considerable support for the Canadian proposal. European Commission President François-Xavier Ortoli engaged the Canadians in lengthy discussions, in which his commissioners participated. Prime Minister Gaston Thorne of Luxembourg travelled to Brussels to join in the discussions. We left Brussels for the flight home confident that the first stages in the forging of the link had been well accomplished.[12]

A monitoring phase then commenced to ascertain the nature of Europe's response to the Canadian overture. By early in the new year, 1975, it was clear in the minds of Halstead and the several heads of mission that the exercise was well begun and justified further calls upon other European heads of government. The courtship could not reveal favouritism, however, and so the next round of visits was scheduled for February and was designed to include as many of the other EEC members as could conveniently be scheduled. The itinerary would embrace Italy, the Federal Republic of Germany, the Netherlands, and the United Kingdom. As planning proceeded, we realized that Ireland would occupy the rotating chairmanship of the community at the time of the trip, and so Dublin was added to the itinerary in response to a warm Irish invitation.

The stop in Bonn gave Trudeau his first opportunity to meet the recently elected chancellor, Helmut Schmidt, an impressive individual with whom common ground would be found on a number of important issues. Marcel Cadieux, then ambassador to the EEC, had reported the existence of some criticism of the Canadian initiative on the part of diplomats displeased with the 1969 reduction of Canadian forces in Europe: "Canada should not expect favours from Europe if it is not prepared to shoulder its defence burden" was the message. This wholly inaccurate depiction both of Canada's NATO posture and of the mutually beneficial nature of the contractual link was not unexpected. What was necessary was to determine whether this view was held by any heads of government, of whom Schmidt was key. We quickly learned that he was as thoughtful as he was realistic. West Germany was fearful of two possibilities, he told Trudeau: (i) an exchange of nuclear munitions, which would reduce central Europe to an uninhabitable wasteland, and (ii) the disappearance of allied forces, which were of such psychological significance. The first concern led Schmidt to understand and laud the Canadian decision to withdraw from the NATO nuclear-strike role, which in our eyes and his could be regarded by the Soviets as provocative and destabilizing. The second concern was conveyed graphically. "A German farmer is not able to detect the identity of NATO aircraft flying overhead as their contrails stream behind them. Besides, he knows that those airplanes can flee westward as quickly as they can fly eastward. He recognizes the maple leaf on tanks and infantry vehicles, however, and knows that there is no escape for them in the event of war. These units are reassuring and important, whether or not there is a persuasive military role for them." This kind of straight talk, intellectually and politically credible, was wholly attractive to Trudeau. He and Schmidt would enter into a comradeship that would grow stronger on each occasion they met.

Notwithstanding the naysaying of the defence community, German hesitation about closer commercial links with Canada stemmed from an entirely different perspective. Both public and private sectors expressed dismay at Canada's recently adopted uranium-export restraints, which were seen as a retroactive diminution of the sanctity of contracts. To a country devoid of indigenous sources of energy, these safeguards raised questions about the reliability of Canada as a trading partner and, in return, prompted doubts about the effect of Canada's recently adopted foreign-investment regulations. Thus did Canada's response to India's nuclear explosion in May 1974, manifest in the world's toughest controls on commerce in fissionable materials, have an impact upon Canada's reputation among its friends and allies.

The visit to Britain was memorable, for it included the colourful medieval ceremony of granting to Trudeau the freedom of the City of London, a ceremony as touching as it is rare. The occasion demanded a very special address in reply, one that related to London, but one that would seize the opportunity presented by an audience as distinguished as any in the world. Crafting the address was a joyful challenge for us.

In no other country in the world has the concept of "freedom" been so debated, its meaning so extended, its practice so protected.

To be a free man anywhere is a condition of great moment, but to be a free man in England – to breathe Lord Mansfield's pure air – is more; it is an exhilarating experience.

The second segment of the speech, Trudeau decided, should convey to this distinguished audience the overwhelming importance he attached to North–South issues. Only then, and briefly, would he touch on the contractual link. It was a decision that attracted sharp criticism from some in External Affairs; it was a speech, however, that garnered attention far beyond what any special pleading about trade arrangements could possibly have done.[13]

It is not the absence from the scene today of a Pitt or a Churchill that causes men and women to wonder in what direction humanity is pointed; it is the nature of the adversary. More than eloquence and more than leadership is required to come to grips with monetary imbalances, nutritional deficiencies, and environmental pollution. Not a Shakespeare or a Wordsworth or a Kipling could translate into stirring words the requirements for commodity price stabilization or nuclear non-proliferation. Yet these struggles are the essence of life on this planet today. They are not struggles that can be confined to a law court or a battlefield or a House of Commons; they require institutions and regimes of immense dimensions and novel attributes; they call – in the final analysis – for worldwide co-operation, for they demand that we struggle not against other human beings but with other human beings. They demand a common cause of humanity.

The events comprising the Freedom of the City ceremony were conducted partly in the Mansion House, partly in the Guild Hall, and reinforced for both of us the strength and vitality of the common law and constitutional practices that Canada had inherited from this gifted society. It was a lifting, as well as a lofty, occasion.

Later in 1975, the formal rounds of all nine members would conclude with visits to Luxembourg, where Prime Minister Gaston Thorne was a stout advocate of an outward-looking Europe, and to Denmark, which expressed concern about the way the Canadian precedent might affect resource sharing within the community.

In contractual-link terms, what was the result of this intense flurry of activity and immense investment of time and interest? The question, in some respects, remains open to this day. Happily, the EEC in July 1976 concluded with Canada a Framework Agreement; a major EEC representational office was opened in Ottawa. It was of a kind that had existed previously only in Washington, D.C. (but would soon be followed in Tokyo). The community representative was of ambassadorial rank, and thus of considerably more influence than a mere information officer. An unprecedented quality of intimacy was thus made possible in intergovernmental consultations relating to a number of bilateral and multilateral issues and events, including the Tokyo Round of GATT, UNCTAD, and G-77 proposals with respect to the then-lively proposals for a "New International Economic Order." We were able to understand better the EEC Lomé Conventions with the African, Caribbean, and Pacific countries. An important joint cooperation committee was struck, with a number of subcommittees to examine specific issues.

All of this was useful and advantageous. In the end, however, business is conducted by businesses. Governments can open doors, offer encouragement, and create hospitable circumstances, but if Canadian firms were not prepared to alter (or add to) their predominantly American-oriented business practices, and to buy from and sell to Europeans, third options and contractual links are of little effect. This phase had been undertaken honourably and pursued thoroughly, but it proved in the period 1974 to 1984, unfortunately, to have had marginal impact upon Canadian patterns of merchandise and capital flows. This was a period of worldwide stagflation and significant international economic disturbances. In the result, no novel business arrangements were pursued; no discernible shift in investment patterns came about. Any strengthening of commercial ties were nominal.

The other immediate channel of third-option activity engaged Japan. While considerably less innovative in the pursuit phase, it proved to be considerably more successful in some respects.[14] The vitality of the Pacific Basin as a region of constructive human activity was becoming increasingly evident, bearing out Trudeau's observation in

Osaka in 1970 that henceforth "Japan and the Pacific countries shall be referred to not as the Far East, but as our New West."

Much more difficult, however, was the initial phase; simply gaining the attention of Japanese policy-makers was a major challenge. What was necessary, pleaded Canadian Ambassador Ross Campbell, was a prime ministerial intervention to put Canada on the agenda of the Japanese government. Several telephone calls from Campbell to Head in the late spring of 1974, encouraging Head to undertake such a mission, persuaded Trudeau of its merit. The Japanese clearly welcomed it; dates were set in April, and appointments were arranged for lengthy conversations for Head with each of Prime Minister Kakuei Tanaka and Foreign Minister Masayoshi O'Hira, as well as with a number of senior officials. Agreement was quickly reached on the desirability of an exchange of prime ministerial visits. Tanaka at once accepted the invitation to visit Canada later in the year. He told Head that the Japanese welcomed the opportunity to create a North American link parallel to that with the United States as part of the diplomatic-diversification policy that had been adopted following the double shocks of 1971: the Nixon–Connally economic policies and Kissinger's visit to China. O'Hira told Head that Japan was part of Asia, but felt more comfortable in the Pacific, and accepted Canada as a Pacific power.

Gratifying as that overdue acknowledgement was,[15] it had done little to spur the transformation of the low-key relationship into something more dynamic. Over the previous decade, relatively regular ministerial meetings had addressed all elements of the bilateral relationship. Bilateral trade remained at a modest level, but had been expanding steadily in both directions, with the balance favouring Canada in 1974 by almost two to one. This imbalance the Japanese did not mind, for it reflected well their basic trade policy: to import virtually exclusively raw or semi-processed commodities, and to export high-value-added manufactured goods. Head's proposal that the composition of the trade package be altered (so as to include a higher proportion of Canadian finished products) was regarded by Japanese officials as going against Japanese interests.

Japanese dependency on imported goods was, and is, overwhelming. In 1974, 86 per cent of its energy needs were imported; Japan's iron-ore imports represented 42 per cent of the world total; 47 per cent of all food was imported, a percentage that was rising rapidly as Japanese tastes became more sophisticated and living standards increased. In the result, Japan was exceedingly vulnerable to supply disruptions or threats to the openness of vital shipping channels. It was our proposal to the Japanese leaders that a deepening and broadening of the bilateral relationship would address not simply the trading interests of each country but as well would permit a greater degree of cooperation in such areas of joint interest as the Law of the Sea Conference (then under way) and multilateral trade negotiations.

To accomplish any adjustment in Japanese policy is a major undertaking, because of the orthodox and powerful bureaucracy, which tends to be resistant to change. The bureaucracy would not admit publicly, for example, even in 1974, that Japan's insistence on processing from scratch the raw materials, which it imported to the exclusion of most finished goods, had had a serious impact upon the Japanese environment. Far from the serenity and beauty so highly regarded in the Japanese culture, industrial activity had transformed much of the country into a smoggy, desolate landscape. If there were to be any acknowledgement of the environmental, as well as economic, advantage to Japan of changing this upgrading policy by importing increased quantities of processed or manufactured goods, as Canada was encouraging, strong political leadership would be required. It was to Prime Minister Tanaka that we were turning for this lead. The visit in September was his first to Canada as prime minister, but was not his first meeting with Trudeau. The two had met earlier in the year in the splendid Japanese Embassy in Paris, where both men had travelled to attend the funeral of French President Georges Pompidou.

Tanaka was a dynamic man, short in stature but bubbling with energy. One of his eyes had a slight cast to it; the other he used to bore in on his interlocutor, particularly during the translation of his remarks, as he sought some clue as to the impact of his statements on the listener. He had visited Canada on several occasions in the past and retained distinct but superficial memories that he nevertheless repeated with considerable gusto and obvious sincerity: glorious autumn colours in central Canada, beautiful golf courses in British Columbia.

Because the Japanese were much more inclined than the Europeans to play one Canadian province off another as a subsidized source for goods and services, and would, on occasion, encourage Canadian capital investment in an export activity without any assurances of a continuing market, it would be Trudeau's task during these discussions to emphasize the value of taking a longer view of our promising partnership. Tanaka's response in this respect was as we had hoped it would be: an expression of dedication to healthy, permanent growth in each trade sector and an endeavour to dampen the short-term cyclical repercussions of quixotic market activity.

The measure of success of the three-day visit[16] was more easily assessed two years later, in 1976, when Trudeau travelled to Japan in response to the Tanaka visit. By that time, Canada–Japan trade had increased by some $500 million annually. In the same period, however, Canada–U.S. trade had increased by more than $11.6 billion annually.

While in Tokyo in October 1976, Trudeau signed with Prime Minister Takeo Miki a "Framework for Economic Cooperation," and reached agreement to create a joint economic committee at the foreign-minister level to guide cooperative activity. The visit had long been anticipated by Trudeau with relish. He admired Japanese culture and was deeply impressed by the economic accomplishments of the disciplined and industrious people who populated this resource-scarce country. More, he recognized the dynamism that stimulated economic and social activity in Japan and in many countries on the western rim of the Pacific. Were stability in the region to be maintained, it was critically important that Japan participate fully. The time was rapidly approaching for a revision of the post-Second World War division of burdens and responsibilities among the world's powers; as Japan became steadily more wealthy and potentially influential, it must be encouraged to enter the international community more deliberately through, for example, an assumption of a larger share of the assistance to developing countries. This theme featured in Trudeau's conversations with Miki and was central in his address to the students and faculty of Keio University in Tokyo, where he was awarded an honorary degree.

The great decisions concerning forms of political systems and philosophy of social structure have yet to be taken in scores of newly independent countries. Our belief in the inherent superiority of our way of life is not shared by the hundreds of millions inhabiting those lands. Those persons are still assessing our motivation, our discipline, our sense of responsibility. In doing so they measure us not with alien criteria, not by standards foreign to us. They watch our competence in governing ourselves. They look to our willingness to care for others. Above all they seek some evidence of our involvement in the great moral issues of our time – brotherly love, fair play, concern.

The attitudes we develop as individuals, as much as the policies we formulate as governments, will contribute to the worldwide growth or decrease of freedom in this century. . . .

Four years had passed since the "third option" was proposed. A sea change in consciousness had occurred at the level of heads of government in Europe and Japan, yet, sadly, there had been no major conversion in the attitudes of officials in the "realistic" ministries – Finance, Trade – in any of the engaged countries, including Canada, and still less in those most realistic of all persons, the members of the business and investment communities.

The U.S. goods and capital markets were clearly so vigorous and so attractive to Canadian exporters and financiers that Canadian government encouragement to diversify would require much more pointed intervention than would be healthy, and certainly more than Trudeau and his colleagues were prepared to mount. The turbulent course of the National Energy Program offered dramatic evidence of the dual resistance to any dilution of American dominance of the Canadian economy. Part of the resistance came, not surprisingly, from U.S. interests that owned 90 per cent of Canada's petroleum production and marketing and were not in the slightest degree sensitive to Canadian concerns about that circumstance. Part came as well from those members of the Canadian business community whose profitable and convenient commercial arrangements with American partners led them to oppose vigorously any measure designed to encourage a greater measure of Canadian self-sufficiency and control. This potent mix was seized upon by Alberta Premier Peter Lougheed, who employed it skilfully as a champion of provincial interests and regional alienation.

By 1984, this combination of U.S. economic aggressiveness on the

one hand and the aggregate of thousands of individual Canadian business decisions strengthening linkages with U.S. goods and capital markets
on the other, effectively set the scene for a reversal by the Mulroney government of a century of Canadian economic and trade policies. By and
large, the Canadian corporate sector clearly had little interest in pursuing a third option, and had joined forces with American complaints
about the structure of Canadian laws and regulations that were designed
to ensure net benefit to Canadians as foreign capital entered the
country.[17] The rare and spectacularly successful exceptions to United
States-dependent corporate policy were simply not influential in the
mainstream Canadian business community. The third option, no matter
how sound in theory, or how basically attractive to the European and
Japanese trading partners it was intended to engage, stumbled on the
unwillingness of Canadians themselves to heed the warnings of the
dangers of non-diversification. Prime Minister Mulroney would seize
the second option: closer ties to the United States.

III

THE DEFENCE CATALOGUE

In no other instance of international relations does pronouncement
and practice diverge so vividly as in the murky sector of arms sales.
Arms vendors are roundly condemned as conscienceless "merchants of
death," sometimes instigating, often prolonging, regional tensions or
hostilities. The volume of weapons and munitions now part of international commerce has long been measured in the billions of dollars.
So accessible in the market are rapid-firing assault weapons, mortars,
light artillery, land mines, and armoured vehicles of one sort or
another, and so potent is their destructive capability, that any half-
dozen combatants in one of the numerous civil wars around the world
are armed with considerably more firepower than was any allied
infantry platoon (thirty soldiers) in the Second World War. It matters
not how remote is an armed struggle nor how seemingly uncreditwor-
thy are the belligerents, modern weapons are available to them, be they
rebels in Liberia, Tamil Tigers in Sri Lanka, or guerrillas in Colombia.
The market rule operates universally: if one is serious about weapons
acquisition, willing suppliers appear. Throughout the period of the

Cold War, the source of this hardware was overwhelmingly from one or other of the two major adversaries or their many allies (principally France and Britain). Whether in Africa, Central America, or elsewhere, arms found their way to those whose interests seemed to mirror those of one or the other of the two great protagonists.

Over the years, however, any number of other countries have entered this seemingly voracious marketplace, not to defend principle but to turn a profit. Weaponry, in the past three decades, has become one of the most broadly traded manufactures. Recessions may come and go, commodity prices rise and fall, yet the demand for weapons – and the profits to those who supply them – reveals steady and constant growth as sophistication increases and prices rise. The existence of this opportunity was quickly seized upon by a number of newly industrialized countries whose expectation of penetrating markets of the North with the products of their recently acquired industrial prowess had been dashed by the reality of international commerce. Where sales opportunities for such wholesome items as kitchen appliances or machine tools or children's clothing have proved limited, the demand for instruments of death and destruction gives every indication of being limitless. The Cold War model of the vibrant U.S. defence industry proved too attractive not to emulate. And so Singapore, Chile, Israel, India, Taiwan, and others became active players. Their products were not the high-tech marvels of the NATO partners, but the deadly and effective small-calibre conventional weapons that are the meat and potatoes of any terrorist, insurgent, or rebel. In the result, police and militia in many countries are simply outgunned by narcotics traffickers or small-scale criminal organizations. Developing countries, desperately short of foreign exchange and the civilian infrastructure necessary for economic well-being, are nevertheless lured by the siren song of "defence preparedness," and find the money to pay for this illusory state.

Hand in hand with the arms race between the superpowers (primarily a qualitative competition), this commerce in deadly goods continued and increased in quantitative terms between 1968 and 1984. In virtually every case, the source of this merchandise was either government-owned or -controlled factories. And always, the rationale was the same. These weapons were always produced – and sold – for "defensive" purposes. Because they were "conventional" in nature, they did not arouse the fear associated with weapons of mass destruction, notwithstanding that their use accounted for a significant percentage of all violent deaths and injuries throughout the world. In many instances these foreign sales represented the margin of profit for civilian arms factories, whose principal customer – the national army – did not purchase a volume large enough to offset costs of production. Reprehensible as was the result of all of this, coming to terms with the cause was a fiendishly difficult task.

Canada was by no means a major international purveyor of weaponry. Neither, however, was it a non-player in this game. The Canadian Armed Forces had long, and understandably, sought a dependable Canadian source for the bulk of their ammunition. Thus came into being the Crown corporation, Canadian Arsenals Limited. That company needed more customers than the Canadian Forces, however, were it to operate profitably. As the Cold War progressed, a dynamic and highly accomplished number of additional Canadian companies emerged, with the primary aim of providing increasingly technologically intensive materials to the Forces, but alert as well to the opportunities in foreign markets.

Limitations on the overseas sale of arms had long been carefully regulated by Canadian governments. With the exceptions of sales to NATO allies, and the special circumstances of the Canada–U.S. Defence Production Sharing Agreement, all arms exports required cabinet approval. Exports to countries engaged in hostilities were automatically barred; conditions on sales to NATO countries demanded Canadian government approval if a further transfer to a third party was contemplated. To many Canadians, however, these rules were simply not adequate. In the late sixties and early seventies, for example, Canada's NATO ally Portugal was engaged in a heinous colonial war in Angola and Mozambique. American participation in the Vietnam War raised the spectre that Canadian-manufactured arms and ammunition might be employed there. In neither of these cases, to the best of our knowledge, were weapons from Canadian sources employed, but the issue was properly of concern to many. Still another avenue of concern related to items that might have military value, such as aircraft engines, and here considerable discretion was required.

To each of us, these limited exports of defence products were part of the reality of commerce and international relations. Canadian sales of weaponry were small, but in our judgement inconsistent with Canada's support for arms control and disarmament measures and for that reason not to be encouraged. Deeply troubling to us, therefore, was our discovery in 1974 that the Department of Industry, Trade and Commerce had created in 1969 the International Defence Programs Branch, which had a mandate to sell arms. To assist the branch in its merchandising task, a catalogue of "Canadian Defence Products" was published and circulated, complete with illustrations, albeit in a relatively modest black-and-white format. Aware that a thriving market existed in the form of foreign-defence procurements, creative minds in the department had decided to identify any item that could conceivably be useful to the armed forces of other countries and to categorize them as defence-related. The list went far beyond STOL (Short Take-off, Landing) aircraft or even outboard motors. It encompassed sleeping bags, snowshoes, ski poles, public-address systems, and chainsaws.

To Head, who first came across this catalogue in late 1974, such an exercise appeared contradictory to basic elements in the Canadian character and foreign policy. He was deeply opposed to Canada characterizing itself as an active merchant of military equipment and supplies, and was not moved by the IT&C argument that this was simply a merchandising gimmick to encourage export opportunities for items that were inherently civilian and intended for non-combat purposes.

He immediately raised the issue with Trudeau, who made formal inquiries of the then-minister, Alistair Gillespie, and in due course was informed that these merchandising activities were not only in Canada's national interest but necessary in order to persuade our allies that we were serious about defence. Unimpressed by the sophistry of these departmental arguments, we pushed again, now to Gillespie's successor, Don Jamieson. There were serious worries in our minds about the adequacy of Canada's control mechanisms on weaponry, and concern that IT&C's decision to count ski poles as arms in its export accounting system could project to the world and to Canadians an image of the country as a big-time arms merchant. Canada manufactured no heavy tanks, but we were major producers of winter clothing.

This contest proved to be one of those unsatisfactory, protracted struggles between ministers and public servants that lend merit to neither. By late 1975, the inevitable had occurred. Through the mechanism of a numbered question in the House of Commons Order Paper, it was revealed that, in dollar terms, Canada was the sixth-largest "arms" merchant in the entire world, with sales to some seventy-three countries. What Head had feared had happened. The government's endeavours to explain that these were not really guns, only one-and-a-half-horsepower outboard motors, was met with well-deserved mockery. Even so, there was stout resistance in IT&C to any change. Finally, in 1976, Trudeau was successful in cancelling the defence catalogue. Thereafter, real arms sales were to be much more vigorously contained and dictionary definitions of everyday items were to prevail. A woolen toque was a form of headgear, not an item of military merchandise. A small victory for policy integrity and commonsense, perhaps, but one that deeply disturbed Canadian manufacturers who had benefited from earlier policies. One satisfying to us, nevertheless.[18]

IV

LA FRANCOPHONIE

In the decade prior to 1968, the map of the world had changed as never before. Major transformations of boundaries and states made centuries earlier, such as the Peace of Westphalia[19] and the Conference of Berlin,[20] pale in comparison with the massive shifts of political responsibility that began with the independence of India in 1947 and gained full momentum in the years 1957 and beyond. Between 1957 and 1968, no fewer than forty-five nation states attained independence and entry into the United Nations. By 1968, UN membership was much more than double the original number of Charter signatories at San Francisco less than a quarter-century earlier. Of these newly independent states, far the greatest number were former colonies of either Britain or France. The former were scattered through Africa, the Caribbean, the Pacific, and Asia. The now-independent former French colonies were concentrated in Africa (with some exceptions, e.g., Martinique, Tahiti, etc.).

In capitals ranging from Abidjan to Dar es Salaam, and Port of Spain to Kuala Lumpur, joy and pride greeted the dissolution of colonial regimes. Hopes and expectations for economic benefits and soaring standards of living marched hand in hand with the visible rise in dignity and stature that accompanied political emancipation. "*Uhuru*," "*liberté*," "*merdeka*," and a dozen other phrases conveyed the magical spirit of this decade – "freedom." The language of the UN Charter was recited by politicians and journalists in every region of the globe "to reaffirm faith in fundamental human rights, in the dignity and worth of the human person, in the equal rights of men and women of nations large and small. . . ."[21]

The expectations of accomplishment and benefit quickly encountered the harsh realities of realpolitik, however, as the burdens of self-government were shouldered, and the unyielding world of trade and commerce encountered.[22] As had long been anticipated, the newly independent states looked to one another as well as to their former colonial masters for guidance and succour. The often common circumstances resulting from geographic propinquity led to the formation of a number of regional organizations loosely patterned on the model of the Organization of American States (OAS), the post-Second World War metamorphosis of the earlier Pan American Union.[23] The largest in terms of membership was in Africa, where Ghana Prime Minister Kwame Nkrumah's vision of a united black Africa took form in the guise of the Organization of African Unity (OAU).[24] There was a host of others, some regional, some subregional, with varying structures and purposes, foremost among them the European Economic Community (EEC).[25] Others emerged, including the Arab League, the Caribbean Community, and the Association of Southeast Asian Nations (ASEAN). The UN Charter had anticipated such regional groupings and had dedicated an entire chapter to their role in the maintenance of international peace and security – Chapter VIII, "Regional Arrangements."

The metropolitan powers were far from uniform in the policies they pursued with respect to their former colonies. Belgium favoured an abrupt schism; Portugal fought protracted and unsuccessful wars to maintain the liege of its African territories. Britain and France, by contrast, each recognized the long-term benefits to be gained by all parties should relationships endure, even if in vastly different form. The British experience had been the longest, of course, dating from 1867, when its British North America colonies acquired a number (but far from all) of the powers of a self-governing state. In the years that followed, a warm association of consultation and cooperation emerged among Britain and its former colonies – Canada, Australia, New Zealand, and South Africa – an association that evolved into the brilliance of the Commonwealth of Nations with the independence of India, Pakistan, and Ceylon in the late forties. Our engagement with this dynamic and original grouping of countries (fifty-one in number at the time of writing) is described in Chapter Four, including descriptions of the function of its most visible elements, the biennial meetings of Commonwealth heads of government and the extensive and active secretariat.

France, by contrast, had in its wisdom maintained its linkages with its former colonies almost entirely in the form of bilateral arrangements. Much more obviously than in the former English-speaking colonies, senior French advisers and technicians remained to assist the new states as they encountered the challenges of independence. Some of these arrangements were of considerable generosity, and some took on a regional complexion, such as the tying of the value of the currencies of several French-speaking countries in West Africa to the value of the French franc. In 1968, however, there was in existence no multipurpose, formal structure binding together all the member states on a basis of equality, only a variety of quite unrelated francophone organizations catering to as many distinct interest groups: academics, journalists, writers, etc.[26]

In late 1967, France had promoted the addition of an intergovernmental dimension to these unrelated associations, an organization of ministers of education, and encouraged Gabon to host an initial meeting in Libreville in February 1968. The mischief-makers in the Gaullist government in Paris, unable to deal other than by force with their separatist elements in Corsica, were nevertheless not opposed to responding warmly to hints of an independence movement in Quebec – even though this followed more than two centuries of virtually total disinterest in this former colony of France. Alain Peyrefitte, the French minister of education, arranged for an invitation to the conference to be extended to the Quebec minister, and the Gabonese prepared to receive the Quebec delegation on the same footing as those from fully independent states. When Ottawa pointed out to the Gabonese the impropriety of this recognition, and proposed a Canadian delegation that would include a Quebec component, thus reflecting the federal nature of Canada, it was met with an impolite rebuff.

The issue was of concern to the Pearson government, but was not regarded with the seriousness it deserved until Trudeau, then minister of justice, sought the opinion of his close ministerial colleagues, Jean Marchand and Gérard Pelletier. Head prepared for him a memorandum, pointing out that much more was at stake here than simply a breach of protocol. Canada had taken its first major step towards full independence in 1923 in not dissimilar circumstances when it persuaded the United States to sign the now famous Halibut Treaty[27] with it, rather than with Great Britain, thus conferring a significant act of international recognition upon Canada as a sovereign state. Gabon's act, concurred in by France and a score of other francophone states, Head argued, would represent a possibly irreversible first step towards Quebec independence. Armed with this memorandum, Trudeau carried the case to the cabinet table, where a shaken Pearson agreed that Gabon should be threatened with breach of diplomatic relations should the issue not be settled to Ottawa's satisfaction. Sadly, the threat had to be carried out, as the Gabonese government, acting as the cat's-paw of President Charles de Gaulle, continued with its plans. It was scarcely a promising omen for francophone camaraderie.[28]

Prior to the Gabon incident, Trudeau had quite recently had occasion to visit a number of the French-speaking states in Africa in his capacity as parliamentary secretary to Pearson. In early 1967, he had visited the Ivory Coast, Dahomey, and Togo (where he participated in a law conference as the representative of Canadian Justice Minister Guy Favreau). Later that year he would return to Africa to participate in a francophone conference in Cameroon, organized by President Ahmadou Ahidjo. He travelled on to Senegal and Tunisia, where he conferred at some length with President Léopold Senghor and President Habib Bourguiba. This was the period in Canada of the ambitious Royal Commission on Bilingualism and Biculturalism.[29] Trudeau recognized the likelihood that Senghor and Bourguiba could entertain some sort of francophone association for an international involvement of French-speaking Canadians. He returned to encourage Pearson to enhance the Canadian presence in these countries and their francophone neighbours as a visible reflection of Canada's linguistic duality. In doing so, he was supporting a position ardently advocated by Gérard Pelletier. The following year, a major Canadian mission toured French-speaking African countries, led by the veteran Franco-Ontarian federal cabinet minister Lionel Chevrier. On the heels of this mission, a number of new Canadian embassies were opened and Canadian developmental assistance made available.

La Francophonie was to re-emerge as an issue shortly following the 1968 election, when proposals for two further ministerial-level conferences gained momentum. The first, another education conference, was scheduled for Kinshasa, Congo (later renamed Zaire). The second was more embracing in concept, a full-scale conference of French-speaking states being organized by President Hamani Diori in Niamey, Niger. The organizers of the Kinshasa Conference appeared at the outset to be following the same formula as had been employed by Gabon, using the rationale that the Canadian Constitution conferred responsibility for education upon the provinces, not the federal government. This simplistic and tendentious interpretation overlooked the fact that the conduct of international relations was the function of the federal government.[30] Among the many gatherings within the Commonwealth, for example, one of the most successful was the series of Commonwealth Education Conferences, at which the Canadian delegations were routinely composed of provincial ministers – indeed were usually led by a provincial minister. They were never, however, regarded by anyone inside or outside Canada as other than representative of Canada, with prime responsibility for their organization resting with the federal government. Indeed, at the third of these conferences, held in Ottawa in 1964, the Quebec minister of education was elected chairman of the conference.[31] The same precedent was employed in any number of other Commonwealth and international activities sponsored by such UN agencies as UNESCO, FAO, ILO, or WHO, where the subject matter to be addressed fell within provincial jurisdiction.

To convey to the Congolese and to African governments generally the propriety of this well-accepted international practice, Trudeau, now prime minister, accepted the suggestion of former secretary of state for external affairs Paul Martin, government leader in the Senate, that he lead a special mission to Africa for this purpose. In December 1968, Martin visited a number of countries, including the two key actors in the forthcoming conferences, Congo and Niger. He travelled as well to Senegal to confer with President Senghor, who had been one of the first of the African leaders to propose an association of French-speaking states. In Martin's words:[32]

> . . . I went to the Congo to try and enlist the assistance of President Joseph Mobutu. He sympathized with the Canadian constitutional position because of his own experience with a secessionist movement in the province of Katanga. . . .
>
> My call on President Diori of Niger was equally amicable. As I was leaving, Diori handed me a reply to a letter that I had delivered from Pierre Trudeau. In this document, drafted after extensive consultations with me, Diori set out his full understanding of the federal government's position as the sole voice of Canada in the international sphere.

The mere fact that the Congolese invitation was extended to Canada did not deter the pretensions of the Quebec nationalists, however. Several weeks of extensive and heated negotiations, led on the Canadian side by Marc Lalonde, then principal secretary to the prime minister, were necessary before Ottawa's suggestion of a Canadian delegation with distinct components, so to be identified, of Canada–Quebec, Canada–Ontario, and Canada–New Brunswick, was accepted by all. As in the Commonwealth precedents, the Canadian delegation was chaired by a provincial minister, Louis Robichaud, the premier of New Brunswick.

The Niamey Conference turned out to be two conferences, one in 1969, the other in 1970. Representation was determined on much the same basis as had been followed in Kinshasa. Because the agenda of this conference would encompass a broad range of cooperative proposals and exchanges, however, Ottawa insisted that the delegation leader be a federal minister, Gérard Pelletier. It was at the second conference in Niamey that there emerged a formal intergovernmental organization: L'Agence de coopération culturelle et technique (ACCT). Provision was made for national, as well as provincial, involvement on the basis of governmental, not state, membership. The language of the statute referred to "government[s] participating in the institutions, activities, and progress of the Agency." Those governments would include Canada, Quebec, New Brunswick, and Ontario. Chosen as the first secretary general was a Canadian from Quebec, Jean-Marc Léger. And so it was that the first secretary general of each of the Commonwealth (after the creation of a secretariat in 1965) and ACCT would be Canadian. (Arnold Smith, in 1970, was beginning his second term in the Commonwealth role.)

Highly disturbing to Trudeau throughout this entire period had been the provocative activist role played by the Gaullist elements in the French government. Happily, this meddling interference was detected and resented by many of the African governments. So dependent were they, however, on French assistance and advice that they were reluctant in many instances to appear to be countering the strongly presented views of Paris. In a period when sub-Saharan Africa was transfixed by the tragic civil war in Nigeria, a war in which President de Gaulle had expressed support for the secessionist Biafran rebels, there was a nervousness about any separatist tendencies, even though these emanated from a country as distant as Canada. For his part, Trudeau had long since concluded that the distasteful position of France was taken only partly on the basis of grandeur and an inflated sense of importance; the other factor was a genuine fear of the pervasive influence of the English-speaking world. De Gaulle appeared to be still harbouring some resentment against the English-speaking Second World War allies, Churchill and Roosevelt, for their refusal to include him as an equal in their deliberations. This may have been an ingredient in his animus towards Canada. In the result, de Gaulle's willingness to sacrifice the francophone communities throughout the balance of Canada in order to promote the nationalist aspirations of Quebec remained always one of the imponderable aspects of this sometimes misinformed and always complicated figure.

La Francophonie continued for many years as a low-budget, useful, but not very influential association. Following the emergence of ACCT in Niamey, the first major conference was organized for the fall of 1971, and the location selected was Canada. The conference was opened in Ottawa by Trudeau, who stated in his welcoming address that, "Our cooperation is inspired not by nostalgia but by a desire for progress. La Francophonie is not a memory but a vision." The signal was clear: Canada would not condone it if L'Agence was employed as a tool to divide Canada or for the resurrection of the French Empire.

In November 1982, Trudeau would address another gathering organized by ACCT, this time in Paris. The tensions that had been so evident in the formative days of La Francophonie were now largely muted, both in France under the presidency first of Valéry Giscard d'Estaing and then François Mitterrand, and in Canada, where the Quebec referendum of 1980 had failed to attract the support of the majority of Quebeckers for an independent future. The interval between 1968 and 1982 had witnessed changes in Africa as well. The grand old father of La Francophonie, Léopold Senghor, resigned in December 1980, following twenty years in office, and in so doing established a precedent much more honoured in the breach than otherwise by his African contemporaries.[33] In May 1980, in Nice, a resolution passed at one of the regular Franco-African summits (much more an aggregate of bilateral relationships than a multilateral gathering) proposed the formation of a full-scale variant of La Francophonie, one which would engage on a regular basis the heads of government of the members, similar to the Commonwealth heads of government meeting, as Trudeau had long proposed. The first such meeting would take place in Paris in 1986, but would assume a form quite different from what Trudeau had in mind.

At the Williamsburg Economic Summit in 1983, Trudeau had suggested to French President Mitterrand that the event consist of two distinct elements: first a heads of government summit, with an agenda addressing international issues, then, a day later, a meeting of officials and provincial ministers organized on the functional base that had evolved. In fact, the 1986 event was reversed, with the functional meeting first, which meant that provincial representatives then participated in the fully "international" summit. And thus does creeping separatism continue when the guard is not maintained by the Canadian government.

The reluctance of the French-speaking countries to experiment genuinely and wholeheartedly in their relations with one another remains, in Trudeau's mind, a disappointment. This attitude of reticence on the part of many would require cajoling and convincing over time. It was as a step in that direction that his 1982 address to ACCT included the statement: "We cannot remain indifferent to anything that contributes to unity or that builds bridges between peoples."

V

THE PEACE INITIATIVE

The explosion of atomic bombs over Japan in the summer of 1945, and the events that followed, released within each of us – as in millions of others worldwide – a cascade of bewildering and often contradictory emotions: admiration of the brilliance of the scientists who penetrated the secrets of the atom; awe at the magnitude of the energy released; horror at the destruction and loss of life that ensued; relief that the prolonged and often barbaric Pacific War had been concluded; hope that this "ultimate" weapon would illustrate the folly of war; and hope, too, that the Baruch Plan for international control of atomic weapons would win the day at the United Nations. Many of those hopes gradually diminished in the months and years that followed, first as Soviet suspicions of the American monopoly hardened into opposition to effective international controls, then as additional countries disclosed their own atomic prowess. Evidence mounted that inventories of atomic weapons were being amassed by each of the United States and the Soviet Union, creating for themselves a new category of influence: "superpower." We were proud of the fact that Canadian scientists were among the few capable of engaging in the complex, advanced research undertaken in the Manhattan Project; even more proud of the fact that the Canadian government in 1945 chose not to become a nuclear-weapons state, even though it possessed the means to do so. "The Canadians had everything at hand – the uranium, the science, and the technical headstart – everything but the desire."34

Increasingly, as the fifties evolved, distress overtook our other emotions. In 1952, Britain disclosed that it possessed an atomic bomb, and the United States exploded a hydrogen device. In 1953, the Soviet Union overcame the U.S lead and exploded its own hydrogen bomb (followed by the People's Republic of China in 1967). In 1960, France had become the fourth nation to explode a nuclear device. Thus, in short order, there were five nuclear powers on the world stage, all professing that their nuclear weaponry was intended only to be of influence as a deterrent, yet each willing to engage from time to time in nuclear sabre-rattling, as they hinted (or boasted) of their second-strike capability. It was during this period that Trudeau expressed in writing in *Cité Libre* his horror of nuclear war and his criticism of nuclear buildups, including the decision of Lester Pearson and the Liberal Party in 1963 to accept nuclear warheads for the Bomarc anti-bomber missiles that had been acquired by Canada.[35]

The nuclear policy of the NATO alliance shifted over time from one of a "trip wire" to that of "flexible response." As part of this latter doctrine, NATO consciously chose not to deny that it would be the first to employ nuclear weapons, reasoning that such a policy would keep the Soviets uncertain, and thus enhance the deterrent effect. Following the 1968 election, as we became privy to increased information about nuclear activities, we observed with alarm the momentum towards ever more sophisticated weaponry intended for employment in "theatre," as distinct from "strategic" (or bomber and intercontinental ballistic missile), circumstances. Hand in hand with these new, smaller, mobile-weapons systems, the strategic weapons became more accurate, more powerful, and more difficult to intercept because of MIRVing (multiple independently targetable re-entry vehicles), leading to counterforce doctrines. All this was accompanied by outrageous claims in the United States about its ability to survive a nuclear attack.

Throughout this period, we endeavoured to remain as aware of these issues and policies as closely held U.S. security regulations would permit. Trudeau received regular briefings from Canadian Armed Forces and NATO advisers, and engaged in occasional discussions with American experts such as Henry Kissinger. Head sought frequent opportunities to inform himself through his association with such insiders as Helmut Sonnenfeldt, counsellor to the State Department, and his engagement in such policy exercises as the World Order Models Project,[36] and the Aspen Institute East–West Study,[37] which gave him access to many of the influential American and European policy-advisers and decision-makers. Supportive as each of us was of deterrence, we became increasingly confident in our belief that neither of the two superpowers would ever consciously employ nuclear weapons, primarily because of their awareness of the horrendous destruction that would ensue to each. Concurrently, however, we were possessed of a fear that a nuclear exchange might be prompted by mistake or by accident, and it was as a step to diminish this possibility that we launched our examination of Canada's withdrawal from a nuclear weapons role as described in Chapter Three.[38]

An influence upon each of us for many years had been the startling call of Albert Schweitzer in 1957, "We must muster the insight, the seriousness and the courage to leave folly and to face reality,"[39] and the constant efforts of those such as Norman Cousins in the United States and Norman Alcock in Canada, who argued with passion and reason against nuclear testing and against nuclear weapons themselves. As the seventies proceeded, we became increasingly concerned that the international community's willingness to build upon the sixties accomplishments of the Nuclear Non-Proliferation Treaty[40] and the limited test-ban treaty[41] was falling ever further behind the increase in the quality and the quantity of nuclear weapons in the world's several inventories. In these respects, the understanding and dedication of Canada's disarmament negotiators, principally among them George Ignatieff, had a profound impact upon us. Ignatieff spared no opportunity to keep each of us informed and sensitive to these issues from the Geneva Disarmament Conference and, later, from the United Nations in New York.

As "the bomb" was increasingly accepted in the mainstream, our worry increased that it was viewed in the minds of the public and national leaders as simply a bigger explosive device, when in fact its destructive potential in the form of radioactive and electromagnetic – as well as explosive – power make it an entirely novel weapon, quite unlike any conventional "bomb." Head was worried, by the mid-seventies, that few, if any, of the world's leaders had ever witnessed a nuclear explosion, and thus were dealing with nuclear-weapons policy in the comfort of the abstract. Certainly, no theatre commander had ever come under attack by a nuclear weapon, yet, in the theology of the nuclear-games players, these soldiers were expected to respond proportionately and prudently, even as their entire horizon was vaporized. The earlier naïveté of Kissinger's likening of atomic exchanges to a naval battle at sea – fought not for territory but for asset supremacy[42] – seemed to have taken hold, even though its author had long since passed on to much more sophisticated concepts. At a 1978 Toronto meeting of Pugwash, an informal, international group of individuals concerned about nuclear issues, attended by each of us and, among others, the chairman of the Strategic Air Command's Targeting Committee,[43] Head wondered aloud whether the time was not ripe to organize a low-yield atmospheric detonation as a command performance for heads of government from all over the world – to demonstrate to them the awesome power of one of these "bombs." Trudeau found the proposal simplistic at the time, but changed his mind somewhat in months to come as persons who were intimately familiar with nuclear weapons independently put forward similar proposals. In 1980, at a reunion of scientists who had participated in the Manhattan Project, which had culminated in the world's first atomic explosion thirty-five years earlier, a proposal was made to have world leaders witness a nuclear detonation. Harold Agnew, second director of the Los Alamos Scientific Laboratory, commented on the fact that soon "there will not be a single leader of a major power who has witnessed a nuclear explosion. When that happens, the balance of terror we have now will go away. And when that happens, we'll be in real trouble." The group agreed that nuclear weapons should never again be used.[44]

Shortly thereafter, at the opening of a Nuclear Non-Proliferation Treaty review conference in Geneva, Dr. Sigvard Eklund, Director General of the International Atomic Energy Agency, made a similar proposal for a demonstration explosion to alert the world's population to the fact that the world's nuclear arsenal at that time consisted of a combined explosive power equivalent to more than a million of the bombs dropped on Hiroshima and Nagasaki. "How I wish that in a way consistent with the limited test-ban treaty the nuclear weapon powers would arrange a demonstration explosion of a weapon . . . to give the news media the world over an idea of the destructive power of the new nuclear weapons."[45]

Our worry that the leaders of the nuclear-armed countries were functioning in a surreal state increased considerably following the assumption of office by both Margaret Thatcher and Ronald Reagan.

Reagan's belief in a shield of antiballistic-missile devices – the Strategic Defence Initiative – seemed to us, and to many experts, not only far-fetched but likely to bring to a sorry conclusion the invaluable Anti-Ballistic Missile Treaty,[46] which effectively ensured the vulnerability of each superpower to a second strike and so contributed to the "balance of terror." Thatcher's advocacy of "modernizing" the NATO inventory of nuclear weapons (at the very time that the remarkable generation of "smart" conventional weapons, so effective in the later Gulf War, were becoming operational) gave us the impression that she was oblivious to the fact that in many instances "modernization" meant not just replacement of intermediate-range missiles but also "miniaturization." As numbers of weapons in the field steadily increased, their bulk decreased to the point that weapons more powerful than the Hiroshima bomb could now be deployed by paratroops in their backpacks. The challenge to authorities to guarantee the security of these weapons against acquisition by terrorists or adventurers was growing proportionately. Seized with similar worries, former U.S. secretary of defence Robert McNamara had declared to the Aspen East–West Study Group[47] that nuclear weapons have no military purpose, and are solely credible in political terms because of their deterrent value.[48]

In 1982, the Soviet Union chose to begin replacing its ageing SS-4 and SS-5 nuclear-armed missiles, targeted at Western Europe, with new, more accurate and powerful SS-20 missiles. This act had quite understandably prompted a wave of fear and uncertainty in the targeted countries and had led to a decision by NATO to respond with a two-track policy: (i) to replace the Pershing I intermediate-range nuclear missiles forming part of the NATO inventory with a more advanced Pershing II missile, and to proceed with the flight testing of a new air-breathing weapon called a cruise missile; and (ii) to pursue vigorously negotiations intended to make unnecessary all of these replacements.[49] Moscow had retaliated by threatening to withdraw from all nuclear negotiations if NATO proceeded.

Trudeau was worried that only one half of the NATO message was reaching the Kremlin,[50] and so – against considerable resistance from Reagan and, particularly, Thatcher – encouraged the G-7 Summit meeting in Williamsburg in May 1983 to issue a declaration emphasizing the peaceful intentions of the West, and its desire to negotiate lower weapons levels with the U.S.S.R. The seven-paragraph declaration concluded with an unequivocal message, submitted to the six other leaders by Trudeau:

We commit ourselves to devote our full political resources to reducing the threat of war. We have a vision of a world in which the shadow of war has been lifted from all mankind, and we are determined to pursue that vision.

In the months that followed, the United States and the Soviet Union put forward arms-limitations proposals, either at the Geneva nuclear negotiations[51] or at the Mutual and Balanced Force Reductions (MBFR) talks in Vienna, but in all instances the other side shunned the offers as inadequate or unrealistic. In an effort to bridge the growing gap, Reagan had, in January 1983, proposed a summit meeting to General Secretary Yuri Andropov, but this had been rejected, which was an element in the American coolness at Williamsburg to Trudeau's overtures.

It was against this background that each of us watched with mounting concern the rise in tensions and the incendiary rhetoric that followed the destruction by the Soviet armed forces of Korean Airlines flight 007 on September 1, 1983. The Boeing 747 with 269 persons on board, en route from Anchorage to Seoul, had inexplicably strayed far from its usual course and had penetrated deeply into Soviet airspace north of Japan. It was destroyed by a missile fired from a Soviet interceptor aircraft.

In the hours following the destruction of the airliner, both Reagan and Secretary of State George Shultz issued strong, but under the circumstances as publicly revealed, proportionate, denunciations of the event. On September 3, Tass wrote that the airplane had not responded to radio warnings to identify itself, and the Soviets were forced to conclude it was engaged in a spy mission over Soviet territory and that the United States was "feverishly covering up traces of the provocation." On September 5, Reagan said that the attack "had pitted the Soviet Union against the world and the moral precepts which guide human relations. . . . From every corner of the world is defiance in the face of this unspeakable act and defiance of the system which excuses it and seeks to cover it up."

In the UN Security Council, the U.S. representative Jean Kirkpatrick argued ". . . the Soviets decided to shoot down a civilian airliner, shot it down and lied about it." Replied Oleg Troyanovsky of the Soviet

Union, Washington is "motivated primarily by its own anti-Soviet instincts and to force up their psychological warfare." On September 7 at the CSCE conference in Madrid, Andrei Gromyko said, "No matter who resorts to provocation of that kind, he should know that he will bear the full brunt of responsibility for it. That criminal act will not be justified either by a dishonest juggling of facts or by false versions donned in the toga of concern for human rights."

On September 9, the chief of the Soviet general staff claimed he had irrefutable evidence that "the intrusion of the plane of the South Korean airlines into Soviet airspace was a deliberate, thoroughly planned intelligence operation . . . directed from . . . the United States and Japan."

On September 14, a joint resolution of both Houses of Congress called the event a "cold-blooded barbarous attack . . . one of the most infamous and reprehensible acts in history." Three days later the governors of New York and New Jersey ordered the Port Authority not to permit the landing of any Soviet airplane bringing Foreign Minister Gromyko to the United Nations.

On September 26, President Reagan addressed the General Assembly and accused the Soviets of a breach of their solemn undertakings in the arms-limitation sector. "Evidence abounds that we cannot simply assume that agreements negotiated with the Soviet Union will be fulfilled." Two days later, General Secretary Yuri Andropov replied, "One must say bluntly, it is an unattractive sight when, with a view to smearing the Soviet people, leaders of such a country as the United States resort to what almost amounts to obscenities alternating with hypocritical preaching about morals and humanism."

All of this was played out against the disturbing reports from Sweden of Soviet submarine activity in Swedish archipelagic waters – stoutly denied by the Soviet Union – and the manic practice of U.S. nuclear-armed attack submarines banging their hulls against submerged Soviet patrol submarines, taunting the Soviets and boasting of their skill in being able to locate the other boat so accurately and to approach with such stealth. These were not adolescents playing arcade games; these were grown men testing the outer envelope of national willpower.

Were the military forces of the superpowers exceeding the previous, cautionary limits set for them by their political masters, or were the contemporary civilian leaders of an entirely new breed, exhibiting none of the prudence and wisdom of President John Kennedy, or the acceptance of reality of Premier Nikita Khrushchev, when they resolved the Cuban missile crisis? Whichever was the case, and there seemed to be no evident third alternative, the chilling prospect loomed of two gunslinger nations engaged in an unconscionable contest of egotism and showmanship. Were the two nuclear powers actually engaged in a real-life enactment of the games theories and scenarios that each played in their war rooms and boasted about in academic circles? If so, in actual situations, the penalty for misjudgement could be a nuclear holocaust. In Washington, the commander-in-chief was a person who impressed Trudeau at every encounter as one who genuinely desired peace but was incapable of distinguishing between screenplays and reality, one who was encouraged to stand tall by a British prime minister proud of her reputation as an "iron lady." In Moscow, a new and untested leadership had succeeded the steel-willed but risk-averse (Afghanistan notwithstanding) Leonid Brezhnev.

Each of us, in common with multitudes of others, were deeply steeped in the tragic events of the summer of 1914, when a succession of misjudgements by proud men inexorably led Europe, and much of the world with it, into a fratricidal contest of will involving the flesh and blood of hundreds upon hundreds of thousands, in uniform and out. "Sucking up lives at the rate of 5,000 and sometimes 50,000 a day, absorbing munitions, energy, money, brains, and trained men. . . . the mirage of a better world glimmered beyond the shell-pitted wastes and leafless stumps that had once been green fields and waving poplars. Nothing less could give dignity or sense to monstrous offensives in which thousands and hundreds of thousands were killed to gain ten yards and exchange one wet-bottomed trench for another."[52] Trudeau was deeply convinced that, in the autumn of 1983, there were no evil conspirators on either side, no megalomaniacs seized of plans for world domination, simply adventurers who pictured themselves as resolute defenders of national principle. Those who viewed current events against the precedent of unopposed Nazi aggression in 1938 and 1939 were, in the judgement of each of us, simply wrong. On October 4, responding to questioning by the new leader of the Progressive Conservative Party, Brian Mulroney, Trudeau replied:[53]

> I do not believe that the people in the Kremlin deliberately murdered or killed some 200 or 300 passengers in the Korean airliner. I do not believe that. I believe it was a tragic accident, an accident of war. It was caused, no doubt, by a reckless pilot and, no doubt, by a misguided commander on the ground. That is what I am afraid of, that the next war that awaits us will be started, not by the people in the Kremlin or by any other people, but, rather by some accident of some pilot making the kind of tragic decision that he made, and the people on the ground making that tragic decision. That is why I am worried.
>
> I can express indignation just as well as the Leader of the Opposition. The difference is that we have done it before him and we have done it before other nations.[54] Now, I think there should be some effort to re-establish communications with the Soviets. I, for one, think that it is in that direction that the superpowers must go. They must try to find some way to stop shouting at each other, when the world is teetering on the brink of disaster and atomic war.

Some months later, in the more formal circumstances of his participation in the Throne Speech debate, Trudeau repeated his concern that tests of strength may be outweighing reasoned decision-making:[55]

> Managing the threat of nuclear war is the primordial duty of both East and West. But Canadians are concerned that the superpowers may have become diverted from this elemental responsibility, that they may be too caught up in ideological competition, in endless measurements of parity, in trials of strength and will.

In the immediate aftermath of the Korean Airline disaster in September 1983, each of us had grown increasingly apprehensive as the bursts of outrage and bravado from Washington and Moscow grew ever more shrill. Head was at IDRC, far removed from any daily responsibilities for the conduct of external relations, but still in close touch with

Trudeau as occasion permitted. The two had shared their misgivings by telephone, and Head volunteered to put his thoughts on paper, to Trudeau's encouragement. An eleven-page memorandum entitled "Nuclear Arms Limitation: A Proposal," dated September 6, was the product.[56] The premise of Head's argument was as follows:

> It must be assumed that neither superpower consciously desires nuclear war. Yet the increasing deployment of destabilizing weapons systems, the increasing reliance on computer analysis and response, the decreasing time for assessment and decision, and the inherent weaknesses in command and control systems make it possible, if not probable, that miscalculation (either electronic or human) will lead to a nuclear exchange within this decade.[57] To reduce that possibility, every effort must be directed by all influential leaders to reducing the superpowers' reliance on nuclear weapons systems. An exchange of fire involving conventional weapons can be contained and concluded. A nuclear exchange cannot, even if commenced with battlefield yield munitions.

He proposed a range of Canadian initiatives, including increased financial commitment to verification activities, new energy in collective undertakings leading to a threshold test-ban treaty, and, in time, the long-sought comprehensive test-ban treaty, a demonstration explosion for world leaders, and encouragement to NATO to adopt a "no early first use" policy. First in his list, however, was an effort to obtain from the two superpowers a declaration of their recognition of the dangerous phenomenon of destabilization and their intention to return to the assurance of second-strike credibility, eliminating the fear of pre-emptive strike systems. The memorandum concluded with a challenge to Trudeau:

> Canada is a respected member of the international community, has an enviable policy record, is regarded as being deeply affected by arms buildups because of its geographic location, and has proved again and again its effectiveness as an actor. We have an obligation to contribute to the impasse. Your reputation and your seniority combine to place an inescapable burden upon you.

The following week, on September 15, we met over lunch at 24 Sussex Drive to discuss the memorandum. The only other person present was Robert Fowler, an External Affairs officer on secondment to the Privy Council Office, where he was a senior staff member responsible for briefing the prime minister and the relevant cabinet committees on foreign-policy issues. Trudeau questioned Head closely about the international climate, as well as about the content of the memorandum. Following lunch, the two of us strolled in the garden to the rear of the house. There, Trudeau voiced his concern that any public activity of the sort proposed would give rise to accusations that it was no more than a ploy to revive his political fortunes in the runup to a federal election, and so would lose credibility.

Head countered by suggesting that multilateral proposals could be undertaken without any major public-relations flurry, and that approaches to each of Reagan and Andropov could be carried out quietly, gaining strength by doing so. He argued that the international climate was so seized with mistrust that the two leaders were politically unable to communicate meaningfully with one another. A quiet inter-mediary, on the other hand, could evoke from each leader four or five substantive statements – of the kind that one or the other may have made in the past under different circumstances – and then release them simultaneously with their permission. This use of self-enforcing under-takings, beginning with a simple declaration of their devotion to peace, could lead gradually to other confidence-building measures. Trudeau listened gravely to Head's arguments, challenging him again and again on premise as well as on detail, repeating what he had told Head on numerous previous occasions, that he was not temperamentally dis-posed to be a diplomat–negotiator, but that he had independently been giving thought to some form of Canadian initiative.

In the end, however, he gave no firm reply to Head. The following day the two of us spoke again briefly during an official reception and dinner for the visiting Prime Minister Robert Mugabe of Zimbabwe, but no decision was taken.

Unknown to Head at the time, another PCO staff member, the highly respected and experienced Brig.-Gen. Maurice Archdeacon, was preparing a similar proposal and would seek out Trudeau in a quiet moment in days to come to express his own deep sense of concern over the state of the international climate. (The United States had declared its refusal to ratify the carefully negotiated SALT II treaty, and was publicly debating whether to accuse the Soviet Union of breaching one of its provisions.) Archdeacon, too, encouraged Trudeau to undertake some initiative to ease the distrust so apparent.

The following week, Head was at the United Nations on IDRC business, and, in the course of lunch with Ambassador Gérard Pelletier, acquainted him with his conversations with Trudeau and sought his support should Trudeau turn to him for advice. The longer-term goal, Head explained, must be the continued withdrawal of certain categories of battlefield nuclear weapons (as had been done by NATO several years earlier)[58] and increased access by the members of each military bloc to new technical services so beneficial to humankind, such as the Soviet navigation satellite, which had already contributed to several successful and dramatic search-and-rescue missions in Canada. At stake was confidence, confidence in the peaceful intentions of one's adversary, and confidence in the quality of one's own weapons and policies. The following day, in Washington, D.C., he called upon Paul Warnke, the veteran American nuclear-arms negotiator to seek his counsel. Warnke viewed the international climate as gravely as we did, and encouraged Head to press Trudeau to lend his considerable international reputation to some high-level interventions. (In the weeks to come, Warnke would make the same appeal to Trudeau in the latter's Ottawa office.)

Following these meetings Head sent Trudeau another memorandum. In it he wrote that the primary statement that the two superpower leaders should be encouraged to make was: "A nuclear war cannot be won; every effort must be devoted to ensuring the avoidance of nuclear war."

The issues that underlay these discussions were by no means unfamiliar to Trudeau. Klaus Goldschlag, one of the most brilliant of Canada's foreign-service officers, had crafted a carefully constructed strategy of "suffocation," which Trudeau presented to the UN General Assembly Special Session on Disarmament in May 1978. The strategy consisted of a coherent set of measures, including the elusive comprehensive test-ban treaty, an agreement to stop the flight testing of all new strategic delivery vehicles, an agreement to prohibit all production of fissionable material for weapons purposes, and an agreement to limit and reduce military spending on new strategic nuclear-weapons systems. In June 1982, Trudeau had returned to New York to address the Second Special Session on Disarmament. His message on that occasion – at a time of the Soviet SS-20 deployment and the NATO two-track response, including the threat of Pershing II and cruise-missile testing – was that all new weapons systems are potentially desta-bilizing. He argued that such new systems "heighten concerns about a disarming first-strike capability, or will tend to blur the difference between nuclear and conventional warfare, or will increase the prob-lems of verification. Instability is the fuel that feeds the nuclear-arms race." Towards the conclusion of that address, he had uttered the state-ment of which Head later reminded him in September 1983:

> This implies that the superpowers agree to communicate, to talk to each other, and to recognize the unquestionable common interest which unites them in a fundamental way; that is, the need to avoid a catastrophe which would destroy them both.

In the final week of September, Margaret Thatcher came to Ottawa on a long-scheduled official visit. A prominent element in Trudeau's discussions with her was his mounting concern over the dangerous downward trend in the international political climate. With his assess-ment she agreed, but she argued that the trend could only be coun-tered effectively by standing up to Soviet threats and intransigence. It was a not-unexpected point of view, but one which added weight to Trudeau's perception of danger.

Allan MacEachen was once again secretary of state for external affairs. From him Trudeau now sought advice and suggestions. As a result, several of Canada's most senior ambassadors, James (Si) Taylor from NATO, Geoffrey Pearson from Moscow, and Allan Gotlieb from Washington, were called back to Ottawa for consultation. They, together with senior officials from the Privy Council Office, External, and National Defence, gathered at Meech Lake on a weekend early in October to discuss the international situation, to report from the several capitals and their individual responsibilities, and to offer various scenarios. Trudeau posed questions to many of them, encouraging discussion, challenging assessments. Head was one of the participants, as were Robert Fowler and Maurice Archdeacon.

Out of the meeting emerged a consensus that a concerted Canadian effort was desirable and appropriate. It would embrace a host of activities and extend over several months; the press would later dub it "The Peace Initiative." An early element was a speech to a conference on peace and security at the University of Guelph where, on October 27, Trudeau mused on the need to engage a "third rail" of high-level political energy to speed the course of agreement sought in the two-track NATO policy with respect to intermediate-range nuclear weapons in Europe, energy that would reverse the disturbing trend-line then evident. What he proposed was a renewed package of confidence-building activities, preparatory to the European Disarmament Conference scheduled to open in Stockholm in January 1984. Among these was an upgrading of that meeting to the foreign-minister level as a clear indication of the seriousness with which the meeting was regarded. He revealed that he had had a discussion to this end with Reagan and would leave shortly for Europe to consult with NATO leaders there.[59] He warned against the danger "of allowing shrill rhetoric to become a substitute for foreign policy, of letting inertia become a substitute for will, of making a desert and calling it peace."

The next three months were dedicated overwhelmingly to this initiative, perhaps with even greater vigour than first intended because of the frightening events that were unfolding elsewhere. In the Caribbean, American armed forces had in October carried out a military invasion of Grenada.[60] On October 23, two hundred U.S. marines and forty French soldiers were killed by a suicide bomber in Beirut. On November 4, sixty Israeli soldiers were killed in similar fashion in Tyre. On October 31, the U.S. Senate defeated a resolution by Senator Edward Kennedy, urging negotiations for a mutual, verifiable freeze on nuclear weapons.

In November, Trudeau visited Prime Minister Yasuhiro Nakasone in Tokyo, was encouraged by the decision of the Commonwealth heads of government meeting in Goa in late November to endorse his efforts in the form of a special declaration on international security, travelled from India to China for talks with Premier Zhao Zi-yang and Deng Xiao-ping, and watched with dismay as the Soviet Union carried out its threat and formally withdrew from the Geneva strategic-arms negotiations with the United States.

In December, against the background of a NATO decision to follow Trudeau's recommendation and upgrade the forthcoming Stockholm disarmament and confidence-building conference to a ministerial level, Trudeau journeyed to Washington to discuss the initiative with Reagan, who received him warmly and wished him "Godspeed" in his endeavours, but declined to offer any specific undertakings. Trudeau told Reagan that, for whatever reason, only the blunt half of the West's message was penetrating the Kremlin, not the message of peace. For example, two weeks following Reagan's speech to the Japanese Diet (November 11), in which he employed the phrase "A nuclear war can never be won and must never be fought," General Secretary Andropov had announced his order to deploy new extended-range tactical nuclear weapons in East Germany and Czechoslovakia and new missiles at sea and to withdraw from the INF negotiations. More efforts to communicate were necessary, urged Trudeau. In mid-December the climate chilled still further as the Soviet Union announced it would not return to the Vienna MBFR talks following the scheduled Christmas recess.

Early in January 1984, Chinese Premier Zhao Zi-yang arrived in Ottawa on the first-ever official visit of a Chinese leader to Canada; while there, he expressed support in public for the initiative. Mid-month, Trudeau flew to New York for discussions with UN Secretary General Javier Pérez de Cuellar, suggesting to him that the UN act as the forum for the five nuclear-weapons powers to negotiate arms limitations. Later in the month he travelled to Eastern Europe for discussions with the leaders of Czechoslovakia, East Germany, and Romania, a highly unusual practice for a statesman from a NATO country. In Stockholm, foreign ministers from thirty-five countries formally launched the "Conference on Confidence and Security Building Measures and European Disarmament." Late in the month the Soviet Union formally complained that the United States was consciously violating solemn arms-limitation treaties to which it had adhered.

To this date, Trudeau had not been able to secure a firm appointment to meet Soviet leaders. Invitations had been extended, but the uncertain health of Yuri Andropov prevented any dates being set. In early February, Andropov died, and Trudeau, attending the state funeral in Moscow, met briefly with Andropov's successor, General Secretary Konstantin Chernenko, and was told by him that the Canadian initiative was "useful and practical." Trudeau was convinced that a window of opportunity was now available for political action.

Shortly prior to his trip to Moscow, Trudeau indicated to the House of Commons that in light of[61]

> . . . an ominous rhythm of crisis. . . . the confluence of three potentially disastrous trends: the resort to force to settle disputes; the risk of the proliferation of nuclear weapons; and the worsening state of East–West relations . . . [he had] decided to use Canada's influence to call international attention to the danger, to try to inject high-level political energy into East–West relations, to turn the trend line of crisis, to work at the crossroads of common interest between the two sides. . . .

In the course of his discussions with leaders North and South, East and West, Trudeau encouraged consideration of both specific acts and general agreements. Again and again he would emphasize that the trend towards destabilizing weapons systems must be reversed, that deterrents must deter – not provoke. He repeated his message that the decision-making process is the ultimate responsibility of government leaders, not of military advisers or arms experts, and that this responsibility must not be shirked.

As winter turned to spring in 1984, some easing of tension was evident. NATO foreign ministers issued a balanced statement on East–West relations in May; the G-7 Summit in London in June approved a declaration drafted by Trudeau that emphasized the overwhelming objective of peace.

Later that year, Trudeau was selected as the recipient of the 1984 Albert Einstein Peace Prize. In his address to the Peace Prize Foundation when accepting the award, he concluded with the following remarks:

> In a world with untold riches yet to be discovered, with countless symphonies and novels yet to be written, with massive human wants yet to be alleviated, in this world a handful of men

and women have dedicated their energies to the design of explosive power so overwhelming that the use of only a small portion of it endangers the continued existence of life on this planet. The decision to destroy the brilliant accomplishments of seven millennia of poets and architects, musicians and scholars, theologians and artists, to destroy all of God's handiwork, to place in jeopardy the lives of almost five billion people – that decision lies essentially in the hands of two men, one in Washington, the other in Moscow.

I know them both. Neither, in my judgement, is evil. Each, in my judgement, profoundly hopes that the vicious genie contained in each of their bottles will never be released.

In the summer of 1985, Trudeau took his sons on a long-promised holiday to the Crimea. While there, much to his surprise, he received a message from the Kremlin conveying a request from the newly appointed General Secretary, Mikhail Gorbachev, that he interrupt his vacation and fly to Moscow on an airplane sent for that purpose. On his arrival in the Kremlin, Trudeau found that Gorbachev was flanked by two familiar figures, Alexander Yakovlev and Georgi Arbatov, director of the U.S.S.R. Academy of the United States and Canada. Arbatov expressed the hope that Trudeau would advise Gorbachev on what to expect from Reagan in the course of the forthcoming summit. Trudeau counselled him to accept at face value Reagan's professed commitment to peace, but to explain that those protestations were simply not being heard by the Soviet people over the heavy interference of military preparations. Though both Reagan and Gorbachev had independently declared their desire for peace, could they not at Geneva jointly do so? Surely, then, sceptical publics in each country would be forced to pay attention.

A few weeks later, Reagan met Gorbachev in Geneva. It was the first U.S.–U.S.S.R. summit in more than six years – since the June 1979 meeting in Vienna between Carter and Brezhnev when they signed SALT II. At the conclusion of the two-day meeting, Reagan and Gorbachev issued a joint statement. The opening lines read: "Nuclear wars can never be won and must therefore never be fought," the very statement that Trudeau had urged each of them jointly to make. The statement continued with a pledge to accelerate negotiations to "prevent an arms race in space and to terminate it on Earth, to limit and reduce nuclear arms and enhance strategic stability."

The negotiations to which they referred would be challenged and contested by the Cold Warriors within each government. Scientists and soldiers alike disputed the wisdom of these policies. The political energy was present, however, and prevailed. In 1988, a new treaty was signed by the two superpowers to eliminate all intermediate-range missiles; in 1991, a strategic-arms reduction treaty (START I) was signed by President George Bush and Gorbachev; in 1992, Bush and President Boris Yeltsin agreed on further reductions (START II). These were the first-ever treaties calling upon the parties actually to reduce, as distinct from merely limiting the size of, nuclear arsenals.

A new era in East–West relations had begun.

CHAPTER NINE

Reflections

In the opening pages of this chronicle, we expressed our conviction that Canada should endeavour to function as an "effective" power in world affairs. By this we meant that Canada should not be content to accept a typecast role based upon past experience or previous self-image, but should be an active, responsible participant in international events on the basis of an evolving interpretation of need and opportunity. We meant as well, moreover, that Canada should not seize upon immediate advantage, no matter how appealing such may be in domestic political terms, if to do so would diminish a longer-term gain in the pursuit of world order and a just international society.

The challenge of balancing the immediate with the future is never easy, but especially was it not in that era of superpower rivalries, when so many circumstances tended to be painted in the garish colours of absolute contrasts. In a period when military preparedness was regarded as the equivalent of wise statesmanship, and prosperity was measured almost exclusively in bare economic terms, unconventional alternatives were interpreted as awkward at the best, and naïve at the worst. Fresh approaches were applauded in political speeches, but not necessarily welcomed when translated into policy initiatives. This was particularly so among those persons and associations engaged in the tradition-rich world of foreign policy, which held constancy and predictability in high esteem.

In large measure, it was the very prominence of the superpower rivalry that prompted us to look beyond, as previous Canadian governments had not always been able to do, in order to better understand the nature of those events obscured by the shadow of the Cold War. Of what potential influence would these be in decades to come? Was a Canadian involvement desirable? Events in this category were not nearly so discernible in 1968 as many became in later years. Such issues as the growing disparity in wealth between the nations of the North and South, the rapid increases in the world's population, and the insidious momentum in the degradation of the planetary environment were not yet accorded the priority they deserved. These issues fell outside the mainstream in another sense as well. None of them were amenable to the application of military force; they demanded instead a sense of shared values and moral principles if they were to be addressed effectively.

It seemed to us that in the same sense that superpower antagonisms required the design of confidence-building measures and the identification of common purpose in order to reduce tensions, these issues evoked the need for an international community, not simply in concept but in practice, one which accepted the role of ethics and the rule of law. The quest for that community would endure as the constant theme of our foreign-policy engagement.

High roads almost always have slippery surfaces, however. In the misty realm of international relations, this is particularly the case. Self-righteousness, so readily attributed by critics, is not an attractive trait in individuals or in states. Veteran diplomats, Canadian and foreign alike, had long been exposed to protestations of high purpose by generations of politicians, and had learned through experience to discount the rhetoric of lofty intention while looking for the reality of the deeds that might or might not follow. The pretentious projection of immediate advantage, clothed in the wrappings of timeless principles, was a device that had been employed by despots and opportunists alike since the dawn of history. Opportunists usually suffered the fate of judgement exercised by weary constituents; despots, on the other hand, could wreak havoc on the unprepared. Little wonder, therefore, that observers had long-warned against the dangers implicit in policies that assume good faith on the part of all. "A man who wishes to make a profession of goodness in everything must necessarily come to grief among so many who are not good," said Machiavelli in the sixteenth century.[1] Hobbes extended the warning to whole societies in the seventeenth century: ". . . during the time men live without a common power to keep them all in awe, they are in that condition which is called war."[2]

Scholars tended to scoff at even the suggestion that foreign policy could or should reflect other than the pursuit of immediate self-interest. Hans Morgenthau, arguably the most influential theorist of international relations in the past half-century, stated that "universal moral principles cannot be applied to the action of states."[3] Some commentators would go further, contending that self-interest was its own moral justification. They employed as an early example the famous declaration of the powerful Athenians to the diminutive Melians: ". . . you know as well as we do that right, as the world goes, is only in question between equals in power, while the strong do what they can and the weak suffer what they must."[4]

The realists, be they observers or practitioners, employed the example of the Melians in another sense, to argue that countries of modest size could not assume to exercise influence on the mighty. In this view, Canada, by definition, is limited to following the lead of others or to reacting to events as they occur. By contrast, the two of us believed that Canada's limited power and its vulnerable geographic position made the quest for community not only more necessary but more possible of success. Canada was not perceived by others as threatening to their interests. We were neither possessed of massive military assets, nor scarred by a historic record of colonization. Canadian society seemed blessed with the gyroscope to which Adlai Stevenson referred: not subject to the vicissitudes and fluctuations of jingoistic instincts. The opportunity was present, should determination be exercised, to look beyond the immediacy of events and the massive size of the major actors in order to shape policies with long-term interests – and moral principles – in mind.

To do so was certainly not a major departure from previous attitudes. Canadian governments had long been deeply influenced by the abhorrence of Canadians to war, by their dedication to fairness, and by their compassion for the needy – all reflections of human values. These had been translated into resolutions at the United Nations and into commitments of human and financial resources abroad. Though often in subdued tone, Canadians had declared that their willingness to resist aggression and to contribute to orderly international processes stems from their conviction that to do so is "right," that there is a place for moral principle in international councils, and that the future welfare of

Canadians is dependent upon an international community respectful of principle.

The two basic elements of realism – the concept of an anarchic international scene and the concept of diffidence as a reflection of size – had nevertheless been of considerable influence in the formulation of Canada's post-Second World War international posture.5 Not large enough on its own to protect its economic or security interests, vulnerable to actors much more powerful (and perhaps less principled) than itself, Canada chose refuge and strength in concert with others. By so doing, the country was able both to enjoy the benefits of membership in a collectivity and to exercise a certain moderating influence from its vantage point within the group. The Canadian public found this associational role to be an attractive one. Canadian diplomats, for their part, excelled in pursuing the organizational agendas now available to them. In the United Nations, in NATO, in the Commonwealth, Canada gained a well-deserved reputation as a sometimes innovative and often effective team-player. In these circumstances, issues of moral principle were by no means overlooked, but they tended necessarily to be muted in the value structure of the collectivity.

So well-suited was this particular policy thrust to the Canadian psyche, and so apparently advantageous to Canada was it in the turbulent postwar period, that Canadians generally paid little heed to the extraordinary sea change in Canada's historic international posture that it represented. A country that had been hesitant in the extreme to undertake international responsibilities during the thirties had been transformed into one of the world's international activists in the fifties and sixties. This metamorphosis was partly the result of the maturation experience of the Second World War, and partly the product of the wise policies of Louis St. Laurent and Lester Pearson. The challenge of positioning Canada advantageously in the international community, while simultaneously building a supportive domestic constituency, was formidable. To have met that double challenge so well was an epic accomplishment.

For two decades, Canada's interests were so coincident with those of the associations to which it belonged that the net benefit of membership far outweighed the occasional muffling of singular Canadian preferences. Canada, as a middle power, came to reflect, and also to represent, the median values of the other members. Professor Paul Painchaud would say that "middlepowermanship" had attained the status of an ideology. "It expresses, beyond each particular decision, an intention and continuing aims which delineate the global international policy of states which claim it."[6]

By the late sixties, however, some strains were becoming evident in this or that grouping, as Canada's sense of international priorities, including its sense of moral principle, failed to be reflected adequately in the group consensus. Most significant in 1968 was Canada's concern over the continued exclusion from the United Nations of the People's Republic of China. That exclusion, in the judgement of each of us, was unprincipled. In the two years following the 1968 election, our conviction grew that Canadian principles were not well served by prevailing group policies in two other sectors as well. In one instance, the issue related to NATO nuclear practices, in the other it grew out of the growing conflict between environmental wholesomeness and the traditional practice of freedom of navigation. By coincidence, each of these three issues distinguished Canada from the strongly held positions of the most powerful of international actors, the United States.

The issue that concerned us in each of the three instances was coloured by an abstract value: the universality of the United Nations; stability in East–West relations; and a pollution-free Arctic environment. More apparent than at any time since Canada's entry into the ranks of international actors, it seemed to us, the Morgenthau thesis was open to challenge. The two of us were seized of the conviction that principle and interest – idealism and realism – were not necessarily inconsistent, and certainly not contradictory. In these three instances, the convergence appealed to us as obvious. These were novel issues, signifying to us that a world of burgeoning populations, nuclear weapons, and environmental degradation demanded new criteria in the formation of foreign policy. Power was no longer subject to traditional measurements; security was no longer solely a derivative of military might. In the circumstances, decisions based on ethical considerations were not simply tolerable, they had become necessary.

These were far from original conclusions. Evidence had been accumulating for some time from reputable monitors and analysts of the hazards and risks represented by nuclear error, by environmental destruction, and by North–South disparities. What we determined to ascertain was the potential impact upon Canadian interests of these novel factors, and the weight that should be given to them in relation to orthodox foreign-policy concerns. Again and again, we found ourselves stimulated in these respects not just by the impressive technical data and interpretations of contemporary scholars, but by the teachings of the great moralists. Kantian and Thomistic premises were particularly familiar to Trudeau; the works of such social commentators as Ruskin and Tawney were well known to each of us. Increasingly, we were persuaded that those international practitioners who were unapologetic followers of the realist school were, in the seventies and eighties, in error. The narrowness of their focus, and the rigidity of their interpretations of national interest, made them all too often indifferent to the oncoming challenges. Policies conceived in such circumstances threatened to be unrealistic as well as morally questionable. We were not willing to accept Niebuhr's reluctant conclusion that irony was the prevailing characteristic of history.[7]

The obvious occasion to reveal a shift in the weight to be given to the two basic foreign-policy elements was the publication of the foreign-policy white paper. In *Foreign Policy for Canadians*, the text noted that Canadian postwar activity in the international arena had "stimulated and substantiated a deep-seated desire in this country to make a distinctive contribution to human betterment."[8] This goals-oriented exercise represented a major step in the process of acquainting Canadians with the new international agenda, and dedicating the government to it. The six major themes were identified as reflective of Canada's national, as well as foreign, interests. Of the six, two were fresh: social justice and, especially, a harmonious natural environment.[9] Each implied much more than a reordering of resources. These goals were assertions of novel values (really, the application of traditional values to novel circumstances), a declaration of major departures from previous attitudes, and a dedication to new principles for the governance of Canadian activities in the international community.

Without question, the simple assertion of these goals by Canada, even a wholehearted dedication to them in practice, would be of marginal effect upon the health of the global biosphere, or upon the diminishment of disparities of wealth and power and well-being as between the

industrialized and the developing countries. To withdraw from involvement on that basis, however, would be to perpetuate the sad truth of
Niebuhr's major contention that humans, when acting in a collectivity,
tend to be less moral than when acting as individuals. We were of the
opinion that Canadians should not be asked to tolerate an ethical distinction between their own personal standards of conduct and those of
their government. Whatever was the magnitude of Canada's activities
worldwide, the thrust should be ethically positive, not the reverse.
Consistency of moral standards and actual practice would hopefully also
enhance the influence that Canada could bring to bear within the international community for the pursuit by other actors with similar goals.
Trudeau would accordingly seize opportunities whenever they presented
themselves to explain to Canadians that these issues internationally were
in large measure extensions of local experience. To non-Canadians, he
would argue that the new reality demanded recognition of the common
advantage to be derived from the acceptance of ethical standards in the
conduct of international relations.

At Duke University, Trudeau reflected on the weight given by the
industrialized countries to the notion of abundance, with its invitation
for waste and obsolescence, and its forgiveness of tawdriness and self-
indulgence, while all the while multitudes in the developing countries
were engaged in poverty-line strategies, frequently overburdening the
carrying capacity of the land. In these circumstances, he argued, it is
illusory to contemplate or practise withdrawal or isolation. "In the final
decades of the twentieth century, social justice can no more be com-
partmentalized than can quality of life be isolated." A "new ethic" of
broad, universal responsibility is required. Then, anticipating the reaction of the realists and neo-realists, he said:[10]

> I find ironical the attitude of some western scholars who profess
> reluctance to push against the outer barriers of social norms, to
> question old values or test new ethics, all because they believe
> governments will not follow the newly-broken ground, or that
> society is too sedentary to change. This diffidence – dare I call it
> irresponsibility? – contributes to the very sedentary condition
> about which the social scientists rightly voice concern. A gov-
> ernment faces an insuperable task in encouraging the electorate

to abandon old assumptions unless it can count upon the exploratory assistance and the philosophical commitment of its university graduates.

Trudeau returned to this theme the following year in London, England, where he stated:[11]

The role of leadership today is to encourage the embrace of a global ethic. An ethic that abhors the present imbalance in the basic human condition – an imbalance in access to health care, to a nutritious diet, to shelter, to education. An ethic that extends to all men, to all space, and through all time.

Stirring phrases, even if honestly prepared and sincerely uttered, are often of only passing moment, however. To be more, to endure, they must induce or stimulate a human resonance that responds with empathy and conviction. Equally as important, as noted earlier, the language must not be so unrelated to government acts as to inspire cynicism. In any society composed of disparate communities and competing interests, the conversion of lofty message into acceptable action is a daunting challenge. In the international community, where the number and distinctiveness of actors tend towards the infinite, the difficulties are compounded and assume a magnitude beyond easy comprehension. Misjudgements abound, shortfalls in performance are frequent, fatigue takes its toll, the ever-receding goals of justice and humanitarianism prompt contentment with half-measures and partial successes. The temptation of "practicality" and the comfort of "the possible" assuage the conscience. Yet, in instances which threaten the survival of humankind, latitude should not be generously offered, either in the form of self-indulgence on the part of ineffective actors, or as absolution for an indifferent public.

Now, as possibly never before, moral principle has become the defining element in effective policy. It must not be an intolerant principle, however, nor one possessed of self-righteousness. More, in an age when human conduct casts shadows so far into the future, the short-sightedness encouraged by the brevity of electoral terms of office must be circumscribed and overcome. To lengthen those terms would be foolhardy; to extend and broaden human awareness, therefore, will be as demanding as will the alteration of human conduct which it demands. Yet not to do so is to accept without challenge the theories of primacy of ego and greed. The philosophical dynamic of human nature – evil or good – was explored and debated in the course of many centuries preceding the emergence of the "modern" religions of Christianity and Islam.[12] No resolution of the debate is likely in this or the next century. To retire from the field of intellectual debate and concede victory to the realists, however, is surely unconscionable.

We write these words in 1995, at a time when the phrases – and the concepts – of a "planetary environment" and a "global economy" are accepted without challenge, as neither were during the greater part of our period in government. Still to be accepted, however, is a concept inextricably related to the first two, that of a single human society. Unless this universal phenomenon is recognized and embraced, the mortal perils facing the human race and its natural habitat cannot be countered effectively.

Trudeau had drawn from a work by Teilhard de Chardin[13] to make this point to Habitat, the UN Conference on Human Settlements in Vancouver in May 1976: "Love one another, or you will perish. . . . We have reached a critical point in human evolution in which the only path open to us is to move towards a common passion, a 'conspiracy' of love."

In this monumental contest of ideas and ideals, of communication and conduct, no state is ineligible. The new measurements of influence are not military, they are economic, scientific, cultural, and, above all, civil. Our future as humans will be influenced immeasurably by our definition of community and our acceptance of the common destiny of our species. Canada and Canadians are as well positioned and as qualified to participate in this magnificent engagement as are any. The effort must be comprehensive and all-inclusive. Those individuals who covet governance roles must not succumb to the temptation of circumstantial morality, and certainly not to the pretentious assumption that national interest defines moral principle.

Ethics are the fibres of civilized conduct. Interwoven with enlightened laws, they become the fabric we call society. A rent in that fabric weakens the structure and the security of all who are dependent upon it. The rent may be caused by the weakness of international legal regimes or the cynical assumptions of patronizing and self-serving states. It is the more heinous, and the more damaging, when done by those segments of society so privileged as to mistake wealth for wisdom, and arrogance for dignity. Conscience is much more than a guide for human behaviour; at the conclusion of the twentieth century, it is the elevated – and only certain – path towards the survival of civilization.

NOTES

✦

Chapter One: The Inheritance

1. Holmes, John, *The Shaping of Peace: Canada and the Search for World Order* (Toronto: University of Toronto Press, vol. 1, 1979; vol. 2, 1982). Holmes was a foreign-service officer in the Department of External Affairs from 1943 to 1960, later becoming professor of international relations at the University of Toronto and counsellor of the Canadian Institute of International Relations. His grace, wisdom, sense of humour, and sense of "Canadianism" made him one of the most admired and most loved members of the foreign-policy community in Canada and elsewhere.

2. As host to a 1967 Francophone conference, Gabon (encouraged by France) chose to recognize the delegation from Quebec in identical fashion to delegations from states such as France or Senegal. For a more detailed discussion of this incident, see Chapter Eight.

3. Only 0.19 per cent of GNP in 1967, compared to the 1-per-cent target later endorsed by Pearson in his World Bank Commission report. By 1978, ODA had increased to 0.54 per cent of GNP, but thereafter subsided somewhat, a result in no small measure of Head's departure from the PMO, where he could exercise policy influence.

4. The other was Regional Economic Expansion, a domestic form of equity.

5. The Treaty of Westphalia concluded the Thirty Years War and effectively concluded the dominance of the Holy Roman Empire. As well, it launched the European system of nation-states, regarded by historians as the commencement of the modern political age.

6. *Canada Gazette*, Oct. 9, 1880.

7. Canada, Department of the Interior, "Southern Baffin Island" 12 (1930).

8. Canada Treaty Series, vol. 1, no. 17, 1930. In 1957, a statue of Sverdrup

was erected in Steinkjer, Norway, to the cost of which Canada contributed. *See* 9 *External Affairs* 270-1 (Ottawa, 1957).

9. Report on the Affairs of British North America; ". . . two nations warring in the bosom of a single state. . . ."

10. MacLennan, Hugh, *Two Solitudes* (Toronto: Macmillan of Canada, 1945).

11. *An Act for the Union of Canada, Nova Scotia, and New Brunswick, and the Government thereof; and for Purposes connected therewith*, 30-31 Victoria, c. 3. Between 1867 and 1931 when Canada finally achieved full independence with the Statute of Westminster, the BNA *Act* was amended a number of times.

12. *An Act to give effect to certain resolutions passed by Imperial Conferences held in the years 1926 and 1930*, 22 George V, c. 4.

13. *An Act to constitute the Commonwealth of Australia*, 63 & 64 Victoria, c. 12.

14. 1155 U.N.T.S. 331.

15. *Re Ownership of Offshore Mineral Rights of British Columbia*, [1967] S.C.R. 792; see also *Re Newfoundland Continental Shelf*, [1984] 1 S.C.R. 86.

16. Article 2(1): "The Organization is based on the principle of the sovereign equality of all its Members."

17. This discussion took place in the fall of 1968 at a meeting of the Policy Advisory Committee of a major research activity entitled "The World Order Models Project," under the direction of Professors Richard Falk and Saul Mendlovitz of Princeton and Rutgers universities respectively. Dillon and Head were committee members, as were such as George Ball and U.S. Supreme Court Justice Arthur Goldberg.

Chapter Two: Manhattan Comes to the Arctic

1. Pearson, Lester B., "Canada's Northern Horizon," 31 *Foreign Affairs* 581 (1952-53).

2. Sergeant Larsen took the *St. Roch* back through the passage from east to west in a single season in 1944. The tiny vessel is now on permanent display in the Maritime Museum in Vancouver.

3. Anik A-1, launched in 1972, and Anik A-2, in 1973.

4. Three parks north of the 60th parallel were announced to the House of Commons by Jean Chrétien on Feb. 22, 1972. Two were located in the Northwest Territories: along the South Nahanni River and on the Cumberland Peninsula of Baffin Island. The third was in the Kluane region of Yukon Territory.

5. "Canadian Claims to Territorial Sovereignty in the Arctic Regions." Published in abridged form in 1963 *McGill Law Journal* 236.

6. The U.S. navy had been active in Arctic waters close to the Canadian archipelago since at least 1958. *USS Nautilus* navigated from the Pacific Ocean to the Atlantic that year, passing beneath the ice of the geographic North Pole and exiting southeast through Davis Strait. *USS Seadragon* completed the voyage in the opposite direction in 1960. *USS Skate* surfaced through the polar ice on March 17, 1959; *Skate* and *Seadragon* surfaced simultaneously at the Pole on Aug. 2, 1962. Each of them had traversed archipelagic waters. (*See New York Times*, Aug. 23, 1962.) In none of these instances had U.S. authorities sought permission from Canada, although notification was given on occasion.

7. Canadian authorities had much earlier begun discussions with Humble with respect to icebreaker escort and other practical assistance.

8. Canadian Press story in *Montreal Star*, Feb. 28, 1969.

9. House of Commons Debates, 28th Parl., 1st Sess. vol. VI, pp. 6057-8. Diefenbaker pursued the question on March 7 and again on March 10. Ibid., pp. 6336-7; 6396.

10. For a brief history of the sector theory, see p. 51, *infra*.

11. House of Commons Debates, 28th Parl., 1st Sess., vol. VIII, pp. 8720-1.

12. *Globe and Mail*, Sept. 5, 1969.

13. 1958 Geneva Convention on the Territorial Sea and the Contiguous Zone, Article 14, 516 U.N.T.S. 205.

14. With the anomalous result that portions of archipelagic waters would lie beyond the territorial-sea zone, amounting to a clear declaration by Canada that it had forfeited its long-held, albeit vague, claim to all these waters as Canadian.

15. House of Commons Debates, 28th Parl., 2nd Sess., vol. I, p. 3.

16. Ibid., p. 39

17. "In Flanders fields the poppies blow
    Between the crosses, row on row . . ."

18. Convention on the High Seas; Convention on the Territorial Sea and the Contiguous Zone; Convention on the Continental Shelf.

19. (1959), 402 U.N.T.S. 71.

20. So similar in outlook were these countries on a number of international issues, including developmental assistance and peace-keeping, that the group came to be called the "like-minded." It consisted of Canada, Denmark, Finland, the Netherlands, Norway, and Sweden.

21. The other, relating to Canadian participation in the nuclear-strike role of NATO, is the subject of Chapter Three.

22. House of Commons Standing Cmtee on Indian Affairs and Northern Development, 1st Report, 28th Parl., 2nd Sess., found in House of Commons Journals, vol. CXVI (1969-70), pp. 207-11.

23. United States Department of State Press Release No. 49, Feb. 18, 1970.
24. *New York Times*, Feb. 26, 1970, p. 78.
25. House of Commons Debates, 28th Parl., 2nd Sess., vol. I, p. 39.
26. Speech to the Annual Meeting of the Canadian Press, April 15, 1970.
27. Speech to the National Press Club, May 18, 1970. These observations generated intense public criticism from within the Alberta oil industry and were branded as factually incorrect and unduly alarmist. Already unpopular within the province for the government's policies on the official languages, Trudeau was now a target of oil-industry spokespersons.
28. Senate Debates, Sess. 1909-10, pp. 179-184.
29. House of Commons Debates, Sess. 1909-10, vol. II, p. 2712.
30. House of Commons Debates, Sess. 1938, vol. III, p. 3081.
31. Pearson, Lester B., "Canada Looks 'Down North,'" 24 *Foreign Affairs* 638 (1945-46).
32. For a fuller description of the widely disparate statements made over the years by Canadian politicians when referring to the sector theory, *see* Head, "Canadian Claims to Territorial Sovereignty in the Arctic Regions," 9 *McGill Law Journal* 200 at pp. 206-10.
33. Among the several ironies of the U.S. self-portrayed position as guardian of international law is its own refusal to accept the jurisdiction of the International Court of Justice, except on its own terms. This is achieved by a "self-judging" reservation. Because international law provides for reciprocity, Canada could exclude any claim brought against it from the United States by pleading the American disclaimer. Claims from other maritime states, encouraged by the United States, could not, of course, be so avoided.
34. Bill C-203 amended *The Territorial Sea and Fishing Zones Act* by providing for fisheries closing lines in the Gulf of St. Lawrence, Bay of Fundy, and Queen Charlotte Sound. In 1976, the United States proclaimed two hundred-nautical-mile fisheries zones off its coasts; in 1977, Canada declared zones of equal breadth in the Atlantic and the Pacific, and shortly thereafter in the Arctic. The UN Law of the Sea Convention would recognize and make regular such zones by calling them "Exclusive Economic Zones." UN Convention on the Law of the Sea, done at Montego Bay, Dec. 10, 1982, UN Doc. A/Conf. 62/122 (1982); 21 I.L.M. 1261. *See* Part V.
35. Transcript of prime minister's remarks to press, Parliament Buildings, Ottawa, April 8, 1970.
36. United States Embassy, Press Release, Ottawa, April 9, 1970, reporting remarks of State Department spokesperson Robert McCloskey.
37. Transcript of prime minister's remarks on "The Nation's Business," April 19, 1970.

38. *Washington Post*, April 24, 1970.
39. Address to Conference on Canadian Studies, Warrenton, Virginia, organized by The Johns Hopkins University, April 17, 1970.
40. The Moscow visit was delayed by the terrorist kidnapping in Montreal of British diplomat James Cross and the subsequent abduction and assassination of Quebec cabinet minister Pierre Laporte. By the date of the rescheduled visit (May 1971), the issue was well contained within the UN Conference on the Law of the Sea preparations.
41. Currently found at R.S.C. 1985, c. A-12.
42. Ged Baldwin, MP, Press Release, Aug. 25, 1970.
43. U.S. Department of State, Press Release, Dec. 18, 1970.
44. UN Convention on the Law of the Sea, *supra*, n. 34, Art. 234:

> Coastal States have the right to adopt and enforce non-discriminatory laws and regulations for the prevention, reduction and control of marine pollution from vessels in ice-covered areas within the limits of the exclusive economic zone, where particularly severe climatic conditions and the presence of ice covering such areas for most of the year create obstructions or exceptional hazards to navigation, and pollution of the marine environment could cause major harm to or irreversible disturbance of the ecological balance. Such laws and regulations shall have due regard to navigation and the protection and preservation of the marine environment based on the best available scientific evidence.

45. Trudeau, Pierre Elliott, *Conversation with Canadians* (Toronto: University of Toronto Press, 1972, p. 127).
46. Holmes, John W., "Most Safely in the Middle," 39 *International Journal* at p. 377.

Chapter Three: Nuclear Weapons

1. Robertson joined the Department of External Affairs in 1929 and by 1941 had been named undersecretary by Prime Minister King to succeed the legendary O. D. Skelton. He served as high commissioner to Britain on two separate occasions in the forties and fifties, and was briefly ambassador to the United States before assuming once again the senior departmental post of undersecretary from 1958 to 1964. In 1949, as clerk of the Privy Council, he hired Trudeau as a member of the Privy Council Office, and supervised his work there for two years.
2. Pearson, Lester B., *Mike*, vol. II (Toronto: University of Toronto Press, 1973) p. 133. Pearson makes a single reference to the review in his auto-

biography, quoting a passage on Canada's UN policy. Of this passage, he wrote, "It summarizes my views better than I could myself."

3. For a commentary on the relationship between Pearson and Robertson, *see* English, John, *The Worldly Years: The Life of Lester Pearson, 1949-1972* (Toronto: Knopf, 1992) p. 20.

4. House of Commons Debates, 28th Parl, 1st Sess., vol. II, p. 1528.

5. Ibid., vol. III, p. 2627.

6. Ibid., p. 2904.

7. Ibid., vol. V, p. 5268.

8. For an account of these negotiations, see Chapter Seven.

9. So secret was the agreement that Churchill chose not to mention it in his public account of the Aug. 1943 conference. *See* Churchill, Winston S., "Closing the Ring," c.5; "The Quebec Conference" (Boston: Houghton Mifflin, 1951) pp. 80-97. For references to the 1945 Washington Conference that pursued atomic cooperation among Britain, Canada, and the United States, *see* Bothwell, Robert, *Nucleus: The History of Atomic Energy of Canada Limited* (Toronto: University of Toronto Press, 1988) p. 72. For a discussion of the tensions that later emerged, culminating in the 1946 McMahon Act, *see* Holmes, John W., *The Shaping of Peace, Canada, and the Search for World Order* (Toronto: University of Toronto Press, 1979) pp. 209ff.

10. The Baruch Plan proposed the creation of an International Atomic Development Authority to have an operational monopoly on all intrinsically dangerous activities in the nuclear field, to be responsible to the political organs of the United Nations without being subject to any nation's veto. *See* "Documents on Disarmament," 1945-1959, U.S. Dept. of State, Publication 7008, vol. I.

11. "So far as possible, from earliest days in the war until the early fifties, the Cabinet was kept in the dark about atomic energy and the bomb. When major decisions had to be taken at Cabinet level, as much of the information as could be was deliberately obscured or made highly secret. After 1945, the principle was that so far as possible atomic energy and the bomb should be left to the personal surveillance of Attlee, guided by the advisory committee of service officials, civil servants, and scientists which had set up under the chairmanship of Sir John Anderson. There was thus no official or political link between the highly important committee and the rest of the ministers in Cabinet." Harris, Kenneth, *Attlee* (London: Weidenfeld and Nicolson, 1982) p. 287. "Attlee consulted the full Cabinet less than ten times in six years and then mainly for purposes of information." Burridge, Trevor, *Clement Attlee: A Political Biography* (London: Jonathan Cape, 1985) p. 235.

12. Pearson refers in his memoirs to the words delivered by Louis St. Laurent,

then secretary of state for external affairs, to the UN General Assembly on Sept. 18, 1947, ". . . a speech which many have come to consider marked the beginning of the North Atlantic Conference." *Mike*, op. cit. *supra*, n. 2, vol. II, p. 41.

13. These were not, however, the only nuclear weapons in Canada. The Second World War base agreements with the United States, which provided for over-flight, landing, port, maintenance, and etc. privileges and facilities, were interpreted in the postwar years as permitting the storage of atomic bombs at the two American bases in Newfoundland: Goose Bay and Argentia. Presumably these two storage sites were utilized for that purpose by the Strategic Air Command of the U.S. air force and navy until these services withdrew many years later.

14. *Cité Libre*, April 1963.

15. An early example of this influence was the decision taken by the government in the sixties to acquire CF-5 aircraft for the Royal Canadian Air Force. No compelling operational role existed for these airplanes; the large contract, on the other hand, was a major benefit for Canadair (which manufactured the airplanes under licence from Northrop, the U.S. designer) and for the Montreal-area labour force.

16. A report that failed to make a single reference to the Canadian nuclear role, but which nevertheless recommended: "3. Canada should continue its present roles in Europe. . . ." The report then recommended, reflecting as it did so the inadequacy of the External Affairs Review, "4. The future long-term military roles of Canadian forces assigned to NATO must be reviewed promptly. . . ." Fifth Report, Part III, tabled March 26, 1969. *See* House of Commons, *Journals* vol. CXV, p. 837 at p. 847. Review following review at a time when the government sought to make decisions!

17. The 1956 NATO "Committee of Three" consisting of Lester Pearson, Halvard Lange of Norway, and Gaetano Martino of Italy. It was created, Pearson later wrote in his memoirs, to answer the question "whether the alliance could successfully adopt itself to a changing political environment in which the likelihood of imminent military aggression had diminished, and whether something other than fear could ensure close and effective co-ordination of policies between member governments." *Mike*, op. cit. *supra*, n. 2, vol. II, p. 93.

18. *See* n. 13, *supra*.

19. Kissinger, Henry A., *Nuclear Weapons and Foreign Policy* (New York: Harper, 1957) at p. 180. "The proper analogy to limited nuclear war is not traditional land warfare, but naval strategy, in which self-contained units with great firepower gradually gain the upper hand by destroying

their enemy counterparts without physically occupying territory or establishing a front-line."

20. Nye, Joseph S., *Nuclear Ethics* (New York: Free Press, 1986). Dyson, Freeman, *Weapons and Hope* (New York: Harper & Row, 1984).

21. House of Commons Debates, 28th Parl., 1st Sess., vol. VII, p. 7869.

22. Ibid, p. 7870.

23. An identical conclusion was reached in the mid-eighties by the Aspen Institute's prestigious East–West Study Group, which included among its members the former ministers of two nuclear-weapons states: Robert McNamara of the United States and James Callaghan of Great Britain. See the group's report, published by The Aspen Institute, 1984.

24. N. 21 *supra*. It would be false to assume, however, that Canada's increasingly entwined armed-forces defence-industry partnership would find so stimulating and rational the process of public debate of first principles that it would of its own volition encourage the practice. Other criteria were clearly more attractive. Out of the era of nuclear weapons, Canada passed in the mid-eighties into the era of industrial lobbyists.

Chapter Four: Commonwealth Paradoxes

1. Wheare, K. C., *The Constitutional Structure of the Commonwealth* (Oxford: The Clarendon Press, 1960) pp. 9-10.

2. Prime Minister Harold Wilson; Secretary of State for Foreign and Commonwealth Affairs Michael Stewart.

3. As compared, for example, with the annual meetings of the Western Economic Summit (G-7), which continue for two days at most (Britain, Canada, France, Germany, Italy, Japan, the United States).

4. Sometimes referred to as the "grandparent" of development assistance cooperation. The plan was adopted in Jan. 1950 and was originally intended to coordinate flows of capital aid and technical assistance from the original Commonwealth members to the newly independent Ceylon, India, and Pakistan. It later expanded to include Japan and the United States as donors and extended to a number of countries in South and Southeast Asia, not all of whom were Commonwealth members.

5. The dinner took place Nov. 12, 1968.

6. *See* the discussion of STAFEUR in Chapter Three.

7. Following a brief procedural event called "Orders of the Day."

8. House of Commons Debates, 28th Parl., 1st Sess., vol. I, p. 13.

9. As with many civil wars, the salient trigger event is buried in historic charge and countercharge.

10. Article 2(7): "Nothing contained in the present Charter shall authorize the United Nations to intervene in matters which are essentially within the domestic jurisdiction of any state or shall require the Members to submit such matters to settlement under the present Charter. . . ."

11. Article 39: "The Security Council shall determine the existence of any threat to the peace, breach of the peace, or act of aggression."

12. The single enforcement measure up to this time was that in Korea. The Security Council decision was made possible by the unusual absence from the sessions of the U.S.S.R., as a protest against the Security Council's refusal to seat the representative of the People's Republic of China. The Soviet representative returned soon thereafter.

13. The Security Council had first seized itself of the Rhodesian issue in Nov. 1965. In Dec. 1966, it voted to impose mandatory, but selective, economic sanctions against Rhodesia. This resolution fell far short of the demands of the African members for forceful, comprehensive measures, as did another in May 1968.

14. The occasion was the dedication of the new premises of the Nigerian Institute of International Affairs, when Gowon delivered the main address.

15. Oct. 29, 1968. In the absence from Nigeria of the Canadian high commissioner, Paul Malone, Head was accompanied by the acting high commissioner, Robert Elliott. Many years later, Elliott returned to Nigeria as Canadian high commissioner.

16. House of Commons Debates, 28th Parl., 1st Sess., vol. III, p. 2345.

17. June 1969.

18. The Charter of the Organization of African Unity was as adamant on this point as was the UN Charter, reflecting the sensitivity of these newly independent states to their colonial past. The OAU did create a consultative committee on Nigeria in 1969.

19. Ferguson at this time taught at Howard University, and would later join the faculty of the Harvard Law School. His missions to Nigeria took him into the Biafran side. In his conversations with Head, he would relate his frustrations with Ojukwu's failure to keep his undertakings.

20. See n. 10, supra.

21. Those countries, for the most part newly independent, which chose to remain aloof from the Cold War adversarial camps. The original leaders of the movement were Presidents Tito of Yugoslavia, Nasser of Egypt, and Nheru of India.

22. The commission was under the chairmanship of Sir Hugh Wooding, chief justice of Trinidad and Tobago. The three law professors were Head, L. C. B. Gower from England, and Zelman Cowan from Australia. Cowan would later become governor general of Australia.

23. To visit his mother, a Canadian citizen living in Toronto.

24. Ramphal told Head that Julius Nyerere of Tanzania had come away from his Sept. 1969 official visit to Ottawa impressed by Trudeau's sensitivity to African issues.

25. The elderly Jomo Kenyatta, president of Kenya, no longer engaged in distant travel. President Milton Obote of Uganda attended the Singapore Conference, but was ousted from office in his absence by the soon-to-be-infamous Idi Amin.

26. The other Canadians were Ralph Collins, assistant undersecretary of state for external affairs (and soon to be named Canada's first ambassador to the People's Republic of China), and High Commissioner James George.

27. Hadwen was Canadian high commissioner to Malaysia; Carter, Dupuy, and Cornett were senior External Affairs officials.

28. "The oldest, established, permanent floating crap-game in New York," from *Guys and Dolls*, music and lyrics by Frank Loesser.

29. Belligerency was suspended for the period of the Games to permit the athletes of the states of Greece to compete.

30. Idi Amin (Uganda), Norman Kirk (New Zealand), Michael Manley (Jamaica), Dom Mintoff (Malta), Lyndon Pindling (Bahamas, which had gained independence in 1973), Sheikh Mujibur Rahman (Bangladesh, which had severed itself from Pakistan), and Gough Whitlam (Australia).

31. Two heads of government were not available: Prime Minister Sir Seewoosagur Ramgoolam of Mauritius was chairing an international sugar conference in Britain and Prime Minister Prince Makhosini Dlamini of Swaziland had been hospitalized with a stroke. In each case Head was received by the acting prime minister. In all instances the resident Canadian high commissioner sat in on the discussions, subject to the agreement of the head of government.

32. House of Commons Debates, 29th Parl., 1st Sess., vol. II, p. 1232. Mitges later pursued the issue in debate, pp. 2147-8.

33. Republished in Ingram, Derek, *The Imperfect Commonwealth* (London: Rex Collings, 1977) pp. 82-3.

34. Kingston, Jamaica, 1975; London, England, 1977; Melbourne, Australia, 1981; New Delhi, India, 1983. The nine-month interval of a Progressive Conservative government in 1978-79 denied to Trudeau the much-anticipated opportunity to participate in the first such meeting held in Africa. Prime Minister Joe Clark led the Canadian delegation to the 1979 Lusaka, Zambia, Conference.

35. Barbados, Guyana, Jamaica, Trinidad, and Tobago. Bahamas attended the conference, but was not a host.

36. Rajasthan Atomic Power Plants I and II.

37. Madras Atomic Power Plants I and II.

38. At this time there were still claims made in the United States under the "Atoms for Peace" program that underground nuclear explosions could fracture mineral seams and release oil from sandy formations in commercially attractive ways. These were never proved feasible. At about the same time, the U.S.S.R. had ceased using nuclear explosives in the digging of a lengthy canal in Siberia because of overwhelming radiation problems.

39. One consequence of the termination of nuclear cooperation was the denial to Canada of any opportunity to assist the Indians with maintenance and repairs. In 1994, AECL was so concerned about the possibility of coolant leaks that it drew the problem to the attention of the UN International Atomic Energy Agency in Vienna. *See The Financial Post*, Sept. 20, 1994.

40. Hard on the heels of a dramatic drop of world prices of Jamaica's two export commodities, sugar and bauxite, U.S. travel agencies in the thousands were counselled anonymously to discourage Americans from travelling to Jamaica because of alleged Communist activities there.

41. Transcripts of many of the statements and press releases of the participants may be found in the volume entitled "Documents on the Invasion of Grenada," issued as Supplement No. 1 to the Oct. 1983 edition of *Caribbean Monthly Bulletin*, published by the Institute of Caribbean Studies of the University of Puerto Rico.

42. House of Commons Debates, 32nd Parl., 1st Sess., vol. XXV, p. 28343.

43. Described in Chapter Eight.

44. "In the last few decades, mankind has been overcome by the most fateful change in its entire history. Modern science and technology have created so close a network of communication, transport, economic interdependence – and potential nuclear destruction – that planet earth, on its journey through infinity, has acquired the intimacy, the fellowship, and the vulnerability of a spaceship. In such a close community, there must be rules for survival." Ward, Barbara, *Spaceship Earth* (New York: Columbia University Press, 1966) p. vii.

Chapter Five: North–South Dimensions

1. Authorship of the term "Third World" is attributed to French sociologist Alfred Sauvy in 1952, who likened the "common" people of the world to the Third Estate of the French revolutionary period.

2. The concept was first discussed at the 1955 Bandung (Indonesia)

Conference. The first Non-Aligned Summit took place in Belgrade in 1961.

3. This category soon became known as the G-77, the number of countries attending the 1964 UN Conference on Trade and Development. As further countries gained independence, the number of members of the G-77 swelled to many more than a hundred.

4. Subtitled "Canada and the Search for World Order" (Toronto: University of Toronto Press, vol. 1, 1979; vol. 2, 1982).

5. Inaugurated at the 1950 Commonwealth Foreign Ministers' Conference in Colombo, Ceylon.

6. A career foreign-service officer, formerly Canadian high commissioner to Ceylon.

7. In Fiscal Year 1967-68, $253 million in volume; 0.19 per cent of GNP, the accepted standard of measurement.

8. At the University of Alberta, June 1968 (see Chapter One), in the presence of UN Secretary General U Thant, himself from a developing country, Burma.

9. Robinson, H. Basil, *Diefenbaker's World: A Populist in Foreign Affairs* (Toronto: University of Toronto Press, 1989) p.78.

10. IRRI, together with the Wheat and Maize centre (CYMMIT) in Mexico became charter institutes in the remarkably successful Consultative Group on International Agricultural Research.

11. CUSO was the largest of several similar organizations. World University Services (WUS) was another.

12. For an account of CUSO's early years, *see* Smillie, Ian, *The Land of Lost Content: A History of CUSO* (Toronto: Deneau Publishers, 1985).

13. The popular name given to the U.S.-sponsored "European Recovery Program," launched by the Paris Economic Conference of July 1947. George C. Marshall was U.S. secretary of state at the time.

14. The World Bank and the International Monetary Fund were products of the UN Monetary and Financial Conference held at Bretton Woods, New Hampshire, in July 1944. The World Bank at that time was called the International Bank for Reconstruction and Development.

15. N. 8, *supra*.

16. The occasion was the conferring on Trudeau of the honour of Freedom of the City of London, March 13, 1975.

17. There is no better example than the so-called Hickenlooper amendment to the U.S. foreign-aid law. This denies all assistance to any countries that have nationalized assets of American citizens and not paid compensation deemed to be adequate.

18. The World Intellectual Property Organization.

19. Culminating in the 1993 conclusion of the Uruguay Round of the General Agreement on Tariffs and Trade (GATT).
20. From 0.19 per cent in 1968, the last year of Pearson's leadership, to 0.54 per cent in 1978, the last year Head spent in the Prime Minister's Office. In dollar terms, the increase was tenfold.
21. The public announcement of the refugee program was made by Trudeau during an election rally in Vancouver, where alleged abuses of welfare schemes was a major issue. The large crowd greeted the plan with sustained applause.
22. N. 16, *supra*.
23. Jenkins, Glenn P., *Costs and Consequences of the New Protectionism; the Case of Canada's Clothing Sector* (Ottawa: The North-South Institute, 1980) p. v.
24. The Multi-Fibre Arrangement of Jan. 1, 1974, involved cotton, wool, and artificial fibres. Seventy-two categories of textiles and garments were monitored and regulated.
25. The National Energy Program.
26. Tin was one example; sugar, wheat, and cocoa were others.
27. Part of the imaginative Lomé agreements between the EEC and the ACP (Africa, Caribbean, and Pacific) countries.
28. Brandt Commission, *North-South: A Programme for Survival, The Report of the Independent Commission on International Development Issues under the Chairmanship of Willy Brandt* (London: Pan Books, 1980) p. 8.
29. The text of the report is found at House of Commons Votes and Proceedings, March 19, 1981.
30. The Bata Shoe Company.

Chapter Six: The Neighbourhood

1. Holmes, John, *Life with Uncle: The Canadian American Relationship* (Toronto: University of Toronto Press, 1981).
2. Queen's Printer for Canada, Ottawa, 1970, p. 20.
3. Ibid, p. 21.
4. Ibid, p. 39.
5. Johnson, Nixon, Ford, Carter, and Reagan.
6. Holmes, *supra*, n. 1, p. 3.
7. So frequent were telephone calls from abroad, claiming to be on behalf of presidents and prime ministers, that the PMO switchboard created a practice of screening the likely authentic ones through Head both for verification and to decide whether to pass them to Trudeau. Such was the

practice on the occasion of this Christmas call, which was then cleared through to the maternity ward of the Ottawa Civic Hospital.

8. The International Commissions for Supervision and Control. There was one for each of Cambodia, Laos and Vietnam, and three countries took part: Canada, India, and Poland.

9. Kissinger Press Conference, Jan. 24, 1973, *New York Times*, Jan. 25, 1973. "Agreement on Ending the War and Restoring Peace in Vietnam," Office of the White House Press Secretary, Washington, D.C., Jan. 24, 1973.

10. In the period 1954 to 1972, several Canadians lost their lives on these missions, including Doug Turner, an External Affairs classmate of Head, killed when a commission aircraft was shot down by the Pathet Lao over the Plain of Jars in Laos.

11. *See*, for example, Taylor, Charles, *Snow Job: Canada, the United States and Vietnam, 1954 to 1973* (Toronto: Anansi, 1974).

12. Among them, such senior diplomats as Marcel Cadieux, Blair Seaborne, and Tom Delworth.

13. The other members: Hungary, Indonesia, and Poland.

14. Not counted here is Canada's engagement in NATO, a close-knit alliance representative of the broad international community, which, at the time of writing, has continued for almost half a century.

15. The former Democratic governor of Texas, until this moment most familiar to Canadians as the person seated next to President Kennedy when he was assassinated in Dallas in Sept. 1963.

16. The vice-president's comments proved to be prescient. He was forced to resign in 1973.

17. *New York Times*, July 13, 1976. Jimmy Carter, the then-Democratic presidential candidate, joined in the criticism, charging that Canada was "playing politics" with the Olympics. Four years later, on the occasion of the 1980 Moscow Olympics, President Carter ordered the U.S. Olympic team to boycott the games because of the U.S.S.R. invasion of Afghanistan, and pleaded with other countries to do the same.

18. House of Commons Debates, 30th Parl., 1st Sess., vol. XIV, p. 15249.

19. France would endeavour to explain Canada's presence as a decision of the United States and based solely on geographic comity. None of the other participants were swayed by this brief campaign.

20. The three flew to Washington together and, when checking in to their hotel, announced themselves casually as Messrs. Hood, Head, and Towe. The registration clerk asked with a straight face if this was a new vaudeville act.

21. Ottawa, National Film Board of Canada, 1976.

22. Nov. 1974.

23. Created by the Boundary Waters Treaty of 1909, U.S.T.S. 548.

24. Brzezinski's father had been Polish consul general.

25. President Lopez Portillo of Mexico preceded Trudeau by a few days; Prime Minister James Callaghan of Britain followed a fortnight after him.

26. An activity sponsored by the Chicago Council on Foreign Relations, drawing together on a biennial basis government and business leaders from Europe, North America, and South America. Head was a member of the Steering Committee from 1970 to 1990.

27. One Canadian had addressed a joint session, but never a prime minister. Vincent Massey, in his role as Canadian minister (Canada's mission was a legation) in the early twenties did so.

28. This phrase would later be utilized extensively by President George Bush.

29. An amusing episode occurred on the eve of departure. Trudeau and Carter had earlier shared their concern over the distinctly Cold War penchant of NATO Secretary General Joseph Luns, and Trudeau wished to learn whether the president intended to raise the issue at the meeting. Head was instructed to call Brzezinski. He saw this as an opportunity to try out the recently installed secure telephone line between Ottawa and Washington. The instant he picked up the telephone, there was an acknowledgement on the other end. Head identified himself and asked to speak to the national security adviser, Zbigniew Brzezinski. "Yes, sir," came the reply, then, "Could you spell that name for me, please."

30. Once again the practice of note-takers was employed. In most instances these were "sherpas." Head was the Canadian. A long-standing acquaintance, Robert Hormats, acted for the United States. To ensure the accuracy of their records, they compared them with one another's. As an assist to the Japanese, Head's notes were transcribed and handed over to the Japanese note-taker.

31. In later years, both Trudeau and Head would become acquainted with Cutler through their involvement with the Salzburg Seminar.

32. Nor would it be revived by the Reagan administration. Reagan withdrew the treaty from the Senate in the early days of his term, as he simultaneously denounced the complex and successfully concluded UN Law of the Sea Convention; both were defiant signals to the international community that the United States was again intending to disregard all but its own immediate interests.

33. The vice-president of the United States is as well Speaker of the Senate, the upper chamber of Congress. Thus the Canadian counterpart for protocol purposes is the Speaker of the upper chamber of Parliament, the Senate.

34. One important segment lay in George's Bank off Maine. The issue was sent to a chamber of the International Court of Justice in The Hague, which later ruled in a fashion satisfactory to Canada.

35. President William Howard Taft was the proponent of reciprocity in trade with Canada. It became the critical issue in the 1911 Canadian federal election.

36. One example was found in the ideological vigour that a Reagan loyalist employed in his verbal attack upon a paper that Head presented to a session of the mammoth and prestigious annual conference of the American Association for the Advancement of Science in Washington, D.C., in Jan. 1982. Head's theme was South–North relations. His paper, "The Issue Is Survival," was published in the *Bulletin of the Atomic Scientists*, vol. 39, no. 5.

Chapter Seven: The Second World

1. Lasswell, Harold D., *The Future of Political Science* (New York: Atherton Press, 1963), p. 168.

2. Gouzenko was a cypher clerk in the Soviet Embassy in Ottawa, who in 1945 defected with evidence of Soviet espionage activities in Canada.

3. The Canadian was Gen. A. G. L. McNaughton, then-Canadian permanent representative to the United Nations. Following a McNaughton intervention in a Security Council debate (The Czechoslovak Question) in 1948, the Soviet representative, Andrei Gromyko, replied, "I am not prepared to listen to the moralizing of the Canadian representative as to whether or not the delegation of the U.S.S.R. is abusing its right. The delegation of the U.S.S.R. will use its rights as it thinks fit in accordance with the terms of the Charter. It is not prepared to take lessons from the Canadian representative." Official Records of the Security Council, SCOR III, nos. 63, 71, 73, and 74, April-May 1948.

4. Royal commission to investigate the facts relating to and the circumstances surrounding the communication, by public officials and other persons in positions of trust, of secret and confidential information to agents of a foreign power. Report released June 27, 1946, by the King's Printer, Ottawa.

5. Most prominent in this respect was Herbert Norman, Canadian ambassador to Egypt. A career foreign-service officer, Norman was cited by McCarthy as a security risk because of his Communist associations as a youth. He committed suicide in 1957. Following the earlier royal commission inquiries, eleven Canadians were convicted of criminal offences.

6. The first visit by a Canadian foreign minister to the U.S.S.R. was by Pearson and did not take place until 1955. It was the first-ever visit by a NATO foreign minister to Moscow.

7. "Canada and the World," XX *External Affairs* (July 1968) pp. 278-84.

8. Hébert, Jacques, and Trudeau, Pierre Elliott, *Two Innocents in Red China*, translated by I. M. Owen (Toronto: Oxford University Press, 1968).

9. Sweden was one of the handful of western countries which had recognized the People's Republic. As a principled neutral state, it was an attractive site for negotiations.

10. Andrew would be followed in Stockholm by Margaret Meagher, the first woman in the Canadian foreign service to become a head of mission when she was named ambassador to Israel in 1958.

11. Only one other negotiation of importance was under way, between Italy and the People's Republic. That negotiation concluded successfully in Nov. 1970, a month following the Canada–China agreement. The final wording employed by the Italians was virtually identical to that negotiated by Canada. A second set of talks, conducted on a desultory basis in Warsaw between the People's Republic and the United States, addressed outstanding issues other than recognition.

12. House of Commons Debates, 28th Parl., 2nd Sess., vol. IX, p. 9273.

13. House of Commons Debates, 28th Parl., 1st Sess., vol. X, p. 11384, July 21, 1969. *See also* Sharp, Mitchell, *Which Reminds Me* (Toronto: University of Toronto Press, 1994), p. 204.

14. House of Commons Debates, 28th Parl., 3rd Sess., vol. I, pp. 49-50.

15. *Foreign Policy for Canadians*, "Pacific" (Ottawa: Queen's Printer), pp. 23-24.

16. Following his tour of duty in Norway, Ronning was named high commissioner to India.

17. When the *New York Times* published an editorial praising the contributions to peace of three men – UN Secretary General U Thant, Pope Paul VI, and Ronning – Ronning chortled with glee. "I can sense my Lutheran ancestors turning over in their Telemark graves, that one of their progeny should be mentioned in the same breath as a Buddhist and a Roman Catholic."

18. Because beavers cannot survive without access to water, a lavatory on the airplane was converted for their use during the flight. Much to the disgruntlement of those seated near it, the beavers quickly made apparent that they are nocturnal animals, and noisy!

19. In the spring of 1973, a Canadian medical delegation led by Dr. Gustave Gingras, president of the Canadian Medical Association, had returned to Canada with strong recommendations to this effect, as had a later delegation led by the Hon. Jeanne Sauvé, then minister of state for science and technology.

20. In all these sectors, considerable progress was achieved. Canadian immigration officials, for example, were permitted entry into China to process applications there, an immense step forward.

21. Joyce was from the Department of Finance; Burns and Petrie from Industry, Trade and Commerce; Dupuy from External Affairs. (One who travelled frequently with us in his role as a security liaison officer was RCMP Supt. Barry Moss, a highly competent and most congenial professional.)

22. Producing prints of the peculiar size 10" wide × 2" high.

23. House of Commons Debates, 29th Parl., 1st Sess., vol. VII, p. 7036.

24. Ibid., p. 7037.

25. Though some Kuomintang supporters in Toronto demonstrated during Zhao's visit there.

26. The single exception of note was a Canadian legal claim against China for the unpaid balance of Canadian-government-guaranteed loans employed to purchase nine shallow-draft Yangtze River ships constructed in Canada. The loans were made in 1948 to the Nationalist government. The ships were nationalized by the Communist government in 1949.

27. 1922 – ". . . the Government certainly maintains the position that Wrangel Island is part of the property of this country." Prime Minister W. L. Mackenzie King, House of Commons Debates, 1922 Session, vol. III, p. 1751. 1923 – in reply to a question as to who owns Wrangel Island, "I should like to know myself." Hon. Ernest Lapointe, minister of fisheries, House of Commons Debates, 1923 Session, vol. IV, p. 3360. 1924 – ". . . as far as Canada is concerned, we do not intend to set up any claim to the island." Hon. Charles Stewart, minister of the interior, House of Commons Debates, 1924 Session, vol. II, p. 1110.

28. Official diplomatic papers relating to this episode are found in Department of External Affairs, "Documents on Canadian External Relations," vol. 3, 1919-1925, Ottawa, 1970, pp. 51-69.

29. *Foreign Policy for Canadians*, "Europe" (Ottawa: Queen's Printer), pp. 18-19.

30. The two countries had entered into diplomatic relations in 1942. The first visit to Moscow by a Canadian foreign minister was in 1955, when Lester Pearson made the trip. He was followed by Paul Martin in 1966. Mitchell Sharp would travel there in November 1973. See n. 6, *supra*.

31. For a full account of this man's remarkable career, see Gromyko, Andrei, *Memories* (London: Hutchinson, 1989). Gromyko's comments on Canada and Trudeau are found at pp. 227-8.

32. By happy coincidence, a shipment of his vehicles would be unloaded in the Port of Leningrad during our presence in that city.

33. Whose formal title was Chairman, Council of Ministers.
34. "Declaration on Principles of International Law concerning Friendly Relations and Cooperation among States in accordance with the Charter of the United Nations," adopted by the General Assembly, Oct. 24, 1970.
35. House of Commons Debates, 28th Parl., 3rd Sess., vol. VI, p. 6184.
36. A fishing fleet that was exceeding catch quotas in the Atlantic Ocean off Newfoundland, and gave rise to a complaint by Trudeau to Kosygin and an earnest plea that this practice cease. Kosygin agreed to look into the issue and to adhere to internationally agreed limits.
37. House of Commons Debates, 28th Parl., 3rd Sess., vol. VI, pp. 6182-5.
38. The assailant was Geza Matra, an immigrant from Hungary. He received a three-month jail sentence.
39. For a fuller discussion of this sequence of events, see Chapter Two.
40. Baskets one and two related to security in Europe and to cooperation in the fields of economics, science, technology, and the environment, respectively.
41. Treaty on Principles Governing the Activities of States in the Exploration and Use of Outer Space, including the Moon and other Celestial Bodies, 610 U.N.T.S. 205; entered into force Oct. 10, 1967.
42. T.I.A.S. 7762; entered into force Sept. 1, 1972.
43. Agreement on the Rescue of Astronauts, the Return of Astronauts, and the Return of Objects Launched into Outer Space, C.T.S. 1975, no. 6; entered into force April 22, 1968.
44. The secretary of state for external affairs, Don Jamieson, was not in Ottawa.
45. It was simultaneously delivered to the Canadian Embassy in Moscow.
46. For a more detailed account of the legal aspects of this incident, see Lee, Edward G., and Sproule, D. W., "Liability for Damage Caused by Space Debris: The Cosmos 954 Claim," 1988 *Canadian Yearbook of International Law* 273.
47. The Soviet ambassador to Canada during the period of the exchange of visits was Boris Miroshnichenko, later named ambassador to Kenya.
48. Yakovlev, like most Russians, was at his jolliest with children, and once entertained the three Trudeau boys following a tobogganing afternoon with their father in Rockcliffe Park.
49. The full explanation of the Canadian decision was revealed to the House of Commons by Secretary of State for External Affairs Don Jamieson on February 9. House of Commons Debates, 30th Parl., 3rd Sess., vol. III, pp. 2697-8.
50. As had happened to other nations in the past and would happen to Canada in the future when the Mulroney government p.n.g.'d seventeen Soviets in

1988 and the U.S.S.R. retaliated by banning five Canadians. Enraged, Joe Clark ordered two more Soviets out of Canada and reduced by three the size of the Soviet Embassy. Not to be outdone, the Soviets promptly withdrew from the Canadian Embassy in Moscow the services of household, clerical, and other essential "local" staff on which diplomatic missions depend, severely hampering the function of Ambassador Verne Turner.

51. We later watched with pride the influential role which he played in the transformation of the Soviet Union under the leadership of Gorbachev.

52. Numbered Question #1369 (Mr. Jones), House of Commons Debates, 30th Parl., 3rd Sess., vol. VI, pp. 6980-1.

Chapter Eight: Hits and Misses

1. Peloponnesian War, Book 1, p. 22.

2. An election that turned on the issue of reciprocity in trade with the United States. The Canadian electorate rejected the proposal.

3. ". . . Canada seeks to strengthen its ties with Europe, not as an anti-American measure but to create a more healthy balance within North America and to reinforce Canadian independence." *Foreign Policy for Canadians*, "Europe," p. 14.

4. *International Perspectives*, Autumn 1972.

5. Ibid at p. 2.

6. Mitchell Sharp had visited Brussels early in 1971, and the president of the commission, Franco Maria Malfatti, later that year came to Ottawa.

7. The goodwill had been enriched the previous December at a Downing Street dinner offered by Prime Minister Heath in honour of the visiting widow of Jean Monnet. The dinner served as a formal sendoff to Soames, who was leaving London to take up his post in Brussels. Heath graciously extended invitations to each of us once he learned that we would be in London.

8. House of Commons Debates, 30th Parl., 1st Sess., p. 786.

9. Ibid., p. 784.

10. A fifth visit, less formal, was to Salzburg in Jan. 1974 for a meeting of the Club of Rome, attended by other heads of government.

11. We had broken our return journey from the Singapore Commonwealth Conferences in January 1971 by landing in Germany. We did not, however, leave the Canadian Forces NATO base at Lahr, and so were, diplomatically speaking, on Canadian soil for that short period.

12. While in Paris and Brussels, calls were made upon the secretaries general of OECD and NATO, respectively.

13. We learned afterwards never to underestimate the tenacity of External Affairs. Notwithstanding that only 10 per cent of the speech text was dedicated to the link exercise, the department indexed and published the speech under the title "The Contractual Link: A Canadian Contribution to the Vocabulary of Cooperation." *See* Statements and Speeches, External Affairs Canada, 75/6.

14. By 1984, the Japanese market was absorbing twice the value of Canada's goods as was Britain.

15. Canada and Japan had first established diplomatic relations in 1928. A Canadian legation in Tokyo opened in 1929.

16. The day that the Japanese party left Ottawa, Trudeau delivered the opening address to the Commonwealth finance ministers meeting. In that same week he would receive official visits from Prime Minister Gough Whitlam of Australia and Prime Minister Olaf Palme of Sweden.

17. *The Foreign Investment Review Act*, S.C. 1973-74, c. 46.

18. It would be a temporary accomplishment. Following the 1984 change of government, the defence catalogue reappeared, now in full-colour glossy format.

19. Concluding the European Thirty Years War in 1648.

20. Attended by the United States, the Ottoman Empire, and all European states with interests in Africa, 1884-85. By the *Berlin Act* of 1885, the boundaries of African colonies were formally fixed and principles agreed upon for future territorial claims.

21. UN Charter preamble.

22. Canada's engagement with these issues is described in Chapter Five.

23. Charter of the Organization of American States, signed at Bogota, April 30, 1948, 119 U.N.T.S. 3.

24. Charter of the Organization of African Unity, signed at Addis Ababa, May 25, 1963, 479 U.N.T.S. 39.

25. Treaty Establishing the European Economic Community, signed at Rome, March 25, 1957, 298 U.N.T.S. 11.

26. Among them, L'Association des universités partiellement ou entièrement de langue française; La Fédération internationale de la presse de la langue française; and L'Institut internationale de droit d'expression française.

27. Convention Between United States of America and Canada for Preservation of Halibut Fisheries of the Northern Pacific Ocean, signed at Washington, D.C., March 2, 1923, 1923 U.S.T. 701.

28. For Prime Minister Pearson's description of this event, *see* Pearson, Lester B., *Mike*, vol. 3 (Toronto: University of Toronto Press, 1975) p. 263.

29. Co-chaired by André Laurendeau and Davidson Dunton.

30. A function hotly contested by Quebec nationalists, who maintained that

provinces possessed an implicit power to act internationally in pursuit of their provincial powers. It was a contention wholly without precedent in the international community. The position of the Government of Canada at the time in question is found in "Federalism and International Relations" (Ottawa: Queen's Printer, 1968), one of the documents prepared for the Federal–Provincial Constitutional Conference.

31. A policy paper dedicated to Canadian practice in such instances, prepared for the Federal–Provincial Constitutional Conference, is entitled "Federalism and International Conferences on Education" (Ottawa: Queen's Printer, 1969).

32. Martin, Paul, *A Very Public Life*, vol. II (Toronto: Deneau, 1985) pp. 664-5.

33. To the date of writing, only one other leader of a French-speaking African country has voluntarily stepped aside – Ahmadou Ahidjo of Cameroon resigned in Nov. 1982. In English-speaking Africa, President Julius Nyerere of Tanzania did so in 1985. President Kenneth Kaunda of Zambia would respect his electoral defeat in 1991, and Olusegun Obasanjo turned his military regime over to an elected civilian government in Nigeria in 1978.

34. Bundy, McGeorge, *Danger and Survival: Choices About the Bomb in the First Fifty Years* (New York: Vintage Books, 1990) p. 149.

35. *Cité Libre*, April 1963.

36. A project of the World Law Fund, 1967-1975. Among the senior Americans participating with Head were George W. Ball (then U.S. ambassador to the United Nations) and Douglas Dillon (secretary of the treasury in the government of President Kennedy).

37. This study was pursued by a group of highly experienced individuals, including James Callaghan, George Kennan, John J. McCloy, Robert S. McNamara, Saburo Okita, Elliot Richardson, Helmut Schmidt, Cyrus Vance, and Shirley Williams. Head and Mitchell Sharp were full members and participated in all working sessions of the twenty-seven-member group from 1983 through 1984. Trudeau and Edward Heath were signatories to the final statement, "Managing East-West Conflict: A Framework for Sustained Engagement" (New York: The Aspen Institute for Humanistic Studies, 1984).

38. As we chose to ensure that the CF-101 long-range interceptor aircraft in Canada be replaced by airplanes not dependent upon nuclear-tipped air-to-air missiles. The replacement CF-18s are armed with conventional weapons. These acts meant that Canada was the first country in the world, having possessed nuclear weapons, to relinquish them. It remains the only country to have done so.

39. The *Saturday Review*, May 18, 1957. Schweitzer's primary concern related to atmospheric testing.

40. Treaty on the Non-Proliferation of Nuclear Weapons, done at London, Moscow, and Washington, July 1, 1968, 729 U.N.T.S. 161.
41. Treaty Banning Nuclear Weapons Tests in the Atmosphere, in Outer Space and Under Water. Done at Moscow, August 5, 1963, 480 U.N.T.S. 43.
42. *See* Chapter Three, n. 18, *supra.*
43. At this time U.S. strategic nuclear policy concentrated overwhelmingly on civilian, as distinct from military, targets. This policy was not changed until Aug. 1980, when President Carter announced a major shift.
44. *Ottawa Journal*, July 17, 1980.
45. *Ottawa Citizen*, Aug. 12, 1980.
46. Treaty between the United States of America and the Union of Soviet Socialist Republics on the Limitation of Anti-ballistic Missile Systems, done at Moscow, May 26, 1972, 23 U.S.T. 3435.
47. N. 37, *supra.*
48. In the fall of 1983, he would express this view with vigour in an article he contributed to the journal *Foreign Affairs*. He wrote, "Having spent seven years as Secretary of Defence, dealing with the problems unleashed by the initial nuclear chain reaction forty years ago, I do not believe we can avoid serious and unacceptable risk of nuclear war until we recognize – and until we base all our military plans, defense budgets, weapons deployments, and arms negotiations on the recognition – *that nuclear weapons serve no military purpose whatsoever. They are totally useless – except only to deter one's opponent from using them.* [McNamara's emphasis] This is my view today. It was my view in the early 1960s." "The Military Role of Nuclear Weapons," 62 *Foreign Affairs* 59 at p. 79.
49. Taken at a NATO Summit in Bonn in June 1982.
50. In May 1982, for example, the Pentagon revealed that it had a strategy in readiness to fight a protracted nuclear war.
51. There were two distinct sets of negotiations under way: START, relating to strategic weapons, and INF, relating to intermediate range nuclear forces.
52. Tuchman, Barbara, *The Guns of August* (New York: Macmillan, 1962) p. 439.
53. House of Commons Debates, 32nd Parl., 1st Sess., vol. XXIV, p. 27720.
54. The reference is to a Canadian withdrawal of landing rights of Aeroflot, the Soviet airline, a boycott later joined by other countries.
55. House of Commons Debates, 32nd Parl., 2nd Sess., vol. II, p. 1211.
56. It would be followed by other policy memoranda in the weeks that followed.
57. In the first week of June 1980, malfunctioning U.S. computers twice warned of Soviet ICBM attacks and, on each occasion, U.S. nuclear forces began to move into responsive positions.

58. And would happen again in late Oct. 1983.

59. In this early November trip, Trudeau consulted with President Mitterrand in Paris, Prime Minister Lubbers in The Hague, Prime Minister Martens in Brussels, Prime Minister Craxi and Pope Paul VI in Rome, Chancellor Kohl in Bonn, and Prime Minister Thatcher in London.

60. This episode is discussed in some detail in Chapter Four.

61. House of Commons Debates, 32nd Parl., 2nd Sess., vol. II, p. 1212.

Chapter Nine: Reflections

1. Machiavelli, Niccolo, *The Prince*, chapter 15.

2. Hobbes, Thomas, *Leviathan*, chapter XIII.

3. Morgenthau, Hans, *Politics Among Nations: The Struggle for Power and Peace*, 2nd Ed. (New York: Alfred A. Knopf, 1954) p. 9.

4. Thucydides, *The Peloponnesian War*, chapter XVII, "The Melian Conference."

5. *See*, in this respect, the forceful observations of Professor James Eayrs in his 1965 Plaunt Lectures, published under the title *Right and Wrong in Foreign Policy* (Toronto: University of Toronto Press, in cooperation with Carleton University, 1966).

6. Painchaud, Paul, "Middlepowermanship as an Ideology," in Gordon, King, *Canada's Role as a Middle Power* (Toronto: The Canadian Institute of International Affairs, 1966) pp. 29-30.

7. Niebuhr, Reinhold, *Moral Man and Immoral Society: A Study in Ethics and Politics* (New York: Scribner, 1932).

8. *Foreign Policy for Canadians*, Booklet One (Ottawa, The Queen's Printer, 1970) p. 6.

9. Ibid., p. 14. The other goals were economic growth, sovereignty and independence, peace and security, an enhanced quality of life.

10. Address to Convocation, Duke University, Durham, North Carolina, May 12, 1974.

11. Address upon receiving the Freedom of the City of London, Mansion House, London, March 13, 1975.

12. "No man is without a sense of right and wrong" wrote Mencius in the fourth century B.C.; "Man's nature is evil" contended Hsun Tzu in the third century B.C.

13. Teilhard de Chardin, Pierre, *L'énergie humaine* (Paris: Éditions du Seuil, 1966) chapter 5.

The letter n followed by a period after a page number indicates that the indexed information is found in a note on that page. The note number follows the period.